The Myth of Moral Panics

This study provides a comprehensive critique—forensic, historical, and theoretical—of the moral panic paradigm, using empirically grounded ethnographic research to argue that the panic paradigm suffers from fundamental flaws that make it a myth rather than a viable academic perspective.

Bill Thompson is a sociologist from the UK, where he was a Practicing Associate of the British Academy of Experts, and taught at Cambridge, Essex, and Reading Universities. In 2004, he relocated to the USA, where he has worked with the local Teamsters Union Chapter while teaching at SUNY and Hartwick Colleges.

Andy Williams is Principal Lecturer in Forensic Criminology at the Institute of Criminal Justice Studies at the University of Portsmouth.

Routledge Advances in Criminology

The Myth of Moral Panics

Sex, Snuff, and Satan

Bill Thompson and Andy Williams

LONDON AND NEW YORK

First published 2014
by Routledge
711 Third Avenue, New York, NY 10017

Simultaneously published in the UK
by Routledge
2 Park Square, Milton Park, Abingdon, Oxfordshire OX14 4RN

*Routledge is an imprint of the Taylor and Francis Group,
an informa business*

First issued in paperback 2015

Library of Congress Cataloging-in-Publication Data
Thompson, Bill.
    The myth of moral panics : sex, snuff, and Satan / by Bill Thompson
and Andy Williams.
        pages cm. — (Routledge advances in criminology ; 14)
    Includes bibliographical references and index.
    1. Moral panics.   I. Williams, Andy.   II. Title.
    HM811.T467 2013
    302'.17—dc23
    2013001400

ISBN 978-0-415-81266-5 (hbk)
ISBN 978-1-138-95284-3 (pbk)
ISBN 978-0-203-06866-3 (ebk)

Typeset in Sabon
by IBT Global.

To the memory of Tony Ham

Contents

Preface
The Dark Side

The concept of moral panic is not only very popular; its proselytizers like to boast about its colonization of other disciplines and the number of hits on *Google* [Goode & Ben-Yehuda, 2010: 29 and 33]. Popularity, however, is no guide to validity, and Stan Cohen's *Folk Devils and Moral Panics* [1973] is no exception. Its account of how horror-headlines turned an insignificant spat between a bunch of bored British teenagers into an irrational societal-wide reaction creating the deviancy that it condemned is a myth. Far from incite widespread alarm, the press was denounced as a "lie factory" by Britain's leading moral entrepreneurs who rushed to the youths' defense, and the horror-headlines were condemned by Parliamentarians who believed that the real trouble makers were the 'law and order' lobby. Instead of panicking and demanding more social controls, the public lined up in an orderly fashion and voted to subsidize the teen's coffee-bar culture at the next general election.

Rather than chart the history of public anxieties since then, the moral panic paradigm reflects and reveals the fears of the mythmakers, telling us far more about the academic construction of reality than the social construction of social problems. Bemused that no one had queried Cohen's account, or the incredible claim in *Policing the Crisis* [Hall *et al.*, 1984] that everyone was panicking about mugging in the middle of a class war; we decided to put the concept to the test by looking behind the horror-headlines about gore-fest horror movies in the third seminal study, Barker's *Video Nasties* [1984]. We then laid our findings before a panel on moral panic at the 1989 American Society of Criminology in Reno [Thompson, 1989]. The paper pointed out that 'moral panic' had become a cliché, a sociological insult thrown at horror-headlines that the author did not like. Although no one applying the label used Cohen's definition, they all subscribed to his consensus model of society even though the UK had long since become a pluralistic one. Case studies not only exaggerated the effects of the horror-headlines, they took public panic for granted rather than demonstrated its existence, and no one considered that the horror-headlines they used were invariably generated by the increasing value conflict between moral entrepreneurs from all sides of the political divide. As the legislation that followed rarely reflected the entrepreneurs' aims let alone what the public wanted, the alleged effects of 'panics' were equally misleading. We concluded that the panic paradigm's problems followed from the fact it was a political rather than a sociological perspective and that it promoted its adherents' values, evidenced by its selective use. Whereas Barker immediately denounced the campaign to censor the violent videos as moral panic, he ignored the much larger furor over sex stores from which it emerged [Thompson, 1994a]. As that inconsistency followed from accrediting the attack on the 50 horror movies to the New Moral Right and the closure of 500 sex stores to feminism, the paradigm's political bias was undermining the concept's academic integrity.

At that point, we thought the concept might be saved if it was drastically revised, but what happened next suggested that was never going to happen. Despite being inundated with requests for the paper, instead of generating a debate about the viability of the concept, we became subject to moral panic beginning with a *volatile* and *hostile* reaction. Publishing proposals died the moment that they were sent to reviewers. New conference papers questioning other panics were systematically blackballed by organizers. Two early articles were heavily censored, removing references to progressive[1] moral enterprise, and substituting "moral panic" for "moral enterprise" [Annetts and Thompson, 1992; Greek and Thompson, 1992]. In 1993, after another promising book proposal died, the US commissioning editor revealed what had caused all the *concern*. While it may have been sociologically correct to point out that progressives engaged in moral enterprise, the current *consensus* ensured that it was politically incorrect to say so. They would publish *if* we removed all criticism of progressives.

When we finally got into print thanks to Peter Tatchell [Thompson, 1994a; 1994b], the paradigmatic journalist Beatrix Campbell appeared, claiming that she wanted to write a review for *The Observer,* although her questions suggested that she had already written it. Campbell was convinced that anyone who did not believe in moral panic, opposed feminist censorship, undermined satanic abuse allegations, and wore *Yves Saint Laurent* suits was not only an over-privileged, bourgeois, New Right, Thatcherite; they were the font of the UK's "anti-feminist backlash". Rebutting that was easy. As we had been born on housing projects, were lifelong co-operative socialists, ran night-classes for working-class women who wanted better jobs, and bought our suits in sales, she was running on erroneous stereotypes. As for the rest, we merely preferred Weber's approach to scholarship than Marxist's to propaganda [Weber, 1970]. Needless to say, no review appeared. Campbell decided to write a book instead, but as that was even more libelous, it had to be pulped as part of a legal settlement [Campbell and Jones, 1999]. While the thought of being *folk devils* amused us; the *disproportionate* reaction did not stop there thanks to an *amplification of deviancy.*

Despite repeatedly telling another progressive journalist, Damian Thompson, that satanic abuse was *not* a moral panic, he claimed that we said otherwise to validate his own account to his editor [*Daily Telegraph*, 20.3.91]. Although we had clearly said the opposite in another 200 newspaper stories and on a dozen radio and TV shows, a panic proselytizer jumped on that single article and blamed us for turning the concept into a cliché even though they listed our Reno paper in their bibliography! While that claim was removed from later editions, it had became part of panic folklore [Hunt, 1997:639], and the damage was done. It provided an excuse for our detractors at Reading University to cut off research and conference funding, block funds we secured elsewhere, exclude our achievements from the Annual Proceedings of the university, and 'encourage' prospective and current post-graduate students to study something else; several students even left. This caused no end of problems, not least the amount of time and effort we could spend on righting miscarriages of justice, our major preoccupation at the time.

When a new head of department tried to stop that display of authoritarianism by backing our research projects and a new criminology stream based around them, he discovered that he could not. Instead of becoming academic heroes for seeing off a Third Party Disclosure Order, making the UK safe for ethnographic research unlike the US [Ferrell and Hamm, 1998], the university's ethics committee banned our new students from talking to folk devils. We were then raided by the infamously incompetent Thames Valley Police who seized our research data anyway. Because that action was based on an anonymous phone call, the police had to apologize, pay our legal costs, and return our files; but the university refused to investigate who had made the malicious call and for why. Worse: despite being granted leave to pursue a judicial review which could have forced magistrates to exercise far greater diligence when considering search warrants in future, our travails meant that we did not have the funds to deposit with the court in order to proceed, losing the opportunity to secure much needed reform.

Although these experiences did not shape our critique, they proved that the paradigm was far from politically neutral [Goode and Ben-Yehuda, 2010: 46–47]. They also confirmed that the claim that "academic politics are so vicious because the stakes are so small" is false, no matter who said it first, [Keyes, 2006]. On the contrary, apart from ruining more than one PhD student's promising career, it ensured that the first half of this book which could and should have been published 20 years ago was not, and helps explain why Reading University's Sociology Department no longer exists. While that may not amount to much in the wider course of history, it is indicative of the approach adopted by many academics today. Despite paying lip service to Kuhn's concept of paradigm shifts, sociology is no different. As well as failing to apply its findings to itself, it only flips when it is useful to do so. Its approach to scholarship is shaped by its politics, rather than the other way around, although it likes to pretend otherwise. Anyone who suggests otherwise, engages in free inquiry uncovering the vagaries of social life, or considers *all* political ramifications of what they find may as well have discovered tectonic plates. In the case of moral panic, the paradigm has spent 40 years defending a concept that was flawed from its inception, and was not even justified by the case study it was based on. This was no cover up. It was worse. No one had bothered to check the original sources because they were too busy using the concept for a political purpose. We have never been able to make up our mind what was the bigger scandal: the original published study, or the fact that thousands of professors and their students took its claims for granted.

We would have preferred to restrict this volume to the foundation of the panic paradigm in the UK, and left the critique of the paradigm shift that followed the colonization of the US and elsewhere to a separate volume as there is so much to cover. However, as our reviewers and publisher thought otherwise, we have tried to squeeze in as much as possible into a single volume. While we are grateful to Routledge for publishing a critique, the amount of space allocated has led to excluding as many issues as we cover, and covering *none* to the depth that we would have preferred. Consequently, we have elected to concentrate on the theoretical and evidential problems that follow from the paradigm's politics, and have adopted a polemical style as it is more economical. We are aware that doing so may offend some hypocritical sensibilities, and will ensure that we will not be invited to the 40th anniversary party; but we are not going to beat about the bush. We have uncovered fraud as well as conceptual confusion, and a preference for political propaganda rather than a regard for evidence. Otherwise, our conclusion and intent remains the same. As the paradigm constructs moral panics rather than uncovers them, any academic concerned with the origins and application of moral legislation would be better served by going back to Becker and starting over by reviewing, critiquing, and updating the concept of moral enterprise [1963].[2] While it is now far too late to warn the US not to buy a pig in a poke, we hope that this volume will finally initiate a real debate about the viability of moral panic rather than another attempt to save a label that has long since made no sense; though that, of course, is up to you.

We make no apology for the amount of space devoted to UK cases for three reasons. As the two seminal studies that established the paradigm were British, we had to dissect them in detail. As our US reviewers did not know what video nasties were, or how Barker's account popularized the politics of panic, we think that it is time that they did. As the new politics of panic was exposed by the myth of the Paulsgrove riots, which like mods and rockers went global within hours, we have no need to plead its case. Although we address more than enough panics from elsewhere to demonstrate particular points, we must apologize to readers 'down under'. The ramifications of Cronulla beach had to go; but as this critique was always intended to be a wakeup call from the home of moral panic, we hope that you will consider this a first step in a worldwide critique, which includes putting our claims to the test too.

Acknowledgments

This account of the moral panic myth would not have been possible without the help of our favorite folk devils: Shaz and the Paulsgrove Vigilantes, the Macs and the Orkney Satanic cult, and Eileen Jones and the New Moral Right. Our accidental ethnography was facilitated by: the mods, Chris and Pip; the Purbrook Park class of '73; Stace and Nik and the *Hawkwind* road crew. We owe a debt to Jason and Roberto for their support, and our moral panic classes at Reading University who debunked the myths about Devil Dogs, Raves and all the rest, so that we could keep our promise about the mods and the rockers. We would like to thank Jane Higgins, whose art is well worth stealing; Vicky for the car, and much more besides; and Eve for Harvard skills.

We send our best wishes to: FACT and United Against Injustice; Honey Kassoy, Dennis, and the habitués of the Empire House for those private showings; Remi Gaillard for the street theatre; Max and Stacey for the tireless tirades; the Seneca nation for Blue100; Joel Ward and the crew of the good ship Pompey for 7 April 2012; Joel and Phil for their advice, though we are saving it for next time.

This version was written to the sounds of *Dead Skeletons, Cherry Poppin' Daddies, Tame Impala, Plan B* and *Saida Karoli*; also, watching *Heisenberg WW* for light relief.

Introduction
Moral Panic for Dummies

DESCRIPTIONS AND DEFINITIONS

The popularity of moral panic can be explained by the passage in *Folk Devils and Moral Panics* cited by most papers, essays, dissertations, theses, journal articles, and books on the subject:

> Societies appear to be subject, every now and then, to periods of moral panic. A condition, episode, person, or group of persons emerges to become defined as a threat to societal values and interest; its nature is presented in stylized and stereotypical fashion by the mass media; the moral barricades are manned by editors, bishops, politicians, and other right thinking people; socially accredited experts pronounce their diagnosis and solutions; ways of coping are evolved or (more often) resorted to; the condition then disappears, submerges or deteriorates and becomes more visible. Sometimes the object of the panic is quite novel and at other time is something which has been in existence long enough, but suddenly appears in the limelight. Sometimes the panic passes over and is forgotten, except in folk lore and collective memory; at other times it has more serious and long lasting repercussions and might produce such changes as those in legal and social policy or even in the way society conceives itself [Cohen, 1973: 11].

Having noticed that one or more of these facets appears in the report below the horror-headline that caught their attention, the authors claim to have uncovered another moral panic even though that *description* can not distinguish between a moral panic and an overreaction to horror-headlines in any other model of the social construction of social problems. In order to do that the author needed to demonstrate that the reaction conformed to Cohen's *definition* of moral panic, with its:

- Three distinct but interlocking phases;
- Nine elements of: media exaggeration and distortion, prediction, symbolization; orientation, images, and causation; the subsequent

sensitization of the public and social control agencies to this media frame; and an increase in the control culture paralleled by the rise of an exploitative culture;
- Dozens of other features, including the 'must have' deviancy amplification, the diffusion and escalation of innovative forms of control culture, the public dramatization of evil and widespread public demand for even more social controls which proved that a panic was in progress;
- Explanation of why the deviants became the symbolic target of the unaddressed but projected fears that facilitated the panic;
- Evidence that the deviants accepted and acted out their ascribed role;
- Demonstration that the phases, elements, and features were mutually reinforcing [Cohen, 1973: 38–39, 87, 95, 11–12, 161–162, 192].

As most of the 'must have' features are also germane to social group value conflict claims-making [Best, 1989]; it was the three-phase, nine-element, transactional process which separated Cohen's moral panic model from other explanations of the same phenomena and *not* the description.

The inability of academics to differentiate between a description and a definition, let alone cover the phased interaction ensures that no one else has ever uncovered a moral panic as Cohen defined them: the societal-wide projection of subconscious fears onto a group of folk devils during a symbolic boundary crisis following horror-headlines about a precipitating event, amplifying the deviancy and increasing the control culture in the process. On the contrary, with the solitary exception of the Centre for Contemporary Cultural Studies (hereafter CCCS) [Hall *et al*, 1984], everyone else claiming to have identified a moral panic in the next 25 years was merely slapping the label on a set of horror-headlines that they did not like. As it took three decades before anyone else noticed that the description was "not a very accurate reflection of the book's contents" [Critcher, 2000: 1], it is no surprise that no one ever explained why they ignored the definition, or why moral panic became so popular.

When those working in other disciplines discovered that it took a lot less research time or analytical effort to boost one's publication record by sticking the label on any reaction they did not like, moral panic became one of the most successful academic fads in history. It spread far beyond the confines of sociology and cultural studies to: criminology and criminal justice [Murji, 1998; Tonry, 2004; Garland, 2008]; feminism [Gelsthorpe, 2005]; gay studies [Herdt, 2009]; geography [Aitken 2001a and 2001b]; history [Abbott, 2007; Dreher, 1997; Lemmings, and Walker, 2009]; law and cyberspace [Akdeniz, 1997; Welch, 2000; Patry, 2009]; media history [Hunt, 1997]; music [Wright, 2000]; nursing and midwifery [Paterson and Stark, 2000]; popular culture [Barker, 1994a; Springhill, 1998]; social work [Parton, 1985; 1991; Winter, 1992]; and youth [Schissel, 1997;

Krinsky, 2008]. In short, the paradigm's popularity reflects its proponents' lack of academic standards.

PANICS FOR DUMMIES

The three major problems with what we call descriptive panics can be illustrated by Newburn's summary of the 1984 Video Nasties panic in the UK:

> The campaign had all the classic ingredients of a moral panic: a stereotypical threat to societal values (the stereotype constructed by the mass media); the manning of the barricades by moral guardians or 'right thinking' people; and the construction of a legislative 'solution' which allowed the panic to subside [1992: 183].

First, as the only reason those three 'ingredients' had become 'classic' was that they were the only three facets being used, that habit exposed descriptive panics' lack of theoretical and analytical integrity. Second, as 'the public' were watching the videos rather than panicking about them, the experts and moral guardians publicly disagreed about the threat, and the legislation *decriminalized* hardcore pornography as well as the gory horrors, descriptive panics had no evidential veracity either. The video nasties episode did not even fit the description! Third, the reference to a 'campaign' highlighted the 20-year failure to quantify the differences and similarities between the effects of moral enterprise and the process of moral panic [Thompson, 1994a]. While the majority within the growing panic paradigm ignored these problems, Goode and Ben-Yehuda [1994], the concept's US boosters, did not. They tried to circumvent them by creating a 'new, improved' definition which helped initiate "the age of moral panic" [Thompson, 1998] not because it was, but because academia had gone moral panic mad. Rather than engage in a real academic debate about theory and evidence, those applying the concept opted for a definitional free-for-all, illustrated by the highbred that emerged on *onpedia*:

> A moral panic is a *mass movement* based on the perception that some individual or group, frequently a *minority group or a subculture,* is dangerously deviant and poses a menace to society. These panics are generally fuelled by *media coverage* of social issues (although semi-spontaneous moral panics do occur), and often include a large element of *mass hysteria*. A widely circulated and new-seeming *urban legend* is frequently involved. These panics can sometimes lead to *mob violence* ... A factor in moral panic is the *deviancy amplification spiral.* Recent moral panics in the UK have included the ongoing tabloid newspaper campaign against pedophiles, which led to the assault and persecution of a pediatrician by an angry, if semi-literate, mob in August 2000, and

that surrounding the murder of James Bulger in Liverpool, England, United Kingdom in 1993 [italics our emphasis—eds. *onpedia*,[1] 2002].

If the video nasties panic was the point when it *should* have been impossible to ignore the paradigm's lack of intellectual rigor, quality control, and evidential standards; *onpedia's* reference to that "semi-literate mob" *was* the point when it became impossible to deny that the paradigm was being used as a political rather than a sociological perspective. As the vigilante lynch mobs were a myth created by a government agency to justify denying the public the Megan's Law that they wanted; logic dictated that the horror-headlines about the riots that never were should have been denounced as a moral panic about phantom vigilantes. Yet the paradigm switched sides, and promoted the myth that the Portsmouth public had panicked and rioted about a nonexistent pedophile threat even though the CCTV tape shown during the government's show-trials proved otherwise, and the peaceful protesters were found 'not guilty' as a result [Silverman and Wilson, 2002; Hughes and Edwards (Ed.), 2002]. The reference to the attack on the pediatrician, which was another myth about another nonevent a month later, 150 miles northwest of Portsmouth, also demonstrated that the paradigm was based on the same media methods that it condemned [Williams, 2004; see Chapter 7 this volume].

Readers raised within the paradigm will object and point to numerous "theoretical developments" and revisions that make our criticism redundant. However, as the friendly critics like McRobbie and Thornton never questioned the concept [1995] and the more critically minded believed that *everyone* was in a permanent state of panic [Ungar, 2001; Furedi, 1997; Waiton, 2008], moral panic continues to avoid the critical scrutiny and debate that academic concepts were subjected to in our youth. As we will demonstrate those claims in the Conclusion, we will concentrate on the most influential 'development' here.

'NEW, IMPROVED' MORAL PANIC

Rather than arrest the descent into conceptual chaos, or correct the problems that followed from the panic paradigms political bias, the 'new, improved' moral panic conceived by Goode and Ben-Yehuda [1994] encouraged both; and it is easy to see why. Moral panic was now applied to *any* reaction by the members of *any* social group over *any* issue that exhibited:

- *Volatility,* by erupting and subsiding in a sudden fashion;
- A heightened level of *concern* about the issue;
- A *consensus* "that a problem exists and should be dealt with";
- An increased level of *hostility* towards the folk-devil; and
- A *disproportionate* fear "in excess of what is appropriate if concern were directly proportional to objective harm" [Goode and Ben-Yehuda, 1994: 33–39].

As the first four elements inevitably appeared during social group value conflict, and disproportionality is innate to public claims-making [Best, 1989], the new definition was even more generic than descriptive panics. Although Goode and Ben-Yehuda tried to avoid that fate by adding some 'must have' features to distinguish between a moral panic *within* a social group and moral enterprise *by* a social group; no one adopting the new generic definition appeared too concerned whether those features were present or not. Even when they did appear, they were more often asserted than proven:

- A pre-existing issue that emerges in 'troubled times';
- Media exaggeration and agenda setting, focusing the above anxiety on the folk-devil;
- The expression of "fear", "stress" or "anxiety";
- Folk-devils symbolizing the pre-existing issue;
- An expansion in the control culture;
- Pandering politicians; and
- The re-imposition of society's moral boundaries [Goode and Ben-Yehuda, 2010: 2–3, 17, 23–25, 29, 31, 35–36, 89, 91].

Likewise, aware that a societal wide moral panic was near impossible in pluralistic societies, Goode and Ben-Yehuda avoided the problems that they claim had caused, by ditching it. Moral panics could now be "sectional", appearing within "specific social circles, sectors, categories, or groups" at the "local or regional level", rather than being societal-wide. However, by also insisting that these sectional panics still restored *society's* moral boundaries, Goode and Ben-Yehuda raised more problems than they failed to resolve. Did the horror-headlines invoke or follow from the social group's concerns? If the hostility already existed, but did not increase after the horror-headlines, did we still have a panic on our hands? The same question could be asked when the control culture was deployed to the max, but no expansion in powers occurred. If the folk devils contested their status, made counter claims, and generated horror-headlines about their detractors, were we dealing with one or two panics? Moreover, how does one section of society panicking because of *its* values, restore *society's* values in a pluralistic society? Rather than worry about these issues, the growing legion of panic fanatics appear to have homed-in on Goode and Ben-Yehuda's claim that one-off horror-headlines and social group urban legends also amount to moral panic in their own right. As a result, these generic panics invariable fail to quantify any of the elements despite the US boosters' insistence that doing so demonstrated the concept's validity [2010: 2, 18, 35–38, 41, 43–45, 89, 91].

The most problematic aspect of the new generic panics was that it discarded the original and *only* justification that the label ever had [Goode and Ben-Yehuda, 1994: 31, 32, 35]. As the "anxiety" in moral panic consisted of the public's "confusion" over the meaning of the precipitating event, which made it susceptible to the *uncontested* media inventory, and led to the projection of the inventory's symbolization onto the folk devil; without a new justification, the label 'moral panic' no longer made any sense! [See Chapter 1 this volume] These and many more problems, along with the ambiguities and contradictions in the new definition follow from the two interrelated problems that provoked the booster's revision: the paradigm's politics and its failure to cover and explain the rise in moral enterprise in pluralistic societies [Thompson, 1989].

THE POLITICS OF PANIC

Instead of resolving the politics of panic, Goode and Ben-Yehuda tried to sweep it under the rug by arguing that "as there is no intrinsic leftist slant to the moral panic concept" it "could" be applied in a neutral manner [2010: 47]. History and practice suggest otherwise. Theoretically, the concept *was* innately political. It could hardly be otherwise, given that it was predicated on the existence of a panic prone petit-bourgeois which instead of facing up to their fear of impending proletarianization panicked about symbolic moral boundaries instead, while the power of the press ensured that the rest of society followed suit. In Cohen's account: once the *capitalist* press had stigmatized the *working-class* mods and rockers and the *petit-bourgeois* police, magistrates, and neo-fascist moral entrepreneurs had amplified the deviance because they were panicking about "permissiveness", the *middle-class* parliamentarians duly passed a new law while the police restored society's values on the beaches [1973]. Hall *et al* [1984] offered us the *capitalist* controlled Conservative party forming an alliance with the panic prone moralistic, crime fearing, racist, neo-fascist *petit-bourgeois* led by Enoch Powell and Mary Whitehouse in order to crush the *working class* while the judiciary and police provided the excuses to do so. Although the revolutionary *proletariat* turned up for a class war, they ran away once the black mugger appeared because of their subconscious racism, although you had to be a *déclassé* 'intellectual' to discern all that. Barker's video nasties panic has the *capitalist class* exploiting the moral entrepreneurs' *petit-bourgeois* fears about the moral corruption of children by amoral *proletarian* parents, while the neo-fascist *Daily Mail* acts as a conduit for the Thatcher Government's alliance with the New Moral Right and masked the real issue: the failure (sic) of Thatcher's law and order policy [1984].

As the never-ending array of panics over youth emerging from the paradigm are supposedly caused by the same structural strains in the three seminal studies [Thompson, 1998: 47]; panics and progressive politics were always inseparable. If that is not enough proof, one merely read some Cohen. In a later edition, Cohen confirmed that *Folk Devils* was an attempt to utilize "critical sociology" to explain the nature of the youths' reaction to the problems generated by society "as presently structured"; and if that was not clear enough, he insisted that "what was really happening on the beaches of Brighton and Clacton . . . was, no less a *political battle ground between classes*" [2002: xlix]. Practically, nothing has changed at all. Moral panic is still used as it always was to label anything deemed Right-wing or politically incorrect, from racism to rich folk's fear of street beggars, as mad as well as bad [Welsh, 2003; Samara, 2008]. Indeed, the prioritization of progressive politics is confirmed by its failure to differentiate between the disparate responses to 9/11 in the US from the heroic sacrifice aboard United 93, through the *real* panic over Anthrax in the mail, to the neo-cons' manipulation of Islamophobia to launch Operation Iraqi Freedom [Rothe and Muzzatti, 2004; Fahmy and Johnson, 2007]. The legacy of the paradigm's politics can be seen by the way one enterprising student pointed out that:

> The Anglo-American invasion of Iraq, "Operation Iraqi Freedom," was politically made feasible in an unusual fashion, which in many ways could be considered a moral panic. While international politics are more complex than the panics which grip societies from time to time, the way in which the case for war was crafted and the way moral justifications were invented bear the imprint of a moral panic.
>
> The five basic criteria . . . that help define a moral panic can be found throughout the war. The war's justification tended to change around from month to month, but **heightened concern, hostility, consensus, disproportional evidence,** and **volatility** were all constructed and exacerbated to support the case for war. [Emphasis in original eds., 2003][2]

The author's lack of awareness that generic panic's core criteria could be applied to any war is less important than the fact that they also describe contemporary progressive politics. Although the US boosters allude to "Left-wing panics" to justify their claim about potential neutrality, it is no accident that they were identified by critics, a cynical academic outsider, and a journalist unaware that he was not supposed to do that: anti-smoking campaigns [Thompson, 1991], HIV [Thompson and Annetts, 1992], pornography, sadomasochism, and Satanism [Thompson, 1994a; 1994b], political correctness, and date-rape awareness [Fekete, 1995], radical feminist satanic panic [Pendergrast, 1995]; and the Paulsgrove pedophile panic [Williams and Thompson, 2004a and 2004b]. Other case studies have also identified progressive panic, (and we suspect we have missed others); but as those we found do not name the group involved like Boero [2007], or questioned whether the reaction was a moral panic like Zajdow [2008] and Lattas [2007], we have not included them. That leaves Jenkins claims about the role of radical feminists in the child-abuse 'panics' in the UK as the major exception within the paradigm [1992]. However, as Cohen subsequently denied that it was a panic [2002: xv–xvi], and the US boosters tried to explain away the radicals' role in the later allied porn and satanic panics in the US, it would appear that the new generic panics are as politically selective as descriptive panics [Goode and Ben-Yehuda, 2010: 84 and 46–47]. What is more, even critics like Furedi [1997] and Waiton [2008], shy away from the sociology of progressive *moral enterprise*.

SPOT THE DIFFERENCE

The booster's attempt to separate moral panic from moral enterprise by pointing to the former's display of disproportionate claims-making is immediately undermined by the simple fact that moral entrepreneurs invariably exaggerate problems for publicity purposes [Best, 1989]. Asserting that moral crusades require moral entrepreneurs whereas moral panics "do not, although they usual usually do" clarifies nothing, especially when the examples offered to illustrate the difference did nothing of the kind [Goode and Ben-Yehuda, 2010: 125, 20–21]. As the local laws against marihuana before 1930 *were* generated by crusading local law enforcement agents, the Orleans panic concerning Jewish white slavers in France never transcended the level of a rumor because of counter moral enterprise, and the Salem village witchcraft trials followed one of the most evil pieces of moral enterprise in history; they undermine rather than illustrate the booster's intent [Himmelstein, 1983b; Sloman, 1979; Morin, 1971; see Chapter 4]. Goode and Ben-Yehuda's account of when and why moral enterprise leads to panic did not help either. Having been told that the "intensity" of the "concern" about the deviants in the moral crusades against drink, sexual psychopaths, and psychoactive drugs in the US was greater than usual, yet offered no more detail than "the panics that they generated is one of their interesting but secondary features"; to then be told that prohibition, sexual psychopathic laws, and the Marijuana Tax Act demonstrate that panic "implies fairly widespread concern whereas crusades do not", is simply not good enough [2010: 125–127]. When those supposed to determine and explain the difference between moral enterprise and moral panic fudge an issue like that, it is no surprise that those who follow are frequently oblivious to how their own evidence proves the opposite of their intent. Samara's [2008] otherwise excellent account of the battle over street beggars in Cape Town's shopping district is a case in point.

The evidence offered shows that instead of *following* a moral panic, the bylaw against panhandling was drafted *before* the horror-headlines appeared and that they were both generated by the interest with most to gain: economic entrepreneurs engaging in moral enterprise to increase their profits. Unfortunately for those entrepreneurs and Samara's thesis, the headlines backfired. Cape Town's administrators' political opponents won the next election, delaying a watered down version of the bylaw by five years. As the public opinion poll cited to demonstrate panic was taken *before* the horror-headlines appeared, and the 70 percent who wanted more controls did not increase afterwards, the incident is bereft of the volatility, the heightened concern and hostility that are supposed to appear. The political backlash provoked by the horror-headlines demonstrated that polls do not reflect what the public will do in an election and that the media orientation does not necessarily run parallel with the reaction it is supposed to encourage. The poll's negative response to street children appeared when the dominant media frame considered the panhandlers to be social victims; the proposed law was *abandoned* when the dominant media frame stressed the beggars threat to safe streets; and the law was finally passed when media accounts were divided equally between victim, threat, and neutral perspectives [Samara, 2008].

LABEL SLAPPING

A large number of panics, descriptive and generic, have no justification whatsoever. Miller's account of the public history of Ritalin is typical [2008]. Although the media was the main source of both public knowledge that doctors were dispensing the drug as a cure all for ADHD despite the lack of scientific evidence, and the subsequent skepticism about both the drug and its need, as we are offered numerous reasons why some parents accepted and others rejected the medicalization of bad grades, sticking the label 'panic' on this issue is completely unwarranted. Millar offers no evidence of a consensus amongst doctors and parents, still less the reading public during either phase of the coverage. Turning media flip-flopping from lauding the drug to questioning its widespread use into volatility, concern, and hostility is obviously a step too far, not least because we are offered no account of its effect on reducing dispensing. As disproportionately is innate to drug claims-making, and there is no sign of those 'must have' features, a powerless folk devil, or a panicking public the label has no merit. And where is the role of Scientology's anti-psychotropic drug crusade?

The worst example of label slapping remains satanic abuse, which also demonstrates how panic is invoked to substantiate an author's belief rather than uncover, describe, and explain what is happening. Although UK radical feminists denounced extensive concern about their false allegations of child abuse as a moral panic about feminism[3] [Campbell, 1989: 217]; Pendergrast had no problem using the paradigm to denounced US feminists' claims-making about satanic abuse as a moral panic, having lost his two daughters to the adult survivor fad [1995]. When the satanic allegations reached the UK, Wiccans, pagans, and occultists alarmed that believers were losing their children because of their lifestyles, claimed that the social workers were panicking about paganism [www.paganlink.org, 1992], and set about supplying rebuttals [SAFF, 1991; Pengelly and Waredale, 1992; Silvermoon, 1992]. Yet, the moment the parents' accusers were faced with critical media comment, they could insist the headlines were a moral panic about social workers [Winter, 1992]. That ambiguity was not resolved by suggesting that the first panic flipped to the second, because no one offered any evidence that the public was panicking either way [Jenkins, 1992]. The same applies to later accounts. Schissel argued that the allegations were part of a larger contradictory Canadian moral panic about vulnerable children and delinquent youth [1997]; de Young offered a convergent panic caused by social strain [2004]; and Gillies proffered that the allegations were a new variant in the endless UK panic about working-class mothers [2006]. While the various 'explanations' on offer may look like a 'debate' to the uninitiated, the fact that none of those using the label reviewed and critiqued the others evidence demonstrates otherwise. Although the definitional free-for-all helps explain how so many people could offer so many different causes without ever querying the others on offer, the core problem remains the poor level of scholarship.

"WHATEVER"

Any attempt to pass the blame for the concept's problems onto internet idiots, silly students, and junk-news journalists would be disingenuous given the amount of misinformation emanating from the paradigm because its level of scholarship is so low. Zgoba attributes Goode and Ben-Yehuda with defining moral panic [2004: 386–387]; Cocca claimed Cohen's description *was* the definition [2002: 57–58]; and others credit moral panic with features it never had, given that no one ever argued that panics always follow moral enterprise [Walsh 2000: 101; Pijpers, 2006: 92]. As even Cohen dare not suggest that the UK media turned the mods and rockers into an "unprecedented threat to public safety", Krinsky clearly made up that claim for affect [2008: 1], and he is not the only one. Given that Cohen's PhD covered societal reactions to vandalism [1969]; *Folk Devils* insisted that both youth groups were working-class; smooth mods preferred *Mike Raven's R&B Show*; and the rockers' deviancy was restricted to road traffic offences before they became part of the counterculture; de Young has some explaining to do. Her claims that "Cohen was looking for a dissertation topic" when he noticed that "hasty legislation" followed a clash between the "middle-class, Beatles-crazed, fashion conscious Mods" and "the working class, politically reactionary, and quite proudly delinquent-prone Rockers" are a bad example to set students [2004: 1]. They owe more to the contemporary coverage in *Time* magazine than they do to *Folk Devils* [*Time*, online, August, 1964].

These problems follow panic proselytizers' tendency to rely on secondary sources rather than critically review what has gone before *in detail*, as academics are supposed to do. Hunt, for example, tells his readers that Cohen believed that moral panics were *created* by "particular interest groups [called] moral entrepreneurs", *Policing the Crisis* claimed that moral panics were *generated* by the elite, and Left realist criminologists *argued* that the public generate their own panics, although none of that is true [1997: 631, 633, 636–638]. With journal editors who published this rubbish merely proving that their peer review process is not guided by academic standards; it is long past the point where anyone could cover every twist and turn in this academic hairball, as every new 'study' adds another knot.

It could hardly be otherwise when the paradigm pays no more attention to the new generic definition than it did to Cohen's. Some rely solely on disproportionality, while others continue to use any definition that suits their purpose [Wright, 2000; Cassell and Cramer, 2008: 65]. Despite new panics supposed need of a "fearful anxiety" and a "legal outcome, one way or another"; Ungar's academic panic, which merely consisted of professors bemoaning their students' poor sense of history, demonstrates that the label *is* being applied to *any* complaint by *any* group about *any* issue the author does not agree with [Goode and Ben-Yehuda, 1994: 32; Ungar, 2008]. That makes generic panics even more vacuous than a cliché.

CONSTRUCTING SOCIAL PROBLEMS

The reason the panic paradigm took so long to breach the US also explains its core weakness.

Social problems, deviants, and even criminality tend to be identified, quantified, and labeled in a social construction process by moral entrepreneurs and/or other interested agents long before horror-headlines appear and are accepted or rejected by other social groups. The process is the same whether the problem is real, relates to values or not, is subject to definitional disputes, or does not really exist:

1. One or more social/commercial/professional groups typify the behavior or beliefs of someone else as problematic to promote their own beliefs about what is desirable;
2. These moral entrepreneurs construct a ready made solution for the problem which reflects their social values/interests and will delegitimize those of the targeted group;
3. The entrepreneurs select suitable horror stories reflecting the adverse typification, proffer exaggerated estimates of the extent of the threat, and suggest dire consequences will follow if their solution is not adopted;
4. The entrepreneurs will then promote one of their own number, and/or form alliances with law enforcement and/or other social control agencies and/or interested parties, to supply the expertise that validates their claims;
5. Armed with the typification, solution, horror stories, estimates, warnings, and friendly experts; the entrepreneurs secure press coverage,

tabloid TV coverage and/or appear on sensation mongering talk-shows to promote their perspective as if they were neutral concerns about a new and dangerous problem to convince the public that the problem exists;

6. Having gained publicity, the entrepreneurs and their allies use it to secure support amongst local, regional and national Government—if they did not do so before—in order to advance their solution though legislation; and

7. The entrepreneurs secure legislation controlling the targeted group, public funds for themselves or associated experts to conduct research to prove their case, and continue to typify the targeted behavior as problematic [Adopted from Rubington and Weinberg, 1989].

In contrast, as the panic paradigm begins its analysis with the horror-headlines at Stage 5, resorts to vague concepts like "social strain" to explain the panic, and rarely covers the intricacies of power in stages 6 and 7; its linear account from strain blame to headlines to legislation is innately fallacious. That is why Klocke and Muschert's proposed solution, delineating and studying *all* forms of reaction in detail, will not save the concept [2010]. To understand a reaction, you need to quantify it first; but as you also need to know what people are reacting to, you need to know how the first four phases shaped the horror-headlines and the coverage that follows. That is why the panic paradigm can not match the ability of the US perspectives to identify when, where and why moral enterprise targeted and typified a specific group or issue, and whether the campaign is part of a larger multi-faceted moral crusade by one or more social groups, or reflects an owner-ship battle over a social problem between moral entrepreneurs and other interested agencies. Being politically neutral, the US approach can cover anyone and everyone who engages in moral enterprise for whatever reason and from whatever part of the social, political, or religious spectrum. It can distinguish between the common process involved and other issues like the extent of disproportionality [Best, 2001]. By treating those initiating the campaign, those exploiting it, and the effects of media publicity as separate phenomena, it can also differentiate between the overt and latent effects of each stage. Likewise, it can account for when and why moral enterprise lead to extensive social conflict like the 1950s disputes over fluoride [Crain, Katz, and Rosenthal, 1969], or when a group like the Legion of Decency can threaten Hollywood with an economic boycott to impose censorship without having to complete the process [Black, 1994; Walsh, 1996]. It has been subjected to extensive theoretical and philosophical debate [Best, 1995; Holstein and Miller, 1993]; and has been independently validated by dozens of case studies covering crusades against 'social evils' from coffee drinking to prostitution, undertaken by historians and others who were oblivious to the sociological ramifications of their work [Sinclair, 1965; De Grazia and Newman, 1982; Troyer and Markle, 1984; Woodiwiss, 1988;

Starker, 1991; Burnham, 1993; McWilliams, 1993; Tate, 1999; Dillon, 2003; and Morone, 2003]. These features also enable and encourage critiques and developments [e.g. Benson and Saguy, 2005].

Our review of the history of the anti-porn crusades on both sides of the Atlantic demonstrated several other advantages of the US model. It can determine when and where moral enterprise serves the interests of the state and/or Capital and when it does not. It can identify and explain alliances within and between the disparate social groups that engage in moral enterprise. It can discern when counter enterprise appears and evolves into those value impasses dubbed culture wars. Contrary to Marxist lore that it could not, we also provided more than enough evidence to prove that the US perspective can account for the role and effects of the unequal distribution of power in society. Indeed, by identifying precisely who was doing what and why behind the horror-headlines the US model is far more faithful to Marx's applied accounts of class conflict like the *Eighteenth* **Brumaire of Louis Bonaparte** and his lesser known *Articles on Britain* than the simplistic economic determinism found within the panic paradigm [Thompson, 1994a; Pearce, 1976; Marx and Engels, 1975]. By coving all forms of moral enterprise, the US model also negates the need for risk or fear theory, which emerged in part to cover the increasing number of progressive panics, and those promoted by what we call "expert agencies", the scientific specialists and their activist acolytes ignored by the panic paradigm because of its political bias.

The means by which the paradigm constructs moral panic is very different.

CONSTRUCTING MORAL PANICS

In order to sell generic panic to the US, Goode and Ben-Yehuda divided the paradigm into three perspectives: "the elite", claiming panics are engineered by the ruling class to protect their economic interests; "the interest group", akin to the US moral enterprise model; and "the grass root" covering spontaneous panics amongst the public. The problems of the past were then accredited to the elite perspective by characterizing *Policing the Crisis* as a conspiracy theory [2010: 62–65]. That was more than disingenuous.

As we shall see in Chapter 3, far from claiming that the elite had engineered the panic, the CCCS spent 400 pages explaining how, during a particular point in history, numerous events converged to produce the mugging moral panic which aided the restoration of the elite's hegemonic control. Indeed, the CCCS emphasized that the panic was shaped by the activities of disparate social and interest groups seeking to secure their own ends before they converged and facilitated the panic. That not only ensures that the alleged gulf between the elite and interest group perspectives is smaller than a babbling brook given that interest groups also seek to generate societal reactions for their own ends; the elite perspective remains much closer to Cohen's original model by continuing to seek out existing social anxieties, amplifications of deviancy, and extensions in the control culture. Its core weakness is its adherents' determination to find an immediate panic pay-off for Capital, amply illustrated by Schissel who argued that Canadian panics about gangs, bullying, and other problems in schools facilitated the exploitation of youth as a cheap, obedient, and disposable labor force by multinational companies during a period of economic uncertainty [2008].

The US boosters' dismissal of the elite perspective is also somewhat hypercritical. They not only retain mugging in their list of moral panics, when they then saddled up and rode out through history rustling and rebranding pre-owned reactions as moral panic they include the 1955 *Boys of Boise* rent boy scandal, supposedly engineered by the local elite to discredit a reformist City Hall [2004: 7 and 62]! Although they explain that contradiction away by insisting that the elite's actions secured "widespread support from the man and woman in the street", they denied that defense to the CCCS who not only invented it, but unlike the boosters could explain why. What is more, the boosters' single source suggested the complete opposite. When people panicked after *The Idaho Daily Statesman* revealed that three "deviates" had "corrupted" ten boys in Boise they did so for real. Gay men fled in the dead of night for obvious reasons, mothers fretted whether their sons had become "queer", and heterosexual men avoided single sex events like poker parties least others thought that they were. This panic was encouraged by the *lack* of published details other than that the "monstrous evil" had "infected" up to another 100 teens and the decision by the city council to discuss the issue behind closed-doors. In the context of the time, the reaction was not disproportionate. Far from arrest the small fry as the boosters imply, second wave arrests included the *married* bank VP, a *prominent* attorney, and a high-school *teacher*; and that would have sent shock waves through any conservative town even if another 500 men had not been questioned [Gerassi, 1966: 12, 24, 45–52, 65, 149–158, 164].

Gerassi, a former *Time* editor, discovered the Boise gang conspiracy was a rumor. The instigators were the Allied Civic Group; a group of Mormon moral entrepreneurs annoyed that the cops were not as enthusiastic about enforcing the blue laws as they were. The ACG also conspired with a probation officer who wanted to end the gay games taking place at the local YMCA in order to force the cops to take action, and employed a private detective who had recently exposed a gay sex-ring at the local military base to do that [Gerassi, 1966: 21–23, 156]. Having been forced to act, the PD hired their own private dic whose resume included uncovering those having a gay time in the US State Department [Gerassi, 1966: 24 and 26]. However, far from undermining the medicalization of deviancy, the reaction that followed promoted it; and as the campaign against medicalization came from out of state in 1963, it was a response to the scandal's legacy rather than its cause [Gerassi, 1966: 181–186].

Despite having panicked the public, the newspaper supported medicalization by editorializing that no one had the right to complain about the "infection" unless society offered a "cure". The Idaho Board of Health earmarked funds for offender and victim programs; and the City hired a psychiatrist, Dr. Butler, who was related to the Boise gang by marriage. Butler promoted medicalization at a public meeting, offered it as a defense as an expert witness in court, and put it into practice when appointed head of Idaho's Division of Mental Health by establishing a mental health clinic [Gerassi, 1966: xvii; 15, 29, 46–47, 63 and 171]. Local women's groups rounded on the DA, the PD, and the local sheriff for failing to protect the City's youth, undermining the control agencies' opposition to medicalization as they did so. A prominent council member who had demanded a cleanup was publicly embarrassed when the local sheriff leaked his son's involvement as payback for the city council's dismissal of the Police Chief for not acting sooner; and the probation officer lost his job too [Gerassi, 1966: 24, 37–38, 118–119, and 126–129]. Meanwhile, the murder of a brutal, overbearing father by one of the youths involved led the public to demand that the probe be restricted to child molesters; and when *Time* covered the scandal, wished it would just go away. The moment the crusading DA left for a political post secured by playing up the threat, his successor offered probation deals to those already charged, and abandoned proceedings against the other 488 men. Although there was no reprieve for those already convicted, their harsh punishment reflected their previous records [Gerassi, 1966: 7–8, 47, 54–58, 65–69; 117, 193–194, Chapters 16–18, 289].

As this conservative city not only adopted a liberal solution, but did so during the era of the sexual psychopathic laws, calling Boise a moral panic demonstrates that the generic panic's theoretical and evidential standards are no better than descriptive panics [Gerassi, 1966: 10 and 72; Sutherland, 1950: 142–148]. Far from increasing "our understanding of social structure, social processes, and social change", this representative example of the paradigm's academic imperialism demonstrates how it does the complete opposite [Goode and Ben-Yehuda, 2010: 28].

IN WHOSE INTEREST?

We need not expend too much space on a critique of the interest group perspective for the simple reason that US moral panics are so under-theorized that there is little to discuss. For example, Jenkins' early work, despite popularizing the label stateside, never really justified applying the label even when sections of the public accepted the typification and solution offered by the moral entrepreneurs. Like other contextual constructionists using the label, he appears to have adopted it to cover cases where the public appeared to believe the horror-headlines at Stage 5 of the social construction process.[4] However, as none of those doing so ever quantified the level of reaction which is almost impossible, or delineated whether the public agreed with the entrepreneurs for rational reasons, overreacted because they did not assess the validity of the claims being made, or 'panicked'; contextual constructionism has been guilty of label slapping too. As a result, once one peels the panic label off case studies of successful moral enterprise, the interest group perspective effectively disappears.

As we cover grass roots panics in the penultimate chapter, where we demonstrate that their spontaneous nature is a function of the author's failure to research the back story, we draw attention here to how it also reflects the author's politics, amply illustrated by Wright's account of the Marilyn Manson-teen suicide panic [2000]. Relying solely on the element of disproportionality, apparently proven by the fact that music is not a recognized clinical cause of suicide, Wright designates neoconservative town administrations' cancellation of a couple of Manson's 1997–8 tour dates as moral panic. Yet he not only fails to explain that the administrations were reacting to demands from the revived Charismatic Christian crusade against demonic music, he makes no mention of the fact that Manson's latest offering, *AntiChrist Superstar,* and the tour's title, *Dead to the World,* would explain why the crusade singled Manson out, or how that secured Manson numerous invites to rebut these complaints on more than one popular talk show. That lack of detail was matched by Wright's failure to explain the context.

The Charismatics were not the only group to exploit the contemporary interest in teen suicide generated by the World Health Organization and government agencies worldwide who palmed off an increase in the percentage of teen suicide compared to other age categories as an increase *per se.* Hundreds of NGOs jumped on the bandwagon in order to secure funding for their pet projects or start new ones, even though teen suicide was actually declining! [TSS/SC 2008] One of the most successful initiatives involved the NYC gay community which took advantage of the US government's *Task Force on Youth Suicide* to promote the claim that widespread bullying of LGBTQ teens in NY High Schools ensured that their rate of suicide was four times higher than heterosexual teens. As that claim could never be substantiated it was innately disproportionate, but despite securing appropriations for the world's first LGBTQ high school, no one called that good idea a moral panic [Gibson, 1989].

If the paradigm had concentrated on the effects of horror-headlines at stage 5 of the social construction process, delineating when, where, and why the moral entrepreneurs' campaigns worked, failed, or led to battles of blame as it did in Boise, it might have justified its existence; but the paradigm's political perspective mitigates against accepting that secondary role.

DON'T GO THERE

From its inception the panic paradigm has relied on several assumptions and ignored several weaknesses that we cover here to avoid constant repetition in the chapters that follow.

The Powerful Press

Rather than demonstrate when, where, and how horror-headlines shape public perceptions and reactions, this is taken for granted as Critcher has admitted [2003: 27]. Schissel's evidence for a nationwide panic about aboriginal youth amounted to five newspaper articles that most Canadians would not have read [1997]. Watney's UK AIDS panic rested on half-a-dozen citations in the press [Watney, 1987]. Payne's panic about the movie *Hounddog* consisted of questions at a film festival press conference [2008]. These examples suggest that the paradigm continues to rely on the Frankfurt School model of media effects despite it being debunked decades ago [Lowery and Defluer, 1983]. Worse, the paradigm never covers the content of popular, seminal prime time TV shows when it comes to typifying and proffering the solutions for social problems being raised by moral entrepreneurs. They played a major part in promoting public 'awareness' about the threats posed by pin-up porn and Satanism covered in Chapters 5 and 6, and which help explain why they did not work. Part I, of this volume, reveals that the media did not have the effects accredited to it by the seminal studies. Part II covers an example when the horror-headlines were a very good guide to what was happening. Part III, a case in which a unanimous media orientation had ambiguous effects.

Stigma

Cohen was well aware that urban society was too diverse for stigma to be applied to deviants as opposed to criminality unless prior prejudice was involved, despite claiming otherwise in *Folk devils* [Lemert, 1964, cited Cohen, 1969: 35]; and the paradigm continues to ignore how non criminalized notoriety often has the opposite effect. If moral boundaries could be maintained by turning the pages of the secular sermons in the UK's Sunday tabloid press, the thirty-year vicarious denunciation of swinging clubs would have led to their demise rather than their expansion [Roberts, 2003]. Indeed, so many British celebrities have been exposed for engaging in drink, drugs and adventurous sex since the 1970s that the younger generation came to believe that this was normal, and made it so. One week's media deviant becomes next week's reality TV celebrity unless they are a member of the British upper-class wearing a Nazi uniform [BBC, 2010]. *Part I demonstrates that the mods and rockers were not stigmatized by the press. Part II that the same applies to inanimate objects deemed evil influences. Part III reveals that even when deviants are stigmatized that does not necessarily have the effect that the paradigm assumes that it does.*

WHO'S PANICKING?

The use of the term panic to describe the public reaction to horror-headlines was always ambiguous and anomalous given that it covered both the outrage amongst the public *and* the determined, instrumental acts of the moral entrepreneurs and social control agencies. The first followed from Cohen's dubious analogy with people panicking in natural disasters [1973: 22–23], and the second from his initial attempt to subsume moral enterprise under the panic rubric. However, while natural disasters can generate collective stress, Cohen's analogy was based on a myth:

> The social activities and processes that occur in a community stricken by disaster are very different from popular representations . . . [People] . . . do not suddenly become wildly disorganized and irrational . . . Panic has been reported in many disasters, but when investigated empirically, such reports have often proven unfounded . . . Contrary to the myth, most people react quite rationally in disaster situations; they do not behave in an asocial, irrational manner as the 'panic' image suggests [Tierney, 1989: 20–21].

As horror-headlines are invariably provoked by moral enterprise, the entrepreneurs would hardly be panicking about them, and as public-order policing has its own motives and dynamics [Waddington, 1993], offering these as indicators of panic is equally dubious. That leaves us with the 'panicking' public, but as no one has justified using the catch-all 'panic' label to cover the disparate reactions that appear, and/or rely on proxies like the number of horror-headlines, we still await any proof that the public ever panicked. Part I demonstrates that even when the horror-headlines were supposedly provoked by a 'precipitating event,' that event was newsworthy because of ongoing moral enterprise. Parts I and II demonstrate that the moral entrepreneurs in the seminal studies exhibited neither the fear nor anxiety Cohen associated with panic. Parts II and III confirm that what the public thinks is often irrelevant, as the success or failure of moral enterprise frequently depends upon the aims of the politicians who take up the cause and whether or not the folk devils fight back.

Common Values and Structural Strain

The belief that disintegrating societal values can be restored by targeting folk devils rests upon Erickson's *Wayward Puritans* [1966], an evidential disaster area that deflected attention from the fact that 'common values' are *recreated* and evolve in each generation through moral enterprise, evidenced by the history of child protection rationales [Rose, 1991 and 2009; Platt, 1977]. Parts I and II prove that the societal values supposedly feeding the panics in the seminal studies had long since been abandoned and were *not* even ascribed to by the segment of society supposed to be defending them. Part II shows that the major account of a new generic 'sectional' panic exhibits the same evidential problems that descriptive panics do. Part III demonstrates that even when 'the public' adopts the typification being promoted in the media it does not always accept the values behind the typification.

The Usual Suspects

Many of the problems exhibited by the panic paradigm reflect the concept's original dependence on the remarkable properties ascribed to the petit-bourgeoisie by the New Left. Forever declining since Marx predicted their immanent fall into the proletariat during the 1840s, this class with its fearful indignation conveniently reappears whenever the New Left needed a scapegoat for its own failings [Weeks, 1985; Levitas, 1986; Kavanagh, 1987; Sked, 1987; Mort, 1987; Murray, 1995]. As the petit-bourgeoisie was and is the organizing class, supplying the leadership of the working-class movements of the past and progressive activists today, the link drawn by the paradigm between this class and the political Right was always simplistic and misleading [Thompson, E.P., 1972; Foster, 1974; Prothero, 1979 and 1997; Royal, 1981]. Although new panics are supposed to have abandoned this bias in favor of political neutrality [Jenkins, 1992: 8], nothing could be further from the truth.

The US boosters' source of panics—elite (ruling class), interest group (petit-bourgeoisie), and grass roots (working-class) perspectives—is not only a class based model, it facilitates the new politics of panic targeting the working-class for failing to fulfill the New Left's expectations of it and for daring to object to the authoritarian aspects of political correctness [Jones, 2011: 116]. The US approach *looks* different because that switch occurred much earlier when progressives blamed the working-classes for putting Nixon in the White House in 1968 and then for undermining their great white hope, McGovern, in the next election [Miroff, 2009]. That is why, when US academics slap the label panic on any Right-wing manifestation of petit-bourgeois politics from the Moral Majority to the Tea Party, they throw in the 'rednecks' for free. They do so for the same reason that President Obama quipped that these classes "cling to their guns and churches" in times of crisis:[5] economic determinism. Similar reservations apply to the role given to the "respectable working-class", supposed to hold the same values as the petit-bourgeoisie. This can be traced to Lenin's claims about the "labor aristocracy", although the working-class historian Trevor Lummis demonstrated that generalization was impossible [1994]. Part I reveals that the real world reaction of these 'panicking classes' to the horror-headlines was the complete opposite of their theoretical determined role in the seminal studies. Part II explains why the role ascribed to the petit-bourgeoisie never made any sense, demographically or politically, and why the US boosters' attempt to explain away progressive panics is in error. Part III covers the origins, nature, and effects of the new politics of panic.

Moral Enterprise, Interested Agencies, and Social Group Conflict

When Goode and Ben-Yehuda attempted to integrate moral enterprise within the panic paradigm, they failed to address the paradigm's limited concept of social values. Despite alluding to societal-wide values, the seminal studies concentrated on those supposed to favor Capital like the protestant work ethic, even though the public and the moral entrepreneurs involved did not perceive the world in those terms. The latter were always more concerned about the demise of the moral values that they had *imposed* upon Capital during the previous century as part of the religious-progressive-feminist alliance which promoted issues like raising the age of consent in the UK and prohibition in the US [Thompson, G. (Ed.) 1923; Pearl, 1955; Blyth, 1963; Boyer, 1968 and 1992; Bristow, 1977; Shiman, 1988; Dixon, 1991, Thompson, 1994a; Petrow, 1994; Tate, 1999].

The paradigm's failure to take that history and its legacy into account when covering contemporary social group value conflict reflects the way new wave sociology during the 1960s reinforced the division drawn by the New Left between the "reactionary" moral crusades of the past and the new progressive social movements, even though the "dual crusades" against pornography and prostitution suggested that division was over drawn. The most obvious example is the exploitation of Gusfield's claim that prohibition was a symbolic crusade, masking the moral entrepreneurs' WASP fears of immigrants [1963], even though prohibition was merely one part of the religious-progressive-feminist agenda which included universal suffrage, the regulation of big business, free public education, and *encouraging* immigration. The major motive linking the Prohibition Party, the Anti-Saloon League, and the Women's Christian Temperance Union was the destruction of the saloon culture of the "roughs and toughs", the "lower orders", and the "sporting bourgeoisie" as well immigrants, because the crusaders believed that saloon culture was the source of the graft and corruption blocking progressive reform [Sinclair, 1965; Woodiwiss, 1988; Burnham, 1993]. Although the Prohibition Party began to demanded programs to Americanize immigrants from 1924 and prohibitionists played on racial fears in the southern states [Link, 1992]; if prohibition was symbolic of anything it was the progressive agenda, in the same way that abortion rights has come to symbolize women's rights in general [Sinclair, 1965, 100]. The panic paradigm could learn a lot from the repeal campaign too.

Repeal followed from the common cause amongst Greenwich Village intellectuals, bohemians, journalists, the NYC cocktail set, and the capitalists opposed to government regulation, who argued that decriminalizing "sauce" would provide a revenue stream to fund FDR's social programs. Once Du Pont was converted to repeal, the precarious power previously enjoyed by the prohibitionists because of the divisions within the major parties disappeared overnight and they became the folk devils! By emphasizing that prohibition had generated more crime and corruption than before, and by contrasting their sophisticated urbane lifestyle to the bland world of backwoods, bigoted, Bible bashers; the repeal movement made moralism synonymous with hypocrisy, and drink with independence, and turned the American Dream into the good life displayed across the glossy pages of Park Avenue magazines and cinema screens. Instead of slumming with "the roughs" as they had done in the past, the sophisticated "smart set" now set the standards for others to follow; and social vices like drinking and smoking previously associated with the lower-orders became *the* fashionable American way, especially amongst the flappers turning against their mothers' Puritanism [Burnham, 1993]. By failing to pay attention to this history, the paradigm failed to learn four lessons from repeal: (i) capitalism had long since abandoned the values that the paradigm associates with it; (ii) what was legally deemed deviant in one decade could easily become the norm in the next; (iii) while societal values reflect the outcome of social group value conflict, not everyone need agree with those values; and finally, (iv) anything less than a detailed study of the cultural-political as well as socio-economic forces at work would ensure that any conclusion drawn would be erroneous.

Once the Charismatic Christians on both sides of the Atlantic embarked on a series of moral crusades in the 1960s against the US Supreme Court's and the UK parliamentary decriminalization of sin, they discovered that the new social movements, victimized ethnic groups, professional lobbies, and even the deviants were out there crusading too. That is why the amount of social group value conflict dramatically increased from the 1960s onwards, along with the amount of moral enterprise *within* social groups as various sections sought to control the direction their movement should take. Part I reveals that Cohen deliberately omitted the seminal role of the Local Government Information Office in provoking the initial horror-headlines about the mods and rockers, and that the CCCS underplayed the role of the London Transport Police in the mugging moral panic. Part II covers the motives behind, and the effects of, local government moral enterprise, and how state agencies were hijacked by progressive moral entrepreneurs to further their group's agenda. Part III covers a case when the local authorities and social control agencies encouraged 'panic' to mask their own failings from the public!

Teen Trouble and Physical Threats

Although horror-headlines about teen trouble are a mainstay in the panic paradigm, they are the most problematic of them all. Goths would obviously pose a much greater threat to mainstream values than the vacuous Teddy boys, mods, and skinheads of panic fame, ever did; but Goths have never generated panic because they do not trash cinemas, trash resort towns, or engage in violent racist hate crimes. Indeed, Goths and other teen groups which generate their own values rather than need a cultural studies professor to invent some for them, have always had more to fear from criminal youth than society, even when the latter is represented by bullying high school jocks [Larkin, 2007]. Exceptions to this rule require extraordinary circumstances as the punks in Jamestown NY, the heavy metal fans in

Lansford PA, and the West Memphis Three all discovered to their cost during the satanic panic in the US [Victor, 1993, Ellis, 1990; Leveritt, 2002].

Even when teen crime waves generate horror-headlines, public support for more law and order could never be taken for granted, as that will depend upon the level of direct physical threat involved. In order to argue otherwise, the paradigm continues to palm off teen criminality as mere deviance in order to dismiss rational concerns about violence as a disproportionate fear, although that exposes its double-dealing with Durkheim. Despite ignoring the implications of Durkheim's observations about value pluralism as Schissel [1997] admitted; the paradigm readily exploited the corollary that *crime* could maintain social unity in otherwise diverse societies by extending that to *deviancy* [see Thompson, 1982]. The paradigm did so by conflating the 1960s sociological truism that most criminalized deviancy consisted of alternative life styles devoid of innate harm with the contentious Marxist belief that teen crime was a rebellion against the imposition of capitalist "time work discipline" [Henslin, 1977; Cohen and Young, 1973; NDC, 1980; Waites *et al*, 1981; Humphries, 1981]. Although Cohen admitted that the threat of physical violence was as important as value transgression when teen deviance provoked horror-headlines; his dubious dismissal of that factor in *Folk Devils,* on the grounds that the mods and rockers fought each other opened the door to dozens of formulaic panics which amounted to little more than a couple of horror-headlines about the latest teen crime wave [Cohen, 1973: 197–198]. We address these issues in Part I, which reveals that fears about teen deviancy in the seminal studies really concerned criminal violence. Part III covers the example of criminal teens who *were* consciously engaging in resistance to authority, but were condemned by the panic paradigm!

Disproportionate Threats and Statistics

The paradigm's tendency to dismiss fears of violence as irrational and disproportionate to the statistical threat of becoming a victim was a political response to counter the political Right's exploitation of the fear of crime, although Left Realism demonstrated that was the progressives' own fault. Even now the paradigm continues to ignore the sources of the public's zero tolerance policy: childhood experiences, precautions taken as teens to avoid becoming a victim, and the growing exasperation during adulthood that previous counter-measures have failed to inhibit the next thug that generates horror-headlines. To ignore the outpouring of "heart-felt victim empathy" that appears during 'panics' verges on callousness as well as exposes the paradigm's failure to appreciate the role appeals against violent criminality [Banner, 2002: 283–284].

The frequency of moral entrepreneurs' appeals to anti-violent sentiments demonstrates the salience of zero tolerance. Without the alleged threat of violence to follow, the demand to restrict the latest manifestation of violence in popular culture like computer war games because they promote the "wrong values" would never get an airing. Likewise, the paradigm has never considered that fears of random violence like the LA freeway shootings or "wildings" follow the fact that the threat can appear out of nowhere irrespective of who is statistically most at risk, making the statistical probability of victimhood irrelevant, and no guide to disproportionality. Indeed, the failure to recognise that random violence *can* happen to anyone, despite its concentration in the lower classes, is an act of irrationality. Part II covers cases when moral entrepreneurs tried to exploit zero tolerance philosophies to amplify the supposed threat; and Part III covers a seminal example where the paradigm made the fear factor look irrational by deliberately omitting the evidence that the threat was real and immediate.

Visibility

The issues of zero tolerance and statistical probability also draw attention to the role of visibility in generating moral panic. The way this initial 'must have' feature was quickly transformed from a property of the folk devil to the horror-headlines about them helps explain why the paradigm has underestimated the relationship between threats, fear, and *invisibility*. Even though the mods and rockers were highly visible whereas the mugger was not, part of their impact was the inability to predict where and when they would appear next; the same fear factor that explains 'overreactions' when serial rapists or killers are at large [Jenkins, 1992]. Today's segmented media markets also makes visibility unpredictable. There is no guarantee issues will have the same coverage on the mainstream media, cable TV, the Web, or the blogosphere. Even when they do, the approach or spin can be very different leading to a wealth of reactions. Although the paradigm appeared to accommodate this problem with the concept of sectional panics, as we have already pointed out, it failed to explain how they could restore society's values as opposed to reinforce that sections values, prejudice, or fears. Consequently, we have reversed this feature of moral panic. Part I covers the invisibility of moral panic in the seminal studies to demonstrate that the authors' ability to discern its existence relied on questionable theoretical assumptions. By demonstrating that entrepreneur's claims-making is also designed to 'prove' their ideological beliefs, Part II demonstrates the similarity between the moral panic paradigm and moral enterprise. Parts I, II, and III all reveal that panic paradigm claims-making relies on making countervailing evidence that points to different conclusions invisible.

Deviance Amplification

Few case studies bother to demonstrate that the folk devils adopted their stigmatized role or that an amplification of the deviance leading to an increase in control culture has occurred, even though these facets rather than the horror-headlines 'proved' that a panic was in progress. Although the US boosters maintained this "no folk devil: no panic" rule to distinguish between moral panic and moral enterprise, that division does not work in the real world. For example, Goode and Ben-Yehuda dismiss the concept of risk panic on the grounds that they do not invoke a folk devil, when they clearly do [2010: 165]. If it is not the money-grubbing corporate world, a mainstay on the Left since Marx's enlivened *Capital* with the antics of "moneybags", it is Monsanto and their Frankenstein food, politicians grabbing lobbyists' cash, the "GW deniers", or the "New World Order globalists" and so on. The boosters' failure to consider those examples is, however, less important than the disappearance of the need for the folk devils to increase in number over the period of panic as Cohen's model required. If one excludes case studies failing to demonstrate an amplification of the threat, be it real or imagined, there would not be many panics left. Part I demonstrates that the folk devils in the seminal studies never played the role ascribed to them. Part II, that demonization does not automatically follow from horror-headlines. Part III, how one person's folk devil is another's folk hero in pluralistic societies.

Panics, Politics, and the Public

It matters not whether the claims or counterclaims come from a social, identity, or professional interest group, Christians or gays, professors or police, whites or blacks, females or males, government agency or a righteously indignant NGO staff member. Behind every alleged moral panic you find someone trying to impose their values on everyone else [Thompson, 1989]. They do so because they are convinced that they know what is best for society. They engage in "coercive reform", criminalizing others' preferences, because they know that in a pluralistic society "assimilative reform", the attempt to persuade others, will not work as everyone has their own values and convictions. 'Minorities' like youth are no exception as they invariably find a champion from a social or interest group wary of how labeling the youths will promote values that they oppose. In most cases the public merely reflects bemused bystanders watching the moral entrepreneurs on either side of the divide battle it out on TV or in the press, whatever poll results might say. In every case we have reviewed, we failed to find any evidence of a panicking public because that feature is function of the paradigm's theory, assumptions, and labeling process. That fact was reinforced in dramatic fashion one night when we participated in a studio debate over Dawn Primarolo's anti-pornography bill in front of a live audience organized by the UK's Central TV in 1992. Despite all the tabloid hype backing the bill and denouncing porn, the 'panicking' public literally laughed the bill's supporters off the stage!

As every sociology and criminology student quickly learns that horror-headlines can mislead the public, can generate the perception of deviancy amplification, and can lead to needless laws; what else but politics would compel anyone to prove that over and over and over, again and again and again? The fact that the US boosters spent most of their time telling readers what the paradigm *could* do rather than what *had* done, is an effective admission that the paradigm *is* political: the attempt to promote an alternative set of values to those supposedly proffered by the horror-headlines. That is why you can learn far more about the dynamics of teen trends, deviant behavior, persecution of minorities, irrational behavior, and social group value conflict by watching *South Park* than reading books on moral panic; and why we put those books on moral panic on the shelf next to those on alien abduction, the Bermuda Triangle, and the prophesies of Nostradamus.

THE MYTH OF MORAL PANIC

The panic paradigm became popular because it offers adherents the opportunity to promote their values and claims-making in what amounts to an uncontested environment, despite the odd disagreement over details. In contrast, this critique is based on our ethnographic experience in the social worlds behind six sets of horror-headlines where *everything* is contested. Although we have utilized every sociological methodology that there is at one time or another, we contend that there is no substitute for being there. In our case, one of us was fortunate enough to have mod siblings, in an area full of mods, and was even taken to Clacton though not on *that* week-end; so, we rely on the historical record apart from our rebuttal of Cohen's "meaning of mod". Likewise, one of us played a bit part in the class struggles of the 1970s, witnessed acts of racial profiling by the police grabbing 'muggers' in Oxford Street, and was fortunate enough to have been frequently invited to one of the epicenters of the counterculture, backstage at *Hawkwind* happenings. So, we have used those insights as well as the historical record to critique *Policing the Crisis*. Having followed the moral crusade against sexstores from which it emerged, we knew that *Video Nasties* was on the Christian crusaders' hit-list two years before the horror-headlines appeared in *The Daily Mail*. Indeed, one of us was even in the room when one of the groups involved handed their list of targeted nasties to local video-store owners and warned them to remove the titles from their shelves. As we had followed the feminist civil war, helped fund one of our PhDs by clerking for an attorney in the eras obscenity cases, and were later consulted by attorneys whose innocent clients were accused of distributing snuff movies, we can easily rebut Goode and Ben-Yehuda's excuses about the progressives' porn panics. As we spent five years on Orkney, the seminal satanic case in the UK, and were asked to review several others, we know that Charismatic Christians were not the only ones responsible for the satanic panic. Then when the panic paradigm swapped sides in 2000, and backed the government's attempt to demonize lawful protest, we were there too: attending a demonstration, watching as the 'vigilantes' drafted their presentation to Tony Blair which changed the law, and were ever present at the trials which proved that no riots took place in Paulsgrove, Portsmouth.

This personal journey through the social worlds behind the headlines supplied the evidence that follows, highlighting the disparity between the social realities we discovered and the descriptions and explanations offered by the panic paradigm. We deliberately undertook that journey because many years ago a group of sociologists proved that you could learn far more about the nature of deviancy by hanging out with deviants rather than social control agents, and we suspected that we would learn more about the nature of 'moral panic' by associating with the moral entrepreneurs and folk devils rather than academics; and so it proved. The end result is damning. Given that Cohen's original intent was to critique and transcend the "vague, subjective, and continually shifting definitions" of deviancy employed in 1960s criminology [1969: 15]; moral panic theory has failed completely, because that is a perfect description of the current state of the moral panic paradigm.

Chapter 1 outlines Cohen's model, detailing the difference between the original definition and what now passes for moral panic despite the lack of justification for the label. Chapter 2 examines the evidence offered for each element, covers Cohen's reliance on a set of theoretical imperatives that were not applicable, and reveals that once one reviews the evidence that Cohen *deliberately* omitted, *Folk Devils* is far more misleading than the media coverage. Chapter 3 presents a summary of the dense text of *Policing the Crisis* in a user-friendly form and outlines the convergence model of moral panic to demonstrate that it remained closer to Cohen's original concept than the "new, improved" generic panics do. However, once we include the evidence that they omitted, it transpires that the only people panicking about the supposed link between horror-headlines, mugging, and black youth were the neo-Nazi British Movement and the neo-Maoist Center for Contemporary Cultural Studies.

Chapter 4 explores the origins and effects of two major cracks in the foundations of the panic paradigm that can traced back to Erickson's *Wayward Puritans* which never justified its thesis that boundary crises generated deviance, the suppression of which restored society's collective conscience. On the contrary, the crises that Erickson covered were *created* by the public's disregard for the norms and laws of the period, and the attempt to scapegoat deviants backfired as the folk devils ultimately won. On the other hand, Erickson's thesis reveals why the panic paradigm believes that it is entitled to "rearrange" the evidence to justify its theory. Chapter 5 covers the background to the 1984 panic over violent videos to explore the nature of the paradigm's political bias. By placing the panic in its wider context, the porn wars between 1975 and 1995, we demonstrate how the myth of the New Moral Right masked the fact that Britain's Christian moral entrepreneurs were not only in constant conflict with *permissive* Conservative governments, but formed a formal alliance with radical feminists between 1985 and 1992. That revelation not only demonstrates how paradigmatic accounts are woefully inadequate, but that the power that the paradigm accredited to numerous moral panics only existed because professional feminists agreed with what they were doing. We will also demonstrate that, despite claims to the contrary, the paradigm's guesses about the role of the state and Capital in panics are inferior to the evidential reality uncovered by contextual constructionism. Chapter 6, which covers the rise and fall of the satanic ritual child abuse allegations on both sides of the Atlantic, enables us to compare and contrast the politics found in the elite and interest group perspectives defined by Goode and Ben-Yehuda, and reveal how moral panics are constructed in the same way that the satanic abuse allegations were!

Chapter 7 finds us on the Paulsgrove housing estate in Portsmouth, UK during the summer of 2000, concentrating on the neglected area of the folk devil. As this grass root panic is the nearest an episode has ever come to conforming to Cohen's original model, the fact that paradigmatic accounts willfully ignored the evidence offered at trial that no riots took place proves that the "mistakes" that we have uncovered within the paradigm are deliberate. The Conclusion reviews the growing criticism of the panic paradigm to piece together an explanation for the myth of moral panic, and draws a link between the politics of the panic paradigm and one of the most insidious forms of control culture that the world has ever seen.

Part I

The Making of a Myth

The following three chapters review the two seminal studies behind the moral panic myth. Chapter 1 outlines the transactional process in Cohen's original model that has been lost to sociology along with the psychological assumptions, which explained and justified the label 'moral panic.' It demonstrates the inability of descriptive and generic panics to justify the label moral panic, and facilitates our critique of Cohen's case study.

Chapter 2 reviews the evidence offered by Cohen for each phase, element, and feature of the moral panic. It reveals that while *Folk Devils* was a "relentlessly theoretical work" it was not "empirically grounded" as Garland claimed it was [2008: 9]. On the contrary, Cohen's approach to evidence not only replicated the media methods that he condemned, his deliberate manipulation of the data should have led to a bigger academic scandal than that surrounding Margret Mead's *Coming of Age in Samoa*.

Chapter 3 demonstrates that while *Policing the Crisis* is not a conspiracy theory, it *is* the paradigm's equivalent of a black hole. In the same way that the astrological phenomenon was uncovered by analyzing the behavior of the galaxy around it; no one saw the mugging moral panic until its existence was revealed by the analysis proffered by the CCCS of the crisis in the heavens of hegemony surrounding the horror-headlines. However, as it followed Cohen's model and merely made the politics of panics more overt it cannot be held responsible for the paradigm's political bias.

1   Constructing Moral Panic

INTRODUCTION

In order to delineate the transactional process which distinguished moral panic from other reactions to horror-headlines, we have used **bold script** for the nine necessary elements and **bold** *italics* for the 'must have' features in the three-phase panic process. To save space and avoid repetition, we cover most of the specific evidence Cohen offered for these elements and features in the next chapter; although it will become apparent long before then that neither the descriptive panics or the 'new, improved' generic panics contain the essence of moral panic as Cohen defined them.

PHASE ONE: THE INVENTORY

The first phase of moral panic concerns the creation of a *media inventory* covering the *precipitating event* with its panic inducing images [1973: 30]. The first element, **exaggeration and distortion** includes the use of *generic plurals* presenting single events as common occurrences, publishing 'facts' known to be false or *rumors,* and *over-reporting* by using *melodramatic language.* In the case of mods and rockers:

> The regular uses of phases such as 'riot', 'orgy of destruction', 'battle', 'attack', siege', 'beat up the town' and 'screaming mob' left an image of a besieged town from which innocent holiday makers were fleeing to escape of marauding mob [1973: 31].

The meaning of the initial horror-headlines and reports were reinforced by the editorials and feature articles that appeared in the *news-cycle sequence* common to major stories, which pass comment on the misleading accounts rather than the real nature of events [1973: 30]. The subsequent *societal-wide reaction* is shaped by the erroneous *putative definitions* that emerge during this reinforcement. In Clacton's case, they consisted of:

- "Gangs"—when most groups present were unstructured;
- Giving the mods and rockers distinct identities—before they had polarized into two groups;
- Inferring a deliberate "invasion from London"—when going to Clacton was a Bank Holiday tradition and many arrestees were local;
- Emphasizing the role of the motor bike and scooter riders—though they were in a minority;
- Claiming that the youths were "affluent"—though most were not;
- Inferring that they were "classless"—when most were working-class;
- Imputing "deliberate intent"—despite a lack of evidence; and
- Emphasizing the "violence and vandalism", "cost of damage" and a "loss of trade"—when there was little serious violence, the vandalism was no greater than usual, the damage was not as excessive as reported, and the poor trading figures were the result of bad weather [1973: 34–37].

The vital role accorded to the feature articles demonstrates that horror-headlines alone are not enough for moral panic. As both are also common to crime reporting, a moral panic requires the other elements, beginning with the **predictions** that shape the next two phases. In Cohen's case, the predictions consisted of the "implicit assumption, present in virtually every report that what had happened was inevitably going to happen again" [Cohen, 1973: 38]. Without that the *social disaster*, the *self-fulfilling prophecy* of *deviancy amplification* creating the problem being denounced, would not occur [1973: 38–39]. Likewise, the third element, **symbolization**, contains far more than the erroneous *stereotypes* found in subsequent case studies. That is because the disproportionality that appeared had nothing to do with the *claims* made as the US boosters contend, but the way that the symbolization process created the *impression* that the problem was rapidly getting worse. That impression also explains what later case studies do not: why the wider public was sucked into the panic; and why the claims and prediction did not appear to be disproportionate.

The first feature of the symbolization process involved the metamorphosis of positive and neutral concepts into *negative symbols*, making the problem appear bigger than it was. For example, the image of the quiet resort town of Clacton was now turned into 'a disaster area' indicated by the expression "we don't want another Clacton here". Second, Cohen drew attention to the three-step process whereby other youths became *guilty by association*. As 'mod' became symbolic of delinquent status, anything associated with mod like their hairstyle came to symbolize mod, and so anyone with a similar hairstyle was believed to be both a mod and a delinquent; making the problem look bigger still. Third, *follow-up stories* turning unrelated incidents into part of the problem encouraged people to believe that the predictions were coming true. By failing to cover these aspects, descriptive and generic panics cannot account for the effects of the

symbolization. Rather than merely *demonize* the folk devil as later studies purport; by creating the appearance of an outbreak of the deviancy
and offering the public an explanation for the precipitating event Cohen's
symbolization ensured that the *effect of the inventory was total,* not least
because *no one offered an alternative interpretation* [1973: 43–44].

As well as demonstrating that horror-headlines and demonizing folk
devils by stereotype are not enough to create a moral panic, these elements
involve far more than the "concern" or "hostility" found in generic panics.
Cohen's first three elements have extensive social effects, fuelling the moral
panic by *creating* the disproportionality which descriptive and generic panics imply is a function of existing anxiety rather than emerging from the
interactive process. As we shall see, the existing anxiety about another sup-
pressed problem is made visible by its projection onto the folk devil through
the moral panic process, which also enhances it.

REACTION: PHASE ONE

The second phase of Cohen's model involved the inculcation of the media
inventory amongst the public creating the societal-wide agreement about
the symbolic meaning of the threat, especially when the deviancy is seen as
a symptom of a "dislocation in the social structure" or a "threat to cher-
ished values". That is why this phase ensured that the reaction concerned
the implications of the event for society rather than merely condemned
the folk devils, and enabled Cohen to assert that moral panics restored
the societal values under threat [1973: 49]. The forth element, the media
orientation, spells out the implications of the deviancy for "society as we
know it" and thereby determines "what is to be done" as a consequence
[1973: 49]. It does this by *reporting the subsequent public reactions* to
the inventory, from public meetings to government debates, reinforcing the
psychological impact of the precipitating event, and linking the deviants
to the *structural strain* creating the *group myth* that now emerges about
the causes and consequences of the precipitating event [1973: 49–50]. In
Cohen's case, this was achieved by the increasing number of disaster analogies and *prophecies of doom* that appeared in the press, which were warning the public that unless "something was done" the situation would get
worse. Although commentators offered several *variants* the public could
consider, their collective effect was to increase the symbolic meaning of
Clacton. It mattered not whether people argued that it was "not so much
what happened" at Clacton but that it "could have been worse, and was
likely to become so"; or, as "various social groups" insisted, that "it's not
only this" but other adverse social trends from teen pregnancy to illicit
drug consumption that constituted the problem. As every comment alluded
to the same structural strain, every reaction increased the size of the apparent threat [1973: 51–53].

As well as ignoring the psychology of moral panic that generated the reactions; it is rare to find any other case study illustrating the reports of the reactions in the press or the fifth element: the **folk devils' new image**. This emerged from the *spurious attributions* and *specific auxiliary status traits* repeated in the press that linked the folk devils to the specific values perceived to be under threat. Indeed, unless one explores these claims emanating from the moral barricades, you can not explain why the folk devils became demonized. Later studies referring to existing stereotypes can not be panics. In Cohen's case, the new labels "mods and rockers" replaced the *emotive symbolic labels* from the past like "hooligans" or "wild ones" used in the initial horror-headlines. In Cohen's case these traits were summarized by a local prosecutor as: a lack of views on serious subjects, inflated ideas about their own importance, immaturity, irresponsibility, arrogance, and a lack of respect for law and peoples' property. They were also encapsulated in a single phrase by the magistrate Dr. Simpson who denounced the youths as "sawdust Caesars".

This *re-labelling process* with its new specific stereotypes could be seen in both the *guilt by association* mentioned earlier and the *legends and myths* about the youths that subsequently emerged. The most widely reported legend concerned the youth who offered to pay his £75 fine by bank check. Repeatedly told to prove that, as "fines won't hurt them" harsher punishments were needed, the legend reinforced the media orientation that the problem was caused by the teens' affluence. In reality, it was a sarcastic comment, given that £75 would take months to pay off [1973: 55–57]. Once again, while there were disagreements on the moral barricades, with some arguing that delinquency was endemic and others suggesting it was only a lunatic fringe [1973: 59–61]; these contradictions did not confuse the public because every claim generated and diffused normative concerns and drew a sharp distinction between the new stereotype of the youths and normal behaviour [1973: 61].

The ability of moral panic to accommodate variations and even contradictions applied to the **causation** element too. A precise diagnosis was less important than the fact that *everyone* agreed that the deviancy was a "sign of the times", part of the wider "social malaise" caused by being soft on crime, a decline in religious belief, and the delinquents' lack of a sense of purpose having been "coddled" by the welfare state. In their turn, these explanations reflected a common reactionary or conservative belief that the permissive reforms of Victorian values had gone too far [1973: 61–62]. As a result, it mattered not that liberals believed that the youths' boredom and alienation followed from a lack of creative outlets, or that conservatives argued that the youths were not using the outlets on offer; everyone agreed that the youths were alienated and bored [1973: 63–65]. While descriptive and generic panics give the impression that the impact of horror-headlines is immediate, Cohen did not. The media inventory did not spread across society in "an absorbed symmetry" and the public continued to disagree over the specific images and stereotypes, the class composition, the precise causes, and the potential longevity of the problem. For example, the informed public of magistrates, teachers, social workers, and probation officers:

> were overwhelmingly critical, if not hostile, towards the mass media: 40.5 per cent felt that the media had exaggerated and blown the whole thing up, and a further 41.3 percent actually attributed responsibility to media publicity for part of what happened [1973: 69].

This *deferential reaction* did not undermine the panic, because these groups were unrepresentative of the wider public whose beliefs and reaction were covered in the third phase of the panic [1973: 74]. Later case studies rarely cover two other features from this phase. Despite offering a social strain to 'explain' the panic, with the exception of the odd US drug panic they rarely demonstrate how the folk devils come to personify the social strain because of the *new* stereotypes generated [Best, 1999]. Likewise, one rarely finds any discussion of the moral panic's *unique features* that reflect the specific nature of the perceived threat in each panic. In Cohen's case this consisted of the *divide and rule tactic* whereby:

> the adult community, faced with an apparent attack upon its most sacred institution (property) and the most sacred guardians of this institution (the police) reacts, if not consciously, by over emphasising the differences among the enemy [1973: 58].

Although Cohen did not say so, these unique features are as important as the nine elements given they not only explain and demonstrate why each panic takes hold, but also help inhibit alternative explanations which would undermine their total effect. In the case of the mods and rockers, the divide and rule feature inhibited a class analysis, deflected blame away from society, and negated the possibility that the reaction reflected a fear of physical violence as the polarized youths only attacked one another. In other words, one is entitled to expect case studies to identify the unique features of a panic that reinforce the nine elements.

REACTION: PHASE TWO

The last phase, the rescue and remedy phase in Cohen's natural disaster analogy [1973: 85] is vital because it is during periods of crisis like moral panic that the common values regarding what is "damaging, threatening or deviant" in societies are revealed, and explain both the success of the appeals for social unity and the panics' ability to transcend any contradictions concerning causation [1973: 75–76].

The focused fear generated by the two previous phases is both a cause and effect of the **sensitization** process that creates the *amplification of the deviancy* which resolves "the anxiety inducing ambiguity" of the precipitating event by "structuring the situation" and making it "more predictable" despite being akin to *mass hysteria* [1973: 77]. In Cohen's case, any act that looked like hooliganism was immediately reclassified as part of the mods and rockers phenomenon, making it look larger than it was by generating a large number of *false alarms,* the cancellation of legitimate activities because they "might lead to trouble", and the reporting of *non events* keeping the issue to the fore [1973: 78]. This hysteria was matched by the *diffusion, escalation, and innovation in police activities,* expanding from the local to the national level, as their pre-Bank holiday preparations for invasions by the youths become increasingly complex and sophisticated. As this *surpassed the normal response to deviancy* and *trampled on civil liberties* it not only offered a standard to differentiate panics from the normal reaction to deviancy, it provided proof that a panic was in progress [1973: 86–87]. The failure of descriptive and generic panics to address these issues, from the initial confusion through to its ironic resolution by the escalation in **social control culture** enables us to argue that they amount to label slapping. They turn a normal level reaction to deviancy into a moral panic and do not contain the appearance and resolution of the psychological response that justified the label.

As well as mobilizing civil defense and other local government resources [1973: 92–93], Cohen argued that the police reaction led to the *dramatization of evil* whereby:

> Deviants must not only be labeled but must also be seen to be labeled; they must be involved in some sort of ceremony of public degradation. The public and visible nature of this event is essential if the deviant's transition to folk devil status is to be successfully managed [1973: 95].

As the police escorted the youths out of town, and the public demanded more controls [1973: 88–91 and 96]; this dramatization reached its peak in the Brighton courts during Whitsun 1965. Although the lack of a threat was indicated by the use of convenient charges like 'willful obstruction' and 'threatening behavior'; the court's recourse to numerous extra-legal measures and punishments such as needless remands in custody encouraged the opposite impression. This *show of power,* with its *ritual outbursts of hostility,* "clamping down hard" and "making examples of offenders" drew approval from the public gallery and was widely reported in the press; whereas the successful appeals against those extra-legal measures were not [1973: 108–109; 97].

This official response was complemented by *the informal elements of public opinion,* another form of social control exercised by the public who were given several active roles by Cohen. It was the *on the spot reaction of the local community,* the "pristine form of public reaction", which led to the disaster analogies in the media [1973: 111]. The public also contributed to the *generalized build up* of the reaction, through statements made by local MPs, those invariably quoted on youth problems in the press, church sermons, and speeches at conferences, school prize-giving days, and passing-out parades. The ultimate effect of the panic also depended upon the *moral entrepreneurs,* the local business owners who held meetings and lobbied their local government and parliamentary representatives who then repeated the entrepreneurs' demands in council chambers and in Parliament. If the entrepreneurs' solution remained at a general level, little would happen. If they created a *specific appeal* reflecting the values transgressed, which was then adopted by *national action groups* exploiting the social control agents' perspective and the media coverage to justify doing so, the moral panic would lead to a new law or social policy change because of the *generalized belief* that now existed about the threat [Cohen, 1973: 111–112].

In Cohen's case, the moral entrepreneurs gained policy changes at the local level like banning beatniks from sleeping on the beaches, but they failed to secure a new law because the two main resort town action groups did not create a specific appeal [1973: 79–81 and 83–85]. On the other hand, after the Whitsun disturbances, these two action groups helped create a *pyramidical conception of blame and responsibility* holding the government responsible for depriving the social control agencies of the powers they needed to resolve the threat. By ensuring that MPs took up their demands and tabled Parliamentary questions, the action groups forced the Home Secretary, Mr. Brooke, to reconsider his belief that the law was adequate. After calling a joint meeting of Chief Constables, and holding a private meeting with one of Brighton's MPs, Brooke introduced a Malicious Damage Bill increasing the penalties for the vandalism [1973: 136]. The fact that this moral enterprise emerged out of the moral panic was evidenced by the philosophy of Blake, the organizer of one of the action groups who, like the nationally known Mary Whitehouse and Lord Longford, personified the typical *moral crusader's authoritarian personality* [1973: 123, 127–132, and 173].

The **exploitative culture**, the final element, is analogous to the "warning and impact phases" in a natural disaster. Whereas warnings about impending natural disasters often led to panic and/or denial that the threat is real making the consequences worse, the opposite occurs in moral panic. While there is no warning about the precipitating event, subsequent warnings about "next time" are not only readily believed, they generated the false alarms and "widening the net" to other acts of hooliganism that make the situation look worse. When subsequent invasions did occur they enhanced the validity of the media inventory and institutionalized the threat through the police's heavy-handed approach [1973: 144–148]. The most important aspect of this element, however, concerned the interaction between the press, the public, the control agents, *and* the deviants on the beaches.

This produced an *in situ* amplification of deviancy and offered a "more sociological explanation" why the public flocked to the beaches despite the horror-headlines. Rather than forming "two highly structured opposing groups (or gangs)", or even exhibiting homogeneous patterns of participation [1973: 149–50]; the youths' polarization, against each other and collectively against the adult community, followed from the media inventory. By promoting the image of "warring gangs", the press turned a "minor antagonism" between the youths that was "not especially marked" given their common working-class origin into "something greater" by offering a deviant role to play and leading the youths into publicity seeking behaviour. Having turned every innocent act that then occurred beachside into an exemplar of the deviancy, the inventory effectively encouraged the escalation of the violence at the beaches and legitimised the heavy-handed reaction to it [1973: 152–154, 158–166]. This link between the media reports, the changing expectations, and subsequent events can be seen in the youths' targets: Easter—the Clacton residents; Whitsun—the other youth group; and, thereafter—the police [1973: 157]. Likewise, instead of being drawn to the beaches by "sheer curiosity" or "vicarious satisfaction", the public went to see "a modern morality play" in which 'good' society dealt with the 'bad' deviants, evidenced by the way that the public's passive fascination was "livened only when the forces of good triumphed" such as "cheering the police when they made an arrest" [1973: 158–60]. Although the immediate cause of amplification was the police who arbitrarily enforced the rules [1973: 166–67], and the courts then fed the panic by "making an example of the offenders"; the ultimate blame rests with the media which promoted the images of the "thin blue line" of the police as saving society from chaos and the magistrates as society's mouth-piece [1973: 172].

The effect of the panic on society involved two types of exploitation. The commercial exploitation of the youths consisted of exaggerating their fashion differences that reinforced their polarization and helped create the youths' self-identities. The *ideological exploitation* of the issue took several forms. Religious groups were able to control their members' behaviour. Government reasserted the social consensus. Social control agents secured more resources. "Other groups" also claimed that the events justified their previous positions on various social issues, and new positions such as the claim Clacton followed from the failure to heed previous warnings about media violence [1973: 139–143].

Delineating Moral Panic

In short, in order to match Cohen's definition of moral panic case studies should have exhibited a vast array of phenomenon including: appeals for unity, mass hysteria, false alarms; the amplification of deviancy *in situ* and/or otherwise; an escalation in control culture activity; the dramatization of evil; courts in action; the appearance of specific moral entrepreneurs; and the widespread condemnation of the deviants across society, as people exploit the issue for other ends, as well as on the moral barricades. The fact that descriptive panics rarely mentioned any of these issues, let alone followed the process by which the elements and features invoked and resolved anxieties, suggests that whatever else they were recording, it was not moral panic. As generic panic has now replaced the elements, features, and process that quantified the meaning of moral panic, they no longer exhibit the psychological dimensions and effect that gave the label its original meaning. Whether or not the amplification of deviancy was the key issue, its frequent failure to appear is seminal because Cohen argued that the crucial stage in the emergence of the folk devil is when the public adopts the symbolization that facilitates the stigmatization, making the negative sanctions much easier to apply. As that process also enhances the solidarity amongst the folk devils, it also facilitates the public's fear that the deviants pose a threat to society [1973: 157]. Without that, the moral panic could and would not turn the original *claims* about the threat into a socially constructed *reality* through the amplification of deviancy that create the "social disaster" that panics always do.

THE CONTEXT AND BACKGROUND

The interactive phases of moral panic did not explain why it occurred, but offered the clues that facilitated an explanation. In Cohen's case, the **boundary crisis**, focusing the anxiety caused by **social strain** on the mods and rockers, can be found in the predominant themes of affluence and youth that had dominated post-war discussions of social change. After Clacton, adult society drew erroneous links between teen affluence, the supposed homogeneity of youth culture, and the aggressive acts of fringe delinquency at the beaches and so became convinced that delinquency was a major social problem [1973: 177–180]. As a consequence, society ignored the **real problem** that led to deviancy. Society had created a large number of secondary modern school graduates facing dull, tedious jobs after a decade of dull, tedious teaching, who adopted a materialistic approach to life, maximizing the aspects of teen culture that they could. Unlike the middle-class adolescent who went to grammar school that offered far more options, the working-class teen had no alternative. As contemporary cityscapes provided few opportunities for legitimate excitement, the youths responded to the leisure goals that they could not achieve by manufacturing their own form of excitement, "making things happen out of nothing", and took this do-it-yourself excitement to the resort towns that likewise offered them nothing. Although this involved engaging in acts of vandalism and hooliganism, the youths were not really responsible for their actions:

> One chose these things, but at the same time one was in a society whose structure severely limited one's choice and one was in a situation where

what deterministic forces there were—the lack of amenities, the action of the police, the hostility of locals—made few other choices possible [Cohen, 1973: 183].

Having identified the real problem, Cohen could now explain the cause and nature of the panic. Drawing on Nuttall's cultural analysis of mod [1970], Cohen suggested that the adults exacerbated an existing jealously induced generation gap between themselves and the youths by their failure to understand the nature of contemporary teen culture:

> The sixties began the confirmation of the new era in adult-youth relations. The Teddy Boys were the first warnings on the horizon. What everybody had grimly prophesied had come true: high wages, the emergence of a commercial youth culture 'pandering' to young people's needs, the elevation of scruffy pop heroes into national idols (and even giving them MBEs),[1] the 'permissive society', the 'coddling by the Welfare State'—all this had produced its inevitable results. As one magistrate expressed to me in 1965, 'Delinquency is trying to get at too many things too easily . . . people have become more aware of the good things in life . . . we've thrown back the curtain for them too soon' [1973: 191–192].

As a result, the mods and rockers' spending power and sexual freedom when combined with their flouting of societal values was perceived as the inevitable result of permissiveness which had placed traditional values under strain, not least because of the mods' apparent incongruousness. They did not conform to previous images of slum louts, yet behaved like a hooligan; and despite looking like a bank clerk, they did not adopt society's values:

> His disdain for advancement in work, his air of distance, his manifest display of ingratitude for what society had given him: these were found more unsettling than any simple conformity to the folk lore image of the yob [1973: 195].

As Erikson said it would, when a boundary crisis emerges it generates deviancy, the punishment of which restores social order by reasserting the values that are under strain [1966]. In Clacton's case, the youths not only became the scapegoats for the decaying resort towns' failure to adjust to the respectable working-classes' tendency to opt for inclusive vacations in Spain with its guaranteed sunshine; but for what the youths had come to represent in the public imagination. This was almost inevitable, given that moral indignation born of wider social change has to have an outlet, and those identifying with societal norms have a lot to lose if the norm breaker goes unpunished. As well as the direct threat to persons, property, and commercial interests, the mods and rockers' moral panic reflected their "violation of certain approved styles of life": the ethics of sobriety and hard work [1973: 197].

THE REAL THING

Neither descriptive panics nor the 'new, improved' generic version capture the essence of Cohen's moral panic that distinguish panics from other over-reactions to horror-headlines and/or deviancy [1973: 11]. This consisted of the *psychological impact* of the media inventory that ensured that the moral indignation generated by pre-existing fears caused by wider social change was projected onto the folk devil. Later studies clearly ignore the role of the transactional process in creating the disproportionate fear regarding the threat, but which is understandable because the panic makes the claims about the threat look real. On the other hand, although Cohen defined what a moral panic was, that does not mean that he uncovered one; and we will explain how Cohen's moral panic model amounted to a myth in the next chapter.

2 Sozzled Students, Drunken Debutantes and the Hidden History of Mods and Rockers

BORIN' CLACTON

Cohen not only constructed rather than uncovered a moral panic; he did so by using the same methods that he condemned in the press. The exaggeration began with turning the Clacton traders' riot analogy into *his* disaster analogy. That false impression was enhanced by using generic plurals, turning *one* reference by an MP into a disaster when referred to as "increasing disaster analogies". That distortion was completed by ignoring those who leapt to the youths' defense and presenting their rationales as his own explanation for events, while constantly claiming that no alternative explanation was on offer [1969: 516; 1973: 51–52, 113–114; Hansard, House of Commons: 23 June, 1964].[1] *Folk Devils* even opens with one of those melodramatic scene settings he complained of, complete with its own symbolism. Cohen turned the myopic outlook of the declining resort town into a thesis about pompous, moralistic, inefficient, decaying Britain, living on past glories, taking out its frustrations on its own creation, the bored working-class teen, perpetuating the very problem that it sought to control. While that analogy was amusing, it grossly misled readers by concentrating on the foibles of a few and condemning society through guilt by association. What makes the success of Cohen's political orientation even more remarkable is that it could and should have been seen as the fiction it was from the get-go; at least by British readers.

Due to the climate, UK resorts open at Whitsun *not* Easter. Like the late season, Easter caters to senior citizens and cash-strapped families willing to take a chance on the weather for the discounts. As the majority of 1960s seaside activities like swimming and sunbathing are not an option at Easter no matter what the weather, and many of the beach stores and cafés remain closed until Whitsun; unless one booked into the Billy Butlin's holiday complex with its heated indoor pool, game rooms, and organized entertainments, boredom in Clacton was guaranteed. Although that should have raised the question, what were the youths doing there, Cohen never asked let alone answered it because he knew that it would undermine his all-important polarization by panic thesis. To demonstrate that, we will also place the horror-headlines in their wider context, but rather than rely on impressionistic cultural commentators like Nuttal, we will draw from the historical record and by teasing out the counter evidence offered by a timely doctorial study into contemporary reactions to vandalism undertaken by none other than Stan Cohen [1969]!

THE PRE-CLACTON INVENTORY

Far from being the seismic shock that Cohen inferred, confusing everyone over its ambiguous meaning—the panic in moral panic; the residents and wider public was well aware of what Clacton could signify because the news media had been full of stories about violent delinquents and destructive vandalism for three long years, and little else for the previous three months. The public had long since stopped being perplexed by delinquency having heard all about the causes and solutions offered by the six major inquires, reports, and conferences on the subject since 1959. Nor had they forgotten the Teddy boys who *had* terrorized towns as well as fought on the beaches throughout the 1950s, and *had* caused a shock when they first appeared because they proved that delinquency was not caused by poverty and slum life, now being eradicated by full employment and the welfare state. No sooner had the aging Teds put away their flick knives and metamorphosed into an Elvis cult, than soccer hooligans emerged in their thousands, becoming a social problem in their own right between 1960 and 1963 when the government responded by establishing attendance center to keep the troublemakers away from the games. Although Cohen was no soccer fan, he was well aware that the hooligans attracted extensive media coverage because of the potential embarrassment they could cause England when it hosted soccer's world cup finals in 1966 [1969: 185–190]. As Clacton involved two rival, mobile factions throwing themselves at each other, not caring who else or what else was in the way, it also raised a rational fear that mass hooligan would no longer end with the soccer season in May. Although soccer hooliganism was nothing new, its mobility was. Until the 1960s most fans could not afford to attend road games, with the exception of the local 'derby' against their nearest rival, or the later stages of the knock-out cup competition when British Rail put on cheap charter trains for fans because of the increased interest. When rising affluence led to British Rail extending these 'football specials' to the regular league games, it inadvertently enabled hooligans like the Merseyside Maniacs to take their "own form of excitement" like bottle and coin throwing with them, and that ensured that hooliganism became associated with mobile mobs invading towns long before Clacton [Lacey, 2010; Taylor, 1971: 156–157; Dunning *et al*, 1988: 141–181].

In 1960 a 3-year-old's drowning was blamed on vandals breaking the safety catch on the gate that would have prevented her from reaching the river Irwell. After that, vandalism began to compete with soccer hooliganism for media space. Reporting effects aside, it was endemic [1969: 126]. Communal facilities, whether publicly or privately owned, were under constant attack. Advertising hoardings, buses, cemeteries, parks, places of entertainment, memorials, schools, and sports fields were all targeted by "bored teenagers" [1969: 103–104]. That "nothing was sacred" was demonstrated by the 250 percent increase in claims from vandalized churches through 1960 to 1964 [1969: 141]. One reason for the attention was vandalism's irritating nature. Although its affects were omnipresent, the culprits were not. They had vanished long before their handiwork was discovered. According to Cohen, that made it a safe crime. The low detection rate followed the lack of personal complaint, and property to carry or dispose of [1969: 88]. Consequently, as Clacton involved a communal complaint about perpetrators caught in the act, and a sudden reverse in typical trends is one of those news values that will hold the front page, the media would probably have been all over Clacton even on a fast news day [Chibnall, 1977]. The fact that vandalism was also headlining the news in the weeks leading up to Clacton guaranteed that it would.

When the UK Post Office claimed that vandalized public telephone booths was increasing [1969: 135–138, 277]; the phoneless public who frequently had to trudge from one ruined booth to another in the rain and the wind did not need to be told what might happen in an emergency. Although the petit-bourgeoisie ensured that the worst case scenario rarely happened by giving the masses access to their telephones in emergencies as long as they wiped their feet on the doormat; it was a different story on the railways where vandalism was posing a *direct* risk to life and limb, the very reason why British Rail began to keep records in 1959. In February 1964, BR announced that 'accidents' caused by vandalism had increased by 70 percent in the last two years and offered reward to anyone naming the culprits. As BR was already considering ending the soccer specials because too many were coming back vandalized, the new announcement reinforced beliefs that there was a symbiotic link between the two [Cohen, 1969: 158, 190, 260]. The following month, local government also declared war on vandalism. One of the vandals' most common targets, local government was caught in a trap. Although patrolling property was more expensive than repairing any damage, the collective cost led to closing facilities which encouraged more vandalism [Cohen, 1969: 219–220, 251–253]; but with Clacton only weeks away, *The Cost of Vandalism to Local Authorities* issued by the newly created Local Government Information Office promoted a get tough policy [1969: 163]. With the estimated cost of vandalism of public facilities, on trains and of telephones now costing the country between £2–3 million a year [Cohen, 1969: 145–150], when the average worker would not make £100,000 over their lifetime, that huge sum may explain why, according to Cohen, the local media, pulpits, speech days, and mayoral inaugurations became preoccupied with *vandalism* rather than the mods and rockers as he later claimed in *Folk Devils* [Cohen, 1969: 161–166]. Either way, as officialdom had already declared war on both, Clacton was the wrong time for mods and rockers to play hooligans and vandals in public.

A WELL-WORN INVENTORY

Even if the reports provoked by Clacton evoked normative concerns; insignificant similarities like the use of the 1960s "sign of the times" cliché, and the fact that liberal and conservative commentators agreed that the youths were bored, does not justify Cohen's failure to record the source of the perspective on delinquency that he claimed amounted to a unified expression of indignant authoritarianism behind the 'moral' in moral panic [1969: 235; 1973: 60, 76, 127–132]. Clacton's column inch count had other causes. The attention given to Clacton is easily explained by the fact that vandalism like hooliganism had already gained grossly disproportionate coverage compared to other crimes [Cohen, 1969: 139 and 149] and the reports' repetitive nature reflects their dependency on a single source: a stringer, the local newspaper reporters who supply the national press with breaking stories in their area via a news-wire service to get a second pay check. The story was easy to sell because it finally put a name to the vandals, and was worth buying because it slotted into existing concerns about mobile hooligans. As the mods and rockers responded to the collective condemnation by putting on a repeat performance the very next day, interviewed youths swore more vengeance, and the two groups clashed again at several resorts over the Whitsun weekend seven weeks later; predictions were inevitable, and it was the youths' own behavior that institutionalized their threat [Cohen, 1969: 452–454]. As Cohen knew that violence is rarely reported with precision but always gains misleading headlines, to argue that the media focus was really on the mods and rockers despite the issues of vandalism and hooliganism hogging the coverage is questionable. Resort town papers like Brighton's *Evening Argus,* and the national bestseller, *The Daily Mirror,* were still not using the monikers 'mods' and 'rockers' in their horror-headlines over Whitsun [Cohen, 1973: 36–37; *Daily Mirror,* 14 May, 1964: 1].

Most adverse commentary emanated from the discredited and marginalized 'law and order' lobby which subscribed to *one version* of the affluent youth thesis. The lobby was indignant that they were losing the delinquency debate in general, and had just failed to stop the liberal leaning Children and Young Persons Act 1963 in particular. So, they jumped on Clacton in a desperate attempt to prove that being soft on juvenile crime would not work. Otherwise, as Clacton's arrest demographics merely confirmed that juveniles were responsible for the majority of vandalism and hooliganism [Cohen, 1969: 226–227]; the media inventory, or rather Cohen's interpretation of it, could not have led to mass hysteria unless the public had previously suffered mass amnesia about the existing delinquency debate that Cohen 'forgot' to mention when he inferred it appeared after Clacton.

NO NEW ORIENTATION

Far from generating panic, the immediate media effect was to send the public flooding into Clacton the very next day despite the horror-headlines and the weather being the worst in 80 years. This intent to watch the youths clash with one another turned into a tsunami across the battleground beaches all summer long despite the predictions, warnings, police presence and changeable weather. The Whitsun clash at Margate even put the town on the map, dramatically increasing bookings despite two stabbings [Cohen, 1969: 446, 451, 561–562; 1973: 38]. As this reaction clearly detracts from panic, it is no accident that we find Cohen introducing the first of his proxies covering other events in other places that appeared whenever he had an evidential problem. In this case, Cohen pointed to the LA zoot suit riots during 1943 to support his contention that the media orientation had encouraged the public to direct their deeper anxieties towards the mods and rockers [1973: 40–43]. However, as prejudicial news reports about the zoot-suiters alleged criminal tendencies had led to the riots, Cohen not only loses his precipitating event, he has a problem with his post-event orientation. Although white readers subsequently blamed the jitterbugging Cab Calloway look-a-likes rather than the marauding racist goon squads from the local naval base for the riots; as blaming the victim for racial violence was endemic in the US since the debacle of Reconstruction, no one would need a new orientation to do that [Gilbert, 1986: 30–31]. If anything, Cohen's proxy draws attention to his failure to explain how the pre-Clacton coverage of vandalism and hooliganism shaped the Clacton reaction. Be that as it may, what did *not* happen after Clacton undermines most of Cohen's inferences and assertions about what did happen.

Although "no show" headlines tried to keep the story alive, the never shows at the other 50 popular resort towns from Bognor on the south coast to the Clyde beaches in Scotland quickly demonstrated that the invasions were irregular, only occurred in a handful of resorts, and after August 1964 were quickly confined to Brighton. As the mods *and* rockers rarely appeared together after Whitsun 1964, that disappointment determined that the headlines quickly lost their hubris of horror, demonstrated that this was a storm in a tea-cup, and that ensured public confidence in the predictions disappeared faster than the rockers had after their Whitsun defeats. That is why most contemporary TV news coverage failed to offer anything more than local Bobbies demanding that anyone looking like a mod vacate the beach and "move along". The *Pathé* news coverage of Whitsun and August

Bank holidays screened in cinemas—complete with a "no show", an obvious fake fight between two modettes, and the commentary playing up the non existing threat—offers an example of how the incongruity between the verbal hype and the visual imagery of this Keystone Cop behavior helped fuel the 'sixties cynicism which we cover below' [MAR1[2]].

Despite resorting to a professional news clipping service after two years, Cohen could only offer a couple of south-west resorts exploiting the horror-headlines to justify banning bongo-bashing beatniks from the beaches, and the extra precautions taken in Skegness after a dance-hall fight without a mod or rocker in sight [1973: 84–85 and 79]. Even if we add every follow up story offered by Cohen to the handful of *mod* invasions of Brighton over the next two years, there is no reason to believe that the public was convinced that the problem was as prevalent or consistent as the Teddy boy's whose infamous knife-fights in city centers, cinemas, dance halls, at fun fairs and resort towns generated the warring gang imagery that Cohen never demonstrated was systematically applied to the mods and rockers [Cohen, 1969: 591; Rock and Cohen, 1970]. As the number of students *charged* with similar offenses on each Guy Fawkes Night in London between 1964 and 1967 was much greater than total number of mods and rockers *arrested* after each beach incident, there is no doubt that the media exaggerated the threat; but Cohen exaggerated the reaction. The 1,500 reports covering vandalism and hooliganism in the local government press between September 1964 and August 1967 suggest they were not that worried about the youths, and continued to concentrate on vandalism. Birmingham and another 20 major cities ran anti-vandalism campaigns, and Glasgow recruited more Special Constables to combat the problem. Not to be left out, the Association of Parish Councils carried out a vandalism audit; and the Council of British Ceramic Sanitaryware Manufactures took advantage of all the interest to argue that it was time to repair vandalized public rest rooms. Meanwhile, soccer hooliganism had become so big that university professors began to turn it into an academic specialism [Cohen, 1969: 64; 79, 133–148, 163–175, 181, 187–195, 537]. Consequently, the claim that the country was gripped by a moral panic about mods and rockers for three years borders on the absurd, especially as the rockers as a group effectively went AWOL after Whitsun 1964. There is, however, a very good reason to pay a little more attention to the rockers than *Folk Devils* did.

ACE

If the omission of the pre-Clacton inventory appears odd given Cohen's PhD, the possibility that the founder of the panic paradigm was oblivious to the preceding publicity covering the rockers defies credulity. The first wave, 1960–61, popularized the 'ton-up boy' label by explaining that the pests roaring up and down UK narrow 'main roads' were trying to reach

100 mph on their bikes: the ton. As one rocker explained, the bikers would meet somewhere like Box Hill in the county of Surrey and then:

> We would leave the lay-by in pairs, race down the road about one mile to a gap in the dual carriageway. When it was all clear we would take off and race back to the roundabout ... After an afternoon's burn-up we used to visit a coffee bar in Leatherhead called *The Tarrola* for the best espresso coffee in Surrey and a well stocked jukebox [Discovery, 2004].

Motorbike riders could and would easily find their way to this extensive café scene:

> We used to go to a café in East Sheen called *La Tatuliar* where they would serve the best coffee ... The best coffee bar for music was in Mortlake and was a typical '60s meeting place full of ton-up boys talking about how fast they could go. The girls were always asking for money to play the latest American records which the owner seemed to be able to get before they were on sale in the shops ... we were spoilt for choice where to hang out. The favourite place was the *Ace Café* [Discovery, 2004].

The popularity of the Ace led to the second panic in 1962 when the bikers gained even more notoriety by turning London's north circular road into their private race track in an even more daring and hazardous challenge:

> someone would drop a coin into the café's jukebox, and the race was on. Whoever was racing would dash out to the car park, fire up their bikes, charge to a fixed point and back to the Ace. The point of the exercise was to achieve the 'ton' along the route, 100mph in heavy traffic, and return *before* the record had finished playing [Discovery, 2004].

The publicity that followed was not always negative, particularly when it included hanging out with the omnipresent 'trendy vicar':

> I was a member of a club based in Hammersmith ... One night we had a visit from the Reverend Bill Sherman of the *59 Club* fame (before it started). He visited our club to check out the interest for the new club and to invite us to a church motorcycle blessing ... Some of our members attended and it made all of the daily papers. Leather jacketed ton-up boys go to church! After that the *59 Club* was started and I was there on the opening night, and to this day still have my original membership number 36. We would always go to the *59 Club* on a Saturday night and it was there that I saw *The Wild Ones* ... After the *59* we would ride back for a coffee at the Ace [Discovery, 2004].

Even if the public was not aware of every facet of the rocker's subculture they would have had no problem discerning the difference between them and the mods. The cinema going public could not have missed the mass publicity surrounding the 1963 exploitation movie *Leather Boys* based on the 1961 best seller by Gillian Freeman, which stared contemporary UK heart-throb Dudley Sutton and featured the Ace as a location. Bike club members were also a common sight at beach resorts before 1964:

> We used to ride to the south coast a lot and the best places were *Brighton, Hastings, Southend or Margate.* Southend had best funfair called The Kursal and we would always go and see the wall of death Brighton was our nearest one and it was always a good fast ride. I can always remember that whenever a road sign appeared saying 'bends,' everyone would change down a gear and accelerate. Great fun with lots of sparks coming from scraped silencers or centre stands. There was a short tunnel through Reigate which always prompted a quick change down and opening up of the throttle to see who could make the most noise. Everyone would be smiling as we came out the other end. The best mad run was Hastings as it had the most bends [our emphasis—eds. Discovery, 2004].

As well as negating Cohen's caricature of the rockers as a consumer style [1969: 569], the rockers' history answers the question: why Clacton? When the armadas of mobile mods on their slower motor scooters suddenly appeared in 1963, they not only presented a hazard on the road for anyone doing a ton; the mods began to invade the rockers' cafés and favored beach resorts too, making clashes common place. Indeed, the enmity grew so fast that stock exchange messengers, the unofficial barometer of changing popular culture in the UK, quickly adopted the moniker mod or rocker [Cohen, 1969: 591]. In short, whether or not reporters had a habit of "turning peripheral youths with varied motives into the image of highly mechanized and organized gangs" [1973: 58]; the mods and rockers could not have been turned into two warring factions by the Clacton reaction because it had already happened!

REWRITING REACTIONS

While Cohen's model of the Clacton reaction may look impressive, it masks his failure to offer any direct evidence that *any* MP, magistrate, police officer, or the general public adopted the media inventory. They did not because there are seven good grounds why they never would.

Pre-sensitization

As the public would have been bored to death with all the perspectives on the causes of hooliganism because they had been covered on radio, TV, and in the press *ad nauseam* over the previous four years, there would be no need to internalize an orientation that had been heard a hundred times before, and certainly not to resolve a nonexistent confusion over what Clacton meant. Given the public's memory of the Teds turning down towns into battlegrounds, their daily dose of visible vandalism, and their need to avoid Saturday soccer hooligans; another pair of youth groups fighting each other would come as no surprise. The confusion allegedly caused by a well dressed mod behaving like a slum lout cannot save Cohen's claims either. As incongruity of dress was *the* major reason for the initial reaction to the Teddy boys, who turned the 1950s Edwardian suit revival into a symbol of delinquency according to a sociologist called Stan Cohen, is debatable if anyone would be fazed by a sharp dressed mod [Rock and Cohen, 1970]. The fact that the slum and street urchin stereotypes had long since been confined to Sherlock Holmes movies and Dickensian dramas on the BBC appears to be confirmed by Cohen's failure to offer any examples of it from the beaches.

Proxy Evidence

Although sudden events reflecting structural strain or threats to values may lead to debates about implications rather than incidents; as the delinquency debate had been in progress for four years, Clacton merely gave the law and order lobby another excuse to promote their ailing perspective for a couple of months. That is why Cohen could not offer any evidence that the lobby switched from the issue of delinquency to permissiveness when they complained about Clacton, and why another set of proxies appeared instead; not that their salience had improved. The popular confusion surrounding the JFK assassination concerned who organized the hit rather than led to debates over the implications for society, and it has proven fertile ground for conspiracy theories ever since rather than resolved anything. The other two examples, concerning senior police officers complaints about criminals shooting cops and demanding greater powers as a result do not even reach the level of analogy [1973, 49–50]. Cohen was well aware that all societies contain a minority who jump on any sign of deviance, claim it is "the thin end of the wedge" and then call for clampdowns. As he also admitted that even when the press set an agenda, *no one* could determine how the public would respond; there is no reason to believe that these two truisms did not apply to the Clacton coverage [Cohen, 1970; Cohen and Young, 1973, (1988 edition): Part Three, Introduction].

Pseudo-Psychological Explanations

Alluding to mass delusion as Cohen did is no substitute for evidence, and should be sociologically unacceptable too [Cohen, 1973: 50]. As the concept has been applied to anything and everything from bull markets on stock exchanges, through witch trials, to Beatle-mania since Mackay's day [1989] even though greed, deadly religious moral enterprise, and post-pubescent stupidity obviously have different causes, the concept has no explanatory value. Indeed, sociologists had long since proven that cases of "mass delusion" need a sociological explanation by debunking the most famous example of them all: *The War of the Worlds* radio panic. Orson Welles' adaptation of the classic Sci-fi novel led to real panic, but only amongst those who had never read H.G. Wells or any other classic, were more religious or believed in little green men from Mars, had missed the beginning of the broadcast or had been told to listen-in by other panicking people. Those who read books, followed the show from the beginning, checked the broadcast schedule to discover what it was or had paid attention to the extensive pre-publicity, and were not paranoid about Reds under beds or UFOs overhead, continued to sit at home and enjoy the show. As only 1 in 6 listeners had been frightened, let alone panicked, the extent of the reaction had always been exaggerated anyway [see Lowery and Defleur, 1983].

The Boundary Crisis

Although some people feared permissiveness; that fear was not subconscious or unarticulated. You could not pick up a paper or watch TV during 1964 without hearing about "the new morality" as it was called at the time. The quiet debate that had emerged since the Conservative government started deregulating moral crimes a decade before became far more vocal during 1964 for two dramatic reasons: an organized opposition to permissiveness appeared at precisely the same time that the justifications for the moral laws of the past imploded because of the Profumo Affair and two other scandals which turned March 1963 into Moralgate.

Despite the war minister's denial that he had an affair with Ms. Keeler, a call girl who associated with Soviet naval attaché Yevgeny Ivanov during this hot period of the cold war, the press would not leave Profumo alone until he resigned four months later. As a result, when a sixteen-year-old youth was cleared of manslaughter, having smashed a wine decanter over the head of former Labour party chairman George Brinham who was molesting him, people wondered whether any politician maintained the standards that they imposed upon the public. The publication of *Honest To God,* a critique of simplistic religious faith by the Bishop of Woolwich also raised the question whether they had any justification.

When the Bishop followed up debunking the Virgin Birth and the Resurrection of Christ in front of a rapidly secularizing society, by declaring on primetime TV that the established Church should abandon its antiquated sexual attitudes too, Britain's moral façade cracked and crumbled overnight [Whitehouse, 1977: 14]. One of the reasons for the rapid collapse was that the BBC's Director General, Hugh Greene had already abandoned his predecessor's promotion of Christian values in favor of value pluralism aired through hard-hitting documentaries, lengthy studio discussions, and the path breaking satirical show *That Was The Week That Was*. These innovations now ensured that the ramifications of Moralgate were debated in every home unlike those of the 1920s and 1930s reprised in Ronald Blythe's *The Age of Illusion* published at the same time [Howard, 1963; Blythe, 1963; Greene, 1969; Whitehouse, 1971]. The reaction was far more dramatic than Edward R. Morrow's contemporaneous *CBS Reports* in the US. In the face of the subsequent maelstrom of mass malcontent on all sides, *The Times*, Britain's establishment mouthpiece, led the media pack in flipping the discourse regarding Britain's "social malaise" that Cohen alluded to, into a 'moral malaise' by reminding its readers that:

> History shows that societies rise and fall, flourish and decay, by what they believe in and by what their way of life stands for [11 February 1963 cited in Howard, 1963: 18].

However, the only people who panicked about this modern fall of Rome were the establishment. Middle-class Oxbridge graduates had long since preferred gainful satire at the BBC to government service at the foreign office, and the students at the new universities were demanding Britain ban its atom bombs. Patriotism and Empire were being abandoned by the masses too, symbolized by their refusal to stand for the national anthem in cinemas playing the latest northern realist movie warning the viewers that abiding by the old rules was self-defeating [Jones, 2011: 110]. While the religious petit-bourgeoisie worried that Britain was on the abyss, they began to organize rather than panic in order to stop the majority of their class gorging on previously forbidden fruit. Enjoying the security of corporate white collar jobs, the majority of the petit-bourgeoisie had turned permissive literature into best sellers, lined up to ensure *Beyond the Fringe* broke box office records for a satirical review, followed the latest political scandals and corruption in *Private Eye* magazine, and watched the champions of the new morality like Dr. Alex Comfort best the hapless defenders of the old on TV every night [Whitehouse, 1977: 13–21].

In this cynical climate, it would have been impossible for anyone to turn anything, let alone mods and rockers into a societal wide reaction against the permissive society, because its pervasiveness reflected its popularity. Although Clacton initially excited the law and order lobby, that did not last long either. The handful of beachside invasions by mods picking on isolated groups of rockers in 1965 and 1966 simply could not compete with soccer hooliganism's increasing casualty list, and the rising body count courtesy of the London gang-land feud between the Kray and Richardson firms, the serial child killing Moors Murderers, and the shooting of three London policemen. That is why the chronicler of law and order news claims that it was during this period that violence replaced youth as the lobby's rallying cry [Chibnall, 1977: 83–88, 93–94]. As a result, long before the last deck chair was stacked away after the August Bank Holiday in 1964, the only people left panicking about the beach invaders were the resort town Guest House Associations, Chambers of Commerce, and Licensed Victuallers Associations. Even though the press promoted their perspective, their proposed solutions were opposed by the police and ignored by everyone else as Cohen once admitted [Cohen, 1969: 516–520, 588; 1973: 84 and 118]!

Moral Enterprise

The public debate after Moralgate polarized between the permissives who emphasized the history of hypocrisy, and the evangelical Christians who warned that while some antiquated laws were past their sell by date, secular humanism would make everything worse because civilization depended upon Christian values. That makes the fact that the decline in religious belief was the most common explanation offered for Clacton very significant given that the latter's' response to Clacton was nothing like the account offered in *Folk Devils* [1973: 61]. By dismissing the Christian moral perspective as reactionary and conflating it with the law and order lobby's concern about crime, Cohen grossly misled his readers. When the Christians drew attention to the delinquents' "absence of a sense of purpose" they were not referring to a lack of a career plan or the decline of the protestant work ethic as Cohen would have you believe, but the youths' godless lives; and far from use the mods and rockers as a *symbolic* means to attack permissiveness, the Christian moral entrepreneurs not only had their own *instrumental* target, they also rushed to the youths' defense. Having wasted the year after Moralgate trying to get the BBC's governors to reign-in Mr. Green, Mary Whitehouse launched a *Clean UP TV* campaign in May 1964 [Whitehouse, 1971: 45]. Making no secret of her religious motives, she quickly became a fixture on TV, the radio, and in the press ensuring that any fears about permissiveness were overt and fully articulated [Greene, 1969; Whitehouse, 1971 and 1977]. Meanwhile, Whitehouse's backers, Britain's independent wing of Moral Rearmament, defended the mods and rockers in a huge double page advertisement in *The Daily Express*. They argued that the rise in delinquency, hooliganism, fornication, and even drug taking followed from the hypocritical example set by the older generation [*The Daily Express,* 14.5.64]. What is more, Longford was a Christian socialist rather than a reactionary and had chaired the Labour party Education Committee, which embraced and promoted the school leaver problem that Cohen presented as his own. Consequently, Cohen's claim that there was no alternative explanation at the time is as false as his claim that the youths symbolized unarticulated reactionary fears about permissiveness [1973: 181–182; Hansard, HOC,[3] 23 June, 1964: 239–240 and 265–271].

Averting Disaster

Whereas one Brighton MP used a disaster analogy, the police set about averting a real one. They were determined to nip any problem in the bud because of the *potential* disaster large crowds presented if anything went wrong, as it had in Lima which gained worldwide attention when a large crowd fleeing from soccer hooligans (and riot police—eds.) had trampled each other to death. This explanation was not only offered by the town's other MP, Sir William Teeling [Hansard, HOC, 23 June, 1964: 274–247]; but Cohen was well aware that it had appeared in the mainstream media after it was offered by the *Police Review* [1969: 461]. Neither source was exaggerating. As Brighton's promenade, on which the crowds had gathered, towered twenty feet above the concrete walkway that bordered the beach, the possibility and fear of another Lima was more than justified.

What the Public Really Thought

The Gallop opinion polls across the summer show a steady rise in the number of people who believed that the clashes were as serious as the horror-headlines suggested; rising from under 50 percent at Easter, to 56 percent at Whitsun, and 64 percent when the mods found some rockers at Hastings and Great Yarmouth over the August Bank Holiday [Mitchell, 2004: 3]. However, as these polls followed immediately after the youths had kept their promise, we have to look elsewhere for the real effect of the horror-headlines. Although Cohen dismissed the results of his contemporary public surveys as unrepresentative [1973: 65 and 114], they deserve a reprise given that the 140 North London (Northview) subjects *were* representative of the control culture, and the second sample covered 65 residents of, and visitors to, Brighton (Southview) whose opinions were not guided by a sudden media blitz [1969: 293–295, 300–301]. The results not only confirms that these samples rejected the media inventory, but their reasons for doing so helps explain why Cohen's analysis in *Folk Devils* is so misleading [1973: 66 and 69]. If you compare the answers to different questions, you quickly find alternative rationales to those offered by Cohen. Less than a third of either sample believed that the teens' behavior was new, and the minority who did was concerned about the nature of the violence involved. Likewise, the 33.9 percent that believed that the mods and rockers were delinquent did not believe they were worse than any others, which is why two-thirds of the wider sample would have had no objection if their son had tagged along [1969: 583; 1973: 69]. The major reason for these results emerged from the London sample, covering everyone from local businessmen to youth workers. Even Cohen admitted that their answers in the interviews demonstrated that you could not always rely on the theoretical devised check-list questionnaire.

What was not in doubt was the revelation that when asked to rank the resort town invaders on a scale of contemporary youth problems, they placed the beachside belligerents below the threat posed by public drunkenness. Likewise, when asked to list juvenile crimes in rank order, they opted for: (1) "theft/armed robbery"; (2) "vandalism/placing stones on railway lines"; (3) "delinquency/armed gang fights"; and (4) "drugs". The mods and rockers came in ninth of fourteen options [1969: 381, Table 35]. This suggests that the professionals shared the popular criteria for assessing any threat—the endangerment of life or limb, and that if they were being influenced by a media inventory it was the *pre*-Clacton one. As the mods and rockers did not engage in *armed* gang fights, they also appear to have been seen as less of a threat than the Teddy boys who had [1969: 466, 591]. While the London sample believed that the invasions were "disturbing and serious", that was because they believed delinquent youth were a symptom of the "general breakdown in law and order" [1969: 343]. As 90 percent also accredited the primary cause of delinquency to the lack of love, attention, and discipline in the delinquent's home, we have a very different rationale from the one Cohen offered in *Folk Devils* [1969: 362–363, 371, Table 34, 378]. This sample appears to have believed that the generation gap had less to do with the youths' conspicuous consumption or sexual jealousy than their total lack of moral sensibility [1969: 329, 337]. The major problem as they saw it was the baneful influence of pop culture [1969: 341], and when it came to sex, the main concern was the rise in illegitimacy [1969: 347]. Otherwise, while they were divided over whether the teens had become more arrogant and demanding, they were clearly preoccupied about property crime rather than permissiveness [1969: 312–313, Table 27, 345].

Cohen appears to have missed the fact that the sample was more concerned with the causes and solutions to *primary* rather than *secondary* deviancy; although the sample was well aware of the dangers of labeling as well [1969: 362–366]. For example, while Cohen condemned the 70 percent who defended dispensing corporal punishment for petty crime in school as reactionaries; they did so because they preferred that solution to calling the police and having the youths labeled in court [1969: 354]. While the majority believed affluence was a problem; that reflected their conviction that contemporary delinquency disproved it had ever been caused by economic deprivation [1969: 369]; a very different reason for the link offered by the law and order lobby. Likewise, while a third of the sample wanted the courts to "tighten up" and ignore the "social workers excuses for delinquents", that answer was premised on reserving the courts for the depraved hard-core delinquent, and dealing with the others in an informal way [1969: 392; 348]. That perspective was reinforced by the magistrates in the sample who warned against acting upon stereotypes, and made it clear that they considered the character and behavior of the individual teen standing before them in the court, reserving punishment for those exhibiting 'signs' of recidivism [1969: 386, Table 36]. Although Cohen interpreted the samples preference for the informal community controls of the past as an "admiration of discipline" and a "closed system of morality"; he ignored the respondents' own rationales which continually stressed the importance of inculcating *self*-discipline and a concern for others. Even the businessmen in the sample preferred informal controls rather than involve the police [1969: 358, 369–370]. That explains why, once one slips past Cohen's cover, 75 percent blamed "society" and adults for the problem in one-way or another [1969: 312–313].

The most important omission from *Folk Devils,* however, was that the sample not only believed that the solution to 'Clactons' was making the guilty party pay financial restitution to the injured party because that would encourage a moral lesson, but that they also believed that magistrates should be recruited from the working-classes, teachers, and social workers as they would have a better understanding of the problems faced by contemporary youth [1969: 379; 392]. Frustrated that his results were "more complicated" than "most theorists predicted", instead of abandoning those theories and inventing a new one to explain the results, Cohen denounced his informants to his supervisor! They had ignored relevant information; failed to frame their answers in line with "known research or theory"; had refused to take a "hard perspective" (i.e. progressive or reactionary—eds.); and had not bothered to read the "relevant debates" in "journals" like *New Society* [1969:337; 420–422]. That display of theoretical fetishism, preference for a neo-Marxist social worker weekly, and contempt for his subjects ensured that Cohen missed a possible explanation for the "inconsistencies" in the answers. It is more than possible that the Christians in the sample were rejecting both the law and order as well as progressive perspectives in favor of their own. They disavowed the former because it did not draw a distinction between the hardcore delinquent and the youth adrift in an increasing amoral society; and they were wary of the latter because they knew that its counterfeit care and medicalization of deviance would lead to the insidious forms of social control that Cohen later lamented in *Visions of Social Control* [1985] when it was far too late. It certainly would explain the problems Cohen had trying to make sense of answers to the issue of predictive testing [1969: 412–413].

What is not in doubt is the cause of Cohen's frustration helps explain the perspective adopted in *Folk Devils.* As trying to force one's perspective upon others rather than allowing them to speak for themselves, dismissing results that do not conform to one's expectations rather than learn from them, inventing excuses for failed theories rather than abandoning them, and imposing simplistic political dichotomies on complex realities hints at a rigid psychological disposition; its easy to see why Cohen preferred Adorno's selective version of the authoritarian personality, rather than Reich's original one which applied to ideologues irrespective of their politics [Reich, 1975; Adorno *et al*, 1950].

FALSE ALARM–REACTION PHASE TWO

Cohen's evidence for the sensitization process linking hooliganism to the mods and rockers relies on half-a-dozen typical reports of Friday night fighting from the action-starved local press, only one of which used the moniker "mod"; and is belied by the fact that the major manifestation of hooliganism during this period, soccer, was not blamed on the mods and rocker panic [1973: 42, 79–80, and 153]. As the police in London's Stamford Hill dismissed Cohen's only example of a false alarm as "people getting jumpy after the trouble on the coast", they had not adopt the media inventory [1973: 79], and although a Blackburn Superintendent alluded to "the type of *behavior* that had been experienced in many parts of the country during the last few weeks" to describe an incident of local hooliganism that does not amount to proof that the courts were consciously guided by the inventory either [our emphasis—eds. 1973: 79–80]. Having pointed out that Clacton "got out of hand" because the town's PD had not been able to cope with the large numbers involved; it was self-serving to describe later precautions, like the patrol of the Woking fun fair, as "over reactions" especially when fun fairs had been the site of teen turf wars in the past. Likewise, given the layout of Battersea Park, cancelling the national scooter rally was a rational precaution as the police would never have been able to cope if those hell-bent on trouble had turned up [1973: 79–80; 170].

As Cohen's evidence in this phase is suspect it is no surprise to find yet another set of proxies from oceans away involving another unsociological explanation, "mass hysteria", being offered to cover his evidential gap. However, even though stories like the phantom anesthetist sometimes made the front pages, Cohen need only have consulted a folklorist to discover that the extent of the "hysteria" is invariably exaggerated, and has other explanations. An obvious comparative example would be Gloss's account of the nonexistent Halifax Slasher [1990]. Like mass delusion, mass hysteria requires an explanation rather than offers one. In any event, as the reports of Friday night fighting were tucked away on the inside pages of the UK's locally orientated evening press they are not comparable with his proxies [1973: 83]; but we can learn a lot from his major one.

While timid old men *were* dragged off streetcars into PDs during the era of the sexual psychopathic laws in the US, Cohen forgot to tell his readers that his case of "mass hysteria" occurred during a highly publicized state-wide manhunt for an extremely dangerous child sex offender [Sutherland, 1950]. That kind of reaction is common when invisible physical threats like serial killers and rapists are at large. What is more, the reason why people were prone to real panic when 30 states adopted sexual psychopath laws between 1939 and 1976 undermines the moral panic model. The legislation's progress was hampered by the fact that the original Michigan law of 1937 was deemed unconstitutional by the Supreme Court, which also insisted that in order to incarcerate anyone because they *might* molest another child, they had to be mentally ill, and ill to the extent that they were completely incapable of resisting their "urges" [Thompson and Greek, 2010]. As a result, the legislative process generated an escalating cycle of fear. Those in favor, like psychiatric and social welfare agencies, claimed that the law was needed because there were a lot of these "sick people" around. Parents' sub-sequent wariness then increased when fiscally conservative opponents countered that as you could not cure pedophilia, the proposal was a waste of time, effort, and money. As parents began to worry about the permanent threat posed by these "out of control monsters", a third fear-ful level was added by liberals wading in defending the offenders' civil liberties as that meant it would take years for the legislation to work its way through the courts [Grubin and Prentky, 1993; Sutherland, 1950]. As that fear cycle ensured that any "hysteria" following another abduc-tion-rape-murder of a child would not be caused by the "precipitating event" but by the *pre*-history; that reinforces our criticism of Cohen's failure to cover the pre-Clacton inventories.

AMPLIFYING THE PANIC

The increase in social control in *Folk Devils,* the escalation from a local to regional and then national response, was a function of Cohen's tendency to exaggerate. Beachside towns with their own small PD in the 1960s would *have* to coordinate with county PDs when faced with crowds as large as 10,000 heading toward them; and that explains the meeting called by the Home Office which only involved the senior offi-cers from the southeast counties and resort towns affected [1969: 550]. Likewise, turning PD press briefings about their preparations for bank holidays into national "warnings" and the "institutionalization of the threat" is no less rhetorical than any horror-headline. Indeed, the lon-gevity of the coverage owed far more to the British summer "silly sea-son", when the news media is deprived of its regular sources of hard news from government to the higher courts and so overdramatizes anything and everything to fill their pages. The routine nature of the warnings and the disappointment amongst the public when they turned out to be "false alarms" ensured it was not long before they were ignored [Cohen, 1969: 549–550; 1973: 199–200].

The "extraordinary measures", from the roadblocks to police officers riding trains, supposed to offer evidence to support his claims were nothing of the kind. Many had already been used to control both soccer hooligans and the contemporary Ban the Bomb demonstrators complete with those "shows of force", "unnecessary violence", "harassment of similarly dressed youths", and the "poor holding facilities" for any "innocent arrested" [1969: 551; 1973: 93–100]. The only real innovation appears to have been the airlift of police reinforcements to Hastings [Cohen, 1973: 86; 1969: 486]. However, Cohen forgot to include the mundane facts that this was the easiest means to overcome the bank holiday gridlock on the UK's pre-freeway coast roads, and that although this flexible back-up squad was sup-posed to be cheaper than mobilizing reserves in every resort town, it failed to reduce the overtime being claimed by the local Bobbies [Cohen, 1969: 492; 1973: 92; MAR1].

The "dramatization of evil" in the courts was true enough, but UK magistrates are always lecturing folk whether devils or not as a visit to *any* court on *any* day of the week will demonstrate. Likewise, while the media published the resort town magistrates' mixed metaphors with approval, as the magistrates referred to the youths as "louts" and "thugs" with their common connotations rather than mods and rockers with their alleged symbolic meaning, and one looks in vain for any references to "gangs", there is no evidence for Cohen's claims about the effect of the media inventory on the courts [1969: 464–465; 1973: 55]. On the contrary, only 24 of the 97 arrested in Clacton were indicted, and the "harsh" penalties reflected that sub group's prior criminal records which would automatically led to a more punitive sentence as Cohen knew perfectly well [1966]. As the alleged "escalating penalties" in Margate and Hastings merely followed in proportion to the seriousness of the offense, no one was playing hardball [Cohen, 1969: 503, Tables 49 and 50; 1973: 102]. That leaves us with the one-off imposition of extra-legal measures by Brighton magistrates during 1965 when the town finally lost their patience with the invaders as the recorder cited in *Folk Devils* explained [1973: 97, 100, 102–106]. The account in the PD is very different. Cases of wrongful arrests were inflated by the typical yobbo's lying lament that they "was doin' nuffink". It was their ignorance that ensured that they failed to appeal against the "no bail" conditions, although that would have brought them instant relief. The police were also reprimanded for being too heavy-handed after *The Times* denounced their behavior that weekend [1969: 496–499; 505]. Indeed, the lack of a crackdown is precisely why the resort town law and order lobbies remained unimpressed and continued to demand more controls. In spite of all the rhetoric, they knew that it was business as usual in the courts, evidenced by the complaint from the License Victuallers Association found in *Folk Devils* [1973: 118].

No doubt some members of the public wanted more controls, but Cohen's use of a third survey to justify his claim that 81 percent did so, having dismissed the other two surveys is not only methodologically dubious, the result is spurious. As over half, 160 of 300, failed to repeat any of the innovations suggested in the media; 32 of the remaining 140 referenced a measure already in use; and only 53 of the remaining 108 mentioned the measures that Cohen referenced such as fire-hosing crowds, the final figure amounts to 18 percent rather than 81! Moreover, as that figure is also inflated by the inclusion of the demand to restrict media coverage because it encouraged the youths; that effectively meant that the only people in the survey demanding "new harsher measures" were the journalists Cohen had included. In short, another survey from a town supposedly under siege undermines Cohen claims about the inculcation of the media inventory [1969: 488–489, Table 45].

WHERE'S THE DEVIANCE?

Cohen's use of the expressions "widening the net", "the amount of deviance recorded", and "an overestimation of deviance" [1973: 105, 111, 143, 199], amounts to an admission that he could not match Young's definition of an amplification of deviancy in the latter's seminal case-study covering a police crackdown on dope smokers in Notting Hill, London which helped create the UK's counterculture [Young, 1971]. As the mods did not develop a critique of mainstream society, still less a political response, there is no comparison. Indeed, the differences are even more marked because Young failed to record the extent of the counterculture which emerged. It included: a political-legal-cultural critique found in a whole rack of alternative newspapers, commix, and books; organizations like Release which campaigned against the drug laws; 'head shops' selling the accoutrements of the culture; fashions copied by the mainstream; and rock bands like *The Deviants* and *Hawkwind*. The latter are important, for whereas indigenous mod bands like *The Small Faces* and manufactured ones like *The Who* produced teen 'anthems', the rock bands from the Hall of the Mountain Grill café along with the *Edgar Broughton Band* not only symbolized the counterculture, they belied the Left-wing myth that the 1970s was devoid of political rock and the equally facile claim that the UK "hippies" were copying those in California [Frith, 1978 and 1983]. On the contrary, these three bands played dozens of benefit concerts for anyone taking on "the establishment", from the emerging ecology movement, through squatters and criminalized bikers, to the National Union of Miners!

Whereas dope smoking also became a central facet of the counterculture, fighting on the beaches never became central to the mods and certainly not the rockers' life-style. Likewise, while the amplification in Notting Hill uncovered a lot more of the original deviance engaged in by the original deviants, Cohen could only offer unconnected follow-up stories, media stereotypes of gangs that did not exist, half-a-dozen beach invasions by youths who denied that they were mods (see below), arrests of innocents who won appeals, and the existing zero tolerance for Friday night fighting in the wilds of outer London. As you cannot turn a beatnik into a mod by simply banning them from beaches, that leaves us with Cohen's account of the *in situ* amplification of deviancy on the Brighton promenade which supposedly proved that the Clacton reaction polarized the mods and rockers, and the youths against adult society.

THEIR OWN FORM OF EXCITEMENT

Cohen's polarization by panic thesis rested on two theoretical tautologies. The first was that the two youth groups did not conform to the gang stereotype in the media because:

in every instance, the young people present constituted a crowd or series of interlocking crowds, rather than a group (or gang) or even less, two highly structured opposing groups [1973: 149].

Yet neither *Folk Devils* nor his PhD offered any evidence that anyone ever believed that *all* those present were mods and rockers, let alone were members of gangs, still less gangs that conformed to Cohen's bizarre criterion: the Jets in *West Side Story*! Like many other questionable features in his account, Cohen's claim relied on his composite of the media inventory rather than any direct citation, or the accumulated evidence that a comprehensive content analysis would provide [1969: 447; 1973: 34–35]. Indeed, the examples offered in *Folk Devils* like his PhD merely consist of generalizations like *The Daily Telegraph's* "grubby hoards of louts and sluts"; and the nearest one gets to a gang reference in the courts is "rats hunting in packs" [1973: 55 and 109].

The second tautology concerns Cohen's insistence that the ever-changing mod fashions prevented the kind of homogeneity required for polarization. He dismissed the clear contrast between the bike and scooter riders seen in *Folk Devils* first edition's photographs on the basis that most mods took the train [1973: 128–129]. However, as the missing history of the rockers suggests that their homogeneity could easily generate a polarization between them and the mass of mods whatever their fashion sense or mode of transportation, we will concentrate on the way Cohen's pedantic stance generates more than one contradiction in his thesis. If the constant changes in mod fashions prevented homogeneity in 1964, the mods merely amounted to those "milling crowds" in 1965, and the invaders in 1966 denied being mods; we never get to see the polarization by panic in *Folk Devils* [1973: 187, 149, and 200]. On the other hand, when Cohen needs to turn the mods into the symbol of unarticulated fears about permissiveness in order to 'explain' the panic, he claims that the mods "sheer uniformity in dress" was "the major factor" in facilitating that symbolization [1973: 194]! Further contradictions can be found in Cohen's account of the *in situ* amplification of deviance on the beaches. Cohen begins by drawing a contrast between his belief that the mods were bored, listless, with no definite plans, and his assertion that the media were adamant that the teens' sole intent was to cause trouble. He then claims that the teens had been drawn to the beaches by an inventory generated "*collective* desire" to be "where the action was", despite his informants' denial that the press played any part in their decisions. Finally, Cohen claims that the police reaction to minor incidents, encouraged by the presence of the paparazzi and adults, led the mods (note: not the rockers) to live up to the *old* stereotype and act out their "normative role" as deviants because of the societal reaction [1973: 150–151, 161, 164–165]. Despite all that, his subsequent exposition of the origins of the mods' delinquency, the school leaver who took their "own form of excitement" to the beaches clearly suggests that they were "looking for trouble"

[1973: 161, 164–165, and 182]; and once they got there, we now discover that the mods had no difficulty drawing a distinction between themselves and others despite their supposed lack of homogeneity:

> if there were no Rockers in sight, the Mods would happily turn on the beat-niks; in the course of one morning, the target could rapidly change from rockers, to beatniks, to police, depending upon the mood of the crowd, rumours of victimisation or actual police interference [1973: 157].

As the moment these targets disappeared, the mods would turn on each other or bait the police, there is no reason to believe that they had to be told by the *Daily Mirror* that delinquents throw deck chairs into the sea or required the encouragement of *The Daily Express* to knock old ladies over as they did so [1973: 152]. We can also dismiss Cohen's ultimate rationale, that the pre-inventory polarization "was not so marked" because of the teens' common working-class origins, as that factor never inhibited soccer hooligans or the Teddy boys fighting each other. On the contrary, as the ultimate sociological question should have been whether the mods would have exhibited "their own form of excitement" without the media inven-tory, and that can be answered by the fact that they had done just that, not once, but twice at Clacton before the inventory appeared, Cohen has no evidence for his polarization by panic thesis.

While *some* adults may have been schooled in the labels mods and rockers by the media and/or believed that the youths' behavior could be explained by their drug consumption, and *some* may even have cheered when the police made an arrest; asserting that *every* adult present went there to watch a "morality play" about re-imposing societal values with the "heavy handed police" playing the lead role is self serving rather than a "more sociological explanation" [1973: 111 and 159]. They could easily have cheered because they finally got to see some irritating, spotty faced lout being egged on by a slut finally get his just desert after a life-time of suffering from his like, but "got away with it". While one could argue that is still imposing values, the morality play was supposed to be about permissiveness, not violence. Once again, you can consider the viability of this part of the thesis for yourself thanks to another newsreel on YouTube which includes an interview with a female café owner, a bunch of bemused beatniks, and the majority of the beach going public ignoring the youths despite all the horror-headlines [MAR2,[4] 2010].

MORAL ENTERPRISE

Cohen's account of the role of moral enterprise is as problematic as it is con-fused. As well as including anyone and everyone who was merely cited in the press, he elevates the *ad hoc* resort town action groups to the status of moral entrepreneurs while reducing Whitehouse's national moral crusade to the status of an 'action group'. That lack of exactitude is exacerbated by his claim that panic didn't lead to specific legislation because the *ad hoc* groups in a couple of resort towns failed to produce specific proposals, when they clearly did; including the proposal to confiscate convicted youths' motor vehicle permits which landed on the Home Secretary's desk [1969: 521; 1973: 115–118, 121–122, 130–131]. As we address legislation below, we concentrate here on Cohen's characterization of the moral entrepreneurs' fears and motives. Despite some equivocation, Cohen clearly inferred that his informant anonymized as Blake and the national moral entrepreneurs like Mary Whitehouse and Earl Longford shared a similar pathology: single mindedness, self-righteousness, and a dual tendency to grossly exaggerate while oversimplifying. He then asserted that this followed from their authoritarian personalities, which he correlated with Puritanism, racial prejudice, fear of the masses, and projection [1973: 127 and 132]. Knowing Whitehouse as we did, that caricature was completely erroneous; an example of Cohen's use of guilt by *no* association. Blake was also an isolated figure within his own *ad hoc* group because he was a fascist; a fact clearly revealed by his perspective on the problem [collated from Cohen, 1973: 115–117; 127–132]:

- The residents had been terrorized by the mods and rockers whose welfare-state induced boredom had lead to the destruction of property which deprived the traders of a living by frightening away the family trade.
- Rather than consider that the public avoided UK resorts because they were 'out of date; Blake blamed the youth's increasing disrespect for authority, hence the need for a clamp down before the country descended into mob rule like China (an oblique reference to the cultural revolution—eds.).
- His solution was to exclude the mods and rockers from the town; and if they still came, use the Riot Act and 'citizen patrols' to deal with them.
- If innocent teens suffered, that did not matter, as the 'rights' of the holiday-makers and residents came first. Making the teens pay fines did not work.

While Cohen presents this as a typical resort town reaction, the account offered by Blake not only explains why he was in a minority of one, it contradicts several aspects of Cohen's account of the moral panic. According to Blake:

The liberals who complained about a police state failed to see that the country was facing an emergency that could only be solved by using the punishments found in Shari law and road gangs. The local authorities and the chief constables were useless, and the police were avoiding arrests to keep the official crime-rate down. The youths were suffering from 'mass hysteria' because they had been overindulged by the welfare state in an affluent society, leaving them with too much money and time on their hands; which was why bank clerks now dressed up as mods and did what they normally would not do.

The ultimate blame lay with the Labour party, the trade unions, and the philosophy of turning the other cheek, which made no sense given that the country was being overrun by yobbos and immigrants, when everyone should know their place both socially and geographically and stay there; although he would probably leave the UK, before it got worse [Summarized from Cohen, 1973: 128–132]!

As well as confirming that law and order advocates believed that the cops and courts were not being tough enough, Blake's reasoning also belies Cohen's claim that those who panicked had drawn a link between the welfare coddling and permissiveness. Black did not address the latter. The difference between Blake's fascism, confirmed by his later conviction for baring blacks from his hotel [Cohen, 1969: 536], and the Christian moral entrepreneurs' perspective on social change is evidenced by the Christian analysis of the contemporary "social strain", published after Moralgate:

> Britain's decline followed the rise of 'humbug and cant' especially amongst Christians who blamed rising affluence rather than their own failure to evangelize for the decline in religious sensibility. The sensational orientated press—'the lie factory', secular humanism, and the denigration of traditional Christianity in government, on TV, in schools and intellectual life had reinforced the growing lack of economic and social justice in the UK whose cause could be traced to: selfish industrialists, Rachmans,[5] fascism, hate filled leftists, the country's obsession with fornication, cross-less Christians, and the neo-fascism of cynicism and satire promoted by intellectuals.[6] Like the poor state of industrial relations, these problems could only be resolved by a religious revival [Adopted from *The Daily Express* 28 June and September, nd, 1963; January 9 and March 25 1964].

This early presentation of "the third way", the Christian alternative to capitalism and socialism, had nothing in common with people like Blake, who were seen as being part of the problem. Following the Whitsun clashes, the Christians not only defended the youths in the form of the open letter to the Home Secretary published in *The Daily Express,* the contents revealed that they considered permissiveness to be a function of economic and cultural materialism [Bold in original; italics, our emphasis—eds. *The Daily Express* May 14th, 1964]:

Dear Mr. Brooke,

. . . You say you do not know the cause or cure of boredom that creates a Clacton. We can tell you . . . **We are bored with Tories** who offer to build schools and houses, to fill our pockets and stomachs. But leave hearts and minds empty of consistent belief or goal.

We are bored with socialists who only promise more of the same thing, and seem preoccupied with class attitudes that are already fading when the Beatles dine with Royalty and debs operate petrol pumps.

We are bored with communists who offer us brotherhood based on hate while their own camp is divided.

We are bored with clergy who press us to fill pews on Sunday, but don't have the guts to speak out against those determined to destroy the conscience and character of our generation.

We are bored with those who through films, TV and books suggest sex is the great god we must worship. We bow down to it and find pregnant schoolgirls, venereal disease, illegitimate children, broken homes and frustration that can lead to suicide.

Having outlined the meaninglessness of modern materialism exhibited by adult society, the Christians homed in on the ramifications of the Profumo Affair and the rise of secular humanism:

Your generation once spoke with patriotism, moral standards, Almighty God. It seems to us that too few of you have lived as if they existed . . . Too many seem to condone the lowering of standards in their own ranks which they condemn in the ranks of youth. Some in high positions seem to be men whose private opinions and lives increase confusion about what is right or wrong . . . All of us would respect your generation more if they showed some consistent belief (whether we shared it or not) and lived it, instead of so often pretending to be 'with it'.

This was followed by addressing the most common complaint about youth at the time, omitted by Cohen, 'ingratitude':[7]

We can not remember the 'thirties when some people suffered so much. We can not remember the 'forties when the whole nation was geared towards victory and recovery.

We are living in the 'sixties and *mean to enjoy life despite the gloom of economic and political prospects. Youth today is bent on a world of its own choosing, free from old fears and full of fun and fulfillment.*

If some of us take to drugs, drink, and violence, out of frustration for the present, it's a sign of intensity of search for the new future.

After covering the global rise of delinquency in the postwar generation living under the shadow of "the bomb" the authors concluded with an invitation to help solve society's problems by joining the Christian crusade to establish a society based on "absolute moral standards of honesty, purity, unselfishness and love" [*The Daily Express* May 14th, 1964].

In short, as those most likely to be concerned about the boundary crisis attacked the press, denounced adult society as hypocritical, and excused the teens' violence as a function of *adult* permissiveness; the Christian moral entrepreneurs were not panicking about the mods and rockers. Neither did the parliamentarians, as a visit to the Palace of Westminster will prove.

PYRAMIDS OF POWER

Cohen's account of the Clacton reaction paid little attention to the parliamentary process, the extensive consultation process that takes place before any legislation is debated, although it appeared in his PhD [1969: 520–521]. Even when legislatures appear to react in haste, the arguments heard in the debating chamber and committee rooms covering amendments are shaped by related issues stretching back years, as the content of any pre legislation *Briefing Paper* published by the government would indicate. Despite mentioning the meeting between a resort town MP and the Home Secretary, Cohen dismissed the demands made by the resort town magistrates on the basis they had only made general appeals. While that may have been true in court, Cohen was well aware that specific appeals would be sent on to the Magistrates Association, which debated and passed-on several that they received from their members to the Home Office. In this case, the association voted to demand building more detention centers rather than confiscate the youths' vehicles [Cohen, 1969, 521; 1973: 119]. Likewise, resort town councils were passing on the demands made by their local traders to the Association of Municipal Councils which would debate them too.

The reason why none of the specific proposals were adopted was that having debated delinquency for four years already, the government and opposition parties had already made up their minds what they were going to do. The Labour party, for example, was intent on expanding social facilities for teens, and they won the next general election held in October 1964 with a manifesto promise that:

> The Youth Service will be developed with grants for youth centres, swimming pools, coffee bars and other facilities without which the present service cannot function [Labour party manifesto, 1964].

As Labour won, and the electorate voted for more coffee bars rather than more social controls, they could not have been panicking about the youths, no matter what the polls said. The defeated Conservative government was not interested in the law and order lobby's demands either. Having already proposed a Royal Commission into the causes of delinquency, the Conservative party's election manifesto concentrated on the root causes of primary delinquency:

> Much juvenile delinquency originates in broken or unhappy homes. We shall continue to support the work of marriage guidance. Local authorities will be encouraged, in co-operation with voluntary bodies, to develop their services of child care for young people deprived of normal home life and affection [Conservative party manifesto, 1964].

The complete lack of any references to the mods and rockers during an election, in the middle of an alleged panic, points to an obvious problem with Cohen's account. That is why the media relied on an aging vicar, a youth worker, a probation officer, a marriage counselor, a psychiatrist, a headmaster, a DJ, and a pop star with an ego when condemning the youths [1973: 119]. If anything extraordinary had been happening, the press would have been full of citations from archbishops, cabinet ministers, shadow cabinet ministers, professors with appropriate research, leaders of national youth groups, chairs of county council associations, senior police officers, chairs of headmaster associations, and the national moral entrepreneurs. It was not that these opinion formers were never cited, but that when they were, like the Bishop of Southwell, they tended to blame adults and society too [*Observer*, 6.4.64, cited in Cohen, 1969: 474]. Likewise, while Cohen may have been impressed by the fact that 400 members of the local law and order brigade could not get into Blake's public meeting in 1965, it is far more significant to note that the only member of the local establishment who attended was the *former* MP who had *lost* his seat in the 1964 general election [Cohen, 1969: 527–528 1973: 125]. The reason why the media and Blake were scraping the barrel can be found in the political response to both Clacton and the Whitsun disturbances.

TODAY IN PARLIAMENT

Cohen's account of the parliamentary reaction is a gross distortion of what occurred. Having highlighted a couple of examples of resort town MPs calling for stiffer penalties and tabling parliamentary questions to do so, Cohen offered a list of debates that included references to the mods and rockers [1973: 133–134]. He correctly dismissed the Drugs (Prevention of Misuse) bill, debated over Easter, as part of the reaction because it was obviously tabled long before Clacton; but drew attention to Frank Taylor's 15th April Resolution, the two-hour debate on Gurden's Motion on the 27th, and the June 4 Statement by the Home Secretary as evidence that the media inventory was being to work, and that once the pressure grew, the

Home Secretary was forced to change his mind, abandon his belief that the existing penalties were adequate, and introduced "an emergency measure": the Malicious Damage bill on the 23rd June. Cohen explained away Taylor's Resolution which merely alluded to Clacton as an example of delinquency [Hansard, HOC, 27 April, 1964: 31–40], and the lack of any criticism of the youths in Gurden's motion on the grounds that the media symbolization process had not had enough time to work; but points to the sixteen speeches referencing the seaside disturbances, including seven that specifically referenced the mods and rockers, during the Malicious Damage bill as proof that that the media inventory had "crystallized" and had its effect [1973: 136]. Although, the bill obviously targeted vandalism rather than the teens, Cohen assured his readers that:

> It was clear from the Home Secretary's original statement and subsequent debate on the second reading that, while the Act was obviously to apply to vandalism in general, it was an emergency measure directed specifically at the Mods and Rockers. As such it may be seen as a normative formalization by the control culture [1973: 137].

The evidence for that claim was Mr. Brooke's comment during his statement that he hoped that the subsequent Act would be operational before the August bank holiday, and that when the bill was introduced, he had declared that:

> I want this Bill also to be a reassurance to the long suffering public. They were long suffering at these holiday places, for many of them had their Whitsun holidays or their Whitsun trade spoilt by these young fools. I want to reassure them by showing them that the Government means business [1973: 137].

Cohen then explained away the lack of draconian measures in the bill by declaring that it was not unusual for parliamentarians to make:

> affirmations and gestures of indignation by which means one aligns oneself symbolically with the angels, without having to take up cudgels against the devil [1973: 137–138].

In this case, while the damage had not been great, the bill targeted vandalism because it was:

> *the most visible manifestation of the phenomenon* and the one *most likely to calculated to evoke social condemnation*. To align oneself symbolically with the angels, one had to pick on an easy target; the fact that the target *hardly* existed was irrelevant; it could be, and already had been defined [our emphasis—eds. Cohen, 1973: 138].

That was because "politicians in office . . . often act to calm things down" during moral panic [1973: 36]. As Cohen's exposition could not be clearer, the failure of anyone to question those claims over the last 40 years is a testament to the paradigm's complete lack of academic and evidential standards. One only had to check the parliamentary record to discover that the bill did not even reflect the pre-Clacton media inventory on vandalism, let alone amount to an emergency measure responding to the demands of the "suprasystem" whatever that was, that "something should be done—and soon" about the mods and rockers.

CLACTON, CHRISTIANS, AND CAUSALITY

As parliamentary resolutions and motions are a means to generate and show support for issues not being addressed by the government, the small numbers turning up for Gurden's suggest that the majority of MPs could not have cared less about the mods and rockers; but those who did had far more to say than Cohen's selective citation [1973: 135]. Rather than panicking about mods and rockers, the debate was shaped by the announcement that a Royal Commission would examine the disparate perspectives on delinquency that had appeared during the four year delinquency debate that had already produced several reports including the Home Office's *Delinquent Generations*, had influenced the Newsom and Ingleby Committees, and had shaped two parliamentary inquires into the youth services, and sport in the Community; none of which were mentioned in *Folk Devils*. Although the announcement effectively made Gurden's Motion redundant, the speeches made by those attending reveal why the media inventory had so little effect.

Gurden wanted the commission to accept the causes offered by the Local Government Information Office which had blamed vandalism on a decline in values and a breakdown in discipline, and he dismissed all those "heard them all before" explanations now being proffered in the press. Although he was convinced delinquency was caused by the new morality that was not for the reasons Cohen suggested. Gurden objected to "that psychological nonsense" about children needing free expression in school, and blamed working-class parents for the necessity to insist schools begin to train children to appreciate public property and understand the value of law based on Christian standards of morality [Hansard, HOC, 27 April, 1964: 31–40]. In other words, he was blaming adults. Sir Richard Thompson also blamed the teens' moral failings on their parents [HOC: 78–79]. Leslie Seymour wanted stiffer penalties, but only because inflation had eroded the punitive impact of existing fines [HOC: 43–45]; and Mr Rees-Davis, a real reactionary, who usually blamed everything on "do-gooders", advocated removing convicted hooligans from school to avoid contagion as well as making vandals pay recompense [HOC: 55–56].

The liberal Christians in the Labour party blamed anything and everything except the teens. While Mr. Maurice Edelman adopted the warring gang motif, he blamed that and the teens' aggressive exhibitionism in front of the news media on TV shows imported from the US which he believed encouraged acquisitiveness and admiration for rule breakers [HOC: 48].[8] Mr Fell from Yarmouth, a battle ground resort, suggested that living under the constant threat of an atomic war did not help; but was convinced that when MPs and religious leaders like Norman Collins set poor examples, it was not surprising that people of no faith, little property, and a poor upbringing did the same [HOC: 63–64].[9] George Thomas opted for the anomie of affluence thesis[10] promoted by the Newsom Committee [HOC, 1964: 72–73]. Mr. Bence blamed modern capitalists for being too materialistic and not taking an interest in the moral welfare of their employees [HOC: 75–76]. Julian Snow concluded the speeches from the floor by targeting "the perverted tastes" promoted by Hollywood movies, which he believed were a perfect example of the baneful effects of private enterprise [HOC: 60–62].

Miss Bacon, the Labour party's shadow Home Secretary, then rose to speak. Bacon had tried to intervene in the debate when Rees-Davies was making his speech, only to be told to "stop grimacing" and that "the nation wants something done (about delinquents—eds.) and you have not got any good proposals" [HOC: 52]. Rees-Davis did not like Miss Bacon because she was a permissive as well as a do-gooder. Consequently, the content of her speech, which explained why MPs were blaming society in one way or another rather than denouncing the mods and rockers, provides a good test for Cohen's account.

Having drawn a parallel between the "social hooliganism" exhibited at the beaches and soccer hooliganism, Bacon raised the issue of Clacton in order to denounce the media, and remind MPs that delinquency *was* classless because there was no difference between what happened on the beaches and upper-class debutante balls or middle-class university rag weeks which she denounced as an excuse for "hooliganism of the worst kind".[11] Like many others, Bacon believed that focusing on the working-class variant was "unacceptable in modern society", which should be making a distinction between the deprived and depraved delinquent. The ramifications of that for Cohen's inferences about 'classless' are obvious; and when Bacon addressed the working-class variant, she argued that as the working-class variant was mainly perpetrated by those in their last year of school, the government needed to address that issue. Having then dismissed the law and order lobby, Bacon proffered the Labour party's wish list including the proposals that appeared in the party's election manifesto. After commenting upon the other speeches, as opposition spokespeople do, Ms Bacon concluded by suggesting that the Government open more attendance centers as they had helped combat soccer hooliganism [HOC: 80–87]. Mr Brooke summating for the government also undermined Cohen's spin on the parliamentary response by making it "very clear" that he would only reference Clacton because it had already been raised. As far as the government was concerned, the newspapers had promoted a completely false picture. There was *no* riot, *no* gang warfare, *no* sacking of the town, and the damage caused by isolated incidents amounted to less than £1000. The government was far more concerned about the growing proportion of young people found guilty of indictable offences. Having already adopted the Ingleby Committee's solutions,[12] proposed a Royal Commission into penal policies for delinquents, and updated the penalties that would apply to any more 'Clactons' in the Criminal Justice Act; he believed that there was no need for a new law. Indeed, as the government was more interested in the stresses and strains faced by teens caused by social change, he had asked his Advisory Committee on Juvenile Delinquency to help determine the origin of modern delinquency by canvassing modern youth on the source of the problem [HOC: 88–97].

In short, the major reason the government and parliamentarians paid scant attention to Clacton was because they were over half way through a comprehensive reform of the juvenile justice system and had no intention of accommodating the law and order lobby's agenda. Like the Labour party, the Conservative party believed that social change had placed pressure on working-class school leavers and wished to avoid locking up any more youths than they had to; which is why the law and order lobby was marginalized during this period. Although Conservative party and Labour party Christians may have disagreed over the precise causes of and solutions to delinquency, they were united in their rejection of more law and order except for hardcore hooligans. The major reason Cohen never mentioned all this, was he could not admit where he really got 'his' explanation from without undermining his thesis. The fact that he purloined it from the parliamentary debate proves that the papers were having no effect; and as he could not have purloined it without reading the debate, it infers the distortions in *Folk Devils* were deliberate.

A MERE TECHNICALITY

Even after the Whitsun disturbances had demonstrated that Clacton was not an isolated incident, only *nine* MPs tabled parliamentary questions about resort town trouble. As these parliamentary questions reflect the contents of MPs postbags from their constituencies, the small number suggests that any panic was confined to the resort towns. That meant making a Statement was unusual, but that had nothing to do with Brooke changing his mind. Back then statements were effectively a means to address to the nation. So the fact that Brooke began by denouncing the press and reiterating that the government was determined to conduct research into the teens' selfish behavior offers the context for what he said next. Brooke reminded the teens that "behavior which may seem amusing to them can develop into an unfair and intolerable intrusion upon the pleasures of other people" and suggested that they should "cease to encourage the perhaps few black sheep among them". Having reminded the rest of society "that there are exhibitionists and trouble makers who thrive on publicity", he reiterated that the government believed that there was no need for a new law [Hansard, HOC, 4 June, 1964: 1250–1251]. The proposals made were either unnecessary, or like the confiscation of licenses were redundant not only because of the legal issues involved, but the fact that most youths took the train. After declaring that the best solution to resort town vandalism was to make the culprits pay restitution, the Christian solution seen in Cohen's London sample, Brooke finally addressed the specific reason for the statement [HOC: 1251–1252].

The eagled eyed Mr. Taylor MP had noticed that the Criminal Justice Act which had increased the level of penalties to cover the inflation of the previous 50 years, and justified Brooke's belief no new laws were needed, contained an error. It had overlooked section 14 of the 1914 Criminal Justice Administration Act, which meant that the fines and compensation orders for criminal damage were still restricted to the 50-year-old maximum ceiling of £20 [HOC: 1250–1251]. Consequently, Brooke apologized for the mistake, and announced that he would correct it by raising the maximum fine and the ceiling of compensation orders to £100 each in line with the previous updates [HOC: 1251–1252]. As that means that the Malicious Damage bill was nothing more than an amendment, correcting a drafting oversight in a previous amendment to a 50-year-old Act, Cohen's argument that it was "an emergency measure" directed against the mods and rockers "aligning with angels" was gobbledygook. Worse, having referenced the real reason for the bill in his PhD, Cohen was deliberately misleading the readers of *Folk Devils* [1969: 69]. Having already spent a considerable amount of time, effort, and energy on the wider problem of delinquency since 1959, the only 'devils' being targeted by Parliament at this point were the press and the law and order lobby; which probably explains why Brooke concluded his statement by reiterating that the government preferred to listen to the teens.

PUTTING THE RECORD STRAIGHT

Summarizing parliamentary debates is not easy. As speakers can address dozens of issues, complete with qualifications and caveats, there is often more than one 'theme' or 'tone' in every speech, and the debate on the Malicious Damage bill was no exception. However, there can be no doubt that in this case rather than promote the media inventory the MPs came to bury it. Brooke began by insisting that correcting the oversight ensured that the courts had all the powers that they needed to maintain order and protect persons and property, before promising to deal with the social strains experienced by youth in their transition from school to work [Hansard, HOC, 23 June, 1964: 239–240]. As the "also reassure" comment that Cohen relied on appeared *after* Brooke had repeated his reasons for rejecting demands for new laws, and reiterated that *apart* from the oversight the courts already had enough powers, evidenced by the fact the Clacton hardcore were already "being taught good behavior and proper manners at a detention centre", Brooke had not changed his mind. If anything, he was reassuring the public that his previous claim had been valid apart from the oversight [HOC:241–242]. After Ms Bacon had responded by offering the Labour opposition's full support [HOC: 245]; the press and the law and order brigade came in for a pounding.

Mr. Morrison (Conservative), like most of the MPs believed that delinquency was on the increase, but he did not blame the teens. He castigated the media for spreading alarm amongst the elderly about the penalties being too light and suggested that those criticizing modern youth would be better employed in voluntary service helping them overcome the problems that came with greater freedom [HOC: 250–253]. Mr. Fitch (Labour) welcomed the amendment as a means to stop vandalism in parks, on railway lines, and especially on "football specials" as well as the seaside, expounded on the anomie of affluence, and concluded that it was adults' responsibility to give the teens "a sense of purpose" [HOC: 257]. Sir William Teeling MP (Con.—Brighton, Pavilion) was still worried about beach invasions, but dismissed the media reports as exaggerations. Although he still preferred higher fines for the "well to do hooligan" and labor camps for the rest to pay their compensation; he believed that the real problem was the size of the crowds with their potential for another Lima. He agreed prison was no place for hooligans, and vandals should pay for any damage done [HOC: 256–263]. Mr. Prentice (Lab.) complained that he had never seen so many "pompous editorials" when it was obvious that compensation was the answer. Having served on Earl Longford's Committee he also argued that the core problem was the decline of the Christian ethic, the rise of a more selfish society, a decline in voluntary service, and the paradox of increasing crime in prosperous societies. He then proffered the Christian perspective on the role of "meritocracy" in creating teen pressure. As society became more sophisticated and less class bound, the emphasis upon meritorious success gave life less meaning to those left behind in secondary modern schools and labeled failures. Their subsequent frustration and a feeling of injustice had led a minority into delinquency [HOC: 265–271]. Mr. Gardener (Conservative) did not agree. As every generation had to deal with "high spirited youth", today's teens were not a major problem. As the time for harsh penalties had passed, he preferred compensation so that the victims did not have to seek redress in the civil courts [HOC: 272–273]. After Brighton's other MP, David James (Con.) had used his disaster-shock analogy, he backed more attendance centers and making perpetrators pay compensation, too [HOC: 274–277].

Although the two Brighton MPs repeated their town's traders' demands as they were duty bound to do, they were the only resort town MPs to do so. A parliamentary consensus had formed around the Christians' solution to delinquency: compulsory restitution and aid for the ailing school leaver. That consensus was not dented by Mr. Awdry (Con.) when he broke the congenial atmosphere with a two-minute attack on the philosophy behind the Longford Committee. Tempering justice with mercy was one thing and improving and modernizing the criminal justice system was another; but he could not allow the way the committee had blamed capitalism for acquisitiveness and promoted the dubious concept of relative impoverishment to excuse the role of temptation in crime to go unanswered. Having got that off his chest, he promptly rounded on the law and order lobby in an equally emphatic manner [HOC: 278–279]. Mr. Paget (Labour) wanted to know why, if the mods and rockers were worse than those on "rugger nights" or Cambridge students fighting on November 5, the casualty departments were empty? He did not believe that the "exuberant types on holiday" were delinquents, let alone criminal; and they needed to be treated differently. Once the culprit had paid compensation that was where the matter should end; not that Paget was going to stop there, for when it came to mods and rockers:

> Certainly, it is something that has to be controlled, and these young chaps must pay for the damage they do. In the sense that this Bill enables the courts to see that these people do pay for the damage they cause plus something more, I am in favour of it. But *I deplore the idea adopted by some magistrates and canvassed and applauded in the newspapers of sending young men of this sort to prison.* That is a lamentable answer to this sort of performance. *We have also had hysterical observations about Sawdust Caesars. These people are nothing of the sort* [our emphasis—eds. Hansard, HOC, 23 June, 1964: 280].

As "the angels" were under attack, and every MP, including Mr. Campbell (Con.), backed the consensus, the claim that this debate was a ritual means to deal with "the devils" is patently absurd [HOC: 281–282]; a fact reinforced when the arch reactionary and scourge of permissiveness Rees-Davis MP rose to speak. Having demonstrated that he was still not in the mood for do-gooders by taking a verbal swipe at Ms. Bacon, he then reminded the MPs that the mods and rockers had paid a visit to his constituency over Whitsun, and that two people had been stabbed. But instead of using that as a spring board for an attack on the youths, he promptly dismissed the episode as "much talk and not very much harm", agreed that compensation was the answer as long as the trade unions would not oppose any work scheme in prison, and sat down [HOC: 284]. That was it. Despite maintaining his record of never speaking without a dig at do-gooders or socialists; he proved that even real reactionaries agreed that the solution to vandalism was compensation.

Mr. Curran (Con.) being a libertarian wanted to know why restitution was not used more often to deal with crime; and argued that as you could not make perfect people or societies by passing legislation, you should not even try. What you should do was lower the age of majority[13] encouraging young people to take more responsibility [HOC: 290–291]. The last speech from the floor by Christian Socialist, Eric Fletcher (Lab.) lamented the decline in religion and proposed more recreational facilities for school leavers [HOC: 293–295]. Miss Pike, the Home Office Under Secretary then closed the debate, by dismissing the law and order lobby, promising more liberal reforms to come, and reiterating that, as the police's *"regular, existing, machinery"* for dealing with outbreaks of public disorder was working, no new laws were needed [our emphasis— eds. HOC: 301–305].

As everyone agreed that the mods and rockers were a case of careless high spirits, Pike confirmed that there had been no increase in the control culture, and the sole purpose behind the bill was to amend an amendment to a 50-year-old Act; Cohen's analysis of the debate is indicative of the rest of his account: a political myth based on very selective evidence. Far from being reactionary, the Christian MPs, the moral entrepreneurs, and those in Cohen's professional sample were acting as a bulwark against the law and order lobby during this period. As for all those alleged inventory effects: beachside vandalism was only one of four types of delinquency mentioned in the debate, and a very poor second best to soccer hooliganism, and no one condemned the mods and rockers. On the contrary, some of those direct references were complimentary:

Morrison:	I have seen a great deal of the age group which is associated with mods and rockers, and I say without hesitation that I am full of admiration for the general fervor and spirit of these young people.
Fitch:	I am not sure of the definition of a rocker and mod. I should like to see groups of those rockers, who, I understand, are the people who race off to the seaside on motor cycles, rushing off on the same motor cycles, to the same sort of places, not to engage in acts of vandalism, but rather take part in such things as Freedom From Hunger campaign.
Teeling:	There will be an unpleasant surprise, I hope, for mods and rockers who go there (Brighton—eds.) on August Bank Holiday.
Prentice:	One's feelings among rockers is that mods tend to be rather goody, goody types, the ones who dress well, the ones who

	become more conventional and be in youth clubs, and that it is rather a brave thing to be a rocker ... I hasten to add that I am in a sense sorry that I introduced the terms mod and rocker because they have become so over worked.

Gardner: One must distinguish between dishonesty ... and the sort of person who goes out in high spirits, undisciplined and irresponsible, and commits the sort of damage that is the grave subject of displeasure when young people go to sea-side resorts and break up deck chairs, damage buildings and make hooligans of themselves.

Paget: I deplore the amount of hysteria engendered by the scraps that took place between the mods and rockers. These young people are not criminals; they are not criminal types. There is nothing either particularly modern or particularly shocking in the fact that young men do today ... have a fight.

Rees-Davis: Since I last spoke on the matter, before the mods and rockers went to Margate, in my constituency, there has been a change.

As Teeling was alluding to the £100 fines and compensation orders that now awaited any trouble maker, none of those comments reflected the media inventory. Bacon, Gardner, and Paget agreed that hooliganism was nothing new; Bacon, Teeling, and Gardener emphasized the difference between the youths and criminals. Bacon, Morrison, Fitch, Teeling, Prentice, and James believed that a very small minority were giving the youths a bad name. And no one dissented from the explanation that young people faced special problems in a changing society that the parliamentarians and the country had to solve. In short, this debate had *less* to do with the media inventory than Gurden's motion; and Cohen's woefully misleading account should have been challenged long before now, as should his "explanation" for this non existent panic.

WIDER CULTURES AND EXPLOITATIVE CONTEXTS

While we agree that the intensity of societal reactions to deviancy can only be understood in their specific historical and cultural context; we do not agree that cherry picking those aspects that fit your preferred perspective and ignoring or distorting what remains is the way to do that. According to Cohen:

a. The youths' deviancy was a rebellion against their dull education, tedious jobs, and a cityscape providing few opportunities for legitimate excitement [1973: 182];

b. The rebellion took the form of their "own excitement", which they took to the beaches [1973: 182];

c. That rebellion provoked the wrath of a jealousy induced generation gap especially amongst the repressed lower-middle-class fearful of the boundary crisis [1973: 198]; and

d. The adults' values ensured that they were incapable of understanding the vital role that clothes, pills and music played in the mod mode of expression, with its subversive potential of living through their leisure time and creating themselves as mods [1973: 188].

The road to perdition then followed from the "facts" that:

e. The youths' "fashion changes . . . *might* be seen as signifying something much deeper and more permanent", the "permissive society" which the lower-middle-classes' irrational fears defined as sexual excess and unisex hair styles, and;

f. This fear then found a symbol in the single dramatic incident of Clacton [our emphasis—eds. 1973: 193–194].

Each assertion—from the *faux* fact about rebellion, through the boorish adolescent stereotype of adults, to that very big "might"—is questionable. As we do not have space to answer them all, we focus on the mythical "meaning of mod" that Cohen promoted to justify his explanation of the panic. The first and most fundamental reason for rejecting his analysis is that every new, unique, and meaningful feature that Cohen ascribed to the mods in *Folk Devils* he had already ascribed to the Teddy boys from the previous decade; making a nonsense of the "meaning of mod" in the context of the 1960s [Rock and Cohen, 1970]. Second, Cohen's 'analysis' is not only factually baseless; it is contradicted by those facts that can be determined. For example, 1960s teens did not enjoy a rise in real income because they married later as Cohen claimed, as the average age of marriage was the same as the previous decade and the trend was towards *earlier* marriage [One Plus One, 2009[14]; Musgrove, 1974: 3]. The reason the teens had more disposable income than previous generations did was because they enjoyed higher wages and higher status jobs [Musgrove, 1974: 4]. As their parents had more money too, the teens' contributed a lower percentage to the family pool than in the past [Thompson, 1983]. Third, although their disposable income may have been used to develop a "style", the sharp Italianate style associated with the London club scene upon which Cohen relied for his incongruous mod was not new at all. It emerged out of the Italian Teddy boys in London who were also instrumental in adopting the scooter [Scala, 2000]. Fourth, the contrast Cohen draws between the mods who threatened society and the rockers who did not is based on several erroneous claims about the rockers, such as the myth about listening to *old* rock 'n' roll records in motorway cafes [1973: 185]. That would have been impossible. Apart from 100 miles or so of the M1, the UK's new freeway system did not exist in 1964, though it did in 1973 when *Folk Devils* was published. As the hidden history of the rockers revealed, the bikers sought out local cafés which were playing the *latest* rock 'n' roll in 1964. These and many more dubious details, belied by the biker subculture [Willis, 1982], undermine the foundation for the "centrality of mod" required for the next step of Cohen's explanation: the mods' personification of permissiveness. Having been surrounded by mod siblings, relatives, and neighbors our unintentional ethnography can take us back into the middle of the world of mods and offer a much better guide than Cohen's theoretical based account that we have already seen is full of erroneous claims.

The very idea that mods, by embracing consumerism, were transgressing commonly-held social values is risible. While the male mod was "flashing the cash" on a scooter, blue beat records, and "fancy clobber" to impress his "skirt"; his "old man", thanks to overtime or a union deal was buying a second suit, a drawer full of bri-nylon shirts, Cyril Lord carpets to replace the linoleum and aiming for, at long last, a car. While modettes were spending their "lucre" on buffoon hair-dos, short garish paisley dresses, and Adam Faith records, "the old dear" was having fun too. She was using her part-time job in the new consumer industries to order that *Rolls Razor* washing machine on credit, save-up for a package-holiday, getting some highlights at the local hair salon, and feeding her perfectly clipped miniature poodle *Pedigree Chum* while waiting for the *Daz* man to call, to give her "a fiver" (£5) for using the right washing powder. In short, as the adult working-class had also embraced consumerism with a vengeance, Cohen's explanation falls at the first hurdle. He also knocked over the second hurdle with his claim that the mods were the first generation to find their "meaning" outside the work ethic. That claim was based on the erroneous academic Marxist myth about a dominant working-class culture centered on hard work and honest labor. On the contrary, the working-class had spent the previous century finding the "meaning" of their class outside work. As well as building the self-help retail co-operatives, friendly societies, and the trade union movement which enabled them to survive the trials and tribulations of industrial capitalism; they also formed thousands of clubs competing with each other breeding pigeons, racing dogs, or playing soccer amongst many others. Just because Leftist historians rarely studied all this activity, does not mean it did not exist [Waites *et al*, 1982; Harris, 1995]. As the pre Profumo "social malaise" which Cohen confused with the post Profumo "moral malaise" amounted to blaming Britain's economic decline on the proletarians' tendency to work-to-rule, strike over any demarcation disputes, and calling in sick rather than Capital's lack of investment; we have another reason to be wary of Marxist myths. Cohen cannot get over any other hurdle either.

What, exactly, was so subversive about wearing an army surplus Parker coat, fighting over tickets for *Juke Box Jury,* making "a prat" of yourself 'dancing' on the *Ready Steady Go* TV show, or popping amphetamine pills "borrowed" from the old dear's prescription bottle in the bathroom? This cultural studies claptrap masks the fact that while they were all called mods the divisions went much further than fashion. The "hard mods", with their own brand of excitement on which Cohen based his excuse for violence came from housing projects; whereas the "smooth mods" and "scooter boys", on whom Cohen based his symbol of permissiveness thesis were just as likely to be found in private housing with their petit-bourgeois parents, doing their grammar school homework. Apart from the lone example of one of their number arrested at the beaches [Cohen, 1973: 105], they tended to avoid trouble, being far more interested in not creasing their "threads", securing a white-collar job, attending art school or one of the new universities. Their disdain for work, was, like most else during their transition from school to college, merely a pose; hence the popularity of the term "poser" during this period. As any adult who watched TV would also have known about "the meaning of mod", having been bored to death by those endless documentaries on teenagers and the generation gap; Cohen's cultural analysis is as mythical as moral panic, and you do not have to rely upon our memory either. Every sociological survey covering teen values during the 1960s demonstrate that despite all that rapid social change, most teens not only held the same values as their parents, they resented the stereotypical presumption that they followed those supposedly held by their peers [Musgrove, 1974: 1–2]. When the generation gap was finally quantified at the end of the 1960s it transpired that the societal divide over values occurred above and below the age of 36 [Musgrove, 1974: 8].

The major reason Clacton could not have had the cultural affect that Cohen accredited to it concerns the changing nature of the lower-middle-class which no longer conformed to the structural-Marxist stereotype that Cohen relied on. Postwar corporate Capital had created a huge pool of educated, tenured, white-collar workers. Like the majority of the working-class they adopted an instrumental attitude to work which they saw as a means to fund their leisure activities and consumption patterns. This reflected the fact that the UK was beginning to catch up with the US' standard of living and leisure ethos [Wallis 1976: 283–28 5; Larkin, 2007: 178–179], and helps explain why "classless" had became a cliché. Superficial commentators confused white-collar jobs with social mobility, rather than the realignment between Britain's manufacturing and service industries that it was.

The old petit-bourgeois most likely to conform to the Marxist stereotype was not only declining, they also had far more to worry about than haircuts. This was the period when a plumber could make more "off the books" than shopkeepers or a local civil servant, and a working-class family enjoying three or four incomes while living in a subsidized public housing project would have more disposable income than those with a mortgage and maintaining the domestic division of labor. That is why the major form of old petit-bourgeois discontent during this period was the rate payer association which opposed subsidizing a working-class that was far more cash rich than they were. Indeed, a fifth of the UK's richest ten percent lived in housing projects during this period [Jones, 2011: 35]. Moreover, if anyone had a cause to be envious or jealous and conformed to Cohen's account it would have been the elderly working-class, who had spent their younger years in deprivation during the depression and then had to survive the 1939–1945 war, and not the petit-bourgeoisie who in their youth would have been relatively privileged and whose moral values would mitigate against sexual jealousy. And yet, one was just as likely to find a working-class grandma subsidizing her grand children's ability to have fun.

If adults erroneously believed that teen culture was homogeneous, it is also easy to see why. An affluent teen did not mean a rich one so much as a self-indulgent one; although there still was not a lot on offer compared to today. As no teen trend could or would have succeeded unless a sizable minority participated, it did not matter if they were: listening to the Billy Fury or Atlantic Soul, they were buying records; wearing polka dot or paisley dresses, turned up or no collar shirts, they were buying fashion; or had a new hair style every week or every month, they had one. Then, when the same records, clothes, and hair-styles turned up on *Ready Steady Go* or in one of those never-ending documentaries about "today's teens", the impression of homogeneity is understandable. While the likes of Blake might rant and rave about youth because of that, Cohen also forgot that the political Left were far more indignant about teens' growing materialism, because they feared the youth's incorporation within capitalism through consumerism [Ross, 1989]. There is also that little matter of sexism that everyone seems to have ignored, for Cohen's concept of a sexual jealously induced generation gap reflected the popular 1960s stereotype amongst young males that any middle-age women who complained about their loutish stupidity must be sexually repressed and would "shut up" if only someone "gave her one"! Finally, as Cohen offers no evidence, whatsoever, that any adult made any association between fringe delinquency and teen culture we need spend no time on that; although if they did, we could blame sociology!

FROM KANSAS TO CLACTON

Britain's delinquency debate followed closely behind the one in the US, which culminated in the 1961 Kennedy Committee after covering the same ground including the concept of the generation gap. While US intellectuals agonized over the teens' materialism and depoliticization, social workers feared familial breakdown, the religious worried about irreligion, and the children's bureau and the justice department battled it out over medicalization or more law and order. The major difference was that US sociologists were able to secure research funds and proffer their explanations in the expanding number of textbooks on deviancy that became *de rigueur* in the burgeoning sociology and criminology departments during the 1960s, and quickly found their way across the Atlantic. Three of the most important were: Erikson and Goodman, who claimed that social change had caused new problems for adolescents in their transition from school to work; Millar, who argued that teens were being made scapegoats for adults' social frustrations; and Vaz who pointed to the adults' inability to distinguish between fringe delinquency and youth culture [Gilbert, 1986]. However, while those explanations may have impressed Cohen, they were not really applicable to the UK. Whereas US society *had* played its part in creating delinquency by raising the age limit at which teens could access adult pleasures, and playing hardball with those who did not conform and engaged in status crimes like under-age drinking; UK teens proved perfectly capable of becoming delinquent without any help from society save one: their impatience, born of watching those US movies and TV shows in which every delinquent appeared to have a wardrobe full of cool clothes, their own hot-rod, and spent all afternoon hanging out with the gang in the local diner [Doherty, 2002]. That is why, far from uncovering a moral panic about delinquents called mods and rockers, *Folk Devils* manufactured one by conflating those US theories with two British myths: the secondary mod school failure and the alienated teen rebel.

Until 1965, most primary schoolchildren (Grades 3–6) had to sit the Eleven Plus exam. Depending upon their score they were directed towards the most suitable form of publicly funded secondary education for their demonstrated ability: grammar schools which led to university and the professions; technical high school for those with a more practical orientation which led to polytechnic and a technical career (Grades 7–13); or secondary moderns for everyone else (Grades 7–11). One year after winning the 1964 election, the Labour Government abolished that system in favor of mixed ability comprehensive schools in a symbolic attack on the class system. The belief that the Secondary Moderns were an innate source of future dead-end delinquents was premised on the Ingleby Committee myth that their primary purpose was "satisfactory social integration rather than attainment of academic distinction" [Howard, 1963: 266]; reality was more complicated.

Secondary moderns not only offered vocationally orientated classes which could lead to apprenticeships in skilled crafts at 15 years of age for anyone who wanted one; for the minority who *were* academically inclined but for some reason had not passed the Eleven Plus, there were other exams enabling a transfer to grammar schools at 13 years (Grade 8) and 16 years (Grade 11). In some counties like Hampshire, where the Conservative party managed to delay the introduction of the comprehensive system for over a decade, grammar school sixth forms (Grades 12–13) would not have been viable or enjoyed their rate of university admission success without the influx of late developers from the secondary moderns. As well as doing a disservice to the many dedicated teachers in the third tier, Cohen ignored the fact that there was nothing to stop any of his failures attending one of the burgeoning technical colleges or the legion of cheap fee night schools to catch up if they wanted to do so. While familial background could make it near impossible for some to take advantage of any form of schooling, and not every local council provided enough funds to make every school a center of opportunity; the Labour party had an obvious political interest in blaming secondary moderns for delinquency, and ignoring the fact that some teens were not academically orientated. Some were not practically orientated either, but most where, and the skill level of arrested soccer hooligans during this period suggests that complete secondary modern failures were in the distinct minority [Cohen, 1973: 105; Taylor, 1971: 155]. Cohen also had a political purpose in maintaining the myth. By merging the school failure with the history of working-class hooliganism, which could be seen as a form of resistance to the imposition of middle-class norms especially in school [Humphries, 1981], Cohen helped create the new myth of the teen rebel, a label handed out to every hardcore hooligan by cultural studies professors who claimed that they were fighting back against "the system" [Clarke, 1996]. In reality, these bullies were doing nothing of the kind, unless one regards terrorizing Pakistanis, other racial minorities, other youth groups, and gays as "the system". As well as disregarding the fact that they had far more opportunities and choices than the hooligans of yesteryear; Cohen also ignored Ms Bacon's warning that one needed to distinguish between the deprived and the depraved. The debate about hooligans' deprivation or depravity was as old as the label itself. While Right-wing commentators argued that hooliganism proved that the masses were innately depraved, far more commentators subscribed to the belief that mass society had alienated the teens from fundamental values and moral fortitude, leaving them so purposeless that they spent their time copying what they read in their generation's popular culture, be it escapist fantasies or turning to gratuitous violence [Humphries, 1981: 3–8]. By 1940 it had become a Left-wing truism that delinquents were:

> victims of rapid social change that has undermined traditional institutions and authority and has dislocated behavioural norms and expectations [and so provided] a model of working class youth that is desocialized and inadequately integrated into society [Humphries, 1981: 6].

While the Christian socialists still held to that 50-year old perspective during the 1960s, they like Ms Bacon knew that unless one separated out the hardcore for special attention they would continue to cause problems in later life. The academic Left was different. They initially switched to the variant championed by Adorno, the long forgotten but highly influential Geoffrey Gorer, and the Communist Party who argued that postwar consumer capitalism had produced a self-centered generation of sadistic neo-fascists; the argument used in the progressives crusade against horror comic books, before they blamed TV shows for the Teddy boys violence [Barker, 1984a; *Tribune*, 4 April 1958]. In contrast, Cohen's generation adopted the New Left version that argued that the teens were heroic if confused rebels reacting against their alienation in a mass society. As a result, Cohen like the CCCS not only failed to distinguish between the deprived and the depraved, but the real teen rebel who was more likely to be found amongst the children of the new petit-bourgeoisie. Be that as it may, Cohen's account was far too inconsistent to make any sense, evidenced by the way he emphasized the mods' distain for authority to justify his claim that they posed a threat to society values despite having previously denounced that distain as one of the new *spurious* attributes [1973: 195 and 54–61]! In short, the myth of mods and rockers was built on a Marxist myth and US delinquency theories that did not fit the UK; though the link between Cohen's theoretical fetishism and his lack of evidence did not end there.

THEORETICAL REALITY

The societal reaction to mods and rockers created by Cohen did not exist, not merely because Clacton was a minor side-show in the wider delinquency debate, but because British society did not conform to the US theories that Cohen lamented were ignored by his London sample. Once we list those theories, you can see why they were ignored, and the extent to which *Folk Devils* amounts to an academic construction of reality:

- The media's role in the panic follows Wilkins who argued that the media had replaced face-to-face labeling [Cohen, 1969: 22]; although Cohen's surveys suggested otherwise;
- The emphasis placed upon the development of the deviant behavior as function of labeling rather than an existing motive was taken from Matza and Becker [Cohen, 1969: 24]; although the amplification of deviance did not match Young's model, and the mods took their "own form of excitement" to the beaches;
- The claim that the youth groups' self definition developed over the panic and was shaped by the audience came from Lemert [1969: 26]; although the polarization between the youths had occurred before Clacton;
- The use of the term "excitement" for violence was a perversion of Tannenbaum's use as a euphemism for vandalism reflecting the alleged motive behind the act [Cohen, 1969: 28]; although Cohen's attempt to apply it led to contradictions in his account;
- The projection of gang membership on miscellaneous youths with marginalized membership came from Yablonski [Cohen, 1969: 468]; although Cohen never offered any evidence that the press emphasized gang membership, and only one MP used it;
- The creation of a self identity in a faltering adolescent by social control activity comes from Erikson and Erickson [Cohen, 1969: 29]; although the period's arrested hooligans' skill level suggests otherwise;
- The stress on the symbolic and unintended consequences of social control activity in the creation of secondary deviance came from Lemert [Cohen, 1969: 30]; although the most violent incidents occurred at Clacton and over Whitsun before the control culture had time to react, and there was no increase in the original deviancy when they did;

- The influence of moral indignation and existence of ritual public denunciation came from Garfinkel [Cohen, 1969: 31]; although Cohen relied on the unrepresentative Blake for his evidence for the first, and standard public order policing practices for the second;
- The role of disassociation from educational and work goals and seeking alternatives in the realm of leisure came from Downs who purloined it from the US [Cohen, 1969: 244]; although that was nothing new and can still be seen today.

The wholesale imposition of US theories on a situation that could not sustain them is matched by a series of theoretical flip-flops that suggest that Cohen was also well aware of what he was doing. Whereas the PhD warned readers that the effects of the Clacton inventory on the mods and rockers was merely "suggestive and *not* proven by the data", *Folk Devils'* readers were told that it was central [Cohen, 1969: 579; 1973: 175]. Although the PhD dismissed the concept of common values in pluralistic society as straining credulity, rejected consensual models of society as untenable, and saw societal-wide reactions as problematic; *Folk Devils* said the complete opposite [Cohen, 1969: 35 and 37]. Despite the PhD rejecting the concept of the amplification of deviancy as inappropriate in the case of the mods and rockers, and pointing out that sociologists often confused an amplification with a mere increase in attention, *Folk Devils* tried to palm off a periodic increase in attention as amplification [Cohen, 1969: 437, 187]. What is more, *Folk Devils* failed to follow the guidelines that Cohen argued had to be followed in order for sociologists to prove that their interpretation was viable. For example, in his PhD, Cohen insisted that in order to justify the claim that a societal-wide reaction had taken place:

> the whole or part of a community must be affected, *a large segment of the community must be confronted with actual or potential danger*, there must be loss to cherished values *and* material objects resulting in death or injury or destruction to property [Cohen, 1969: 438].

Cohen also insisted that whenever sociologists addressed the social construction of social problems they should specify *which* social group was directing the widespread concern, and identify *whose* norms and boundaries were being defiled. *Folk Devils* not only ignored his own guidelines, Cohen deliberately omitted the evidence that would prove those supposed to be most adversely affected blamed society rather than the teens. Likewise, while the following prescriptions shaped the analysis in the PhD, they disappear in the more politically orientated *Folk Devils*:

- Deviancy is created by social groups not society [Cohen, 1969: 18];
- You cannot assume a consensus over social problems, hidden behind using terms like "society", which are used by groups to affect consensus [1969: 115–116];

- One needs to identify who makes the rules, and worries about rule breaking, and engages in moral enterprise when they do so [Cohen, 1969: 19, 37, 41, 46–47, 52, 72];
- One should draw a distinction between rule breaking and deviance [Cohen, 1969: 21, 72–78];
- Creation and enforcement of rules are subject to disagreement, conflict, political maneuvers, and cross pressures [Cohen, 1969: 35–37];
- There is a difference between the cause of the behavior and labeling, and the objective existence of a social problem and the labeling process [Cohen, 1969: 40–49];
- Deviancy defies economic determinism [Cohen, 1969: 41];
- The outcome of societal reactions are not guaranteed, and deviants will not always adopt the role ascribe [Cohen, 1969: 45–50]; and
- Theories should emerge from the data [Cohen, 1969: 51].

As Cohen did not listen to his own advice, it is no surprise that the panic paradigm never did. On the other hand, as we have always worked on the basis of similar guidelines, we can draw the following conclusion. As many forms of deviancy are exploited ideologically by moral entrepreneurs, interested and social control agencies, local and national Government, and commercial interests; and the news media frequently "plays both sides of the street", simultaneously castigating folk devils while entertaining their readership with the deviants' exploits; none of that indicates that any extra-special reaction was taking place after Clacton. On the contrary, as Cohen claimed that the anxiety which generated the psychological projection label moral panic was created by the ambiguity of the precipitating event [1969: 476], and that his model of moral panic was proven by the lack of alternative explanations, undefended folk devils, an escalation in control culture, and an amplification of deviancy; we can say, with no fear of contradiction, that there was no moral panic about the mods and rockers. The threat was a silly season media story invoked by a previous media frame denounced by parliamentarians and moral entrepreneurs, and ignored by the public. Although models and theories are not disproven by a failed case study; in this case they were. The concept of moral panic was not only based on a series of myths, its founder was well aware that he was promoting them; and the failure of anyone to expose that before now demonstrates the lack of integrity within the panic paradigm.

3   Mugging Reality

Whatever Goode and Ben-Yehuda may say, if it was not for *Policing the Crisis* and the elite perspective, the panic paradigm would not be as popular as it is [McRobbie and Thornton, 1991]. Endorsement as a *tour de force* by the *British Journal of Sociology* ensured that moral panic became *de rigueur* in sociology, cultural studies, and media studies courses, and its focus on race made it a mainstay in black studies. It was also used by critical criminologists to indict the sociology of deviance for failing to denounce crime as a function of capitalism and to explain how "the myth of the criminal" enabled the ruling class to secure consent in contemporary societies [Hall, *et al,* 1984: 195; Pearce, 1976]. As the CCCS did not claim that the elite used the press, the law, the courts, and the police to create "a red herring" frightening the masses with a nonexistent rise in street crime to protect their economic interests as Goode and Ben-Yehuda claim, characterizing the thesis as a conspiracy theory is misleading [2010: 63–66]. Despite exhibiting the standard weaknesses found in structural analysis, the following summary demonstrates (by placing the elements and features of the mugging panic in *parenthesis*), that the CCCS remained far more faithful to Cohen's definition than anyone else ever has. As they also argued that the fear of crime and subsequent panic reflected the public's personal experience of crime, the major issue raised by *Policing the Crisis* concerns whether or not common societal values amount to a dominant ideology. If they do, it would not matter where the horror-headlines came from, or if the panic was contested or not; a moral panic that restored common values *would* enhance the hegemony of the ruling elite. That, of course, is a very big 'if', not least because the concept of a dominant ideology is also contested [Abercrombie and Turner, 1978]. By failing to address and resolve that question the panic paradigm is caught in a trap because if the elite perspective does not fit, the mugging moral panic could not exist!

A MUGGING GONE WRONG

The CCCS account of the history of the panic is no different from many others. The *misleading media coverage* of mugging, from the fatal stabbing of elderly Arthur Hills at Waterloo Railway Station in August 1972 to the 1973 trial of three Handsworth teens, engendered a *disproportionate* fear of street crime compared to the official figures, and higher incidences in the past [Hall *et al*, 1984: 3–16]. By *exaggerating the threat, relabeling* every street-crime a mugging, and *overemphasizing the extent of the violence involved,* the media encouraged an *escalation in the control culture* [Hall *et al*, 1984: 28; 72–74]. That increase included special anti-mugging squads, a clean-up of London's royal parks and mobile patrols in provincial parks, the Home Secretary demanding reports from provincial police departments, the Duke of Edinburgh denouncing mugging as a disease, a public opinion poll recording 90 percent in favor of tougher punishments, and three year sentences for mugging becoming the norm. After the Handsworth case, security on London's subway system was increased yet again before the prime minister finally announced in July 1973 that mugging had declined [Hall *et al*, 1984: 8–9].

The major difference between the CCCS account and Cohen's model was that the muggers' *visibility* depended upon the press reports, which instead of creating a new *inventory* drew on a previous one from 1968 which had pre-sensitized the public to the black mugger as the symbol of economic and social crisis in the US. Consequently, the moment that the media dubbed the murder at Waterloo "a mugging gone wrong", the black mugger came to personify "the race conflict, the urban crisis, rising crime, the breakdown of 'law and order', the liberal conspiracy, and the white backlash" in the UK too [Hall *et al*, 1984: 18–27]. That *image* was effective because violent crime is one of the *consensus boundaries* restored by the *"dramatized symbolic reassertion of the values of society" through the stigmatization and punishment* of the criminal. Although the reasons offered by the CCCS for the panic's effects are overtly political, they conformed to the original model by replicating Cohen's analysis of the origins of teen crime and the reaction of the panicking classes. The fact that the CCCS argued that the media inventory promoted the "interests, values, and concerns" of the judiciary and the police as well as the petit-bourgeoisie makes no difference. Neither do their claims about coverage's inter-related effects: it reinforced the growing belief that the permissive, socialist, Labour government of 1964–1970 had encouraged the rise in violent street crime; and that *deflected public attention away from the real cause of the problem,* the economic and social crisis besetting the UK. Doing so then encouraged the public to support the coercive social control measures adopted by the 1970–1974 Conservative government which criminalized anyone challenging ruling-class hegemony as the economic crisis got worse. Indeed, far from offering a conspiratorial account, the CCCS argued that the panic was the latent effect of the *transactional process* linking moral panic to the politics of the period.

According to the CCCS, the *image* connecting permissiveness to black crime first emerged in the UK during 1969 when senior judges' demands that violent street crime be tried in the crown courts rather than the softer magistrates' courts coincided with an anxiety inducing crime wave involving blacks from Brixton mugging Londoners on the city's subway system. The anxiety caused by that then fed anti-immigration sentiment which already blamed blacks for the social consequences of the economic crisis, even though the crime wave was caused by the London Transport Police (LTP) and the Metropolitan Police's Special Patrol Group (SPG). Their practice of racial profiling made every black youth *guilty by association,* and reflected the politicization of the police during the 1960s following previous moral panics. Although the liberal media had criticized these developments, and the *prophesies of doom* about levels of UK street crime by the Metropolitan police commissioner and two senior officers, that opposition disappeared when the mugging moral panic appeared as it *inhibited counter explanations* [Hall et al, 1984: 29–35; 38–55, 66–67].

HANDSWORTH

In order to illustrate their thesis, the CCCS concentrated on the "massive coverage" of the *harsh sentences* given to three teens from an immigrant area, Handsworth in Birmingham, which the CCCS claimed exemplified the rest of the mugging media. The apparent balance between the liberal and 'law and order' perspectives covered in the press was a sham because the *consensus* justifying the 20-year sentence for the ringleader Storey reinforced the conservative perspective that defeating crime was in everyone's *common interest,* undermined the *deferential reaction,* and justified the *increase in the control culture* by blaming crime on criminals [Hall et al, 1984: 85–93]. Although the subsequent *newspaper features* addressed the environmental factors behind the Handsworth teens' turn to crime, as they did not explain how those factors were the consequence of the racial-class structure under capitalism, they reinforced the *symbolic meaning* of black muggers, evidenced by *The Sun's* random use of the predominant panic images: violence, race, drugs, theft, and youth. The local press was no better. The *Sunday Mercury's* assertions that people could transcend their slum conditions and that crime followed the decline in the traditional family amounted to a "deep affirmation of the existing social order". Its *'common sense' diagnosis, ignoring what sociologists, criminologists, community workers or voluntary agencies had to say,* and prioritization of peoples' *'lived experience' over intellectual analysis or professional concern* also offered it readers a *morality play* [Hall et al, 1984: 113–115]. The effect of the panic press was evident in the content of the subsequent 'letters to the editor' and the thirty hate letters sent to Storey's mother. The latter's references to corporal and capital punishment, lynching, castrating Storey, sterilizing his mother for "spawning monsters", and the need for repatriation did not come from a minority of cranks; but reflected what was really being said in:

conversations between neighbors, discussions at street corners or in the pub, rumor, gossip, speculation, 'inside dope', debate between members of family at home, expressions of opinions and views in private meetings, and so on, all the way up to the more formal levels, in which the mass media intersect [Hall *et al*, 1984: 129].

Likewise, the *authoritarian personality* behind the hate mail was also evident in the "call for discipline, the tendency to scapegoat, the drive for re-moralization, and the rigidity of stereotyping" seen in many of the published letters [Hall *et al*, 1984: 133]. In short, the CCCS argued that the authoritarian personality Cohen claimed motivated the UK's moral entrepreneurs was rife amongst the wider public as well; and the reason for that could be found in the UK's common values.

COMMON VALUES

According to the CCCS, the public reaction followed from the common values, that produced an "immensely powerful conservative sense of Englishness" shared by *everyone* because they could accommodate contradictory class and life experiences [1984: 140]. That claim was seen by contemporary sociology as an extension of Cohen's model because the CCCS quantified what those values were:

- Thrift, self-discipline, decent conduct, self-help, self-reliance—the social standards set by the upper classes;
- Deferred gratification—making leisure, pleasure, and security a reward for diligence;
- Social discipline, self-discipline and control—especially concerning sexual pleasure;
- The centrality of the family—the predominant image and guide to societal do's and don'ts, particularly those concerning crime and ill disciplined youth; and
- The conception of "the City" as the "tide-mark" of civilization [Hall *et al,* 1984: 141–146].

These values were reinforced by a two-faceted "master image" of England. One side consisted of the belief that the English were tolerant and moderate, while the other reflected an "assumption of superiority over all other peoples, particularly the colonized or enslaved especially if they are black". Behind that master image lay the values of practical common sense based on experiential truths which ensured that everyone rallied around when needed, and an anti-intellectualism, distrust of experts, sociologists, and theories which made the English incapable of grasping any alternative ideology other than that promoted by the ruling-classes. These ideological values and the belief that British justice was the best in the world were so powerful that they neutralized any reservations or criticisms people had about the country [Hall *et al*, 1984: 147–155]. As a result, the black mugger was a ready made folk devil, the permissive opposite of Englishness: the product of a dysfunctional family and the breakdown of social order in the city, he sought reward without work, had no respect for discipline and authority, and was prone to impulsive, gratuitous violence [Hall *et al*, 1984: 161].

THE POLITICS OF THE MORAL PANIC

In order to explain the effect of the mugging moral panic, the CCCS had to address the politics of race as well as the socio-economic context in which the mugger appeared. The economic crisis that emerged in 1966 undermined the postwar "social democratic consensus" whereby Capital had accepted a state managed economy, rising wages, the creation of a welfare state, and social reform in return for an end to class conflict [Hall *et al*, 1984: 227–232]. Although the consensus and it *myth of classlessness* had been challenged by the rise of the New Left, extra-parliamentary protests like the Campaign for Nuclear Disarmament, and increasing working-class militancy during the late 1950s [Hall *et al*, 1984: 233]; it was the response to the economic crisis that destroyed the consensus. Whereas most progressive commentators concentrated on the political divisions that appeared, the CCCS concentrated on the state, which they argued became increasing coercive but secured consent through moral panic.

According to the CCCS, having gained nothing from the postwar boom, the petit-bourgeoisie expressed their *indignation* that the bourgeoisie had adopted permissiveness through a series of *envy* induced *moral panics about violent youth;* gaining the support of the press, the police, and the courts as they did so because those institutions still held to the common values too. Between 1964 and 1969, the petit-bourgeois responded to the Profumo Affair, the Labour government's failure to arrest the economic crisis, and the return of class struggle in three ways. The *moral entrepreneurs* engaged in a moral crusade against "pornographic Britain", the Labour government's permissive reforms covering abortion, censorship, divorce, and Sunday observance. The 'law and order' lobby gained ground because of the Police Federation's protestations about rising crime, the abolition of capital punishment, and the horror invoked by the Moors murders. The anti-immigration lobby grew because of an influx of Asians fleeing from Kenya. These three displaced responses to the crisis were then reinforced by the moral panics over hippies and drugs in 1967 [Hall *et al*, 1984: 163–164, 223–228; 237–240; 234–235; 237–240; 263–272]. When the student revolt against "the privatization of politics"[1], the anti-Vietnam war demonstrations, record strikes, and Catholic demands for civil rights in Ulster posed a threat to ruling class hegemony in 1968, the issue of race and immigration became predominant following Enoch Powell's infamous 'Rivers of Blood' speech warning of the race war to come. Further politically-orientated panics in 1969 covering the counterculture and its anti-Protestant work ethic, feminism, which exposed the oppressive nature of the family, and Trotskyite revolutionary politics had several effects. The panics facilitated the media marginalization and police repression of student and Black Power activists, led to a convergence in the petit-bourgeois response to the crisis, and encouraged the public to "lurch to the Right" because of their *subliminal fears* about race. These developments led to the return of a Conservative government in 1970, on a law and order platform with racial undertones, which was determined to suppress the urban and class warfare in Ulster and on the UK mainland [Hall *et al*, 1984: 242–249; 253–273].

Once they gained office, the Conservative party set about creating the law and order society, a particularly British form of fascism [Hall *et al*, 1984: 321–323], by overseeing an increase in *extra-legal measures in the courts, exemplary sentencing, and widening the net* turning political opposition into crimes through a series of coercive Acts. The most important were: the Industrial Relations Act—attacking union power; Emergency Powers—introducing interment in Ulster; Misuse of Drugs—raising sentences; Criminal Damage—making sit-in protest illegal; and the Immigration Act—imposing guest worker status on those entering the country. However, as these attempts to crush opposition merely increased the level of protest, something more was needed, and that was supplied by the mugging moral panic, which reflected the switch in the nature of moral panics from the late 1960s.

Whereas earlier panics had followed a "bottom-up" process, from the public's *"on the spot reaction"* to an increase in control culture and a new law, the political panics tended to be "top down", with the media promoting the control culture's definition of the situation. This switch included a *signification spiral,* complete with *prophecies of worse to follow,* which made the new political folk devils *guilty by association* with those of the past. So, for example, student protest was linked to violent hooliganism to produce *the new stigmatizing label, based on spurious attributes* of the violent student hooligan, which delegitimized the students' political protest and helped justify the increasingly coercive control culture [Hall *et al*, 1984: 221–226]. Evidence of this switch was provided by *Mary Whitehouse* who became more political over time. She associated with the political Right in the form of *Lord Longford,* William Deedes, and Malcolm Muggeridge; blamed the demise of the National Health Service on permissiveness rather than underfunding; and denounced the leaders of the counterculture, the Left, and Civil Libertarians like Gerry Rubin, Tariq Ali, and Bernadette Devlin. National VALA also aligned with the government and the London Obscene Publications Squad (OPS) who attacked the counterculture and the political Left by prosecuting their publications, movies, and artworks using obscenity legislation, including the attempt to outlaw the revolutionary *Little Red School Book* [Hall *et al*, 1984: 287].

This account of the increasing role of moral panic in UK politics proved very popular, and no one worried that it depended upon including the social trends Cohen omitted from his account or question the claims about the ideological effects of the mugging moral panic.

THE MOMENT OF MUGGING

Although the amateurish Angry Brigade's bombing campaign encouraged popular support for government coercion; the CCCS believed that was far less important than Powell's racist crusade against immigration, which was boosted by a *Sunday Times'* feature "Must Harlem come to Handsworth" blaming the social problems caused by the capitalist crisis on immigrants by pointing out that "second generation blacks are beginning to show a resistance to all authority" [Hall *et al*, 1984: 273, 275–276, 298, 280–281]. When the 40,000 Asians expelled from Uganda then threatened to undermine the new Immigration Act, the mugging 'gone wrong' at Waterloo became:

> one of those moments in English culture when the suppressed, distorted or unexpressed responses to thirty years of unsettling social change, which failed to find political expression, nevertheless surfaced and took tangible shape and form in a particularly compelling symbolic way [Hall *et al*, 1984: 162].

The black mugger became such a powerful symbol for all Britain's ills that even committed socialists were not immune [Hall *et al*, 1984: 162]. That symbol also explains how and why the mugging moral panic served the interests of the alliance between the ruling class, the moral entrepreneurs, racists, and the law and order lobby, led to the imposition of the coercive strong state, and undermined any political alternative to the crisis of capitalism [Hall *et al*, 1984: 313–315]. Although the "top down" ideological panics obviously diverged from Cohen's model, no one worried about that at the time because the CCCS convinced its readers it reflected reality and furthered the ideological role of panics.

THE STRONG STATE

In the same way that Cohen argued that moral panic exposed the role of social consensus in society, the CCCS argued that the mugging moral panic had exposed panics' ideological role [Hall *et al*, 1984: 310]. The growing consensus in favor of law and order encouraged by moral panics undermined political protest, re-legitimized the capitalist system, and justified the authoritarian society that emerged including: arming the police, *eroding civil liberties*, the dismantling of the welfare state, the shameless advocacy of social inequality, and the backlash against abortion and progressive education. This became more obvious when the panicking moralists, racists, and Right-wing radicals in the petit-bourgeoisie moved from the political fringe to the center in Thatcher's first Conservative government, 1979–1983, with its "full elaboration of the moral-political program of the petit-bourgeois Right" [Hall *et al*, 1984: 312–316, 321–323]. However, the effects of the panics could be seen long before then.

Although the socialist Labour party returned to government in 1974, it had also appealed to "common interest" and opposed militancy in all its forms, having no answer to the economic crisis, not least because of the second mugging moral panic in 1975 [Hall *et al*, 1984: 308 and 313]. This second panic followed media revelations that crime in Lambeth, London had tripled since 1970 and that 85 percent of muggings were committed by black youth on white victims. The harsh sentences handed out in court cases amounted to a "declaration of war on young blacks", the neo-fascist National Front improved its election performance, white youths murdered an 18 year old Asian in Southall, and the Notting Hill Caribbean Carnival ended in a race riot. By isolating the black communities, this panic ensured that white and black working-class solidarity became impossible, and that there was no alternative to the strong state or the mentality behind it [Hall *et al*, 1984: 327–339].

REVOLUTIONARY MUGGING

This overtly political conclusion was more than acceptable because the explanation offered by the CCCS followed Cohen's model of cause and effect almost to the letter. Mugging frightened the white working-classes because of their *inability to understand black youth* who were *badly served by schools* and *could not obtain the skills needed* to transcend their ascribe role as a "reserve army of labor", hired and fired at will in the changing economy. Being worse off than Asian teens with their different colonial experience, more cohesive culture, and employment within the Asian community, black teens saw the "hustlers" in the black community as role models. These "unemployed, semi-employed, club keepers and domino men", who made money through "informal dealing, semi-legal practices, rackets, petty crime" or "brothel keeping, drug selling, and illegal distilleries" offered an alternative to the badly paid jobs, harassment, discrimination, and hostility which had destroyed the teen's respectable parents' aspirations [Hall *et al*, 1984: 380; 340–359].

In other words, the CCCS account of the black teens' adoption of their own form of survival replicates Cohen's account of the mods' "own form of excitement". The effect of the subsequent *in situ deviance amplification spiral* on the streets of immigrant communities replicated that on the beaches, and the teens' subsequent criminalization had a similar effect, although it relied more on Young than Cohen. While criminalization *resolved any ambiguity* the public may have had regarding the cause of the crime, deviance amplification on the streets involving the black youth and the police encouraged the former's race-class consciousness, uniting the youths against the racist society in the same way that the "social crimes" of the past that had helped create working-class consciousness. By failing to see how labeling the black teens as criminal would then lead to their "recruitment into a life of professional crime", whites did not understand that muggers need not see their actions as a conscious political act because class or race consciousness does not always work that way.

On the other hand, as mugging led to an increase in "African conscious-ness" it revealed the revolutionary potential of wageless blacks like those in the Caribbean, it replicated the way the dispossessed survived on crime in South American favelas, and it expressed the same revolutionary conscious-ness found in the US Black Panthers; all of which ensured that the youths' turn to crime was not a reactionary, lumpenproletariat, response [Hall *et al*, 1984: 351–387]. Indeed, mugging was the teens' contribution to "the growing cohesion, militancy and capacity for the struggle" amongst blacks worldwide. As each class had to confront Capital as a class for itself before united struggle is possible, the meaning of the politicized black mugger was not the same as a reactionary white mugger [1984: 389, 392, 395–396]. That dramatic claim with its worldwide implications helping to sell moral panic to Marxist academics across the globe remained within the model as it was based on the same theoretical reasoning as Cohen's "meaning of mod" and the counterculture alluded to by Young. Likewise, the link the CCCS drew between society's common values and goals and the legitimacy of the elite, hidden from public view by common faith in the rule of law, merely amounted to spelling out the politics behind Merton's explanation for crime adopted by Cohen and the panic paradigm [Hall *et al,* 1984: 184–190; 194–208; 215].

CLASS WAR AND COMMON SENSE

As the CCCS had followed Cohen's model very closely, and the claims about the switch from "bottom up" to "top down" moral panics merely made the police a major source of media horror-headlines, if *Policing the Crisis* was a conspiracy theory, the US boosters would have to dismiss dozens of drug and crime wave panics which take the same route. Consequently, we would argue that the switch in the source of the horror-headlines is less impor-tant than the fact that the CCCS replicated the problems we uncovered in Cohen's account. Our criticism concerns the theoretical construction of the mugging moral panic, the omission of a vast amount of countervailing evidence, the exaggeration, and distortion of what remained and the same assumption that the public drew the conclusions from the media coverage that the authors insist that they did. As a result, the real question to ask is why no one had ever considered the role of the mugging panic in undermining the class conflict during the 1970s before *Policing the Crisis* ? The obvious answer is they did not because the panic never happened. As everyone huddled around kerosene heaters, eating camping-cooker food by candlelight in the power-outs during the miner's strikes, no one we knew worried about muggers; they were far more concerned about who was going to win the class war once the powerful miners union decided to take on the Conservative government. Having also played a bit part in all that "intensifying social conflict", we can vouchsafe that structural analysis is a poor guide to the how that conflict which looked "intense" condensed in the pages of a book appeared in experiential reality. Although the CCCS would no doubt dismiss our unintended ethnography as the futile folk wisdom of white working-class folk, the fact that none of our neighbors or teachers ever mentioned mugging despite railing against everything else that appears in the CCCS account, from "the unions being too powerful for their own good" to the "murderous IRA", draws attention to how the CCCS projected the politicization of mugging in 1975 back to the horror-headlines of 1972. If they had done that in a misguided attempt to expose the level of racism amongst the UK police at the time that would have been bad enough, but the truth is that the CCCS thesis on race is itself a form of exploitation.

Far from offering an account of the negative effects of racism in UK society, *Policing the Crisis* amounts to an elongated excuse for the failure of 'the student vanguard'; the embarrassing belief that bourgeois students and their 'demos' would lead to the working-class overthrowing capitalism. The evidence for that can be seen in the claim by the CCCS that the "ideological signification of student protest" became "a dominant signification paradigm for the whole gamut of social conflicts and political troubles" [Hall, *et al,* 1984: 243]; a reflection of the arrogance of the students who subscribed to the vanguard theory. Everyone we knew believed the students were a bunch of posers. When the expected revolution failed to materialize, the CCCS searched around for an excuse, finding it in moral panic's "forgotten island" of white lower-middle class and working class respectability [1984: 244], and Cone's [1969] claim that all whites were racist, which they promptly anglicized. However, the structural connections the CCCS drew between the horror-headlines, those provoking them, and the rise of the strong state to put the thesis together were a mirror image of their critique of the political right which believed disparate forms of emerging protest presented a united threat to society [Hall *et al,* 1984: 309–317].

> The fact is that the [examples used in the *Sunday Express*] as a peg to hang a thesis on are not 'connected' in any tangible or concrete way at all, except rhetorically, ideologically. They may be part of the same

nightmare: they are only in the most metaphorical manner part of the same historical phenomenon. It is not the similarity of the events, but the similarity of the underlying sense of panic in the mind of the beholder which provides the real connection [Hall *et al*, 1984: 300–30 1].

The Marxist Left was no different. The common cause the CCCS claim existed amongst those on the fringe of the political Right—the racists, neo-fascists, moral entrepreneurs, libertarians, Rhodes Boyson—was as fanciful as the Right-wing fears that the students, militant workers, socialists, feminists, stoners, the IRA, the Angry Brigade, and unionized school kids shared a common cause. By hanging the fears and reactions of the disparate and divided Right-wing on the pegs labeled "the strong state" and "the mugging moral panic", *Policing the Crisis* created the convergence they claimed to have uncovered in the horror headlines. They were not even being original. Their thesis reflects the political panic amongst the extreme Left at the time.

A MUGGING THEORY GONE WRONG

The lack of moral panic should have been evident from the beginning as the CCCS failed to demonstrate that the mugging horror-headlines matched their own minimalist definition:

> A massive blaze of publicity in the press . . . widespread public comment and anxiety, a strong and vigorous official reaction . . . the scale and intensity of this reaction is quite at odds with the scale of the threat to which it was a response [Hall *et al*, 1984: 17].

Media mugging mania between 1972 and 1973 was far from systematic. It consisted of four small outbreaks erroneously referred to as "peaks" by the CCCS during a thirteen month period: the *murder* at Waterloo, a couple of deterrent sentences for *violent street robberies*, the alleged 129 percent increase of mugging in London, and the *attempted murder* in Handsworth [Hall *et al*, 1984: 7–8; 30]. That is why the CCCS could only offer an average of one report per week, buried on the inside pages of a couple of newspapers. Though there were more, the reports' direct effect was pitiful. Prince Phillip, infamous for racially orientated gaffes, did not make one. The royal park police merely added mugging to their century old excuses for the *existing* dusk to dawn curfew [Dreher, 1997]. Provincial authorities had long since been replacing on-site park keepers with cost-cutting mobile patrols to cover them all. As Cohen [1969: 173] pointed out, they had previously used the excuse of vandalism, even though by doing so would increase rather than reduce both problems. That's not a lot given periodic feature articles also questioned the sensationalism, the provincial police could not cobble mugging stats together, and although that instant poll found the vast majority in favor of more control, it is far more pertinent to note that the Senior Citizens Conference that year was preoccupied with hooliganism [Hall *et al*, 1984: 5–8]. As the police's anti-mugging squads and the judiciary's campaign against violent crime also preceded the panic, the response is not enough to constitute a "strong and vigorous official reaction" [Hall *et al*, 1984: 17]; let alone enough to undermine the "coming British revolution" [Ali, 1970]. It does, however, explain why mugging did not go political for another three years; and when it did, it was mainly confined to the political fringe [SWP 1976; *Britain First*, 1976]. The evidence offered by the CCCS for each component part of the political origins of the panic does not withstand scrutiny either.

THE DISAPPEARING SYMBOL

The fact that the alleged panic was bookended by the *Daily Express* insisting that "today's footpads are no different from their predecessors" and *The Daily Mail* denouncing the label as a trendy term for street crime suggests that the media did not believe that mugging was new or black—the major rationales offered by the CCCS for its newsworthiness [Hall *et al*, 1984: 183]. Indeed, race was rarely mentioned except when defense attorneys attacked the LTP's racial profiling. That is why the meaning of mugging discerned by the CCCS relies upon their interpretation of the newspapers' "subtext" which rests on the pre-pre-sensitization, which in turn is dependent upon the innate racism supposedly found in that strong sense of "Englishness". However, as the pre-sensitization only appeared in two papers that most people would not have read, and a review of the content cited does not support the interpretation offered by the CCCS, their meaning of mugging, like Cohen's meaning of mod, is highly contentious [Hall *et al*, 1984: 6, 21–23, 91, 248–28 9].

Neither of *The Sunday Times* articles cited from 1968 and 1969 made black muggers the symbol of the "Disunited States" [Hall *et al*, 1984: 21]. When the black mugger appeared in the next two articles, they were symbolic of "the crime explosion" undermining Nixon's election promises not the crisis of capitalism [Hall *et al*, 1984: 22]. Even when the themes of economic crisis and muggers finally merged two weeks before Handsworth at the end of the alleged panic in the *Sunday Times* magazine only read by the elite, it still does not support the claims made by the CCCS. George Fiffer's *New York: a Lesson for the World* argued that mugging the well-to-do by "the poor" was new in 1973. As "poor" was not a "code word" for black in the UK during 1973, it is questionable what effect the article would have had even amongst the minority who read it [Hall *et al*, 1984: 24]. Angus Maude's *The Enemy Within* published in the *Sunday Express* during 1971 cannot save the CCCS either. For far from warning readers that black muggers and American "diseases" were a boat-load of immigrants away from the UK, Maude made spoilt white brats the symbol for the US crisis. He not only blamed the "violence, drug-taking, student unrest, the hippy cult and the pornography" on white, liberal professors' secular humanism, he also insisted that the UK was *already* suffering the same fate [Hall *et al*, 1984: 25–2 6]. The connections drawn by the CCCS between the issues that supposedly encouraged everyone to blame crime on Left-wing permissiveness and demand more law and order as a result are also problematic [Hall *et al*, 1984: 23].

LAW AND DISORDER

The judges' wanted violent street crime dealt with in the crown courts [Hall *et al*, 1984: 32–33] for the same reason that the do-gooder Ms. Bacon wanted to draw a distinction between the viciously violent and the deprived delinquent: the violent were not suitable candidates for soft-options. They proved that by undermining the effectiveness of the therapeutically orientated care homes during this period, although that cause behind the later scandals concerning the countermeasures taken against the contagion of bullying and violence that followed is often overlooked [Webster, 1998 and 2005; Corby *et al*, 2001]. As the simultaneous crime wave involving black youth was confined to a couple of London boroughs, and the legality of the "stop and search" methods adopted by the police promptly provoked a parliamentary inquiry, the claim that everyone would have linked the issue of black crime and the judges' concerns is questionable. The CCCS account masked the fact that the mugging horror-headlines appeared at the same time that the London mugging trials raised the issue of racial profiling in the UK. Even if the police had deliberately claimed that the death at Waterloo was "a mugging gone wrong" to deflect attention away from that, it would not support the analysis offered by the CCCS. It was just as likely that the public would see the murder as another consequence of crooked cops failing to do their job following the extensive media coverage of the endemic corruption in London's Metropolitan police that the CCCS also forgot to mention.

Between 1969 and 1972, *The Sunday Times, The Sunday People* and the popular *World in Action* TV show revealed that the OPS were "licensing" illegal porn stores, the Drug Squad was importing and recycling drugs, and the famous Flying Squad were entrapping Britain's dumbest criminals rather than catching real bank robbers. Public confidence in the police plummeted when it became apparent that those in London spent more time trying to cover their tracks than fighting crime, and further still when *hundreds* of cops were allowed to retire early rather than face the music. Only twenty ever faced prosecution [Cox *et al*, 1977]. Consequently, far from panicking when the outgoing commissioner, Sir John

Waldron, and those two "top cops" warned that crime was out of control [Hall *et al*, 1984: 50]; many would have held Waldron responsible for failing to control corruption, and would have ignored what those cops had said because they were retiring early as well. As the Police Federation had also embarrassed itself by defending the corrupt officers, any pronouncements from that quarter would have only excited those prone to appeals to law and order [Cox *et al*, 1977].

Similar caveats can be applied to the alleged influence of senior judges' pronouncements during this period because the public believed that they were "out of touch". Although the tabloid press promoted that perspective as part of their law and order agenda whenever they considered a sentence was "too light"; as the petit-bourgeoisie were turning John Mortimer's *Rumpole of the Bailey* novels into best sellers, even though Rumpole constantly clashed with judges and exhibited sympathy for the criminal classes, the CCCS had no right to draw their self-serving interpretation. Indeed, Stevenson, whose rant against the Cambridge student riot is accredited by the CCCS with marginalizing the student protest rather than the students' own stupidity, was even regarded as mad in the legal fraternity. His admonition during one of the police corruption trials shows why.[2] Livid that the jury had returned "not guilty" verdicts on half of the indictments because of prosecution failures, Stevenson took his annoyance out on the defendants, blaming the cabal of corrupt cops for the widespread public distrust of the police, while simultaneously asserting that distrust was unjustified despite all the evidence revealed in court:

> You poisoned the wells of criminal justice . . . What is equally bad is that you have betrayed your comrades in the metropolitan police force, which enjoys the respect of the civilized world—what remains of it—and not the least grave aspect of what you have done is to provide material for crooks, cranks and do-gooders who unite to attack the police whenever the opportunity occurs [Stevenson cited Cox *et al*, 1977: 127].

Similar questions can be raised about the alliances the CCCS used to prove the convergence on the political Right, especially the claim that the government, Mary Whitehouse and the OPS were working in tandem. The attack on the counterculture by the OPS was designed to deflect attention away from their corruption, and was counter to official policy at the time. The Metropolitan Police hierarchy was correct in their fear it would further undermine confidence in the police. Although the moral entrepreneurs welcomed the prosecutions for their own reasons, they had no love for the corrupt OPS because it had advised the government to *ignore* Lord Longford's anti-porn crusade in 1971. Like everyone else, the entrepreneurs were far from impressed that the main function of the OPS appeared to be supplying smut and sluts for police parties, hence their moniker "the Dirty Squad" [Cox *et al*, 1977: 178; Tomkinson, 1982; Thompson, 1994a]. What is more, the denizens of the Right supposed to prove that Whitehouse had turned political were also involved in exposing police malpractice and corruption. Deedes had chaired the 1968 parliamentary committee which denounced the use of "stop and search" tactics as an abuse of civil liberties, and Longford's New Horizons drug rehabilitation charity align with Release, the counterculture's legal advice center, to expose further corruption in the drug squad [Cox *et al*, 1977: 94]. The heavy—handed policing the CCCS accredit to the strong state also followed from the corruption scandals. They were promoted and defended by Robert Mark, who had been appointed to clear up the Met, but quickly proved that he was not the "liberal pragmatist" that the CCCS claim that he was [Hall *et al*, 1 984: 312].

MAKING HIS MARK

Unless one ignored the news media, it was impossible not to know that Mark, a former Special Branch Inspector obsessed with communist conspiracies because of his cold-war Christianity, was responsible for turning public order policing into police riots. Mark gave his Bobbies free reign against students and industrial militants, opposed political accountability, denounced defense attorneys and civil liberties watchdogs, demanded the abolition of unanimous jury verdicts, and insisted that anyone criticizing his reformed police was on the side of the criminals. Nor did he make any secret why he did so. Mark wanted to turn the police into a paramilitary force; hence the joint operations with the army, use of demonstrations as riot practice, and letting the armed special patrol group loose on immigrant areas that so worried the CCCS [Cox *et al*, 1977]. The SPG did not single out Brixton blacks either. They turned up in every "high crime area", stopping and searching over 18,000 thousand Londoners most of whom were white in 1975 alone. Likewise, being stopped and searched with no probable cause, having drugs planted on you, and being verballed[3] in court was an equal opportunity hazard for UK teens during the late 1960s and early 1970s, which is why it became a political issue. The major reason the police began to rely on that method in black communities was that they had lost the informants the corrupt drug squad cops had generated by granting snitches the license to recycle seized drugs in return for ratting-out black political activists [Bunyan, 1977: 95–96, 146; Cox *et al*, 1977: 90]. The impression given by the CCCS that the Conservative party was monolithic and that every piece of legislation proved they were single minded is also false. For example, Michael Havers, a future Conservative MP backed Mike Jagers' claim's that he had been framed and propositioned for a bribe by the drug squad officers raiding his home in May 1969 [The Guardian, 23.2.04:3].

RATIONAL FEAR AND STREET CRIME

The continuing dispute over the extent of the period's rising crime rate [McRobbie and Thornton, 1991: 563] is less important than the way the CCCS played up race and played down the violence involved. The reaction against street crime in the UK can be explained by the fact that while the crime rate between 1970 and 1980 only increased by 5 percent per year, violence against a person and robbery increased by over 135 percent and that was only reported cases [HMSO, cited in Hill, 1982: 129; Bottomley and Coleman, 1984: 39–43]. As the CCCS also admitted violence is experienced as "a basic violation of the person", has news value, and offers an obvious appeal to unity, that would also militate against sudden panic. What appears to have worried most people was that although the statistical chance of being mugged remained small, anyone who was had a 50–50 chance of being injured [Hall *et al*, 1984: 68 and 72]. This fear of violence as opposed to robbery was also identified as the major factor in the New York mugging 'panic' during 1973 [Hacker, 1973].

The precious few examples offered of the panic press before Handsworth also raise questions about the interpretation placed on them by the CCCS. The *Killed for 30 Pence* horror-headline concerned the white perpetrators throwing their white victim off a coastal cliff [Hall *et al*, 1984: 72–73]. Citing *Muggers Pick on Wrong Man* is also ironic, as the only reason the constabulary would have concerned itself with the hospitalization of the three failed muggers was that they were considering prosecuting the victim for daring to defend himself; an odd thing to do during a moral panic [Hall *et al*, 1984: 72]. The prime example, offered by the CCCS, *The Sun's* editorial from the October, 1972 'peak' also undermines their account:

> WHAT ARE the British people most concerned about today? Wages? Prices? Immigration? Pornography? People are talking about all these things. But the *Sun* believes there is another issue which has everyone deeply worried and angry: VIOLENCE IN OUR STREETS
>
> If putative jail sentences help stop the violence—and nothing else has—then they will not only prove to be the only way. They will regrettably be the RIGHT way. And the judges will have the backing of the public [Capitals in original—eds. Hall *et al*, 1984: 75].

Apart from demonstrating how the press was emphasizing generic violence during one of the alleged peaks of mugging media coverage, the CCCS ignore the fact that the editorial would have had salience for Asians and blacks, gays and counterculture youth as well as the elderly, because they were constantly forced to play *Escape From New York* in British cities every time they ventured outside because marauding skinhead gangs constantly belied the CCCS myth that they were merely defending their turf from other skinheads [Clarke, 1991].

CAN YOU READ THAT AGAIN?

Presenting the Handsworth coverage as typifying the panic press, and Storey's twenty-year sentence as the "climax to the earlier exemplary sentencing", is questionable evidentially, methodologically, and theoretically. The reason the CCCS did so was that they knew a bonafide content analysis of the wider mugging media would not support their claim that it targeted blacks [Hall *et al*, 1984: 84]. In any event, the initial "harsh" sentence was for *attempted murder* rather than mugging, and it had nothing to do with the judges' alleged clamp down. On the contrary, Storey was sectioned under s53 of the Children and Young Persons Act 1933 by one of those experts that the paradigm lauds as the antidote to panic who had declared Storey psychotic [Hall *et al*, 1984: 82]. Likewise, the failure of the bourgeois press to blame Storey and his victim's plight on capitalism only amounts to a "complete ideological closure" if one foolishly believes that crime is solely a function of capitalism, and overthrowing the system would offer *the* solution. As the tabloid press *were* committed to law and order, the fact that *The Daily Mail* offered a "fairly straight rendering of the opinions of three 'experts'" and *The Daily Express* ran a headline "The boy who was sentenced before he was born" suggests that the press was being unusually balanced [Hall *et al*, 1977: 100].

Given the area's racial history, including electing fascists and a race riot, the local press was very liberal too. The *Birmingham Post* dismissed demands for more law and order. *The Mail* could not have *exemplified* the pre-sensitization when we are not offered any other references to US levels of street crime, and the paper only appears to have done so to warn that there was still time to avoid them if the authorities addressed the *indigenous* causes of social deprivation. *The Mercury* definitely did not affirmed the existing social order, because being a Christian newspaper it blamed crime on the *dominant* secular, materialist, value system [Hall *et al*, 1984: 106–115]. This habit of imposing untenable readings on evidence that clearly suggests the opposite is most evident in the case of race, and that approach can easily be questioned by reviewing the prime example offered by the CCCS taken from *The Sun* :

> Handsworth, the sprawling Birmingham *slum* where the three muggers grew up is a *violent playground*. Paul Storey, son of a mixed marriage, tried drugs, then theft—and finally violence in a bid to find excitement in his squalid environment. Paul's mother, 40 year old Mrs. Ethel Saunders, said "What chance have young people got in a lousy area like this" [Hall *et al*, 1984: 94]?

In order to turn the reference to mixed marriage into racism rather than a comment on a double dose of discrimination, the CCCS used the same form of triangulation that Cohen denounced when it was used by the media to turn everyone with a mod haircut into a delinquent. Similar problems can be found with the other examples offered by the CCCS to prove the racist subtext, typified by turning *The Daily Express's* observation that the children at-risk register reflected the area's demographics into a racist one, when it implied that the effects of deprivation were uniform. The alleged "code words" for race do not stand scrutiny either, not just because references to "grotty little streets" could not invoke images of Harlem's wide avenues or because "ghetto" was associated with the persecution of the Jews in Europe rather than a breeding ground for black muggers. The major problem is that the CCCS never offered an example of a stereotypical black mugger in the press that would invoke the pre-sensitization [Hall *et al*, 1984: 102, 103, and 110]. If they could have, they would have, but they could not because the black mugger did not even appear in the popular movies of the period like *Shaft* or *The French Connection* which would have had far more influence than obscure feature articles in the *Sunday Times* or *Sunday Express* [1971]. When the image of 'the black mugger' finally emerged in *Death Wish* during 1974 *after* the mugging panic, the well dressed 20-something black muggers *with guns* were also outnumbered by their well dressed 20-something white counterparts *with guns* by 4:1.

Other alleged panic effects, such as *The Times* contradicting itself by supporting the 20-year sentence despite having opposed exemplary sentencing for delinquents in the past, merely illustrate the spurious nature of the examples used by the CCCS. Delinquency was not the issue, and even if it had been, there were obvious aggravating circumstances in this case. Indeed, as the pre-sensitization on which their analysis rests did not exist, the assertion that it "undermined the highly varied arguments that the media contained" proves the opposite [Hall *et al*, 1984: 105 and 112]. The interpretation offered for the meaning of the hate mail, supposed to prove the influence of the press is even more incongruous, and does not support a racial reading. Terms like "monster" had been used to describe perpetrators of vicious crimes since *Frankenstein,* expressions like "lynch" did not have the same connotation in the UK as they did in the US, and as President Obama lauded experiential reality and the ability to transcend disadvantage by holding to firm moral values in his autobiography 40 years later [2004: 49]; turning them into evidence of subconscious racism suffers from the standard weaknesses found in deconstructionism [Washington, 1989]. They invariably reflect the authors' theoretical logic rather than the original author's intent. Likewise, as the only letter that referenced the "US crisis" came from the US, and all three pieces of hate mail championing repatriation came from authors associated with nationalist organizations like the Ulster Loyalists, that would suggest that the only people making overt links between Storey, race, murderous mugging, and immigration were the extreme Right and the neo-Maoist CCCS [Hall *et al*, 1984: 134–135].

THAT WAS THE BELIEF THAT WAS

The Pythonesque, a-historical, depiction of the English value consensus proffered by the CCCS could be questioned by any student of history, given that these values were not even predominant during the Victorian period [Houghton, 1957; Inglis, 1971]. Even if those values could accommodate class differences that can not explain away their internal contradictions. For example, as "keeping up appearances" in the postwar period would require one to become somewhat materialistic that would undermine the value of "deferred gratification". Similar conceptual problems beset the "master symbol" too. Given the problems we have found in their thesis and the apparent inability of the CCCS to differentiate between the need for evidence and 'empiricism', it is just as well that the British preferred "practical common sense" to faddy French philosophy. Even when the caricature had some truth, like the racist legacy of Empire, the CCCS omitted that this was being challenged by the rising generation as we reveal below. Faced with a lack of space for a polemical critique we will rely on pointing out that the CCCS account is weakest where it is supposed to be strongest. For far from displaying a total "respect for law" *everyone* in the 1970s appeared hell-bent on ignoring it. While capitalists were hiding their loot in off-shore tax havens despite exchange controls, organized labor continued its tradition of political strikes, Mary Whitehouse and the law and order lobby both insisted that the law was wrong, and the police were mugging the law by engaging in illegal stop and searches, turning peaceful demonstrations into police riots, committing perjury, and framing innocents. At the same time: the army was murdering unarmed demonstrators, torturing the survivors, and terrorizing the Catholic community in Ulster [McGuffin, 1974]; Judges were lecturing magistrates for hearing cases that they were not supposed to; social workers were making a mockery of the law by sending budding Jack the Rippers to care homes rather than in front of crown court judges; university professors were telling their students that blacks were entitled to pimp women, sell drugs, and mug people because everyone else was a racist; real racists were breaking the Racial Discrimination Act 1968; and every other teen was smoking dope because they thought that being a folk devil was "cool".

There are also two simple reasons for dismissing the arguments that as the public wanted to see street thugs punished they must have capitulated to the law and order agenda, and as trade unionists expressed a distrust of "shirkers, scroungers, and loafers" they must have had "lurched to the right" simply because the word "scrounger" turned up in a piece of Handsworth hate mail and conservatives attempted to exploit welfare fraud for political purposes [Hall *et al*, 1984: 151–156; 161; 169–177, 188–189; 194–208]. First, as Laurie Taylor finally accepted after he had been shown the error of his ways by a proletarian bank robber, the working-classes' attitude to criminals depended upon whether they, like capitalists, preyed on the weak [Taylor, 1984]. As trade unionists' attitudes to welfare fraud would follow from their experience of shirking colleagues, loafing family members, and scrounging friends who never reciprocated, that reinforces the fact that working-class ideology, be it sensible, silly, or stupid is no one's but their own. While the proletariat may not always have the ability to make the most of their experiential reality and their subsequent common sense is often one-dimensional; when the academic alternative turns violent assaults on elderly women to steal their social security cash into "racial consciousness" we'll ask for a second opinion, rely on our experience, and go out to dinner [Hall *et al*, 1984: 184].

SOCIOLOGICAL BANDITS

Violent bag-snatching in a recession-hit, but welfare orientated, late-twentieth-century industrial economy was *not* comparable to socio-political banditry in pre-capitalist Corsica, the petty crime of the destitute London proletariat during the mid nineteenth-century, or the desperate plight of the rural poor whose customary rights to subsistence were being turned into crimes by the landed classes to extend their property rights [Hobsbawm, 1972; Hobsbawm and Rudé, 1973; Rudé, 1981; Bushaway, 1982]. Whereas social historians can offer *evidence* for their claim that social crime sometimes aided working-class consciousness, especially when it involved collective protest like food riots, sheep stealing, and poaching [Rudé, 1981; Thompson, 1975]; the only 'evidence' the CCCS actually offer for the politicization of muggers is that the collective incompetent of the armed robbers that led to the six-day Spaghetti House restaurant "siege" by armed police claimed to be members of the Black Liberation Army [Hall *et al*, 1984: 185]!

The structural analysis behind the claim that blacks were being turned into a reserve army of labor is not justified either [Hall *et al*, 1984: 370–377]. Although racism in hiring policies ensured unemployment was twice as high for black teens; violent crime, selling dangerous drugs, and pimping women were *not* the only options available. Although older immigrants were often employed below their skill level [Fryer, 1988: 374]; the fact that blacks were *over* represented in skilled trades like metal work, the engineering industry, *and* the professions demonstrates that the situation was not quite as drastic as the CCCS contend [Moore, 1975: 6]. The question to ask is why black youth preferred to "hustle" rather than do what unemployed white and Asian teens did. They took advantage of free courses in the technical college sector while working part-time, and then took vocationally orientated degrees at a polytechnics which were not only fee-free but came complete with means tested allowances that never had to be repaid. As these colleges were full of all races gaining skills while riding out the recession, that ensures that mugging is not comparable with starving unemployed agricultural laborers in the mid nineteenth-century being criminalized for picking up a piece of dead wood for their winter fire [Hall *et al*, 1984: 191]. The suggestion that Caribbean teens' recourse to crime can be explained by their different colonial experience, familial form, and social traditions to the Asians is fatuous. If Fanon and Fryer were right, Caribbeans were more attached to the values of their "mother country" than the indigenous population [Hall *et al*, 1984: 353–358; Fryer, 1988: 374–375; Fanon, 2008]; and alternative explanations, that black teens who frequently followed their parents to the UK after a five or ten year interval found it difficult to "fit in" makes far more sense. In any event, the Asian teen's experience was not as uniform as the CCCS would have us believe as much depended upon their area of origin, religion, and the industry in the area they had settled in.

There are also good reasons to believe that mugging would inhibit rather than enhance political consciousness amongst blacks. As *Race Today* editor, Darcus Howe pointed out, far from being romantic figures, hustlers like Danny Williams were more than happy to "work for the man" when he came in the form the corrupt drug squad officer [cited in Cox *et al*, 1977: 96, 112–113]. Targeting blacks for specific crimes was not linked to the recession either. They had long since been associated with pimping and drugs, and had suffered constant harassment from the police as a result, evidenced by Hunt's deliberately provocative entitled exposé *Nigger-Hunting in England* which covered the boom years [Moore, 1975: 60–64; Fryer, 1988: 391–393]. That is why the failure of the CCCS to cover the Mangrove 9 trial is the equivalent of Cohen ignoring the history of the rockers [Hall *et al*, 1984: 281]. As the owner of the Mangrove restaurant, which was the unofficial HQ for London's black activists, tells the story it will become obvious why the CCCS never let black activists speak for themselves:

> We took a stand against the police in the Mangrove 9 trial . . . In the first year we had seven raids . . . they never found any drugs, because there was none. They used to raid the restaurant at half past ten or eleven . . . Friday night when it was packed. They would search and everybody would leave their food, we couldn't ask them to pay. So what the police were doing was destroying the restaurant. They didn't want us to have too much respectability. So the feeling was running high . . . It was the first demonstration of its kind seen in London. It was held in August 1970. It was a very important demonstration . . . 500 people came out. We made speeches and marched off to the police station that was carrying out the raids. We went to Notting Hill . . . Then we said we were going over to Harrow Road police station. The police went in very heavy and about 26 people got arrested on small charges. Reggie Maudling was the home secretary at the time and he made a mistake. After the demonstration he said he wanted an enquiry into who had organised it. After he got the results he said "arrest the organizers" and nine of us were arrested. That day we nearly had a race

riot. I was charged with affray, carrying an offensive weapon, threat-ening behavior and inciting members of the public to riot. We were looking at a lot of jail. The trial was about a year later in 1971 and we won it. It was a massive trial, nearly 60 days in the Old Bailey. It was black power time and people were looking for something to identify with. We had telegrams from people all over the world. They were saying the nine people had stood up against the whole establishment. It was after the Mangrove 9 trial that they started introducing law cen-tres. We had a lot of support and we won it outright. The police were embarrassed—they saw that what they had done was bring a lot of black people together. A lot of youngsters identified with us and began to come out on the streets . . . That trial was a turning point. A lot of political people who were asleep began to wake up. That was the start [Crichlow, 2010].

As the police excuse for racial abuse and the criminalization of blacks was nothing new, and we could add other examples of prior politicization in the black community like the battle of Atlantic Road[4], the political role ascribed to mugging by the CCCS is not contentious: it is a fiction.

DISAPPEARING PANICS

While we do not disagree that 'panics' could have political effects, the meta-morphosis of moral panic from the symbolic to the political and from the disparate to the convergent on which the existence of the mugging moral panic relies for effect was a function of the label slapping engaged in by the CCCS [Hall *et al*, 1984: 158–165]. Several panics listed, like "long hair", never generated horror-headlines. Others that did are as contentious as those over rock festivals. Bigger than Woodstock and far more common, British festivals were frequently subject to "silly season" stories in the press. However, while the press jumped on any violent incident, the perpetra-tors were clearly denounced as a minority, and the police played down the threat [see Phillips, in Cohen and Young, 1973: 321–333]. As most of the other panics listed consist of reports about new laws, public order policing, and court verdicts; these panics merely became political because the CCCS labeled them 'panic'. That is why the CCCS failed to offer any evidence that examples like the jailing of the half-a-dozen Cambridge University stu-dents, who *had* turned a 'demo' outside the Garden House Hotel into an unnecessary orgy of destruction inside, followed from, or caused public panic [Hall *et al*, 1984: 250].

In any event, there is no reason to believe that every middle-class house-wife from Hull, or working-class socialist from Salford would have read a tenth of the stories covered by the CCCS, still less panicked because they drew the same inferences that cultural studies professors believed that they would. On the contrary, newsreels and TV reports could be ambivalent, ambiguous, and even contradictory as the one covering the police attack on the anti-war protest outside the US Embassy, Grosvenor Square, reveals [Hall *et al*, 1984: 243]. One can clearly see that the Maoist students were determined to provoke a confrontation, and a retrospective interview with the counterculture's Mick Farren explains the effect at the time [YouTube, Grosvenor Square; You Tube, Mick Farren]. The all important "lurch to the Right", supposed to offer proof that a panic was in progress is undermined by the original caveat offered by the CCCS which drew a distinction between the mobilization of the moral entrepreneurs and the rest of the panicking petit-bourgeoisie:

> For those moral crusaders used to formulating their discontents in organized ways, there was the possibility of joining movements—to clean up TV, cleanse the streets of prostitutes, or eliminate pornography. But for those whose traditional forms of local articulation had never assumed those more public, campaigning postures, there was left . . . only nagging bitterness [Hall *et al*, 1975: 159].

As racists and the law and order lobby had plenty of organizations and campaigns to occupy them too, that does not leave too many people left to panic over mugging other than the "bitter old folk" the CCCS claim were still worried about youth, affluence, and permissiveness. The most that they could have done was switch votes from Labour to Conservative at election time which would have made little difference [Hall *et al*, 1984: 159].

When the country began to polarize over dozens of issues from the mid 1960s, elections became too close to call; a fact lost in the myth of Thatcher's "landslide victories". The Conservative party always lost the popular vote by 6 percent or *more,* and only attained and remained in power for four elections because of the split in the Centre-Left vote which enabled Conservative candidates to win dozens of marginal constituencies with less than a couple of thousand votes in the UK's first-past-the-post system [Jones, 2011]. What is more, Labour still won the two elections held in 1974 despite the alleged effects of the lurch to the right. As they always called upon consensus, and had denounced the seaman's strike in 1966 for being politically motivated; the fact that they did the same between 1974 and 1979 does not offer evidence for a lurch to the right at all; and neither does immigration policy.

MUGGING RACE

Using anti-immigration sentiment as a proxy for the rise of neo-fascism that did not appear after 1968, is as contentious as the rest of the evidence proffered by the CCCS. Although the 1948 British Nationality Act gave everyone in the colonies British subject status with a right of entry, when the colonies became independent during the 1960s, only those declining citizenship in the new countries retained that status. When Kenya, Uganda, and Malawi expelled the Asians who had been used as a buffer between the colonizers and the indigenous population, the obvious moral obligation whatever their status became lost in other issues [Moore, 1975: 47–51]. Two-thirds of the UK had originally opposed immigration primarily because of ignorance, stupidity and racism, evidence by those citing disease, black magic, and educational inferiority (sic) for their opposition [Fryer, 1988: 376–381]; but there were others who were worried that immigration was being used to maintain a low wage economy. Marxists refused to address that issue even though they started it [Lewis, 1984: 109; Engels, 1969: 122–125]. The concentration of immigrants in 60 inner city areas, where the housing stock was poor and government services were already underfunded did not help either [Moore, 1975: 19].

As liberals responded to postwar racism with a case by case attack on color bars in pubs and dance halls, and a campaign for anti-discrimination legislation [Cox, 1975], the Conservative government responded with an Act in 1962 designed to "ease tension" by requiring immigrants to have a guaranteed job before arrival; although anyone who had *registered* as a British subject before 1962 could still enter. Racists responded to the new restriction by complaining that immigrants' higher birth-rate would still defeat any "balance", and that governments had massaged the figures. Once it became apparent that whereas the first 14,000 employment voucher holders had brought an average of 2.4 dependents with them in 1963, but that the 5,000 turning up in 1967 brought an average of 10 dependents, immigration became a major issue. As the Left responded to that by foolishly dismissing people's fears as "a numbers game", they handed the initiative to the racists at the very moment that the postwar boom went bust; though what followed also undermines the CCCS account. While the readers of *Race Today* may have worried about Caribbean youth [Moore, 1975: 93], the predominant public debates at the time concerned the ramifications for 'integration' and employment. Racists pointed to the lack of integration to justify their demand for more controls, as if Hindus, Muslims, and Sikhs should have abandoned their culture. The hostility directed at Caribbeans, often "more English than the English", was hardly likely to aid integration anyway. Once the boom went bust, indigenous workers also began to demand more curbs in a determination to safeguard their position in the job market. That response ensured that the Labour government's Commonwealth Immigrants Act 1968, which restricted employment voucher holders' residence to the period of employment like most other countries did, did not dampen demands about restricting dependents, especially as anyone who had registered as a British citizen before 1962 was still allowed to enter [see Section (d) CIA, 1968]. Indeed, while the Act is often seen as a panic measure, racists were annoyed that it *extended* the right of entry by clarifying previously ambiguous issues like the rights of children of former colonial service workers in the immigrants' favor. In short, the immigration laws were more generous than many other countries, and were only "restrictive" if one believed that *anyone* should have right of entry *anywhere* at *anytime* which apparently the CCCS did.

That distortion is reinforced by the failure to inform readers that level of racism was *declining,* and that every manifestation of racism after Powell's infamous speech in 1968 fed a fast growing anti-racist movement. Although 75 percent recorded their support for Powell in 1968, that support concerned his "right to speak" and reflected the fact that the public wanted an open debate on immigration and the Anti-discrimination bill for the same reason that they also demanded an open debate on the proposal to join the European Economic Community. The public was "fed up" with MPs ignoring the wishes of their constituents. In any event, the speech concerned anti-discrimination laws and not immigration. The moment that the public was polled on Powell's *immigration policy,* his level of support fell to 48 percent, far lower than the level opposed to immigration only 20 years before. Likewise, the CCCS forget to mention that half the Conservative party's shadow cabinet threatened to resign unless Powell was demoted, the Liberal party demanded his prosecution, and the media *denounced* his speech *en masse* [Lewis, 1984: 113–114; 122–125; Powell, 1971: 199–200].

Far from making racism respectable as the CCCS would have you believe, Powell provoked an anti-racist backlash which expanded experientially after the anti-mugging squads' racial profiling was exposed in 1972. Striking immigrants now found allies in organized labor which took on the racists within its ranks. The staff of the race relation organizations, originally deployed to help employers find a cheap labor force, now became a major source of support for immigrant communities and anti-racist propaganda. Radical Labour councils funded black activists who encouraged immigrant youth to organize socially and politically rather than turn to crime [Moore, 1975: 70–102; Fryer, 1988: 386]. Whereas the Labour government left most of the 100,000 Asians with British subject status stranded around the world when they had to flee Kenya in 1968; the Ugandan Asians were granted automatic entry by the Conservative government in 1972 whether they had British status or not, *despite* the efforts of the anti-immigration lobby and the new 1971 Immigration Act. When mugging finally went political in 1975, the small increase in the neo-fascist vote highlighted by the CCCS was swamped by the massive *Rock Against Racism* and the *Anti Nazi League* movements which emerged, and the Labour government passed a new, effective, Anti-discrimination Act which also promoted positive discrimination [Solomos, 1989].

Although it took another twenty years before a UK government finally addressed the endemic racism in the UK police, the failure of the CCCS to address this "other reaction" distorts their account of the nature and level of racism in the UK [Fryer, 1988: 392 and 394]. Having been part of the anti-racist movement at the time, we have no intent to mislead our readers about the level of racism in the UK during this period. It was appalling, but the CCCS exaggerated the extent and its effects. While the minority led by skinheads were engaging in racist chants at soccer games, the rest of the proletariat were happy that Lenny Henry from Handsworth won the TV talent contest *New Faces* in 1975. The CCCS ignored all these indications because *they* panicked.

PROGRESSIVE PANIC

Although many of the problems found in the thesis reflect the dubious nature of any association found in structural analysis, the problems in the case of race are enhanced by the Left-wing panic that followed the march on parliament by a couple of hundred London dockworkers in support of Powell following his infamous speech. Despite the lack of growth in organized fascism, evidenced by the pathetic turnout for the "national" demonstration against Ugandan Asians in 1973 [Knight, 1982], the Left believed that the dockers march heralded the first manifestation of the fascist mass movement their Marxist theory told them would emerge during an economic crisis [*International Socialism,* cited in Widgery, 1976: 407]. Having become overexcited by the revolutionary potential of the student "revolts" in Europe and the US during 1968, the Left feared that it was only a matter of time before the ruling-class would encourage a fascist response [*International Socialism,* cited in Widgery, 1976: 408]. With the revolting students incapable of doing anything apart from squabble amongst themselves [Widgery, 1976: 378–386], Trotskyite groups like the International Socialists took the initiative and set about generating their own horror-headlines and panic about the dockers' demonstration:

> The outburst of racialist sentiment and activity since Enoch Powell's Birmingham speech marks a new phase in British politics. A section of the ruling class (although not yet the dominant section) is resorting to the crudest form of prejudice in order to confuse, divert, and divide workers from the real struggle ... When *confronted with the racist tide* ... An *urgent reorganization* of these socialist forces is necessary *if the onward march of racialism* is to be checked and any longterm fascist development fought against ... Socialist alternatives to the *frustrations and anxieties created by capitalism* must be presented and linked to systematic ant-racist propaganda on a massive scale. A SINGLE ORGANIZATION OF REVOLUTIONARY SOCIALISTS IS NEEDED TO FIGHT THESE URGENT BATTLES [Capitals in original, italics our emphasis—eds. *International Socialism* cited in Widgery, 1976: 411–412].

This political panic, turning Powell and the dockers into Left-wing folk devils out of all proportion to the threat that they really posed, explains why the CCCS insisted on making race and immigration controls the key issue during the escalating class struggle [Hall *et al*, 1984: 245–246, 276, and 333]. It was a proxy for the fascist movement that never materialized. However, while the International Socialist group quickly discovered that the dockers demonstration was a false alarm given that those same dockers could be found protesting the government's economic policies less than a year later, the rest of the Left did not [Widgery, 1976: 409 and 411–412]; and that explains the perspective adopted by the CCCS. The amplification spiral involving all those political panics which the CCCS insist followed from the dockers' demonstration was really a *political* amplification spiral involving Left and Right-wing ideologues. While those on the political Right saw every new form of protest as part of the growing revolutionary threat and were encouraged to do so by the covert cold war policies of US government agencies [Lobster[5]], the Left became obsessed about the threat of fascism, armed militias, and military coups [Jenkins, 1992: 29]; and both groups' fears were enhanced by their respective interpretations of the IRA insurgency in Ulster [Bunyan, 1977]. Yet one look at the strong state demonstrates that the CCCS were panicking about nothing.

THE WEAK STATE

The 1970 Conservative government's law and order agenda merely amounted to recruiting more police officers, building new prisons, and a plan to make criminals and strikers pay compensation for any property damage caused. Their program for dealing with the economic crisis was far more drastic, including as it did the outlawing of wildcat strikes. Yet the moment the government attempted to put their policies into practice, they provoked the "lurch to the Left" which led to the class war of 1971–1974; not that there was anything new about government "coercion". The convergence of crime, violence, and politics in the press which the CCCS imply was something new was no different from the more passive 1950s and 1960s [Chibnall, 1977]. Public order policing in the UK had always been heavy-handed despite the official philosophy of minimum force [Reiner, 1985]. The Special Branch, like MI5, had been spying on the political Left for decades, and special units in government services like the Post Office which opened letters, read telegrams, and bugged phones were as old as the service itself. The SPG had been active and armed since 1964 and warrantless searches began in 1967, under the Labour government. Most of the "emergency powers" adopted had ancient origins. The harassment of peace activists relied on the Incitement to Mutiny and Incitement to Disaffection Acts of 1817 and 1934 respectively. The two States of Emergency implemented by the Conservative government after 1970 were authorized by the 1921

Emergency Powers Act, which had been invoked no fewer than nine times during the supposedly placid 1950s [Bunyan, 1977]. And when the Conservative government tried to impose the rule of law it failed miserably.

The Government lost the vote on the clause that would have forced aliens to register with the local PD during the debate on the 1971 Immigration bill. The OPS attack on the counterculture backfired. They lost more cases than they won, and even more on appeal. The increase in use of conspiracy charges, and the proposed Criminal Trespass bill reflected the government's failure to secure convictions by any other means. John Russell and Mia Caley, who definitely broke the Official Secrets Act by publishing the Ministry of Defense's *Operations Manual* covering the Governments counter-revolutionary plans, were acquitted. The government dare not purge the civil service like it did in the 1950s despite constant leaks. Special branch "fishing" raids were annoying, but mostly led nowhere; and the use of *agent provocateurs* failed too given that all one had to do, as one Welsh nationalist student discovered, was throw away the planted gun before the impending police raid found it. Less than 20 people were prosecuted under the Prevention of Terrorism Act targeting the IRA. Apart from the rare jailing of students and unionists, which immediately led to more militancy; working-class juries used their common sense, exercised their right to reject "bad law", and acquitted most of the revolutionaries, peace activists, trade unionists, and black activists who were prosecuted during this period. Those found guilty tended to be convicted on lesser charges with less drastic consequences. This was also a good time to be a major drug dealer or bank robber because, given all the publicity about police corruption, juries were reluctant to convict them too [Cox, 1975; Bunyan, 1977]. The laws inhibiting protests like sit-ins were so weak that the Directors of Polytechnics could still be found lobbying government for some form of control in 1975 [Miller, 1975].

AMERICAN THEORY AND BRITISH MALPRACTICE

Although the dockers' protest came to nothing, rather than admit that they had been over excited about the "coming British revolution", the CCCS desperately searched for an excuse for its failure to appear and found it in "forgotten role" of the panic prone "authoritarian lower-middle class and respectable working class" in *Folk Devils* [Hall *et al*, 1984: 242–244]. They then set about constructing a united neo-fascist movement out of all the competing demands found on the Right-wing fringe, even though the political Right was as divided as the Left [Hall *et al*, 1984: 242–244, 252–278; 3 13–316; Lewis, 1984]. That is why it was the CCCS rather than the press that "imported" the black mugger as the symbol of the US crisis, exaggerated Powell's influence, turned the demand for immigration controls into a proxy for the fascist movement that did not appear, and omitted the far bigger anti-racist movement which did. Like Cohen, they also drew on US theories that did not apply to the UK. Mesmerized by the US ghetto riots of 1968, and impressed by the US anti-war movement's propaganda that they had forced President Johnson to stop the bombing in Vietnam [Hall *et al*, 1984: 245]; the CCCS used the subsequent defection of the racist white working-class Democrats to the Nixon-Agnew law and order ticket as the model for the UK [Hall *et al*, 1984: 240, 246, 357]. The Warren Supreme Court rulings, enforced integration in schools, the summer of love, Students for a Democratic Society, Black Power, and Nixon's law and order campaign now became permissiveness, immigration controls and Powell, the counter-culture, the student vanguard and workers militancy, black muggers and the Conservative's law and order agenda. Other erroneous parallels found in *Policing the Crisis* include: the government, OPS, Whitehouse alliance—Nixon's rejection of the Commission on Pornography Report; the Misuse of Drugs Act—Nixon's war on drugs; British horror-headlines—"the language of crime, violence, chaos, and anarchy" in the US media; public order polic-ing—the Chicago police riot; the moral panic over drugs, squatters, and the counterculture press—Agnew's speeches concerning the counterculture and drugs; the English fear of muggers—whites frightened by the Black Panther party; the counterculture squat in Piccadilly protesting housing shortages—the Chicago conspiracy trial; the SPG and LTP anti-mugging squads—the police's assassination of Black Panther leaders.

The desire to make UK politics match the New Left's analysis of the US crisis explains why the CCCS backdated the politicization of mugging from 1975 to 1972, although the UK was far more preoccupied by the class conflict and the ramifications of Bloody Sunday at the time. In doing so they turned a valid concern about violent street crime into a panic about muggers in the same way that Cohen turned the delinquency debate into the mods and rocker panic [Hall *et al*, 1984: 280]. Nor is it a coincidence that the public's alleged fear of the black mugger rather than mugging *per se* ultimately relies on psychobabble:

> The symbolization of the race-immigrant theme was resonant in its subliminal force, its capacity to set in motion the demons which haunt the collective subconscious of a superior race; it triggered off images of sex, rape, primitivism, violence and excrement. Out there in the great suburban world of money and power, where few black men or women walked, a suitably high-minded view of 'racial integration' in the lower depths could be taken; what *these* white men and women feared above all was that they would suddenly lose their position of power—that they would suddenly become, in all senses of the word, *the poor*. What the white poor feared, however, was that after all this time, they might become *black* [Italics in the original, Hall *et al*, 1984: 244].

The problem with that attempt to replicate Cohen's psychological dimension of moral panic, is that it turns Fanon's interpretation of dreams in *Black*

Skin: White Mask on its head without explaining how or why that worked. The most important defect in the thesis, however, is that the CCCS never offered any evidence that anyone stateside made black muggers *the* symbol of the US crisis in 1968; and one wonders why no one ever considered that you cannot import a concept that does not exist. The closest the US came to blaming muggers for the country's ills was the government commercials and planted TV plots blaming drug addicts for mugging amongst a host of other crimes during Nixon's war on drugs; but none of those commercials or plots concentrated on blacks. The *black* mugger finally appeared in NYC in 1973, and it was their continuing presence in the NYC economic meltdown of 1975 that popularized their existence, which is why mugging went political in the UK following the horror-headlines about mugging's demographics in Lambeth. Even then, the second panic does not justify the label, as the reaction amounted to even less than the first:

- An increasingly isolated Powell making a speech to the racist Police Federation;
- *One* example from the provincial media in which the mugger was merely one of four problems besetting Birmingham along with "bullies, vandals, and exhibitionists";
- A judge who was forced to publicly retract his comments linking muggers to immigration; and
- The attempt to exploit the issue by neo-Nazis, which immediately provoked the successful counter-reaction we covered above [Hall *et al*, 1984: 330–333].

THEORETICAL PANIC

Once one reviews the nature of the evidence offered for its existence, the mugging moral panic amounts to another academic construction. The racist nature of the mugging horror-headlines depended upon a pre-sensitization that never happened, a back-dated stereotype, and an anachronistic value system that no longer existed. Even the Right-wing press denounced the new label. The judge's "war on black mugging" was really a war on violent street crime. The police's mugging crime wave backfired. It was condemned in Parliament and boosted the growing anti-racist movement. Racism and anti-immigration sentiment were falling rather than rising. The increasing number of moral panics was a function of the CCCS labeling process. The Right-wing alliances did not exist. The control culture operated independently from the state. The seminal Handsworth case concerned *attempted murder* by a psychotic teen, and exhibited an unusual amount of balance in the press. The evidence for public panic relied on a self-serving interpretation of hate mail, which as we will see in Chapter 7 was tame compared to that produced by progressives. The politics of mugging was belied by the

Mangrove 9 trial. Whatever else governments were doing, they were all desperate to avoid a large pool of unemployed, be they white or black, by offering free education and subsistence to anyone who wanted to acquire the skills required for the labor market of the future. As a result, it is not surprising that no one noticed the mugging moral panic had taken place until the CCCS clamed that it had because *they* had been panicking about a nonexistent fascist threat.

Having debunked the first two seminal moral panic case studies by explaining their theoretical origins and their lack of evidence, the next chapter considers why they adopted the perspective that they did, and the ramifications for the myth of moral panic.

Part II

Progressive Panic

Having established that the seminal studies owed far more to theoretical imperatives than social reality in Part I, Part II explores the foundations of the moral panic myth, its politics, and the hidden world of progressive 'panics'. Chapter 4 reviews the assumptions behind the seminal studies' approach to moral enterprise, subsumed within the panic rubric by way of the boundary crisis. By exploring the reasons why the paradigm continues to associate moral enterprise with Right-wing politics and the defense of dominant societal values, it reveals why moral panic is a political rather than a sociological perspective. Chapter 5 covers Martin Barker's account of the *Video Nasties* panic which popularized the concept in the UK. By taking the horror-headlines about 50 horror videos out of their context—another stage in the social value conflict over sex, symbolized by the debate over pornography, between 1975 and 1995—Barker reinforced the politics of panic by spreading an irrational fear amongst progressives that 'society as they wanted it to be" was threatened by the New Moral Right [Barker, 1984b: 6]. In reality, the political situation was far more complicated. The alliance formed by the National Viewers and Listeners Association and the Conservative party in 1978 was one sided and led to constant conflict. No sooner had Barker published his account, than CARE Trust, by now the major force in the Christian community can be found forming an alliance with radical feminists and other Left-wing groups. As the paradigm continues to pretend that this never happened, or that CARE was far from Right-wing; this Chapter exposes more sources of error. The paradigms' fallacies follow from prioritizing structural political theory over experiential reality and evidence. The feminist-religious alliance's crusade against pin-up pornography offers a counter factual rebuttal to Goode and Ben-Yehuda's ambivalent rationales for dismissing these crusades as panic [2009: 243]. As the crusade attracted as much media attention as video nasties, and was backed by professional progressives too, the fact that it failed because of the extensive opposition from progressive and libertarian *activists* questions the assumption that successful 'panics' like video nasties have public support.

On the contrary, the video nasty and pin up porn campaigns demonstrate that these 'panics' were an internal battle amongst the campaigning classes, and that the outcome depends upon the balances of forces during 'panics.' As the elite supported the first and divided the middle-classes over the second, the key issue would appear to be the balances of forces mustered by either side. As the video nasties Act decriminalized triple X porn in the UK it also debatable whether the paradigm has the ability to identify and quantify a successful panic.

Chapter Six covers the ramifications of the panic paradigm's politics for sociological analysis by examining its approaches to satanic abuse allegations in the US and UK between 1983 and 1993. As well as exposing another example of the paradigm's failure to address progressive panics, it reveals that no matter what perspective was adopted, be it the grass root, elite or interest group, moral panic was being used to cover up the fact that progressives were not only adopting the politics of fear, they were more than willing to promote miscarriages of justices and incarcerate innocents to further their political agenda. The means chosen to do so, blaming public panic and the Christian community, will prove invaluable when we consider the politics of panic in the next section. The evidence offered in these three chapters question Goode and Ben-Yehuda claims concerning the paradigm's potential to be politically neutral, and their attempt to explain away progressive 'panics'. It reinforces the fact that the academic problems found within the paradigm reflect its politics.

4   Witch Hunts and Moral Enterprise

Part I demonstrated that the concept of moral panic relied on a panic prone petit-bourgeoisie which projected its economic anxiety in an indignant fashion onto a proxy target following horror-headlines which created a moral boundary crisis. And yet it was never made clear whether the social strain concerned the panicking petit-bourgeoisie's fear of proletarianization, the 'generation gap', or 'permissiveness'; three very different levels and forms of 'social strain'. Cohen was far from specific. Given his use of the term "wider social change", we would suggest the first, but cannot be sure. What is not in doubt is that without the 'real' source of 'panic' in the petit-bourgeoisie, there is nothing to distinguish the interest group perspective from moral enterprise or the grass root perspective from an overreaction. Although the elite perspective avoided that problem by turning the "structurally located groups" referenced in the seminal studies[1] into "the New Right" or "the New Moral Right", it still relied on an untenable linear and structural link between social change, moral boundary crises, and subsequent panic.

This chapter reviews the origin of the seminal studies assumptions about the panicking petit-bourgeois and the concept of boundary crises in order to explain the paradigm's innate political bias and failure to consider either moral panic or moral enterprise from a neutral sociological perspective. In particular, it draws attention to the paradigm's tendency to equate religious moral enterprise with Right-wing politics, and its conviction that 'panics' restore consensual values despite all the evidence to the contrary.

CLASS, MOTIVES, AND MORAL ENTERPRISE

There can be no doubt that moral panic was a political perspective. Both seminal studies associated moral panic with "reactionaries" in general and Christian moral entrepreneurs in particular. Moreover, they promoted the myth of upright, uptight petit-bourgeois and the "respectable working-class" panicking about "traditional values" even though *sociology* had demonstrated that was impossible.

As we saw in chapter two, the "common sentiment" which the model of societal-wide panics relied upon, did not exist during the 1960s. As large sections of the middle-class, the established church, and the judiciary had embraced permissive values, as had the majority of the new petit-bourgeoisie, Wallis suggested that Whitehouse's National Viewers and Listeners Association were defending the disappearing values held by an ever-decreasing minority. He also dismissed the popular psychological explanations for National VALA's apparent overemphasis on sexual permissiveness—moral indignation, resentment towards youth, and sexual repression—because they were not sociological. Instead, he suggested that as sexual permissiveness was the most prominent feature of moral change, National VALA had mobilized in an attempt to stop the rising generation becoming even more permissive [Wallis, 1972; 1976]. However, the moment he surveyed those attending the Nationwide Festival of Light (NFOL) rally in 1971, which the CCCS had used to demonstrate the "lurch to the right", Wallis quickly changed his mind. Having discovered that the majority of attendees were young, highly educated members of the *new* postwar petit-bourgeoisie, and the reason that they opposed permissiveness was their religious belief, Wallis concluded that opposition to the new morality amounted to a form of cultural defense [Wallis and Bland, 1978].

Tracy and Morrison, who spent three years following National VALA, agreed that sexual repression had nothing to do with mobilization [1978], and also emphasized the importance of religion. As National VALA's religious beliefs explained their interpretation of the world as a whole, those beliefs were paramount; evidence by the conviction that the economic crisis in 1966 was caused by the "greed, rampant materialism, envy, and social divisiveness" that secularization had unleashed [Morrison and Tracey, 1978: 42, 46–47]. On the other hand, they also insisted that as National VALA had no hope in hell of stopping secularization, they were engaged in a symbolic crusade [Tracey and Morrison, 1979]. While the paradigm paid little attention to these critics' observations about the extensive change in cultural values and role of religious belief in mobilization, it readily adopted the concept of symbolic protest to boost the claim that UK moral enterprise was irrational. Then, when the American Moral Majority appeared, the paradigm quickly adopted the label New Moral Right to maintain the myth that moral enterprise served the interests of Capital and bourgeois values [Levitas, 1986; Barker, 1984b]. It completely ignored the subsequent debate in the sociology of religion over the nature of Britain's moral minority [Bruce, 1988; Thompson, 1992; 1997]. As far as the paradigm was concerned VALA and the NFOL were no different from their Right-wing US cousins [Thompson, 1998: 83–85; 123–138]; even though *Policing the Crisis* had effectively admitted that Wallis was right!

Long since forgotten, the CCCS agreed that the switch from industrial to consumer capitalism would inextricably lead to a more pluralistic society and an increase in social group value conflict, especially between the old reactionary and new progressive petit-bourgeoisie. The fact that it was already under way, was dismissed on the grounds that although the counterculture was a portent of things to come, the time lag between the cultural conflict on the superstructural level and its cause within the economic base ensured pluralism was not extensive enough to undermine their analysis at that point in time [Hall *et al*, 1984: 235–258]. Despite the subsequent lip service paid to increasing pluralism by panics major 'theorists' [Goode and Ben-Yehuda, 1994; Thompson, 1998], they have not revisited the issue, defined the nature of the social conflict that rages amongst the petit-bourgeoisie both old and new, religious and secular, progressive and socially conservative. This has led to numerous problems across the paradigm, and we will discuss some of them in the coming chapters. Here we concentrate upon the cause.

The major reason why the paradigm ignored Wallis' data reveals another aspect of its simplistic approach. By equating the 'moral' in moral enterprise with religious 'moralism', it maintained a sharp, political, distinction between moral enterprise, and the activities of the progressives in the "new social movements" without considering that the latter are promoting their values too. That tendency can be traced to the paradigm's approach to history because the only thing new about 1960s progressive movements was the increasing amount of secularism [Chen, 1996]. Even the gay movement had decades old antecedents in Woodstock, upstate New York [Evers, 1982].

RELIGION AND PROGRESSIVISM

The political division drawn by the paradigm between irrational, religious, Right-wing moral enterprise, and rational, secular, progressive movements was based on New Left histories, which ignored the fact that Victorian religious moral enterprise was both progressive and feminist [Weeks, 1981; 1985; Mort, 1987], despite the overwhelming evidence found in traditional histories which the radical feminists readily utilized to promote their perspective on sexual morality [Jeffreys, 1985; 1987; 1993]. Those determined to save the degraded masses from evil influences like abortion and alcohol, ice-cream parlors and ice-rinks, smoking and Sunday trading were often the same people trying to elevate and civilize the masses by providing free primary education, ending child labor, replacing the slums with parks, playgrounds, and museums and protect everyone from 'banksters' and speculators [Pearl, 1955; Jaeger, 1956; Pearson, 1972; Trudgill, 1976; Bristow, 1977; Boyer, 1968; Banks, 1981; Lansbury, 1985; Thompson, 1994a]. The Women's Christian Temperance Union, for example, targeted demon drink in order to alleviate social problems, poverty, and cruelty to women and children [Morone, 2003]; although it also served to deflect the leaders' capitalist husbands from any blame. This religious-progressive-feminist alliance, which was responsible for most 'traditional' moral values, fell apart following the split in the religious community between fundamentalists and modernists during the 1920s over the implications of evolutionary theory; and that enabled New Left historians to credit the censorious, moralistic aspects of the alliance to religious fundamentalism. This revisionism created a series of Left-wing myths that had a direct influence on the panic paradigm and its politics, the most important being prohibition [Gusfield, 1963].

By adopting Gusfield's conclusion that the Volstead Act was a symbolic crusade, masking WASP fears about their loss of social power to immigrants rather than a social group conflict over the political aspects of salon culture, the New Left histories adopted the position that religious enterprise was reactionary while the allied feminist enterprise was progressive. So, for example, while they readily emphasized the racial elements in prohibition, they turned a blind eye to the anti-Semitic and racial elements in the simultaneous 'feminist' crusade against white slavery [Bristow, 1982; Thompson, 1994a]. The propaganda of the repeal movement, especially that penned by the H.L. Mencken, was also presented as reality in order to turn every religious moral entrepreneur into a bigoted Bible basher desperately trying to save bourgeois moral values from urban sophisticates and liberal professors. The problem with doing that, of course, was that far from proving economic dissonance, moral indignation, and symbolic targets are endemic features of religious moral enterprise; Gusfield [1963] warned against doing so.

SYMBOLIC POLITICS

Progressive sociologists ignore the fact that Gusfield discussed more than one form of symbolism in social movements. The first concerned the distinction between 'instrumental' campaigns which offered satisfaction through success, and 'symbolic' campaigns which did so by taking part, even if the participants failed to secure their objectives; hence the label 'expressive politics' [Gusfield, 1963: 19]. Second, Gusfield did *not* believe that prohibition was a symbolic crusade because it ultimately failed, but because alcoholic beverages had became a symbol for the wider rationales and goals of the movement [1963: 32, 57, 121–122], in the same way that abortion has become a symbol for women's rights in general. Aware that the distinction between these two forms of symbolism may be ignored or misunderstood, Gusfield specifically warned against imposing secular interpretations on religious motivations and drew attention to the dangers of the "generalizing tendency" in sociology:

> When we maintain that drinking has become a status symbol, we do not imply that religious movements were merely cloaks for status interest . . . A function of Temperance activities was to enhance the symbolic properties of liquor and abstinence as marks of status. This is not an assertion that this was the *only* function nor is it an assertion about

motives. It is merely pointing out that *as a consequence* of such activities; abstinence became symbolic of a status level [Our emphasis—eds. Gusfield, 1963: 59].

In other words, as social movements and political crusades can have more than one symbolic meaning and these can be latent effects, one needed to avoid confusing the symbolic aspects of moral crusades with their cause; and yet that is precisely what the panic paradigm has done. The panic paradigm has always emphasized Gusfield's third form of symbolism, the way that some campaigns act as proxies for the participant's loss of social prestige, and it appears to have done so by relying on the popular summary offered by Zurcher and Kirkpatrick:

> When an individual's prestige is less than he expects as someone who has pledged himself to a usually prestigious style of life, he becomes a *status discontent*. The public acts in which the status discontent participates in order to raise or maintain his own or his group's status are *status politics*. When acts of status politics reach collective proportions, a *status movement—a symbolic crusade*—emerges [Zurcher and Kirkpatrick, 1979: 7].

Although that would have caused no problem for anyone who had read Gusfield, the panic paradigm took no account of how the prohibitionists' perspective changed over time; and that the symbolic role of abstinence was more consequence than cause [1963: 4–10]. Likewise, the paradigm also ignored the fact that Gusfield like most other sociologists in 1960s also criticized economic determinism *and* the tendency to adopt pseudo psychological explanations [1963: 113] like Adorno's methodologically flawed 'proof' that authoritarian personalities were restricted to the political Right. In short, even if status discontent supplied a motive for action it did not follow that the target or the movement was symbolic. It could just as easily be an instrumental one. Consequently, while adverse socioeconomic circumstances can encourage both an increase in religiosity, and a tendency to engage in social action amongst the downwardly mobile [Toch, 1971], the paradigm had no justifications for dismissing religious moral enterprise as symbolic politics generated by status discontent, or its failure to consider, account for, and accept the ramifications of the entrepreneurs' religious perspective or their values, based upon their religious socialization [Wood and Hughes, 1984].

RELIGIOUS POLITICS

The failure of the paradigm to pay attention to the history and nature of moral enterprise is matched by their failure to consider the differences between the US Moral Majority and the UK's moral minority when they emerged. Having decided that atheistic "reds" rather than Catholics were the modern manifestation of the anti-Christ in their eschatology [Marsden, 1980], US fundamentalists readily joined the revived KKK during the 1920s because it was just as concerned about white bootleggers, fornicators, and dead-beat dads as it was about the uppity blacks being used as communist pawns, which became more important during the 1950s [Chalmers, 1976; McGuire, 2011]. As the fundamentalists also supported McCarthy, and Phyllis Schlafly's grass roots conservative revival in the postwar period, it is easy to see why US fundamentalism became associated with Right-wing politics [Wood and Hughes, 1984; Critchlow, 2005; Livesey, 1986]; but it is far more difficult to draw a political line between the modernist and fundamentalist tendencies in the UK.

Members of the Church of England were just as likely to join the Holiness Movement with its emphasis on individual salvation, as they were to promote Henry George's *Progress and Poverty*. While the *Methodist Weekly* folded in 1903 because its socialism alienated readers aligned with the Liberal party, Manchester's Methodist Central Hall experienced phenomenal growth precisely because they promoted women's equality as well as campaigned to close local brothels. Despite their social conservatism, Salvation Army members stood as Labour party candidates in depressed areas, and the Social Gospel movement had both conservative and progressive tendencies like its Baptist founder, the Reverend F.B. Meyer [Bebbington, 1995; Brown, 1995; Randall, 1995].

We suspect that the major reason why this history was ignored by the paradigm followed from the sociological misconception that religion was a declining force in the 1960s because of the popularity of the secularization thesis. However, from the moment that Hollywood's *Inherit the Wind* and *Elmer Gantry* implied that every Bible bashing fundamentalist was a fool or a fraud, and the sociologist of prohibition insisted that fundamentalists were estranged from mainstream society [Gusfield, 1963: 144], to when Zurcher and Kirkpatrick [1976] suggested they were studying the crusaders' death throws and the historian of moral crusades concluded that we would never see their like again [Bristow, 1977]; Christian moral enterprise reemerged to stem the tide of the supreme court's deregulation of sin and parliamentary permissiveness on both sides of the Atlantic.

It did so because of the contemporaneous charismatic, or "born again", religious revival amongst the new petit-bourgeoisie. Although the clashes with progressives over issues like abortion and gay rights should have alerted the Left to the religious nature of the protest, it did not. Progressives were more concerned that Falwell's Baptist based Moral Majority, Christian Voice's Pentecostalists and Charismatics, and Religious Roundtable's Presbyterian and Methodist ministers allied with the political Right without ever asking why. In the US, the alliance can be accredited to both the tendency in cold war Christian to see religion, freedom, and capitalism as the opposites to atheism, state control, and communism; and the fact that the religious had to deal with "dismissiveness", the supreme court rulings suppressing religious expression in public facilities despite the First Amendment's free exercise clause, as well as permissiveness [Guth, 1983; Himmelstein, 1983b; Liebman, 1983; Ammerman, 1987]. Once again, the situation in the UK was somewhat different.

Although the division between fundamentalists and modernists led to the reduction in extra-parliamentary activity, dubbed "the great reversal" by later moral entrepreneurs [Stott, 1984; Bebbington, 1995], the lack of major moral crusades between 1920 and 1960 can be accredited to a lack of need. Although the National Vigilance Society continued to keep a watching brief, Christian Home Secretaries, magistrates, and police chiefs ensured that society tended to conform to the law, until permissiveness changed all that.

BRITAIN'S MORAL MINORITY

Although National VALA's aging pastors, elderly females, fundamentalist cops, returning colonials, and sprinkling of earnest young social workers from the Anglican Church conform to the stereotype of the old petit-bourgeoisie [*The Viewer and Listener,* Spring: 1991], the NFOL and the influential Community Standards movement, ignored by the paradigm, never did. As Wallis discovered, these two factions drew on the Pentecostal and new Charismatic traditions whose congregations were more likely to consist of the working-class and the new petit-bourgeoisie respectively [England, 1982; Walker, 1988; Gibbs, 1984; Griffiths, 1985]. The three groups were able to work together because their common beliefs transcended any doctrinal differences. The most important were: an inerrant Bible; God has a personal plan for everyone; the born again are blessed with God given gifts from prophesy to healing; sacrifice is part of the Christian experience; Jesus' second coming would be proceeded by end-time lawlessness; and heaven and hell literally exist [Thompson, 1992]. The common cause that followed from those common beliefs also ensured that the community building that paralleled the growth in Charismatic churches was far more extensive than that built by the women's movement, which tended to rely on public funding, and the more libertarian gay community, which did not.

This "para Church" community included a vast network of stores and services providing everything from bookstores to vacations; week-long festivals like Spring Harvest which attracted thousands who went to hear moral crusaders like Clive Calver and Lyndon Bowring; the gospel rocking Greenbelt festival, one of the largest musical events in Britain; dozens of magazine and video publishers; and religious schools and colleges. Christian Unions, dominated by Charismatics, also formed the largest student societies in the public university sector. If we include those who remained in mainstream denominations which also began to experience revival, the

UK's moral minority could draw upon some 300,000 to 400,000 people by the mid 1990s [Gibbs, 1984; Walker, 1988; Forster, 1986; Thompson, 1987; Brierley, 1989;]. From the get-go, this community, and the moral enterprise that emerged from it, attacked mainstream values rather than defended them [see Caulfield, 1975; Whitehouse, 1977; 1982; Johnston, 1976; Thompson, 1987]. The refusal of the panic paradigm to recognize that fact is one of the reasons why the NFOL believed that most sociologists were demonically possessed [Johnston, 1979]; another indication that the entrepreneur's religious outlook was more important than their economic and status dissonance. The failure of anyone, including Tracey and Morrison, to notice let alone explain the reasons why National VALA members' pronounced the acronym VALA '*Valour*' draws attention to just how misleading the paradigm's perspective was.

That pronunciation reflects the fact that Britain's religious moral entrepreneurs' saw themselves as fighting the "good fight" against the forces of darkness irrespective of its political guise. They did so because they believed that God's judgment is collective, effecting whole cities and nations as well as individuals, and that they are duty bound to warn the rest of society that judgment is coming. The trans-historical, and trans-class nature of that religious imperative is evidenced by the way it was also used by the aristocrats and the *grande bourgeoisie* who convinced the king to issue a Royal Proclamation for Preventing and Punishing Immorality and Profaneness back in 1698:

> the open and avowed Practice of Vice might provoke God to withdraw His Mercy and Blessings from us, and instead thereof to inflict heavy and severe judgments [cited in Bristow, 1977: 12–13].

Although Tracey and Morrison stumbled across Valour's belief that the economic crisis after 1966 was a judgment from God for the spread of permissiveness; what they failed to understand was that Valour also believed that "the new morality" was a judgment too: a sign that the UK had failed to repent following its deliverance from the Nazis in the Second World War [Gardner, 1983]. While this belief may appear bizarre to secular readers, that is precisely why secular explanations are futile when it comes to considering the motives behind religious moral crusades.

Valour members mobilized because they were convinced that when warnings and judgments are ignored, they become progressively more severe [Gardner, 1983], eventually leading to the complete collapse of civilization [Hill, 1982]; and that religious imperative makes the concept of symbolic crusade redundant when it comes to motive. Although sociological concepts have their uses, they are no guide to motive, and one also has to be careful when applying them. Far from having to reverse the tide of secularization completely, as long as Christians warn everyone what is going on, they will have *succeeded* as the Book of Ezekiel explains:

The word of the Lord came to me: 'Son of man, speak to your country-men and say to them: "When I bring the sword against a land and the people of the land choose one of their men and make him their watch-man, and he sees the sword coming against the land and blows the trumpet to warn the people, then if anyone hears the trumpet but does not take warning and the sword comes and takes his life, his blood will be on his own head. Since he heard the sound of the trumpet but did not take warning, his blood will be on his own head. But if he had taken warning, he would have saved himself. But if the watchman sees the sword coming and does not blow the trumpet to warn the people and the sword comes and takes the life of one of them, that man will be taken away because of his sin, but I will hold the watchman account-able for his blood [Ezekiel, 33: 1–6].

This 'Ezekiel factor', and supplementary rationales, such as Samuel's mes-sage to Eli that "if the Christian knows of an evil and has the power to restrain it, then he must do so" [cited in Johnston, 1990: 34], negate the need for other explanations.

Likewise, rather than defending bourgeois or capitalist values, Valour promoted the *same* Christian values that one finds behind every other reli-gious moral crusade since the 1700s, as the adverse effects of the free market on morality, the family, and the community became increasingly apparent. Even Mort's [1987] observation that the state was sometimes a subordi-nate or passive partner in moral crusades can be misleading. The crusades from the 1880s frequently involved forcing the Government to enshrine Christian values in law, evidenced by the battle over the age of consent featuring William Stead's famous *The Maiden Tribute of Modern Babylon*. Indeed, the moral values the paradigm erroneously associates with Capital would not have existed without the late Victorian crusades, which *began* with an attack on the upper-class brothels and courtesans' apartments in Maida Vale, London [Pearl, 1955]. By insisting that Valour were helping the state re-impose bourgeois values in the interest of Capital rather than the Christian's own agenda and values [National Deviancy Conference, 1980]; the paradigm not only misrepresents the entrepreneurs' perspective, but demonstrated its failure to understand that finance capital has no inter-est in religious morality, unlike the entrepreneurs, who do [Johnston, 1976; Schaeffer and Koop, 1982; Johnston, 1990].

In any event, the initial problem facing Valour was not secularization, but the need to rouse the wider Christian community out of the compla-cency that the entrepreneurs believed had enabled permissives to gain the upper hand and "normalize sin" [Caulfield, 1975; Whitehouse, 1975; 1977; 1982; 1985; 1993]. As everything that happens from the entrepreneurs' perspective does so for a God given reason, and the final victory is assured at Armageddon, Valour did not have to defeat secularization at all. Their initial target, TV content, was also as instrumental as it was symbolic, because it *was* a major source of secular humanist values thanks to Greene's BBC [Thompson, 1987]. Valour had no need for secular affirmation of their beliefs as symbolic crusade theory also infers that they would, because the 1974 International Congress on World Evangelism provided more than enough validation by also declaring war on secular humanism [Stott, 1984]. Valour did not even target sexual permissiveness because it was the major manifestation of the new morality as Wallis suggested. As pornography and sexual minority practices had yet to be decriminalized, they offered a bastion from which to begin the fight-back against permissiveness [Thompson, 1994a; Whitehouse, 1977: 15–16]. In short, unless one understands and considers the religious moral entrepreneurs' religious perspective, any account of their motives and beliefs will be misleading, as the following history and the next chapter demonstrates.

ENTER RIGHT: EXIT LEFT

During the 1970s, Valour's crusade was reinforced by the rise of the Community Standards Associations (CSAs); local groups of moral entrepreneurs who turned single issue campaigns in urban areas like Portsmouth and Liverpool, and rural counties like Devon and Dorset into permanent organizations. With memberships ranging from a score or so of dedicated activists to hundreds, the CSAs performed three important functions: they supplied platforms for other crusades like Victoria Gillick's campaign against doctors dispensing contraception to underage girls; they mobilized for national rallies and signed national petitions like Valour's 1977 petition in favor of child pornography legislation; and they also organized their own local campaigns against evil influences from abortion to video game violence.

To secure their ends, CSAs held their own meetings and addressed others like PTAs, published newsletters, organized letter write-ins to local newspapers, phone-ins to radio shows, and secured tickets for TV studio debates, as well as lobbied their local councilors and MPs. Local government elections were exploited for propaganda purposes too. Worthing CSA forced all the candidates to declare their positions on moral issues by circulating a moral manifesto to every 47,000 homes in that south coast town during the 1983 election. These activities were very effective. Several local councils prevented cinemas from playing movies like *Caligula* and *The Life of Brian*. Portsmouth schools opened their doors to the local CSA's presentation on *Sex and Personal Relationships* promoting premarital celibacy. The most dramatic intervention, however, was Liverpool CSA Chairman, Charles Oxley's infiltration of the Pedophile Information Exchange to collect the damning evidence that led to that organization's prosecution [Thompson, 1992; *Family Magazine,* 1985: 14–15].

The rise of the CSAs led to a shift in the nature of moral enterprise in the UK. As their Pentecostal and Charismatic activists placed a greater emphasis on spiritual warfare, CSAs began to target Dungeons and Dragons games, "occult stores" selling New Age paraphernalia, and Halloween habits as well as social issues including crime victims, cruelty to animals, domestic violence, care of the elderly, and environmentalism. This move away from Valour's political conservativism became even more pronounced after the NFOL metamorphosed into Christian Action, Research, and Education (CARE), during 1983; a fact that many in the paradigm still have not noticed. From its inception the NFOL had belied the panic paradigm's characterization of contemporary Christianity as reactionary. Although the founder Peter Hill relied on established figures like Whitehouse to speak at the founding rally, the participation of the popular, radical vicar David Huddleston and the Labour party stalwart and life-peer Lord Beswick demonstrated that the NFOL was not so conservative. Five years on, a second Wallis survey of the 1976 NFOL rally found that 62 percent of participants came from the professions, and another 21 percent from the working classes, rather than the old petit-bourgeoisie. They were also young, with 60 percent under thirty years of age, and over half were single. Although Anglicans remained the largest single group, they were vastly outnumbered by those coming from the Baptist, Pentecostal, and Charismatic traditions [Wallis and Bland, 1979]. Once Lyndon Bowring took over from Raymond Johnson, his comprehensive program for reform in the UK using US organizational methods enabled CARE to go on the offensive in a way that Valour never could.

Members were provided with extensive educational material, advice on effective political activism, and a series of immediate initiatives for those employed in the key medical, teaching, and social welfare sectors. Utilizing a mail shot system similar to the US group Focus on the Family, members were inundated with campaign magazines and prayer guides, political briefings and resource packs, campaign posters, leaflets, conference notices, books for background study, and updates on previous initiatives. CARE's comprehensive campaign handbook and briefing papers surpassed anything ever produced by a political party or trade union, including as they did: theological justifications for campaigns, legislation briefings, relevant statistics, practical action check-lists, as well as detailed guides and check-lists covering planning meetings, gaining media contacts, organizing press releases, and the best method to lobby different levels of government. CARE also practiced what it preached, coordinating a nationwide network of Christian welfare programs for the casualties of the permissive society. They were not simply anti-abortion, but provided homes for full-term mothers, and while everyone else was talking about it, they established the first AIDS hospice in the UK. Politically, CARE had far more in common with the Liberal Democratic and New Labour parties than the Conservatives, although they were prepared to work with anyone.

Valour, the CSAs, and CARE's moral enterprise secured numerous new laws, including: the Child Protection Act 1978, which outlawed making child pornography; the Indecent Displays (Control) Act 1981, which curtailed public advertisements containing sexual imagery; Clause 3 of the Local Government (Miscellaneous Provisions) Act 1982, closing 500 sex stores; the Cinematographic Acts 1982 and 1985 eliminating sex cinemas; the Video Recordings Act 1984 which controlled the content of video releases of movies; the new criminal offense of possessing child pornography in the 1988 Criminal Justice Act; and the 1990 Broadcasting Act's provision for a Broadcasting Standards Council. These measures were symbolic only in the sense that they promoted Christian values and declared what was right and wrong. As progressives also wanted more controls on sexual representations and screen violence these measures were not "right-wing" *per se*, and if the law's subject matter make the entrepreneurs look puritanical, that is because the panic paradigm ignored these crusaders' social-economic agenda which also raises questions about the 'New Moral *Right*' label.

Although Whitehouse had always been a Conservative, and the founder of the CSA movement had some friends in the Right-wing Freedom Association; that, as Durham suggested, followed from the older generations' cold war anti-communism [1991: 147, 168–173]. CARE believed that the best means to avoid collective judgment was to place a greater stress on the concept of "stewardship", reflecting the growing communitarian tendency amongst evangelicals in the 1980s [Marshall, 1984], and the allied belief that Christians who ignored their social responsibilities were not serving God's will [Eden, 1993]. Based on the Christian obligations of neighborly love and the dominion mandate found in Genesis 1:26 and 1:28; stewardship offered a solution to the cultural contradictions in capitalism and the growing monopolistic tendency which undermined whole communities as well as the family. Stewardship also led to a greater emphasis on progressive causes including environmentalism, third world debt, human rights, and combating racism [Stott, 1984]. This appealed to the rising generation of Christian activists, raised on a decade of *Buzz* magazine offering a Christian perspective on everything from anorexia nervosa to urban legends [Goddard, 1986], which had became increasing frustrated with Whitehouse's strategy. Contrary to the claims of the CCCS [Hall *et al*, 1984], Valour only formed an alliance with the Conservative party in 1978 when the Conservative Party Lawyers Group, and Ian Lloyd MP in particular, convinced Margaret Thatcher that the party might find more votes in moral issues [McCarthy and Moodie, 1981]. Whatever else preoccupied voters in UK General Elections between 1979 and the early 1990s, some 50 to 60 parliamentary constituencies were always so close to call that it only required a shift in a couple of thousand votes to change hands, giving the crusading Christians a level of power far beyond their numbers. Their votes could flip a seat even though moral issues never reached double digits in those "most important issue" polls held before elections. In return for moral legislation, Mary Whitehouse would tour the marginal constituencies with large Christian communities encouraging them to vote for the most 'moral' candidate, who invariably, though not always was the Conservative party nominee [Whitehouse, 1985]. However, as it became increasing obvious that the Conservative party had no intent of keeping to the deal, let alone addressing the contradictions between its new free market philosophy and the crusading Christians' wider agenda on issues like abortion, embryo research, lotteries and Sunday trading, a rift developed between Valour and CARE, with the CSAs caught in the middle. CARE finally lost patience with Valour's pandering to the Conservatives in return for next to nothing, and Valour was equally horrified that CARE formed an alliance with professional and radical feminists; a subject we cover in the next chapter.

Indeed, far from supporting the Conservative party, CARE had always encouraged supporters to join whatever party they wished and promote themselves rather than rely on party hacks. As well as publishing *Becoming a Local Councilor,* and drawing up a list of key issues,[2] CARE established groups in every constituency as a first step to creating a pool of experienced people with a support base from which future Christian MPs would appear. Failing that, members were to continue to quiz prospective candidates on vital moral issues, and prioritize 'God's manifesto' in order to end the "moral *cul de sac* of party politics" as a prelude to "taking back every area of society" [*CARE News*, 1987 and 1988]. Meanwhile, an allied group, the Jubilee Center, launched an attack on the economics of Thatcherism. The *Family Charter* targeted Thatcher's polices undermining families and communities, promoting instead:

- Tighter controls to stop credit card companies encouraging debt;
- Government investment in the depressed areas laid waste by Thatcherism;
- The introduction of more family orientated personnel policies in industry, starting with more statutory maternity leave;
- Tax breaks, and an increase in government allowances for family careers to avoid impoverishing those caring for elderly relatives;
- Tougher controls on leveraged buyouts and asset stripping to protect family businesses; and
- Opposition to increasing Sunday trading [Family Base, 1987].

While the panic paradigm would no doubt dismiss that as petit-bourgeois because it defended family businesses, progressives also supported issues like tax breaks for domestic bound care givers and more maternity leave, and were also in favor of more regulation on shaper business practices like asset stripping. That is why the *Family Charter* was endorsed by socialist trade unions and the Cooperative party, as well as Christian MPs across party lines. The entrepreneurs' economic perspective like their social program had less to do with class than morality, the general frame in which debates within the Christian community took place [Griffiths, 1982], and led to the calls for the Christian community to become politically active irrespective of party preference [Miller, 1982]. Their major motivation, however, concerned the state of spiritual warfare.

SPIRITUAL WARFARE AND PLURALISM

The increasing number of Charismatics involved in moral enterprise led to a growing emphasis being placed on the state of spiritual warfare in the UK. This warfare occurred on three levels: the *cosmic*—with God and the angels battling out against Satan and his minions; the *earth*—where unbelievers are blinded to the word of God by deceiving ideologies that had to be opposed; and the *personal*—where demons try to entrap the churchgoing Christian in numerous ways, from spreading doubt to sexual temptation. The Christian moral entrepreneurs were primarily concerned with the second level, although that also affected the personal. They saw themselves as opposing the Devil's strategy to:

> undermine values, promote Godless ideologies and moral decay— anything that pollutes the minds and perverts the wills of people. The communications media, school curricula, political and religious bodies, educational institutions, powerful leaders, each can become potential avenues of Satan's influence that touch the life of the believer. This is the predominant form of spiritual warfare we face. It is formidable and subtle. It has potential to seep into the lives of the best of us [White, 1990: 22].

As well as adding another reason to ignore secular explanations, this motivation helps explain the imperative to legislate rather than merely warn secular society of God's displeasure. Instrumental campaigns would help undermine:

> the strong, invisible hold which Satan has in the lives of many, in many of our nation's institutions, and in those clear cut situations where God's influence and law is directly or subtly challenged [*CARE News*, 1987: 23].

Although crusades against evil influences like popular culture gained the attention of the panic paradigm, it never addressed the motivation behind them. From a social-political perspective they were an integral part of defending the family as an institution the basic building block of the religious as well as the wider community [Thompson and Greek, 1992; Ault, 1987]. When it came to spiritual warfare, these campaigns were a counterattack against the efforts of the demonically possessed to ensnare others through culture [Porter, 1986; Johnston, 1976]. Likewise, social policies that undermined Gods design were emerging from institutions dominated by the demonic. The same applied to the demands of social movements and social trends.

The entrepreneurs believed that the family was under demonic attack in the form of the "cult of individualism" and feminism. These tendencies not only undermined God's design for human relationships but were also believed to generate "the cogitative dissonance" that pluralism in values, ideals, roles, and expectations had led to. The answer came in the form of laws reflecting God's design and would restore the concept of parental sacrifice, ensure that motherhood became "the norm, the duty and the path of obedience as well as fulfillment for married women", and enable fathers to reoccupy their divinely ordained patriarchal tasks [Johnston, 1979: 58–60, 85–87, 106]. Laws eliminating abortion, wife battery, child abuse, divorce, desertion, euthanasia, the "glorification of one parent families", promiscuous sex and related diseases, pornography, and welfarism were needed to guide the nonreligious towards God's design through the maze of demonically inspired ideologies that emerged in pluralistic societies. This "declaratory or standard setting function of the law" is vital if one wants to understand what motivated the nature and direction of moral crusades.

The crusaders were not stupid or naïve. They knew that passing legislation would not change anything overnight. Putting laws on the statute book may fulfill their Ezekiel mandate and provide a guide for Godly living, but ultimate success would require convincing the masses to return to God. That required moral enterprise within the Christian community as well as mainstream society, as only a "renewed grip on scripture at every level of our churches" would alert Christians to their God given task of transforming themselves and then society. In order to do that, the entrepreneurs had to grasp a "renewed vision of the spiritual battle, one appropriate for our time", which included recognizing "the demonic control of the unconverted" [Johnston, 1979: 115, 125–135, 144]. Ironically, their success in that area proved to be the entrepreneurs' downfall.

THE FALSE PROPHET

During the early 1990s, Liberal Democrat MP David Alton deluded himself that God was calling him to jump the gun and establish a Christian political party, and he founded the Movement for Christian Democracy to do so. This attracted support from the charismatic leader Gerald Coates, Reading University academic Phillip Giddings, The Relationship Foundation, the Mission in Hounslow Trust, and the Jubilee Center's Michael Schluter, who had turned the concept of stewardship into a specific *Charter of Human Responsibility* with the aim of creating a "free and just society" [*The Christian Democrat*, 1991 and 1995].

The first most people heard about this initiative was when it joined forces with the *Daily Mail* to launch a Video Violence campaign in 1993, trying to exploit the public horror that followed the abduction-murder of toddler James Bulger by two young teens, Venables and Thompson, who had supposedly got the idea from watching *Chucky 3* which *The Sun* promptly invited people to burn [26.11.93:1]. Inevitably denounced as a moral panic by the paradigm, complete with the usual misleading suspects and causes, it amounted to a bid by Alton to put himself at the forefront of Christian politics in the UK, although the paradigm paid no more attention to that than the mainstream media did.

Despite the subsequent lukewarm reception he received in the wider Christian community, Alton proceeded with his plans to form a Christian Democratic party. Having received prophetic insight, Alton was convinced that after the next general election in 1997 the Conservative party divisions over European issues would lead to a minority Labour government introducing proportional representation in return for Liberal-Democrat support, opening the way for guaranteed seats for Christian MPs, dramatically changing the UK's political landscape [Chaplin, 1992; *The Christian Democrat*, 1995]. As it did not work out that way, Alton was clearly not being given his insights by God. When eighteen years of Thatcherism finally came to an end amid exposes of how Conservative MPs had made personal fortunes out of Thatcher's privatization program and their hypercritical sex lives, New Labour romped home without anyone's help; and what happened next dealt a severe blow to religious moral enterprise.

THE END TIME

As the millennium drew ever closer, an increasing number within the Christian community became obsessed with the second coming, foreshadowed in charismatic eschatology by the mobilization of the forces of the anti-Christ. Watching for signs of "the end time" was nothing knew, but the effect was.

During the 1950s, pre-revival fundamentalists had seen the end time signs in communism, the United Nations, and the World Health Organization; all perceived as steps towards the Anti-Christ's one world government [Wood and Hughes, 1984]. During the 1960s and 1970s those fears gained a life of their own, merging with other Christian community legends to produce many of the popular conspiracy theories that captivate the secular as well as the religious today, such as the concept of the New World Order; which makes them an effect rather than the cause of mobilization as one progressive has suggested [Durham, 1991]. Back then the religious community's attention was focused on its immediate rivals including eastern religions which were denounced as cults and the growing New Age movement seen as a manifestation of the occult, as well as the threat to the Christian kingdom by the now independently minded Arab states [Watson, 1989; Miller, 1982]. In the 1980s and 1990s, these end time signs were joined by more personalized forms of Satanic influence like listening to demonic rock music, New Age influences in TV cartoon shows and movies, and the allegations concerning satanic ritual child sexual abuse [Livesey, 1986; Pulling, 1989; Harper, 1990].

While the religious moral entrepreneurs had gained a boost from the rise of Charismatic churches within the Christian community, they also suffered from its downside. The lack of a clear theology [Smail *et al*, 1995], and the nature of the phenomena began to cause disquiet as "Charismania" turned into "charismatic chaos" [Masters and Whitcomb, 1988; Howard, 1997; MacArthur, 1992]. The major complaint was that this tendency was becoming obsessed with proving that God's 'magic' was stronger than its demonically inspired New Age counterpart and in its own way led to "worldliness" and worse. While Health and Wealth ministries promised that God would ensure one secured a tenfold return on one's 'investment' in church giving, 'power evangelists' were putting on spectacular 'signs and wonders' stage shows offering bogus healing and other modern miracles. As the pastors of some Charismatic churches often became more important than God, that led to numerous scandals over their abuse of power [Enroth, 1993; Gilbert, 1993; Parsons, 2000]. As well as create division in the Christian community, when Charismania began to effect secular society it backfired.

The US Charismatic literature flooding UK Christian bookstores made the secular world appear a very unsafe place, not because western economies were increasingly dependent upon market speculation for growth, or because the US neocons' foreign policy was creating another generation of terrorists, but because the Devil was apparently working overtime to target the Church and its children. As a result, the entrepreneurs' traditional targets like abortion and euthanasia [Schaeffer and Koop, 1982], began to lose out to numerous ministries warning of the dangers found in: cartoon shows like *Masters of the Universe* and *Mighty Mouse* because of their alleged occult symbolism [Phillips, 1991]; the barbarization of children through toys like *Care Bears* to *My Little Pony*, with their emphasis on magic, charms and astrology [Phillips, 1986]; anti-religious, "mind manipulation" in public schools [Kjos, 1990]; Halloween festivities opening participants to the occult [Phillips and Robie, 1987]; secret satanic messages in rock music [Larson, 1987; Lawhead, 1989]; as well as the profanity and vulgarity, gratuitous violence, negative role models, and explicit sex in modern comic books [Fulce, 1990]. It was also becoming difficult to see where spirituality ended and superstition began. Deliverance ministries exorcizing one's personal demons became a growth industry [Parker, 1997], despite having already caused disquiet [Perry, 1987]. Peretti's *This Present Darkness* [1986], a fictional account of spiritual warfare in a US town, went through six reprints in the UK in twelve months sensitizing the Christian community to immanent demonic attack. David Porter beat the Americans at their own game when it came to the exposing the demonic doorways in home computers [1986], before divulging that demons were hiding in UK toy boxes too [1989].

As the millennium drew ever closer, these tendencies ensured that fewer Christians mobilized around CARE's new progressive agenda concerning racism, unemployment, and homelessness, not because the Christian community was Right-wing, but because demons were apparently easier to deal with individually than collectively, and that led to double trouble. The obsession with satanic signs helped generate the infamous satanic abuse allegations supposed to offer the secular evidence to convince even the most skeptical that the end-times were upon us. Although the crusade owed as much to the fundamentalist feminists as it did to the Christian community (as we will show in Chapter 6), it was the religious community that was demonized by the media when the allegations rapidly collapsed in the UK during 1991. As the revival that had led to great optimism [Wright, 1986] petered out, evidenced by the paltry 269 converts following a major drive by Pentecostal churches in 1994 [Eden, 1993; Howard, 1997: 129 and 131], more and more Christians took the first plane to Toronto, Canada in their desire to be part of the bizarre scenes in the local Vineyard church. Known as the Toronto Blessing, everyone involved hoped it would herald the start of the world wide religious revival that they assumed would preceded the millennium [*Christian Democrat*, 1995: 16], and the Second Coming. At the same time that Jean La Fontaine's report exposed satanic abuse for the fraud that it was in 1994 [La Fontaine, 1998], no fewer than 30,000 credit card Charismatics turned their back on social action in their determination to get some of God's grace in Toronto for themselves [Roberts, 1994]. The moral entrepreneurs' support base began to shrink, and their campaigns dried up almost as fast as their funding. The emphasis upon spiritual warfare that had helped create the most effective moral crusade in the UK in almost a century ultimately helped undermined it.

WITCH HUNTS AND MORAL PANIC

The panic paradigm's failure to cover and accommodate the changing nature of Britain's moral minority and the role of spiritual warfare is indicative of its lack of research into the world of moral enterprise in general. That weakness is caused and compounded by its reliance on a direct relationship between social strain and the reaction that follows horror-headlines, which it takes as given, rather than explores and explains. As society is in a constant state of flux, these "sudden" reactions are more often a function of the author's failure to cover the history behind the reaction. This propensity can be traced back to Cohen's reliance on Erikson's *Wayward Puritans* [1966], which never justified the claim that boundary crises generate the deviants whose demonization and punishment offered the means to restore societal values.

Although the Massachusetts Bay Colony offered a test for Durkheim's observations about the role of crime in creating social solidarity due to its relative isolation and rich documentation [Erikson, 1966:4], that test should never have applied to non-criminalized deviancy because with rare exceptions, like wearing one's hair long, deviancy in New England was also a crime [Wertenbaker, 1945: 174–176]. Even if that were not the case, the examples offered by Erikson had far less to do with the collective conscience of the community, than what worried and concerned the ministers in what was a very hierarchical society [Wertenbaker, 1945; Bercovitch, 1980]. Instead of offering three societal-wide boundary crises to consider, Erickson merely charted how the same fears amongst the ministers continued to grow as their vision inevitably fell foul of the normal vagaries of economic and social developments. There was nothing sudden, dramatic, or unusual about each new challenge to their authority, and there was no link between the alleged 'social strain' and the events that occurred. That misnomer can be attributed to the way Erickson made no secret of having "rearranged" the evidence to fit "the logic" of his "approach", and his lack of understanding about the nature of the religious belief system he was dealing with [Erikson, 1966, vi and x].

BOUNDARY CRISES OR MORAL PANIC?

Theoretically, boundary crises are *not* so much a feature of moral panic as the same thing. According to Erickson, when deviancy threatened to undermine part of a society's traditional boundary network, and the threat had been defined, the reaction led to an amplification of deviancy which was perceived as "something akin to a crime wave". The community then censored the behavior, which may have been present but had not attracted any attention before, and did so by taking "emergency measures". The severity of the crime wave was not "measured by the number of deviant offenders" but the reaction: the "rash of publicity, a moment of excitement and alarm, and a feeling that something needs to be done" [1966: 24—27, 69–70]. As all Cohen did with that description was drop the "New" in England, turn the 1690s into the 1960s, and add the proposition that the perception of the threat did increase, it is no surprise that Erikson's account of the Antinomian controversy of 1636, the persecution of the Quakers in the 1650s, and the Salem Village witch-hunt during 1692 was a portent of the failings of the panic paradigm. Instead of being offered any evidence of widespread public concern, we are merely presented with the Calvinist ministers' escalating fears that their original mission, running a community on Biblical guidelines and fulfilling their end time mandate, was being undermined by the vagaries of life in general and the values generated by commerce and trade in particular.

The Puritans who settled in New England to establish their Community of Saints not only believed that they were "the elect" destined for heaven, but that they had been chosen by God to prove that a society could be run on Biblical lines. They were convinced that their inevitable success would ensure that their theology was accepted as the true one. Palming off that belief as the social conscience of the colony, when the ministers and elite only amounted to ten percent of the population and acted like the dictatorial ruling clique that they were, ensured Erickson's account was fatally flawed throughout [1966: 72]. The fear of God's wrath on the community led the ministers to try and enforce their will through barbaric forms of social control: the stocks or whippings for first offenses; branding and maiming for the second; and hanging for the third. Their plan, however, was under threat from the very beginning. Having been deceptive, they were constantly wary that the Crown could take away the charter it had granted for another part of the continent, and as the rapid increase in population over the first two decades undermined the village system on which the ministers' social control depended, their original fear was constantly being enhanced by others. High status newcomers came to resent the elect's power as much as indentured servants with no stake in the minister's religious vision, and rule breaking steadily increased. Even God's blessings, in the form of commerce and trade, worked against the elect. It led to divisions amongst the elite in the major towns as well as the importation of evil influences through the ports. As the magistrates' refused to impose the strictest penalties, fining rule breakers to fund local governance, an increasing number of colonists stopped following the rules. Consequently, the minister's moral boundary crisis was caused by the community and that included a growing number of disputes between property owners concerning where their boundary ended and their neighbors' begun. What is more, whenever the ministers tried to reinforce their power, the deviants had a habit of turning the table and undermining Erickson's thesis, despite all his "rearranging".

For example, although the Antinomian crisis emerged while the elite was under increasing pressure to introduce a secular legal code and a bill of rights as Erickson noted, that had nothing to do with the threat posed by Ms. Hutchinson's allegations that the ministers were backsliding which galvanized the Boston elite. As Hutchinson was theologically correct in her criticism, it was the ministers who were deviating from the original mission rather than Hutchinson as Erickson contends. Although the ministers responded to being voted from the pulpits by Hutchinson's supporters with martial law, using the clergy dominated general court to declare her supporters guilty of sedition, unseating Governor Vane for supporting freedom of speech, and putting Hutchinson through two show trials, that did not help. As other ministers refused to impose the list of heresies drawn up by the synod precisely because they feared that it would generate more disputes, and Boston developed a reputation for independent thought, the boundary under threat in Erickson's account was further undermined rather than restored [Campbell, 2004].

What is more, by dismissing the religious nature of the court battles as an exercise in theological hair-splitting, which the majority of the population did not understand, Erickson appears oblivious to how that demonstrates the Antinomian controversy was an internal dispute amongst the elite rather than an example of societal wide boundary crisis [Erikson, 1966: 74–81; 108]. Our interpretation is reinforced by the fact that Hutchinson's complaints followed closely behind those of the Cambridge minister Thomas Hooker who founded Connecticut because of his objections to the other ministers' arcane authority and restriction of suffrage, and Salem's Roger Williams who founded Providence rather than suffer religious intolerance and his fellow ministers' worldly attitudes. The community had no say in those disputes outcomes either.

MINISTERS 0–DEVIANTS 2

According to Erickson, the second boundary crisis, the Quaker invasion appeared because of death of the original leaders, dwindling immigration, and the threat was external rather than internal [Erikson, 1966: 109–110]. However, the lack of an obvious link between those "causes" and the nature of the deviancy displayed reflects the way Erikson had to "rearrange" the chronology of the colony to create the crisis. The refusal of the magistrates to impose the ministers' religious code meant that the veneration of the original leadership amounted to an attempt by the ministers to enhance their dwindling status. Towns had been passing laws against unsanctified immigrants since 1637, and Governor Bradford had constantly complained about the quality of the profligate sons of the UK middle-classes being dumped in the colony as well as the "untoward" servants being brought over. By the time the Quakers turned up, every town was trying to steal each others' blacksmiths, millers, and physicians, who like good servants, apprentices, and journeymen were in short supply because immigration had been curtailed by the civil war in the UK, which posed another threat to the ministers that Erickson ignored. If the parliamentarians defeated the king's forces, they would be able to set up a rival "experiment" to that in New England. Meanwhile, the number of those real boundary disputes increased and no one was seeking the advice of the ministers about what to do about that [Wertenbaker, 1945: 68–71 and 169]. Moreover, far from putting pressure on the community, Quakerism offered the non-elect a means of salvation.

Erikson's account of the effects of this second crisis is even more strained than his causes. First, Erikson's insistence that the persecution of the Quakers' proselytizing was "quite out of proportion to danger that it actually posed" rests upon numbers rather than the potential destabilizing effect of allowing religious pluralism, effectively contradicting his own definition [1966: 108]. Although small in numbers, the missionaries kept returning after deportation, deliberately courting the martyrdom that the ministers wished to avoid because back then dying for ones faith was widely seen as proving its validity, and encouraged conversion. Converts also suffered, and in greater numbers too, because the constables enjoyed the house raids, confiscations, public floggings, and mutilations ordered by the ministers. Despite that, the end result was a disaster, despite taking some time. Charles II revoked the colony's charter, imposed a new governor, *and* religious freedom all of which ensuring that the boundary transgressed was never restored [Erikson, 1966: 124 and 135]. What is more, you can draw a direct link between the ministers' awareness of that fact and the third crisis.

SALEM MYTHS

Although the events in Salem Village is the nearest Erikson gets to offering a boundary crisis generating deviance, the reason for that completely undermines this foundation stone of moral panic. Erickson began by offering his readers examples of the increasing number of dreadful prophesies appearing in New England sermons after the intervention of the king as evidence of a new social strain [1966: 137]. He then presents the previous challenges to the ministers' power and the terrestrial boundary disputes as if they were a recent development in order to support his claim that they were now forcing 'society' to cast around for a new mission to replace the original one. Finally, he tells his readers that this new mission consisted of the effort to defeat a symbolic wilderness in the same way that the colonizers' had originally set themselves the task of overcoming the geographical wilderness:

> the character of this wilderness was unlike anything the first settlers had ever seen, for its dense forests had become a jungle of mythical beasts and its skies were thick with flying spirits. In a sense, the Puritan community had helped mark its location in space by keeping close watch on the wilderness surrounding it on all sides; and now the visible traces of that wilderness had receded out of sight; the settlers invented a new one by finding the shapes of the forest in the middle of the community itself [1966: 157].

In plain English, Erickson was arguing that the community having tamed Satan's domain—in the form of indigenous 'savages', weird looking animals that did not exist in Europe, and heretics like Hutchinson—now combined to fight an imaginary threat posed by "demons and incubi, specters and evil spirits" as a means to reinvent their identity and mission [1966: 158].

The obvious problem with that explanation is that it does not recognize that the increasing references to spiritual demons in New England sermons reflected the ministers' desperate attempts to frighten the community back to the fold by invoking the threat of the end time. They did so because they were fearful that unless they could reverse the increasing worldly course the colony had taken, God was going to judge *them*. What is more, Erickson's grade school account of the subsequent witch hunt which supposedly demonstrates how the deviants were complicit in the crisis by acting out their assigned role, providing the model for moral panic adopted by Cohen, is completely erroneous.

According to Erickson, a group of girls in the Salem Village minister's house were introduced to the demonic arts by Tituba their black slave, and subsequently fell about screaming and exhibiting convulsions. Once the doctor concluded that they were bewitched, the girls began to reveal their tormenters. When Tituba then confessed and named others, the girls quickly concurred and were believed because their afflictions were seen as signs of malfeasance. Some of the accused then began to name relatives in a desperate effort to deflect attention from themselves, before the girls began to denounce respectable people whom they had never met in places they had never been to. Although the first half-dozen witches were hung, when the allegations went up the social ladder reaching Samuel Willard, the President of Harvard, the magistrates brought the allegations to an end [Erickson, 1966: 141–152]. The mutual dependency between the deviants and those who persecuted them is supposedly demonstrated by Cotton Mather's observation that "the witches who terrorised the countryside were really very similar to the honest men who persecuted them" [cited in Erickson, 1966: 21], the fact that many of the accused not only made voluntary confessions, and their description of the coven paralleled the organization of the congregational church. Erickson then generously admits that he was bemused that this incident occurred somewhat late in the century, that he was nonplussed that the colony had not shown much interest in witches before, and that given the extent of the accusations, he could not understand why the magistrates did not act as if a state of emergency existed [1966: 154–155]. He concludes by arguing that no other form of crime in history has been a better index of social disruption and change [Erickson, 1966: 153]. Unfortunately for Erickson and the panic paradigm, the historical record suggests otherwise.

REALITY CHECK

Fear of a failed mission had sent the ministers rather than society looking for devils, and there is nothing mutual about confessing during torture and telling one's inquisitors what they want to hear. While Salem Village, like satanic abuse in our own time, *is* a perfect example of how deviants can be manufactured; the way it occurred completely undermines the moral panic process because Salem involved false allegations by several interested parties for very particular ends.

First, the girls made their allegations to avoid personal punishment, because they had been engaging in divination, (fortunetelling), a serious sin in Puritan New England, and had done so without any help from Tituba. Second, the allegations began the moment a former minister pointed out to Rev. Parris, whose daughter was a ringleader, that the girls had committed a crime *unless* they had been bewitched. Determined to avoid the consequences of that, the Rev. Parris secured the agreement of the local doctor that the girls had indeed been bewitched and exploited his position as pastor to encourage his congregation to unite against the unknown (sic) menace within their community, reminding them as he did so of Calvin's appeal that the preservation of the church was worth a hundred innocent lives if need be. Third, the Putnam family took over the allegations once the girls had run out of the usual suspects like beggars, whores, and known diviners, and not surprisingly added anyone that they did not like to the list. For example, although Sarah Osborne had been subject to gossip about fornicating with her second husband before they were married, the reason she was targeted was that the marriage took her inheritance outside the Putnam extended family. Indeed, more than half of the accused were known to have cross swords with the vengeful Putnams in the past; the biggest group of offenders being friends of the Porter family who invoked envy because they had preferred to build their family fortune rather than get involved in village politics and dissipate their resources as the Putnams had done. That is why Rebecca Nurse, whose husband had been involved in a terrestrial boundary dispute with the Putnams and had joined the Porters' opposition to the Putnam's scheme to found the village church, was named. The fourth interested party were the accused who confessed and named others in the hope of saving their own skins, which they could do because only those denying the allegations were hung [Hall, 1999; Boyer and Nissenbaum, 1974]. The final party to the allegations was none other than Cotton Mather himself.

Far from creating a new mission, Cotton Mather was engaged in moral enterprise to save the old; invoking end time demons to encourage the masses to repent. The school system was falling apart; teens were ignoring the law "playing, uncivil walking, drinking and travelling from town to town", adult women were showing too much flesh on their forearms, and the wealthier wives of Boston were adding lace or silver thread to their dresses and hat bands [Wertenbaker, 1945: 95–97, 162–167]. The law forbidding the drinking of toasts was widely disregarded; and immodest dress, rude and lewd behavior could be seen in the sea towns full of foreign sailors. The synod had been bemoaning the extent of Sabbath breaking as far back as 1679. Indeed, the fact that it had become obvious that the original mission was falling apart probably explains why

Wigglesworth's *The Day of Doom* had become a best seller amongst the elite [Wertenbaker, 1945: 165–180].

Consequently, four years before the Salem Village episode, when Mather was called in to uncover the source of possession in the four children of the Goodwin family in Boston, and uncovered the family's Irish washerwoman had a set of poppets,[3] he immediately published *Memorable Providences* to convince the skeptical public that witches were real, only to discover that even the elite did not care. Mather claimed that some even advised him that the problem could be solved by recourse to white magic! Having failed with the Goodwin incident, when Mather heard about Salem Village he was determined to exploit it to the full. He placed three of his acolytes on the five-judge panel, which then admitted spectral evidence in court. This involved the claim that the accused person's spirit, *spectre,* appeared to their accusers in a dream or vision to negate the accused person's alibi that they were elsewhere, which is why no other court accepted this form of evidence. When the jury acquitted Rebecca Nurse, the judges ordered them to deliberate again until they changed their minds. Once Mather had decided that the former minister was the ringleader, George Burroughs was subsequently accused too. When Burroughs was able to recite the Lord's Prayer on the gallows without a mistake, a clear sign he could not be a witch, it was Mather who insisted that the execution go ahead anyway [Wertenbaker, 1947: 269–290]. That history, Erickson's decontextualized use of texts like Mather's *Wonders of the Invisible World* as evidence for the boundary crisis, and the erroneous claim that no witch craze had appeared before when one had in Hartford, Connecticut, reveals how far Erickson's model was based on misnomers. The real reason why there were so few *successful* cases of witchcraft before Salem village was that they tended to be brought to court by the *accused,* who sought judgments against the gossips spreading falsehoods. As most New England magistrates followed the law, they had refused to accept the spectral evidence on which the gossip relied, and that ensured that most "witches" put to death before Salem Village were those like Mary Johnson who had committed a real crime like murdering a child [Hall, 1999: 24]. Otherwise, although the authorities were reluctant to trawl over the cause of the tragedy for fear of causing further problems, far from restore any boundary, the minister's influence dissipated even faster than before.

SO MUCH FOR THEORY

Rather than demonstrate that societal wide boundary crises generate the deviants whose punishment reinforces the collective conscience of society, Erikson's examples suggest the opposite. The deviants were upholding the boundary in the first crisis, they secured their aims in the second, and the boundary fell apart after the third. These crises also demonstrate that social control is far more important than any concern about common values when dealing with deviants. Hutchinson's criticisms were subdued by the intervention of the militia, a *new* set of backdated rules, and show trials. Those offering the Quaker missionaries shelter were dragged around half-a-dozen local towns, flogged at each one, and had their property confiscated. The members of Salem Village accused of witchcraft were subjected to torture which killed one, and if they refused to confess they were hung. Even then, these measures did not work. The ministers dare not impose the new rules they had used to defeat Hutchinson, the Quakers continued to secure converts, and a pamphlet war over the lessons to be learnt from Salem Village appeared, undermining the ministers' influence even further. In short, without force behind them, the "dominant values" were as meaningless 300 years ago as they are today. If a collective conscience did not exist in New England, it certainly was not going to exist in the UK during the swinging sixties, and definitely not in the polarizing class war of the 1970s. On the contrary, Cotton Mather's recourse to moral enterprise, exploiting the problem in Salem Village to overcome the fact that even the elect did not worry about witchcraft, justifies drawing a completely different set of conclusions from those arrived at by Erickson's omissions and his manipulation of history.

Like Cotton Mather; Valour, the CSAs and CARE mobilized because society did not share their values, and those values concerned spiritual warfare and God's judgment rather than any economic anxiety.[4] The reason why the seminal moral panic case studies argued otherwise is that their authors like Erickson "rearranged" the evidence to suit their purpose, and ignored the entrepreneurs' own motivation for mobilization. The panic paradigm has done little else ever since. When the evidence does not fit, it omits it and manipulates what remains to fit its existing theoretical convictions. In contemporary societies where one social group's norms are another social group's deviance, making conflict between them inevitable, in order to label something deviant, someone not only has to publicize it, but create a justification to convince enough social groups, interested agencies, and politicians that they would also gain if the deviancy was curtailed. If a social group suffers as a result, that is because it has not secured enough allies. So, for example, teen crime attracts attention because it is against most peoples' interests, abortion rights remain a battle ground because those on opposite sides cancel each other out, and Marijuana smoking in the US is still illegal in most states because it still upsets enough government agencies whose existence depends upon the war on drugs, and worries the legal drink and drug companies who would lose out if the weed became widely available.

This facet of contemporary society becomes apparent if you consider why it is that you cannot call someone "nigger", "queer", or "slut" without becoming a public pariah, but you can call people "trailer park trash" as much as you like. That reflects the fact that blacks, women, and gays are not so 'oppressed' as progressives contend, and that the balance of power between social groups does not conform to the model of society promoted by the panic paradigm. Something does not "add up". There is a disparity between "common values" and progressives' account of them. This can only be resolved if one recognizes that "hate speech" conventions reflect the fact progressive moral enterprise has had some success, because "common values" are those imposed upon society by whichever coalition of groups and interests exhibits the most power at the time, even though none of the groups involved have secured its complete agenda. As rednecks have little power, and no one wishes to associate with them apart from Jerry Springer, they will continue to suffer from hate speech for some considerable time to come.

In order to understand this feature of contemporary society and the failure of the panic paradigm to reflect this social reality, we devote the next two chapters to various examples of social group value conflict involving different levels of power in order to explore the world of progressive moral enterprise ignored by the panic paradigm.

5   A Very Nasty Business

Martin Barker's account of the panic covering new wave Italian and US horror movies available for daily rental on videotape in 1983 is a milestone in the moral panic myth in more ways than one [1984b]. Written in a simple style, on a familiar subject, its attack on Thatcherism and Mary Whitehouse sold the concept of moral panic and its political perspective to a non academic audience which subsequently associated panic with irrational Right-wing politics and moral crusades; despite grossly misleading its readership.

According to Barker, the panic which followed *The Daily Mail's* horror-headlines about the video's gory content, the moral barricades built by the Parliamentary Video Inquiry (PVI) [Barlow and Hill, 1985], and the MPs subsequent "emergency measure" drastically increased censorship, but the panic had less to do with children's access to the tapes than the "particular conception of the family ideal" that the newspaper promoted to mask the failure of the government's law and order policy [1984b: 3]. The reality behind the newspapers' role point to very different conclusions, and questions the paradigm's myth of Thatcherism, "emergency measures", its ability to deal with the role of Capital, and its approach to social value conflict in the UK between 1980 and 1994. If anyone was panicking it was Barker, with his disproportionate fears about the power and effects of "right-wing moralism" [Barker, 1984b: 6]. Contrary to Barker's account the papers horror-headlines about young children watching adult videos did not appear from nowhere. They were the last step in a two-year campaign by the Christian moral entrepreneurs who had added videos to their 20-year crusade against pornography, as this local Community Standards Association (CSA) recruitment flyer reveals:

> Much more radical legislation will be require if the perverse, sadistic, and bestial is to be dealt with, in magazines, on video tapes and in the cinema [Cornish Community Standards Association, 1982: 3].

The bill was not an emergency measure in response to *The Daily Mail's* headlines. The paper was publicizing the entrepreneurs' public rationales for a bill that had *already* been announced and amounted to a *quid pro quo,* payback from the Conservative party for the Christian community's votes during the 1983 General Election. However, although the entrepreneurs had targeted this new technology because it made their previous efforts to control popular culture redundant [Thompson, 1994a], the Video Recordings Act that emerged was more concerned with resolving the fears within the film and TV industries that video would drastically undermine their profits, and the moral entrepreneurs did not get what they wanted.

Imports of videocassette recorders had increased from 12,000 to 2.5 million per year between 1976 and 1982, as the lack of 24-hour and cable TV in the UK made it the largest per capita market in the world. This phenomenal growth in hardware was paralleled by an explosion in rental outlets, from dedicated stores to gas stations, offering movies before general release, uncensored versions of those that had been released, and many never seen in the UK before. While the moral entrepreneurs were worried about the public using VCRs to copy and distribute video versions of old European 8mm and US 16 mm porn movies, making existing controls useless; the corporate world was more concerned about declining cinema attendance, the free market in video rentals which they did not control, and the perceived threat to TV ratings. Consequently, while *The Daily Mail* was playing the protection of children 'card' that the entrepreneurs had used since 1978 to circumvent reservations about censoring adult pleasures, it had nothing to do with deflecting attention from law and order policies. Another aspect of the 'panic' not covered by Barker was that it led to the revival of the religious-feminist-progressive alliance of yesteryear.

In order to demonstrate all this, and consider why these issues were ignored by the paradigm we have to return to the myth of the strong state. It will take some time to return to the horror-headlines about gory videos, but when we do, it will be apparent how misleading the panic paradigm is when it comes to social group value conflict and the exercise of power.

PERMISSIVENESS PORTSMOUTH

Between November 1970 and June 1971, when the paradigm insists that the strong state was engaged in a moralistic backlash against permissiveness, Portsmouth City Council (PCC) discovered that it was powerless to stop the burgeoning number of sex stores catering to the permissive public despite complaints about their window displays and "immoral influence" from the local Christian community [PCC. File 1/27 1970].[1] Although the Fire Services & Public Control Committee, a body with its origins in the Watch Committee of yesteryear, automatically sided with the complainants against the five stores; council officers warned the committee that they could do nothing because of "the present state of the law and public acceptance" [Personal Communication, Officer Dunn to Cllr. S.A. Fiddy, nd]. Undeterred, the council lobbied the Association of Municipal Councils (AMC) to put pressure on the Conservative government, only to discover that the AMC had already tried to secure a change in planning law and a new one covering indecent displays to prevent "the corruption of youth" following complaints from other councils. However, these overtures had already been dismissed by the Minister for the Environment (DOE), Mr. Heseltine because "the current climate of public opinion would not support more censorship" [1/27 LFWB/AFB1 13.1.71; F.S. & P.C.C. 23.2.71. min. 223]. The mayor wrote personal letters to the couple-of-dozen complainants promising to continue to lobby the Government and to work with the city's PD which had already prosecuted one store for breaking the obscenity laws [P.C.C. 1/27 AJD/B; P.C.C. 1/27 AJD/JM/36/18]; though when two council officers attended the next AMC law committee meeting, they discovered that Heseltine had already excluded sex stores from his new planning law too, on the grounds that the stores were a moral issue. The local MPs who had also been active then informed the council that a recent parliamentary motion and a bill had merely revealed "the deep division" between the pro and anti-censorship forces in Parliament, making another attempt pointless [P.C.C. 1/27; letter 23rd July]. As the AMC had given up the fight, Portsmouth City Council did likewise [F.S. & P.C.C. min 200 1972].

When the Portsmouth public got its chance to demonstrate what it thought about permissiveness, the result undermines the CCCS account of the strong state as well. The jury's "not guilty" verdict during the trial of *His & Hers*, a local contact magazine prosecuted for conspiracy to debauch and corrupt morals by carrying advertisements from sexual minorities demonstrated that they did not agree with the judge that these magazines threatened the institution of marriage and civilized society. As that verdict reflected the trend across the country at the time [Whitehouse, 1977: 147]; the failure to reign in the sex stores and the trial demonstrate that the morality of the strong state was also a myth. Ironically, when everything *appeared* to have changed ten years later, and a 'panic' over sex stores appeared, the paradigm's politics ensured that it was ignored.

THE MISSING PORN STORE PANIC

In February 1981, horror-headlines in *The Times* drew attention to a sex store protest in Barnsley provoked by a "loophole in the planning law" that had turned violent: the roof had been ripped off and threatening phone calls made [10.2.1981]. That protest was merely one of a hundred others attracting local horror-headlines:

> Demo At Sex Shop (Bristol *Evening Post*); Anti-Porn Protesters Plan Sex Shop Demo (Burnley *Evening Standard*); Sex Shop Protest—No, No, No! Says Town (*South Avon Mercury,* Clevedon); Sex Shop Vigil Plan (*Western Mercury*); Group Mount Picket On Porn Shops (Bristol

Evening Star); Churchman In Anti Porn Action Against Sex Shop, Fears Of Rape If Shop Opens (Bedford *Times*); An Emphatic Rejection Of Sex Shops (St. Ives *Times*); Sex Shop Customers Are Filmed (Shropshire *Star*); Spies Film Sex Shop (Kent *Evening Post*); Nothing Good About This Idea, City Sex Shop Not Wanted (Exeter *Express & Echo*); Council Of Churches Join The Protest Against Sex Shop, and Sex Shop—A Step Backwards (Hitchen *Comet*); Stop Sex Shop Plea (Grimsby *Evening Telegraph.*); Schools Plea To Close Sex Shop (Sandwell *Mail*); Churches Attack Sex Shop Plan (Wolverhampton *Express & Star*); Thanks, But No Thanks, Pornography Dangerous (Dudley *Herald*); Degrading To Have Sex Shop In Town (Lancashire *Evening Telegraph.*); Sex Shop Protests (Birmingham *Post*); Call For Sex Shop Curbs (Bristol *Evening Post*); Are These Shops Of Any Real Value? (Staines & Egham *News*); Sex Shop Bid Gets The Boot, City Gives Sex Shop The Thumbs Down (Lichfield *Mercury*); War On Porn Hots Up (Southampton *Evening Echo*); "No" To Sex Shop (Haverhill *Echo*); City Leaders Say "No" To Sex Shop (Salisbury *Journal*); Stop Spread Of Sex Shops Say Women (Shropshire *Star*); Sex Shops The Target As Porn Storm Grows (*Press & Journal*: Aberdeen); Fury Grows In Sex Shop Row (Romford & Havering *Observer*); Liberals Press For Curbs On Sex Shops, MP Joins Move To Block Sex Shop (Colchester *Evening Gazette*); Unsavory Shop Will Degrade, Protect The Vulnerable (*East Essex Gazette.*) Petition Against Sex Shop, Sex Shop Plan Comes Under Fire (Maldon & Brunham *Standard*); We Must Do Our Best To Prevent It (*East Essex Gazette*); Sex Shops Exploit Females, Honour Must Be Restored, Avoiding Sex Side Of Street (Colchester *Evening Gazette*); Sabotage Attempt On Butt Rd. Sex Shop (Essex *City Standard*); The Sex Shop Protesters Go To Whitehall, Partial Control Is Not Enough, Pickets In For a Long Hot Summer, Pickets To Stay Until Sex Shop Is Closed (Sale *Guardian*); War Hots Up On Sex Shops (Kent *Evening Post*); No Call For Sex Shops In Our City (Kentish *Gazette.*); Council Supports Porn Pickets (Kent *Messenger*); Sex Shop Plans In Bad Taste (Lytham St. Anne's *Express*); Storm Rages Over Sex Shop Cinema (Lancashire Evening *Telegraph.*); Women Porno Protesters Defy The Boo-Boys, Sex Shops Must Be Closed—Council Boss (Lancashire *Evening Post*); Battling Gran In Fight Against Porn (Lytham St. Anne's *Express*); Sex Shop Now—Change The Law (*South East London Mercury*); Sort Out This Porn Shop Mess Says MP (*Sunday Mail* Glasgow); Sex Shop? No No No (Surrey *Daily Advertiser*); Help Stop Sex Shops (Surrey *Comet*); Churchman Rap Sex Shop Plan, Degrading To Women and to Family Life (Camberley *News*); Residents Anger At "Illegal" Sex Shop, Dean's Attack On Sex Shop (Surrey *Comet*); Tunwell Slams Plan For Town Centre Sex Shop (Eastbourne *Gazette*); Anti Sex Shop Campaign. Now 6000 Say: Close It (Eastbourne *Herald Chronicle*); Clergy's Reasons For Porno Protest (Yorkshire *Post*); No

Sex Shop Please—This Is Guildford (Surrey *Daily Advertiser*); Profitable Does Not Mean Acceptable (Kent *Evening Post*); Sex Shop Firm Drops Plan After Protests (Wolverhampton *Express*); Over 6,000 Sign Against A Sex Shop In Clacton (*East Essex Gazette*) [extract from Nationwide Festival Of Light, 1981].

The "loophole" referenced in *The Times* concerned the failure of Heseltine's 1971 Town and Country Planning Act to cover sex stores. The Act had given every building in Britain a Use Class Order that could not be changed without obtaining planning permission. Residential property could not be converted into offices or *vice versa*; but if the building had a retail order, you could change the product being sold without planning permission, enabling anyone to buy or lease retail premises and reopen as a sex store. Some sex stores had opened in buildings without the appropriate order and were illegal; but most had not. Although the Government preferred a pilot program licensing sex stores in London's Soho, when Mr. Raison introduced the Local Government (Miscellaneous Provisions) Bill in the House of Commons on 25 November 1981, MP after MP wanted to know why sex stores were not included along with the pop festivals, wrestling exhibitions, street trading, tattoo parlors, ear piercing, electrolysis facilities, and acupuncture services that would now require a special license.

Michael Neubert led the revolt. Concentrating on Soho when sex stores selling offensive material were springing up everywhere made no sense. The government should stop the buck passing between the DOE and the Home Office and give the stores their own Use Class Order as well as require a license. Apart from Matthew Parris, the Conservative party's libertarian, every MP backed Neubert's suggestion. Tony Durant, for example, highlighted the lack of action following previous complaints that he believed reflecting the "widespread concern" across the country. Rodger Moate emphasized the need to give local authorities the power to make the final decision regarding any sex stores in their area. Gordon Oaks summed up the mood. As so many MPs demanded a change in the law, the Government could not say "no", especially as the stores were invading main streets and could be seen by children. His opinion carried more weight because he was also the Vice President of the Association of County Councils (ACC) [Hansard, HOC: 25.11.81: Col. 923–969].[2] The deputy minister, Giles Shaw rigorously defended the pilot program, yet within a week the government *really* did change its mind and introduced a separate clause imposing a license provision on sex stores, which subsequently put over 500 out of business.

PLASTIC PANICS

The furor over sex stores demonstrates how easy it is to construct a moral panic. The violent Barnsley picket could become the precipitating event;

the increase in the number of highly visible stores in spite of the moral barricades, the amplification of deviancy; the subsequent police raids, the morality play; the new clause following the MPs revolt, the emergency measure; and the closure of 500 stores, the restoration of societal values under strain from permissiveness. For once, the local protests would also supply proof that a panicking public existed. Yet no one has ever claimed that the public was panicking about sex stores, because academics accredited their closure to feminism [Manchester, 1986], and progressive causes cannot be moral panics.

As we have explained elsewhere, the sex store clause was merely one of several pieces of legislation secured by Britain's moral minority during the 1980s after two decades of frustration [Thompson, 1994a]. Individual moral entrepreneurs had tried to limit the effects of the 1959 Obscene Publications Act since its inception. They were appalled that had led to a dramatic growth in heterosexual pin-up magazines and cheap paperbacks. Despite having joined the fight in 1964, Valour had little effect. Valour's attempt to stop the promotion of minority sexual practices in stage shows, sex cinemas, and in the counterculture between 1969 and 1977 was no more successful. Despite the occasional sensational victory that the paradigm parades as typical to create its myth of the strong state, Valour's campaign was ailing and failing until Whitehouse secured the passage of the Protection of Children Act in 1978 which opened the way for the successful third phase of their crusade against the 1959 Act by making an alliance with Thatcher and playing the protection of children 'card'. This led to several pieces of legislation, although not—as critics contend—to defeating the recommendations of the Williams Committee, one of those Royal Commissions that tended to lead to permissive legislation [Thompson, 1994a].

Established in 1977 under the chairmanship of Bernard Williams, precisely because there was no consensus on porn, the committee provoked "the great pornography debate", which produced a steady stream of news stories, editorials, general articles, feature articles, and comment in columns, book reviews, and letters to the editor from academics, medics, and Christians over the committee's lifetime. The level of interest is indicated by the fact that when Parliament finally considered a Conspiracy bill during May 1977, *The Times* report highlighted the Attorney General's remarks about sex cinema clubs in Soho rather than what he said about conspiracy! Fearing the worst case scenario, Valour launched their 1977–78 ABUSE campaign to outlaw the making of child pornography in an attempt to discredit the committee's inevitable liberal recommendations; but while no one objected to criminalizing child pornography, the press and the public did not accept that reading *Penthouse* inevitably led to pedophilia because "porn addicts" needed increasingly "harder" material. However, when the new 1979 Thatcher Government did not officially endorse Williams' report and the entrepreneurs secured an Indecent Displays Act during 1981, commentators convinced themselves that the committee's recommendations had been shelved [Thompson, 1994a]; an erroneous belief that is still held today.

David Sullivan, who had made a fortune selling pin-up porn magazines through convenience stores, knew otherwise and set about building a sex store empire between 1979 and 1981 by leasing retail stores, and deliberately informing the local press that he was going to open a sex store. From Alton to Whitestable, the effect was predictable. Following the initial front-page story, editorials, letter pages, and further articles provided his company, Congate, with a vast amount of publicity for the cost of a postage stamp. Having paid closer attention to the politics of porn than most, Sullivan correctly surmised that whatever the critics said, decriminalization through designated sex stores would soon follow and he would make a lot more money. That was until he opened a store in Portsmouth; and what followed led to the Video Nasties episode in 1983.

HEAVEN'S LIGHT OUR GUIDE

By the time Sullivan's *SVEN* store opened in September 1980, the complaints about sex stores a decade before had evolved into the powerful Portsmouth Association for Community Standards (PACS), which had just stopped two sex cinemas from operating in the City with the aid of their ally, Planning Committee Chairman, Mr. Williams. Closing the 32 seat *Apollo Club* in 1977 had been fairly easy because it did not have the correct Use Class Order [*The News*, Portsmouth, 1.8.79: 1]; stopping the second complex from opening proved more difficult, but it turned out to be a local and national game changer. When the Holloway family sought to expand their mini porn empire in Soho to Portsmouth they picked the wrong building. Although the Royal Sailors Rest (RSR) had housed a cinema, negating the need for a new planning order, its previous history as a Christian hostel offering an alternative to the secular entertainment found in naval ports galvanized the local moral entrepreneurs. This letter to the editor of the local paper explains why:

DEPRAVITY

I am sure that many responsible citizens, especially those who are charged with the care of young people, will be alarmed and I may say amazed, that anyone can open a club and exhibit films which would not be permitted in a public place. There is certainly something wrong with those in the highest authority that they pass their responsibility to the unfortunate local council.

Those of us who are familiar with the Soho area of London are saddened and ashamed of the open depravity of that area. It all began with the secret backroom projectors that crept in as far back as the

First World War. From there it has grown, gradually spreading into publications, strip shows, massage parlors, take your own photos and whatever you want, you can have it. Soho is a disgrace to any city. If the authorities cannot contain it there, we in the provinces should at least have some sort of power to keep such depravity from spreading. With a large number of young sailors and an even larger number of other temporary residents of tender age (students—eds.), Portsmouth has a responsibility to their parents to see that, while resident in our city, they are not exposed to contamination by ideas or behaviour of the lowest and animal intellect [*The News*, Portsmouth. 13.4.80].[3]

Although the protest from the Christian community enabled Williams to justify denying planning permission on the grounds that it posed a threat to a long delayed shopping mall; everyone knew that rationale was an excuse for a moral objection and that meant a DOE Inquiry would follow [*The News*, Portsmouth. 5.4.80].

With the local constabulary refusing to become involved, Williams relied on PACS to maintain public pressure and find more viable reasons, which they did, including a possible link to the American mob [*Private Eye* #490; *The News* 17.07.80]. With the aid of *The News*, which published a two part exposé on the Holloways' Soho sex stores and the history of the RSR, PACS and Williams promoted the impression that the Holloways were fleeing from London to Portsmouth because the local Soho Society had put the squeeze on sleaze in the capital city [*The News*, Portsmouth. 16/17.10.80]. The Holloways' lawyers, overconfident that moral objections were illegal, were ambushed at the Inquiry by the appearance of William Wearne, the Assistant Planning Officer of Westminster Council, who pointed out that the Holloways had persistently ignored planning laws like the rest of the sex industry in Soho, and would do so in Portsmouth; and that justified denying the appeal [Proof of Evidence, DOE Inquiry; DOE T/APP/5237/A/80/07227/G5]. The alliance formed by PACS and Councilor Williams, which produced the 600 protest letters, two dozen petitions from churches, and a packed public meeting at the local Wesleyan Hall not only proved unstoppable, it raises important questions about the explanations offered by the panic paradigm for similar moral crusades during this period.

DEAR COUNCIL

A content analysis of the 600 protest letters to the council offers a good reason to query the paradigm's tendency to ignore what newspapers and people actually say in favor of imposing its "more sociological explanations". Once we had proven, quantitatively, that the letters came from the Christian community as opposed from the general public; qualitative analysis suggested that the motive behind mobilization followed directly from the authors' religious beliefs [Thompson, 1987]. There were 147 letters that drew a direct link between their objection and their faith:

> With regards to the application to allow adult films to be shown in the 'Old Sailor's Rest' I must as a parent *and a Christian* voice my strongest objections to this proposal. As a parent I do not want my two sons exposed to such entertainment and *as a Christian* I want to see Portsmouth Clean and God fearing [Letter 32].

Twenty protestors mentioned working or staying in the RSR, and another 126 protestors alluded to its religious use. Forty-seven referenced the city's Christian motto:

> If you allow this to go through I suggest that our motto "Heavens Light Our Guide" be removed, it is a mockery of our God [Letter 91].

The major complaint was that the cinema would "corrupt" the city's youth, students attending the local polytechnic, and young recruits from the local naval bases:

> It would constitute a threat to the morals and future behaviour of the younger people who would attend and become corrupted by it [Letter 12].

This corrupting influence was linked by 37 writers to the lust provoked by the movies; providing a sharp contrast between that, and the spiritual stimulus offered in former years:

> I would suggest there would be a very definite change in use of the building; 'Stimulating erotic feelings and actions' is vastly different from stimulating thoughts and actions towards God [Letter 544].

Eighty-one letters claimed that the City was corrupt enough already, and feared more problems as a result of the movies' effects:

> If this club is allowed to operate, *it can only make a bad situation worse, as passions are bound to be* inflamed, and who knows what the consequences would be? [Letter 86]

The specter of subsequent sex attacks was mentioned directly by 69 authors, and indirectly inferred by another 67 who feared that the cinema would open the doors for other sexual establishments, perverts, and organized crime. Fifty-three believed it would turn Portsmouth into another Soho.

This overt religious motive undermines the self-serving analysis offered by the CCCS concerning the meaning of terms like 'filth' when they appear in public protest. Far from prove a sexually repressed authoritarian personality at work, terms like "filth" and "cesspit" used by 72 authors, had Biblical roots [e.g. Galatians 6: 8]. As research has also proven that authoritarianism, rigidity of thought, and intolerance of ambiguity is no greater in religious circles than outside [Brown, 1987], claiming that these terms automatically prove that their authors are authoritarians is more than debatable. As this protest against a potentially new evil influence was also an instrumental one, we have no need for strain blame or references to unconscious fears to explain mobilization either. This was spiritual warfare in action, and every aspect of those "more sociological explanations" can be accounted for by the protesters' religious belief system. The crusaders indignation followed from the sacrilegious threat to the RSR, and their symbolic references to Soho were analogies with Sodom. Any role accorded to "respectability" or "status discontent" can also be explained in religious terms, given that you can not find a more status enhancing act than playing the role of the watchmen in front of the only audience that matters: God. As the media inventory was based on PACS and Williams' beliefs about the Holloway's motives, there is more than enough evidence to demonstrate that moral entrepreneurs never need the media to orientate their beliefs about events, or explain situations that from the entrepreneurs' perspective are far from ambiguous.

The addresses found on the largest, 632 signature petition from a church congregation also demonstrates that the UK's religious moral entrepreneurs were drawn from all classes rather than the petit-bourgeoisie:

- 17 addresses were from the exclusive 18th-century properties occupied by the upper-middle class in Old Portsmouth;
- 155 from the solidly middle-class areas of Southsea and Craneswater Park;
- 143 from Widley, populated by the professional classes;
- 143 from lower-middle-class areas like Copnor;
- 82 from upper-working-class areas with their smaller privately owned houses such as North End; and
- 92 in rented property or working-class housing projects [Thompson, 1987].

This crusade also demonstrates the problem with projecting social group moral enterprise onto the public and calling it panic. The Portsmouth public were hardly involved at all, but the volume of protest generated by PACS was designed to give the impression that it was. That is what moral entrepreneurs do. PACS and Williams victory over the Holloway family enabled the former to return to the sex store protest that went nowhere in 1971, and one can trace a line between the opening of the *SVEN* bookstore in Portsmouth and the complaints made during the MPs revolt against the government over sex stores. That line reveals how concentrating on horror-headlines rather than tracing their origins back to stage one of the social construction process is extremely misleading, and debunks the claim that you need structural Marxism to address the role of power in society.

THE SEX STORE ACT

When the Portsmouth Planning Committee met to discuss the increasing complaints against the *SVEN* and existing sex stores in March 1981, the contrast with ten years before could not be have been more marked. The council officers now advised the committee that:

> the climate is now right to secure improvements in the legislation for dealing with problems arising from the growth of sex industry activities [PCC, 1/27; KJW/VSW/5.2.81].

That climate had nothing to do with feminism changing public attitudes to pornography, Thatcherite morality, or public panic. It concerned the growing organizational strength of Britain's moral minority that we outlined in the previous chapter. With rare exceptions, the public protest against the sex stores was generated and coordinated by the NFOL which encouraged the protesters to lobby their councils and MPs for both planning and licensing controls. CSAs like PACS provided examples of best practice. No sooner had the Liverpool CSA established a permanent picket outside one sex store than they helped the Christian communities in St. Helens and Southport do the same. Liverpool and Enfield CSA raised petitions which they presented to their local councils, 10 Downing Street, and Parliament. East Dorset Family Concern based in Poole mobilized residents in neighboring Bournemouth to picket the *Private* store, another of Sullivan's company trade names. Mrs. Joan Carlisle from Southend CSA ensured that the local council objected to the Government's pilot scheme. Plymouth CSA mobilized the Christian councilors in the city. Havant CSA organized protests, pickets, and prayers. Worthing CSA held a public meeting, raised a petition, and formed an alliance with a local feminist group to maintain the pressure; a portent of things to come [Thompson, 1987; CCSA #11].

The growing number of protests was matched by the increasing number of MPs willing to support planning and licensing controls. Whereas 68 had voted *for* Dr. Mawhinney's parliamentary motion following the Barnsley protest, 114 MPs voted *against* the Government during the Scottish Local Government Act because it did not include controls on sex stores [Hansard, HOC 23 March 1981].[4] With the government refusing to consider planning controls, the campaign was dependent on PACS and councilor Williams' ability to add planning controls to an impending

Hampshire County General Powers bill and convince the Association of District Councils (ADC) to back it by arguing that a pilot scheme in Soho would lead to an exodus of sex stores to the provinces. Despite constant set-backs, including the Government leaning on the ADC to withdrawal their support, PACS crusade enabled Williams to transcend them all, including opposition when it emerged on the planning committee [PCC 1/27 letters 23.03. and 27.04. 1981; PCC Planning Committee Minutes: 186 and 470, 1981; ADC Planning Committee, Item 12. 22 July 1981:116].

Williams and PACS were also becoming suspicious of the government's intentions. Although the DOE had rejected his request for a delegation to discuss sex stores on the grounds that they were a national issue, the DOE was simultaneously justifying the pilot scheme in London by emphasizing the local nature of Soho's problems [Letter from Giles Shaw to councilor Williams, 3.07.81]. However, as pressure continued to mount, including a flood of petitions to Parliament from the provincial protests, Williams discovered that the Greater London Council (GLC) had not yet approved the pilot scheme and would prefer planning controls anyway. Consequently, he was not surprised that when Lancashire County aligned with Hampshire to force a debate over planning controls, the Home Office and the DOE hastily arranging a meeting with the GLC, Westminster Council, and the London Borough's Association to speed up the pilot scheme. He was also prepared when the government suddenly backtracked and offered Portsmouth and Lancashire counties a meeting too. Knowing that the Government would insist that he drop the planning clauses in the Hampshire bill, he decided that the price would be a national licensing law [PCC 1/27 MAA/DEC/23/440/1. 13.8.81; and MAA/JJ/23/40/1. 10.9.81]. Williams and PACS were convinced that they could not lose, because the NFOL was coordinating the counties' lobbyists and briefing friendly MPs to maintain the pressure.

Although this hidden history explains the MPs' revolt during the Local Government bill, the revolt did not force the Government's hand as Manchester's account assumed [1986: 178 and 182]. The government's *volte-face* followed the intervention of a small group of lawyers, artists, and actors who called themselves the National Campaign for the Repeal of the Obscene Publications Act (NCROPA). A constant thorn in Valour's side during the great pornography debate, this group raised a legal petition against the GLC Bill covering the pilot scheme, and this little known right threatened havoc [Ouvry, Goodman & Co., 1992]. By ensuring that a public inquiry would have to be called to consider the petition, that not only meant that the debate over planning controls would take place first, an inquiry would expose the extent and reason for the government's double dealing over sex stores. In short, the back story to the MPs' revolt over sex stores demonstrates that in order to understand any legislation, including "emergency measures", one has to explore the wider parliamentary process. In this case, the NFOL,

CSAs, PACS, and Williams had generated the horror-headlines that led to the MPs revolt; but it is also clear that serendipity, represented by NCROPA's intervention, often plays a much larger role in UK politics than anyone admits.

THATCHER'S SODOM

Any inquiry into the situation in Soho would have proved very embarrassing for the Conservative government, which contrary to panic lore was far from moral as the residents of Soho had discovered to their cost [Thompson, 1987; 1994a]. Having been formed to force the Conservative party dominated Westminster Council and the GLC to stop property speculators burying Soho's rich historical heritage, including London's theater-land, under a mass of concrete office blocks and car lots, the Soho Society quickly discovered that the corrupt Obscene Publications squad were not the only other problem. When the property boom went bust, the two councils were deliberately standing by while the sex industry began to replace the traditional restaurants, businesses, and craft workshops, despite breaking building codes and Use Class Orders while doing so. By 1981 there were 54 sex stores, 39 sex cinemas, 16 strip/peep shows, 11 illegal 'girly bars', and 12 licensed massage parlors fleecing the naïve from the provinces while contributing nothing to the community. Westminster Council blamed the AMC, the DOE, and everyone else for inaction despite owning several of the properties concerned and the GLC could easily have closed the massage parlors and sex cinemas if they had wanted to. One of the reasons they did not is that London's Conservative councilors ruthlessly exploited the sex industry at election time, promising cleanups that never came to the wider electorate; while Conservative MPs found the sorry state of Soho useful when they wanted to berate the previous Labour Government for being too permissive. This double dealing became so blatant that even the conservative-leaning *London Standard* was forced to comment; but that was not the worst of it.

Once the Soho Society, which included community members from all classes and political perspectives, began to stand their own independent candidates in 1978 and aligned with other London residents' groups to secure legislation, they uncovered the reason why Heseltine at the DOE, William Whitelaw at the Home Office, the GLC, and Westminster Council had been blocking planning controls. Far from being reactionary moralists, the Thatcher Government intended to turn Soho into a Reeperbahn, the famous Hamburg Red Light District [Thompson, 1994a; Soho Society *Clarion* #1, #3, #5, #9, #19, #20, #30 and #31; London *Evening News* 29.09 and 27.10.77; *Telegraph* 25.10.1977, *Screen International* 8.10.1977; *Times* 3.9.77 and 4.5.77, Hansard HOC. 26 January 1979[5]; *London Standard* 14.01.81; Hosken, 2007]!

HUSTLERS FOR THE LORD

Although those "informed" commentators prophesied failure because the new Clause 3 of the Local Government Act 1982 covering sex stores after the MPs revolt was discretionary [Manchester: 1986; James and Goudie, 1986; Sutherland, 1982]; having ignored the role of CSAs and the NFOL in securing the Act, they had no idea that these groups would immediately lobby councils to adopt the clause. Sullivan, well aware that this would hit his profits, fought the implementation of the Act equally as hard, ensuring that it took much longer to apply than usual [Martin, Walsh, and Cherer, 1984]. As the NFOL metamorphosed into CARE, one of their first acts was to send every authority a copy of *Community Standards and Public Responsibility,* a comprehensive guide to implementing the law. Where these guidelines were followed to the letter, problems were kept to the minimum; but where they were not, Sullivan ruthlessly exploited every mistake to secure favorable rulings and save some of his empire [*Local Government Chronicle,* 25.3.83]. Ironically, Portsmouth became embroiled in a legal dispute, although that was not PACS' fault. Their activities were typical of dozens of CSAs and local Christian groups who having ensured that the Act was "enabled", mobilized formal objections to every application for a license, helped authorities draw up the "conditions of operation" that councils could impose, and mobilized for the license hearings [PACS Newsletter, February 1983]. Unfortunately, as one councilor who had not registered a formal objection insisted on speaking, that one illegal action helped keep the Castle Road sex store open for another three years, finally closing its doors on 5 March 1987, 16 years after the first complaint about its appearance back in 1970 [Portsmouth *News* 6.3.87].

The battle in Soho took even longer, not least because when Westminster's General Purposes Committee met in November 1983, they proposed to hand out 44 sex store licenses, which together with the remaining massage parlors, peepshows, and the rest would still turn Soho into a Reeperbahn. It took the exposure of the corruption in the Westminster Council, another DOE inquiry, Section 12 of the GLC General Powers Act 1986 which licensed all sex related premises in London, and an enforcement war to finally bring the sex industry under control in the capital city [*Clarion* #35; DOE No. 5034/C/78/2128; *Clarion* #41]. Otherwise, the campaign against the sex stores was a major success.

In short, the crusade against the sex stores succeeded *in spite* of the Thatcher Government, and the Video Nasties episode which immediately followed, offers further evidence that when it comes to Thatcherism and the New Moral Right, the panic paradigm is a completely useless form of analysis.

BEFORE THE MAIL ARRIVED

The Christian campaign against video nasties emerged out their wider crusade against pornography and the sex stores, and was well underway before

The Daily Mail's horror-headlines appeared. The term 'nasties' had first appeared in *The Sunday People,* which used it to describe a pedophile's surreptitious video of children playing at a holiday camp [13.12.81]. It became associated with horror videos following a two part exposé during May 1982 in the *Sunday Times,* which also published 'Seduction of the Innocent' by Valour supporter David Holbrook [10.1.83] on which *The Mail's* horror-headline "Sadism For Six Year Olds" and the editorial reproduced by Barker was based [1994b: 28]. The tone of these articles planted in the press by the moral entrepreneurs was set by the first *Sunday Times* report:

> Uncensored horror video cassettes, available to any body of any age, have arrived in Britain's High Street . . . They exploit the extremes of violence, and are rapidly replacing sexual pornography as the video trades biggest money spinner [they] are far removed from the suspense of the traditional horror film. They dwell on murder, multiple rape, butchery, sadomasochism, the mutilation of women, cannibalism, and Nazi atrocities [*Sunday Times, 23.5.82*].

The first parliamentary bill attempting to control the videos on the basis of that interpretation was proposed by Mr. Wardell in December 1982 long before *The Daily Mail's* horror-headlines. It had been blocked by William Whitelaw because he preferred a voluntary, advisory, rating system in line with the Conservative government's *laissez faire* policies. However, that plan was undermined by the reformed OPS which had seized over 22,000 nasties like *SS Experiment Camp* from London stores, secured a conviction, and defeated an appeal; and that panicked the film industry because it meant that a voluntary rating system would not prevent prosecution [Hansard, HOC. 11.7.82[6]; *Sunday Times* 30.5.82]. Consequently, with an election pending in June 1983, the Conservative party offered Valour another deal.

In return for a manifesto commitment to control the videos, Whitehouse would take her video nasties campaign to 50 marginal constituencies where a couple of thousand evangelical votes could make all the difference in a tight contest, and send letters to the provisional press in another 150 towns and cities to secure the Christian community's vote there too. One of the beneficiaries, Luton's Graham Bright, returned the favor by introducing a Private Members bill the moment that the new parliament sat [Whitehouse 1985: 36–56]. Meanwhile, CARE set up a propaganda coup by creating the official sounding Parliamentary Video Inquiry to prove that the law was needed. The members were long established moral entrepreneurs including Tim Sainsbury MP who had secured the 1981 Indecent Display Bill, and the research into children's viewing habits was overseen by Dr. Clifford Hill who had just published the apocalyptic *The Day Comes* [1982]. That had covered the moral dangers of media for children without mentioning the videos once, but Hill was hired to produce the social scientific evidence to now blame the videos for the impending doom [Brown, 1984]. Without all this activity, *The Daily Mail* would never have had its horror-headlines.

These national developments were replicated in the provinces where CSAs like PACS were busy securing support from local councils and other bodies to put pressure on the government. No sooner had they secured the sex store legislation than PACS lobbied Portsmouth Council to close the video rental stores that had sprung up in the City; and the Policy Committee lobbied the Home Secretary to pass a new law to do just that in October 1982 [PCC1/27, file 4; Portsmouth *News* 3.12.82]. At the same time, complaints from members of "the public" led to a series of raids by the Portsmouth PD Vice Squad looking for some 60 titles including *I Spit on Your Grave*, and *Cannibal Apocalypse*. These raids culminated in a coordinated attack on the *Network Video* chain the same day that the new Home Secretary, Leon Brittan, announced that legislation was immanent. PACS placed several sensational letters to the editor in the local paper, naming nasties like *Driller Killer* and asserting that three-year-olds were watching them [*The News* 28.3.83]; and also participated in a Christian film company's documentary on video nasties broadcast on Channel 3 during May [PACS Newsletter, July 1983]. As a result, Portsmouth and numerous other towns were bereft of the nasties long before *The Daily Mail's* horror-headlines appeared; and that is also why two trials during November 1983 in Portsmouth Crown Court, covering the videos seized the year before, conveniently made horror-headlines at the same time that the debate on the Video Recordings bill got underway, although no one could have predicted how useful the verdicts would be. Despite involving the same videos, in adjacent courts, at the same time, the juries returned contradictory verdicts: guilty for one retailer and complete acquittal for the other [Portsmouth *News* 1.7.83, 14.7.83, 18.8.83, 15.9.83, 26.11.83]! As those verdicts justified the need for a new law to impose uniformity, we have yet another example of the failure of the panic paradigm to cover, let alone explain, what was really happening and for why.

WHERE'S THE PANIC?

While Barker's account proved extremely popular and spread the concept of moral panic beyond academia, no one noticed that the video nasties episode did not even match descriptive panics. As the public were renting the videos, there could be no moral consensus. On the contrary, the campaign to outlaw the 'nasties' demonstrates how moral entrepreneurs try to *create* the impression of a public demand to impose a 'consensus' on society. The media can not be used as a proxy for public panic in this case as it was divided over the merits of the bill. Several papers and journals even denounced the bill as 'moral panic'. Guy Cumberbatch, Britain's leading authority on media effects was given plenty of space to question the validity of Hill's research in the liberal *Guardian,* which also held a week long series 'Where Do You Draw The Line' with only Poly Toynbee dissenting from the general condemnation as she tried to ingratiate herself with professional feminists having been a member of the now politically incorrect Williams Committee. The conservative *Daily Telegraph* argued that the state had no business playing censorious policemen, and *The Times* did likewise. Indeed, our review of the first 100 articles, features, and editorials on the subject published in those newspapers and *The Daily Mail, The Daily Express,* and *The News Of The World* found 25 in favor of the bill, 48 *against*; and 23 factual accounts about the bill. As well as demonstrating that there was no media engendered panic, those figures help explain why Graham Bright quickly distanced himself from the PVI and scrabbled round for a new justification for 'his' bill [compare *The Times,* 8.3.84 and *The Listener* 14.6.84].

Likewise, Barker's claim that the entrepreneurs were working hand-in-glove with the Government does not stand up to scrutiny. His claim rested on Whitehouse's initial praise for David Mellor at the Home Office reflecting her relief that the libertarian William Whitelaw had finally gone, and Sir Bernard Brain's amendment to ensure that video versions of movies had more cuts than those seen in the cinema to make them more "suitable for viewing in the home" as children might be present. However, Barker's political selectivity ensured that he failed to record that Whitehouse quickly changed her mind once she realized that Mellor was promoting the interests of the film industry, or the reason why Sir Bernard and Mellor constantly crossed swords during the committee stage of the bill, particularly over the introduction of an 18R certificate making hardcore porn legal, giving the permissive British Board of Film Censors (BBFC) the job of rating the videos, and excluding British movies for export from the Act. Sir Bernard, who was gracious enough to treat one of the current authors to lunch in the Commons, confirmed that more than one MP backing the bill in public on the grounds that children needed protection was really "money mad" having a direct pecuniary interest in the bill; and that completely undermines Barker's interpretation of the MPs' public statements, and his rationale for the bill [1984b: 19]. That came as no surprise to us because in complete contradistinction to Barker's account, the panic paradigm's analysis of Thatcherism, and all those "informed" critics, the Thatcher government *was* implementing the William's Report on Pornography:

- The *Indecent Display (Control) Act 1981*—restricting public display of nudity, and introducing warning signs outside sex stores: recommendations 8(i), and 8(b);
- The *Local Government (Miscellaneous) Provisions Act 1982*—licensing sex stores, and making hard-core porn available in them, with no access to those under eighteen: 8(b);
- The *Cinematograph Act 1982*, and the *Consolidation Act 1985*—controlling sex cinemas: 45 and 49.

Far from banning anything, the Video Recordings Act was permissive and introduced even more of the committee' liberal recommendations: 35, 36, 37, 38, 39, 41, 42, 43, 44(a) (b), 51, 52, 53, and 54 [Home Office, 1979: 159–166]. Rather than being censorious, as long as a movie was submitted to the BBFC and was granted a certificate it became legal, and the other provisions safeguarded corporate interests.

By making the cinema industry's investment in multiplexes safe, the Act ensured that it could now cash in twice by phasing in video release *after* a less censored cinema run. By having the finance to stock multiple copies of popular movies, major video rental chains like Blockbuster working in tandem with the film industry's distribution network put the independent video rental stores out of business. By *not* stocking independent movies they also maximized the mainstream industry's profits. Although the BBFC made it clear that they would not countenance any nasties depicting Nazi-style atrocities; as long as distributors were willing to pay the cost of cer-tification, every other nasty could be back on the shelves in no time at all. And they were. Although the Obscene Publications Act 1959 could still be activated, the fact that the OPS spent the next five years bemoaning the increasing number of porn movies steadily securing certificates, the 1959 Act was becoming redundant. Yet again, by failing to distinguish between who, exactly, was complaining and why, the panic paradigm got it com-pletely wrong.

In short, far from being an "authoritarian moral regime" based on petit-bourgeois values [Sked, 1987; CCCS, 1984], Thatcherism established a framework for liberalization and ignored what the moral entrepreneurs wanted. That led to the division in the crusaders' ranks, and led to CARE's alliance with progressives and feminists. But rather than encourage the panic paradigm to adjust to this development in the politics of pluralism, the paradigm deliberately ignored it, because of what it revealed.

SYMBOLIC CRUSADERS

If any group could be described as petit-bourgeois symbolic crusaders dur-ing this period it was the UK chapter of Women Against Violence Against Women (WAVAW), which Manchester accredited with changing public opinion about pornography, despite no evidence of that other than a new law, and two Reclaim the Night marches and two pickets outside sex stores in Leeds and Oxford [1986: 72–74]. That evidential shortfall is the least of the problems with his analysis.

Manchester, like other academics and the professional Left appeared to assume that WAVAW's was *the* feminist perspective on porn, even though the movement had divided over the issue of sexuality a decade before, activ-ists like Selma James provided plenty of alternatives, and an increasing num-ber of women who identified as feminists were wary of WAVAWs rationales, reductive approach to politics, and behavior [Assister and Carol, 1993; Carol, 1994]. WAVAW infuriated sex workers, one of which later recorded the effect and futility of the marches through Soho [Roberts, 1986].

WAVAW asserted that pornography "misrepresented" women's sexuality, as if there was only one, which they believed there was. As heterosexist society prevented women expressing that sexuality by colonizing women's bodies through penetrative sex, heterosexual sex was *de facto* an act of violence; and as women could not consent to anything, let alone sex, in an oppressive heterosexist society, heterosexual sex was *de facto* rape. *Ergo* pornography, the representation of heterosexual sex *had* to promote violence and rape, was a major source of sexism, and was effectively a hate crime [CAPC, 1989: 2–3]. Despite that simplistic logic being promoted by academics in women's studies, sociology, and cultural studies courses, WAVAW were well aware that they were losing both the argument and the younger generation of students because of it; and spent most of the 1970s indignantly denouncing those who did not agree with them as "male identified" in the "women only" *WIRES* newsletter, which insisted that the heretics should be excluded from the women's movement [WIRES #105, #140, #144, #151, #152, #153]. When WAVAW tried to put that policy into practice in publicly funded gay centers during the 1980s [LGYM, 1985] that increased the division between their "prescriptive feminism" and groups like The Sexual Fringe and SM Dykes who opposed the attempt to prescribe political correct[7] sexual practices within the lesbian community, and questioned all forms of sexual labeling [Carol, 1994]. As a result, the women's movement became as divided as those in the USA and Canada [Wilson, 1983; Vance, 1984; Burstyn, 1985].

There *were* other feminist protests against the sex stores. However, as fire-bombing like assaults on "male identified women" in London's lesbian clubs undermine the feminist perspective on violence, Manchester ignored them although they help explain why WAVAW had no impact on the 1982 Act whatsoever. WAVAW did not focus on sex stores until their national "Sex Shops and Strategies" workshop in November 1981; and even then they were more concerned about the symbolic meaning and the alleged effects of pornography *per se* rather than the means of distribution through sex stores [WAVAW, 1985: 6, 13–17]. By the time WAVAW began to organize feminist pickets in May 1982, the Local Government Act was well on its way to securing royal assent; and the primary purpose of the pickets was to convince the feminist movement that focusing on porn would transcend the doubts and divisions that had appeared as the recession undermined the potential of the Sex Discrimination and Equal Pay Acts [Banks, 1981].

Having deluded themselves that the failure of patriarchy to collapse after 1968 was due to the "pornographic backlash" training men how to rape women back into submission, rather than their simplistic structuralism and separatist life-style, WAVAW argued that if the feminist movement followed their lead and mobilized women's "natural abhorrence" of heterosexual sex, "uniting women as a class" as Valour had done over child pornography, the women's revolution would quickly follow:

> A feminist attack on porn would not just be reformist. As the frightening realities of sex-war and sex oppression which are exemplified in porn come into focus, the class consciousness of women will be built. A main object of action around porn would be to mobilize that anger and hate of all women in the fight against male supremacy. Until now the natural horror and disgust of most women at porn has been labeled puritanical and prudish and derided by the ruling male ideology of sexual revolution. Now we must validate that disgust, identify its real cause (the obvious humiliation and degradation of women in porn, which each woman knows applies to her) and enlist the 'prudishness' of all our sisters in the struggle [WAVAW, 1985: 14].

The long haul strategy of the Christians was not for WAVAW either. The means chosen to wean women off Valour's "moralism" was to raise women's consciousness through direct action, as one of the fire bombers explained:

> I really think that direct action against sex shops is the most effective way of hitting back at this degrading industry . . . It hurts men in a way that laws and restrictions can't [WAVAW, 1985].

Fire bombing and causing other forms of criminal damage did not help when it came to practical politics like implementing the 1982 Act, even though professional feminists in local authorities agreed with WAVAW's philosophy. Oxford, site of a WAWAW picket did not even "enable" the Act. When Newham Council did, their haste to outlaw the stores ensured that they ignored the necessary legal requirements to do so, and so the stores remained open [*Newham Recorder,* 8.3.84]. Lambeth, bereft of sex stores, wanted to make a stand and so treated Asian-owed convenience stores selling pin-up porn as if were sex stores, wasting tax dollars in a very deprived area by forcing the issue all the way up the UK's legal ladder before Lord Justice Mustill inevitably ruled that 53 pin-up magazines on a top shelf out of reach of children did not fit the Act's definition of a sex store [*New Lambethian*, Jan, 1986]. This symbolic approach, like the tendency to inflict criminal damage on the premises being targeted, was typical of WAVAW's politics.

In 1985, WAVAW members lined up to offer 'evidence' before the GLC's Licensing Committee having objected to the Curzon Cinema Club's license renewal application. They insisted that the Club in north London had contravened Rule 116 (d)—discriminating against women, of the license code by showing porn movies. That was a lie. The Curzon was a legitimate cinema club and it did not play porn at all, but second runs of mainstream movies like the 15 Certificate[8] *Chose Me*. Yet the protesters from WAVAW insisted that the title alone ensured that London women were seen as being subordinate to men, and that the content led to sexual violence across the capital city. Although the male "moralists" on the licensing committee voted not to renew; Mr. Taglani, an affable Asian gentleman who could not understand why he was being singled out, inevitably won his appeal in the local crown court precisely because the GLC had never applied the rule to anyone else, let alone the major cinema chains for playing the same movies. That was not the only feature of the episode that made it symbolic. None of the protesters, or Sharon Lawrence who had coordinated the affair on behalf of the GLC's unelected Women's Committee, or the GLC's feminist lawyers appeared at the appeal court, which was informed that the objection was really "pay back". Those protesting had been convicted of criminal damage during a previous protest against the cinema during a WAVAW week of action. What made this episode even worse was that it had undermined Mr. Taglani's grant application needed to turn the club that he had only recently acquired into a much needed Asian community centre and cinema [Thompson, 1987].

The same form of symbolism was also evident in Portsmouth where the local student Woman's Action Group completely ignored the sex stores until the WAVAW weeks of action in 1983 and 1986. Having been indicted for criminal damage during the latter, they raided the store in April, stealing petition sheets designed to demonstrate a public demand. Their threat to name and shame those on the list backfired when the working-class women who accounted for half of the petitioners publicly criticized the protesters whose subsequent defense in court, that they had been wolf-whistled at by men 18 miles from the store, did not save them from a £400 fine [Portsmouth *News* 15.4.86; Portsmouth *Journal*, 1.5.86].

Ignoring this overt and self professed symbolism of radical feminist politics, while turning the instrumental efforts of the religious moral entrepreneurs into symbolic authoritarianism provides further evidence of the paradigm's political bias, but it does not reveal its extent. To do that, we need to consider "what happened next" after the video nasties Act.

TV, PAGE 3, AND THE CHURCHILL BILL

In 1985, Winston Churchill MP, grandson of the famous prescription drug addict, offered Valour what it had always wanted: withdrawing TV shows' exemption from the 1959 obscenity law. As the new Home Secretary, Douglas Hurd and cabinet enforcer Norman Tebbit had made high profile speeches about morality, TV violence, and bad language it was assumed that the Obscene Publications (Protection of Children) Amendment bill would pass as easily as the video nasties bill had [*Times* 22.11.85]. After all, it appeared to conform to the Thatcher-Whitehouse alliance popularized by Barker. However, with the Law Lords having just dismissed Victoria

Gillick's case against doctors dispensing birth control pills to underage teens without their parents' knowledge [*The Sun* 18.10.85], the bill had a dual purpose. The Government hoped that it would keep the increasing disillusioned Christian community on board while they could use it as a means to reign-in the increasingly critical BBC, which had refused to stop pointing out the adverse effects of Thatcher's policies despite being constantly threatened with the loss of the TV license fee, the UK tax on TV viewing which was turned over to the public service provider. The only people initially objecting to the bill was NCROPA [*Daily Mirror* 4.11.85; *Daily Express* 18.12.85; *Times* 8.11.85, 22.11.85; *Telegraph*, 2.12.85].

However, once the Royal Shakespeare Company pointed out that the bill's definitions would deem a considerable amount of classical drama obscene; criticism exploded. David Sullivan, tongue in cheek, broadcast the official figures to show that sex crimes had *increased* after the sex shops and sex cinemas had been closed, inferring censorship led to sex crime. *The Times* thundered in denouncing the bill's supporters as Mrs. Grundies, a very damning insult in educated circles, and insisted that Thatcher should explain the apparent contradiction between her free-market and supposed moral philosophies, knowing that she could not. A public forum at the Institute for Contemporary Arts, featuring BBC Controller Michael Grade, TV art critic Melvyn Bragg, film producer Michael Winner, and Geoffrey Robertson, Britain's leading attorney condemned the bill. Mary Hayward, a housewife from Portsmouth who helped found the Campaign Against Censorship pumped out the most reasoned attacks on censorship ever seen. And *everybody* suddenly wanted a copy of NCROPA's critique of the bill. The few remaining civil libertarian Labour MPs wanted them to for amendments to filibuster, and some Conservatives wanted to go on the offensive, because the bill would undermine the corporate control that they had secured through the Video Act. As a result, for the first time in 20 years, Britain might have had a debate on censorship, values, and MPs hypocrisy; but it did not work out that way [Directors Guild, press release 26.2.86. *The Listener* 20.3.86, 27.3.86, 29.3.86, 10.4.86; *The Times* 19.2.86, 24.2.86; *London Standard* 20.2.86; Hansard, HOC 25.4.86 Col 608[9]; NCROPA, 1985].

When the debate begun, Clare Short, a Labour MP, stole the headlines by arguing that if Churchill was serious about adding harmful media images to the obscenity law, he should start with "Page Three"; the topless pinup models that appeared in *The Sun*. Although she later denied any intent to do so, word quickly spread that Short would table an amendment to that effect, and that had an instant wrecking effect [Short, 1991: 2]. "Moralistic" Conservative MPs jumped ship, and when Churchill considered accepting an amendment on pin-ups to secure Labour party support, Whitehouse distanced herself from the bill too. What had appeared inevitable before Christmas suffered an embarrassing death in the spring [*Times*, 3.3.86]; although the next Conservative administration removed

TV shows immunity from the 1959 Obscene Publications Act, the collapse of the Churchill bill a little more than a year after the video nasties affair demonstrated that the panic paradigm had always exaggerated the size and power of the moral lobby in the UK. Far from gaining power through an alliance with the government, the moral entrepreneurs' Parliamentary success had followed from the chill factor inhibiting any effective opposition to their campaign's because the academic and professional Left had endorsed WAVAW's perspective on sex and pornography. Short's intervention, however, ensured that the UK would have a debate about women, sex, and porn instead.

OFF THE SHELF

Encouraged by the apparent effects of Short's intervention because they did not consider the other reasons for Churchill's failure, WAVAW and professional feminists encouraged Short to promote her own bill, turning WAVAW's previous symbolic campaign into an instrumental one. Further encouragement came from the professional Left who saw opposition to Page Three as another source of support in the Wapping dispute, the last major set-piece battle between the once powerful militant trade unions and Thatcherism. This conflict pitched *The Sun's* owner Rupert Murdock against the printers union, the NGA. By making a deal with the Right-wing electricians' union whose members would use computers to set the type and run the presses at much lower rates of pay than the NGA had enjoyed for decades, Murdock became a double headed folk devil: a pornographer as well as a union basher. For some reason the Left completely ignored the fact that the NGA were in their precarious position because Brenda Dean's Left-wing, feminist, graphical workers' union, Society of Graphical and Allied Trades (SOGAT), had been making similar deals with provincial newspapers for several years. Worse, any working-class women in SOGAT, like Monica Key who did not agree with Dean stabbing the NGA in the back, lost their job too [Jones, 2011:50; non-participatory observation, Portsmouth, 1984].

Short's Indecent Displays (Newspapers) bill which appeared the following year ran out of time, though not before the country was treated to the spectacle of Conservative MPs including Graham Bright endorsing their favorite topless model by posing with them, fully suited in *The Sun* [28.3.86; 31.3.96; 7.4.86; 8.4.86; 11.4.86; 12.4.86]. Undeterred, Short joined forces with *Woman's Own*, a supermarket magazine, which surveyed its readers and discovered that they were "offended" by topless pin-ups and convinced that it encouraged sex crime; although a later volume of the magazine's postbag suggests that this custodian of conservative culinary culture had suddenly become WAVAW members' favorite publication [Short, 1991]. Citing the survey as evidence that the women of Britain were with them, Short and her allies in the professional and academic Left promoted another bill in 1988, creating the Campaign Against Pornography (CAP). Its purpose was to promote the erroneous claims that 'new' social scientific research had proved that pin-up porn had become more violent and led to sex crimes; and with the aid of friendly professional feminists secured extensive coverage in the elite press, *New Scientist* magazine, and in TV shows like *Dispatches* as well as in the feminist and socialist press [Thompson, 1994b; e.g. *Observer* 16.4.89: 35; *Spare Rib* 18.5.89: 39–41].

SNUFF 'N' STUFF

Although that new bill ran out of time, Short and WAVAW, guided by US separatist feminist icon Andrea Dworkin, were convinced they could not lose having formed an unheralded alliance with both CARE which had lost patience the Conservatives, and the OPS which wanted a new definition of pornography so that they could remain in business, and which promptly went off in search of snuff movies to further the crusade.[10] The Left-wing dominated Cadbury Foundation funded the publication of the 'evidence' offered in Minneapolis during 1983 to justify the city ordinance that had divided the feminist movement stateside, under the imprint of *Everywoman* magazine which supported WAVAW's perspective [1988; Thompson, 1994a; 1994b].

The feminist crusade was enhanced by committed Christians working in government agencies like HM Customs who spent most of the 1980s seizing hundreds of thousands of books, magazines, video cassettes, films, and other articles under the lesser legal test of indecency, while looking for snuff movies to prove their case. Crazy confiscations included copies of the Deutsche AIDS Hilfe poster funded by the German Government, and the Dutch safe sex education video *In the Heat of the Moment* imported by gay AIDS activists; and our copy of the 1988 US Department of Justice Report on Pornography, which was returned, well thumbed after we threatened legal action. The "snuff movies" seized in these cases invariably turned out to be items like *The Killing of America*, a documentary about the rise of serial killers, or European cult horror movies like *Nekromantic 2* [*Daily Sport*, 25.6.93:11]. None of this did anything to advance the cause of women's equality, as the female students from West Surrey College of Art discovered when the police seized six "pornographic" items from their Diploma show held at the St. Martin's Gallery in London in July 1990.

The next step in this third attempt to impose a complete ban on cheesecake was Catherine Itzin's attempt to neutralize Liberty, the British ACLU, on the advice of Dworkin who blamed the defenders of the first amendment for her failures in the USA. CAP suddenly metamorphosed into the Campaign Against Pornography *and Censorship* (CAPC), and claims about "new research" in the quality press began to appear again in the run up to Liberty's 1989 General Meeting. Once the trade union block vote ensured that a motion to support *any* parliamentary initiative against pornography was passed, Short launched the Off the Shelf campaign which initially consisted of high profile professional feminists seizing copies of *Playboy* and *Penthouse* from the shelves of main street stores, and Dawn Primarolo MP presented a motion in the Commons, rewriting the obscenity law. It gained the support of 200 MPs, the Labour Party shadow cabinet, and the National Union of Students. However, as professional supporters outnumbered feminist activists, this "feminist" campaign relied on CARE and CSA members who had suspended their own "Picking Up the Pieces" initiative targeting pin-up porn in convenience stores [*The News*, 31.3.90: 5]. That provoked the private row between Valour and CARE because the latter had also agreed not to promote any anti-abortion bills as part of the deal; though once WAVAW activists inevitably engaged in criminal damage during their protests CARE began to have second thoughts, especially as the radicals' were unable to keep their side of the bargain.

Motions at Liberty were ratified at the following year's Annual General Meeting, but the 1990 AGM reversed the previous decision. During the intervening twelve months a picture of Short at a CARE meeting emerged along with the text of a speech she had given elsewhere lauding Lord Longford and Mary Whitehouse as champions of women rights. This provoked feminist activists and some academics into forming Feminists Against Censorship (FAC), and their subsequent publications and mainstream media contributions demonstrated that there was more than one feminist perspective on sexuality and pornography. That forced WAVAW to rely upon the professional Left and the conservative Town Women's Guild. The subsequent debate in the media and numerous TV shows including *This Week* and *Up Front* ultimately turned on an exposé of the extensive methodological flaws and the politics behind the US psychological effects studies being touted as the new evidence that pin-up porn led to violence [King, 1993], and a methodologically sound content analysis comparing UK, European, and US pornographic magazines which demonstrated that UK pin-ups did not even make the lowest level of pornographic material by the definitions offered by the Meese Commission and, ironically, WAVAW in the USA [Thompson and Annetts, 1990]. The steadfast refusal of the claims makers, including Dworkin and McKinnon, to debate these issues with the authors despite the constant attempts by TV producers to arrange one on shows like *Devils Advocate*, and the way that *Dispatches* avoided covering these issues, destroyed the credibility of Short's campaign in TV land. When the Labour party Lawyers Group voted against the proposed bill ensuring that the endorsement of the party's Women's Conference would not be enough, Short turned to the Conservative graduates group for their support, but was shocked to discover that they did not conform to the progressives stereotyped encouraged by the panic paradigm. They long since adopted the Libertarian Alliance's position, which was the same as FAC's: no more censorship.

Although Ms. Itzin tried to revive the campaign in 1992 with the aid of Ray Wyre, a former Baptist minister and probation officer, and promote her edited collection of WAVAW and Christian anti—pornography arguments [1992], she was literally laughed off the stage by the working-class studio audience in a live televised public debate. As the campaign fell apart, CARE and Valour who were now on opposite sides of the political divide went back to trying to get MPs to push through Private Members bills, but subsequent attempts by Liberal Democrat MP Liz Lynne, and the Conservative Robert Spink MP to rewrite the definition of obscenity came to nothing. Another campaign to secure a commitment by the Conservative party to ban pin-up porn in the next election only secured the support of 70 MPs [*Daily Mail* 27.6.91: 42–43]. Clare Short, however, could be found lining up with David Alton when his campaign to clamp down on videos following the James Bulger episode led the government to add new clauses to the Criminal Justice bill [*The Independent* 12.4.94: 3; *Daily Mail*, 13.4.94: 1–2].

One of the most bemusing features of the campaign was the way that Ms. Itzin, the power behind CAP/CAPC, continued to deny that the radical feminists had ever aligned with CARE [Itzin, 1992: 15], despite CARE having committed their rationales to print, simultaneously revealing that the progressive Campaign For Press and Broadcasting Freedom had also been involved [Williams, 1991]. *Everywoman* had also boasted that they had convinced CARE to switch from emphasizing the effects of pornography on the family to prioritizing the feminist position [Dec. 1990-Jan. 1991]. Those revelations, however, were surpassed by the way that the campaign had been built deliberately built around the moral panic model, with horror-headlines and TV shows about violence in pin-up porn, and reviving the urban legend regarding the existence of snuff movies, to panic the public into supporting its bills.

As men have been exploiting women, sexually and otherwise since the dawn of time, WAVAW's structural logic was unlikely to convince the public that pin-up porn explained sexual violence. Consequently, in the same way that Whitehouse had argued that *Penthouse* ultimately led readers to pedophilia; WAWAW had argued that pin-up porn led men to crave snuff movies, and they were constantly insisting that they or the OPS had found one. Their own exposition, however, merely demonstrated the legend's metaphoric and symbolic use in radical feminist circles illustrated by the claim that all women supposedly had to "live in fear" knowing "that while rape, degradation and dehumanization of women is filmed and sold as entertainment, women's status in society is worthless" [Corcoran, 1989: 4]. It mattered not that the reappearance of this myth ensured that six British mothers had to contend with the possibility that their missing children had become snuff movie victims during July 1990, following claims by the police to have uncovered the remains of those used for such purposes, when they had merely unearthed some animal bones [*Evening Standard* 27.7.90; *The Sun* 28.7.90]. As we have covered the origin of the snuff legend elsewhere [Thompson, 1994a; 1994b], we merely need to draw attention here to CAP/CAPC's method of planting stories in the elite press was no different from the methods used by religious moral entrepreneurs. One of the major sources of the snuff movie legend was a planted story on the UPI news wire service by a Christian cop, Detective Joseph Horman of the NYPD's Organized Crime Control Bureau; and when the story was ignored by TV news, Citizens For Decency's had the temerity to complain to the Federal Communications Commission [Gallagher 1981: 221]. WAVAW, however, could always count on the *Dispatches* TV show, which even tried to palm off performance art pieces by Genesis P-Orridge's rock band as satanic rituals involving aborted fetuses eaten by the participants to panic the UK public; a subject we cover in the next chapter [*The Mail on Sunday* 1.3.92: 9–10].

ACADEMIC NASTIES

The myth of the video nasties panic which bore no relationship to the bill's origins, and its blatant political selectivity draws attention to several issues. It demonstrates once again that concentrating on horror-headlines not only masks the role of moral enterprise, but enables the paradigm to promote its politics and values even when it is on the losing side. By accident or design, that inhibits awareness of what is really happening, needed to make a viable assessment of events, engage in viable analysis, and respond accordingly. In this case, we could not have chosen a better example if we tried: the paradigm promoted a completely false picture of 'Thatcherite' morality. By concentrating on the immediate form of censorship, Barker missed the complexity behind it. The Conservative Government was implementing the permissive Williams committee recommendations covering the means to distribute material previously deemed obscene. They would have had to do that eventually to confirm to EU regulations anyway. Although the number of sex stores was drastically reduced, that reflected the right of local government to determine their own community standards, while allowing the stores that did exist to stock decriminalized hard core pornography in all its forms; a perfect example of pluralism in practice. Otherwise, the back story to the sex store Act and the video nasties Act reveal that while the Christian moral entrepreneurs had forced a reluctant government to legislate, the end result was the opposite of their intent: the creation of a legal distribution network removing the threat of prosecution from both hardcore pornography and the gory horrors. Having misled his readers regarding the politics of the moral entrepreneurs, Barker thereby ensured that the paradigm could continue to ignore the politics of pluralism, and "what happened next" really meant. While they disagreed over the politics of reproduction rights, progressives were more than willing to align with the Christian crusaders from the new petit-bourgeoisie, and the state in the form of the OPS to turn their symbolic crusade against pin-up pornography into an instrumental one. The results, as we and others have explained elsewhere, were extremely unpleasant for sexual minorities [Thompson, 1994a; 1994b; Carol, 1994], but nowhere near as unpleasant as what this form of alliance was to lead to, as we are about to see.

Apart from demonstrating the superiority of the US social constructionism when it comes to explaining the origin, nature, and effects of moral enterprise, legislation, and government policies, our review questions Goode and Ben-Yehuda's approach to feminist anti-pornography crusades. The fact that they failed does not make them symbolic. The symbolism they contained and the claims that they made reflected WAVAW's interpretation of the world, which they tried to enforce upon society like every other moral entrepreneur through legislation which would effectively turn their claims into reality by criminalizing transgressions. If that did not amount to panic, even a sectional one, then video nasties legislation was not the result of a panic either. However, by finally, reluctantly, accepting that feminists 'panicked' [2009: 244], the US booster's avoided facing up to the fact that progressives engage in moral enterprise, and are no different from anyone else who does. Either way, generic panics can not deal with moral enterprise and the politics of pluralism. They are as misleading as descriptive panics, and worse. WAVAW's crusade exposed the fact that their claims-making was an attempt to define sexism and equal opportunities from *their* perspective. Opposing that perspective did not mean that one was 'against' sexism or equal opportunities; it merely meant that one had a different definition and a different solution. However, WAVAW demonstrated that they are not willing to debate and discuss those definitions. On the contrary, they wished to impose their definition on everyone else. As the means by which they attempted to do so is deemed moral panic and symbolic crusades when undertaken by others, the paradigm is avoiding the issue. WAVAW moved from assimilative reform to coercive reform, including engaging in violence and picking on Asian minorities, because their indignation that the younger generation was well on its way to becoming 'third wave' feminists despite what they were being fed by academic feminists at college. In an attempt to get their way, WAVAW also promoted the junk science of effect studies, and publicly lied about their alliances. Worse still, far from failing to have any wider effects on society as Goode and Ben-Yehuda claim, WAVAW's activities had two. First, they aided the rise of the "New Moral Right" by undermining any organized opposition from the Left. The moment other feminists organized in the form of FAC, like FACT did in the USA, they helped bring the religious entrepreneurs' decade of sexual law reform to an end [Assiter and Carol, 1993]. Second, rather than reconsider their political positions when the division amongst the feminist movement became too obvious to deny, a large section of the professional and academic Left carried on regardless, even though their definition of 'victimhood' was debatable and decidedly anti-academic. One of the results of that was one of the biggest "social disasters" in living memory: satanic abuse.

6 Who Needs Satan?

SATANIC PANIC

Goode and Ben-Yehuda maintain that "on the whole, believers of the Satanism tale", were "largely fundamentalist Christians" who lived "in rural areas or small towns, and tended to have rather low levels of education" [1994: 59]. That claim, based on 'grass root' panics in a couple of dozen small towns in the US, was not substantiated by its source which offered no evidence that those running up and down the streets looking for the satanic cult had not attended college and were economically distressed because agribusiness, corporate welfare, and outsourcing had destroyed their local economies [Victor, 1993: 330–354]. Even if they were, as the major manifestation of the satanic panic was the hundreds of false allegations of child sexual assault worldwide between 1983–1993, generated and perpetrated by progressive academics with PhDs, medics with MDs, social workers with MAs, and DAs with law degrees, one obviously needs to reconsider the boosters' claim. This chapter does that by concentrating on two case studies.

The first, Karen Winter's elite perspective covering the UK's biggest satanic case draws attention to the role of radical feminists in spreading and legitimizing the satanic tale. As her dissertation was published by East Anglia University as well as secured a Masters Degree from Leicester University, it also offers a good example of the politics of panic in UK academia [1992]. By affecting a politically neutral position, Mary de Young's interest group perspective covering the US Day Care Center cases (DCCs) [2004], provides a perfect opportunity to test that perspective, compare it with Winter's elite version, and assess the viability of Goode and Ben-Yehuda's claims about the politics of generic panic.

ORKNEY

Winter begins with a brief resume of events. Three children, removed from the abusive W family during November 1990, "disclosed" the existence of a satanic ring on Orkney, a group of islands off the north coast of Scotland. Having secured Place of Safety Orders for the children in four other families as a result, the social workers saved them from their satanic parents during February, 1991. Winter reasons that as the "grounds for referral" justifying the orders were accepted by the local Children's Panel which dealt with family issues the allegations must have been true; but laments that although the local sheriff's[1] decision to dismiss the allegations was overturned on appeal, the Satanists could not be prosecuted because the media generated a moral panic about the social workers [1992: 17–18]. The media apparently did so by exploiting the UK public's reliance on common sense in order to secure support for the Thatcher government's New Right family philosophy, which resolved the crisis of hegemony caused by the feminist exposure of extensive abuse in proletarian families by covering up the satanic abuse in the same way that it had the endemic incest in Cleveland, England during 1987.

Winter's evidence for this cover-up begins with her assessment of the horror—headlines like "Search for satanic evidence begins" [*Telegraph* 5.4.91: 1][2], "US theory imported with evangelical zeal" [*Daily Mail* 5.4.91: 5], and "Islanders pray for deliverance from scandal" [*Independent* 4.3.91: 3]; which betrayed the abused children.[3] Like the reports denouncing the social workers as "devils in disguise", the horror-headlines convinced the public that there was no evidence to justify the allegations [*The Sun*, 11.3.91: 6]. Winter was particularly indignant that the media insistence that the social workers had abused their powers having been deluded about satanic abuse by the fundamentalist Reach Out Trust; although she also complained about the way that the media reports:

- Criticized the conduct of the house raids and the social workers' hostile attitude towards the families;
- Had confused "no evidence" with "no medical evidence"; "reducing the definition of child abuse to physical injury";
- Used biased analogies like "kidnappers";
- Labeled the children's interviews "interrogations", implying that "the children were persuaded to say what social workers wanted to hear"; and
- Criticized the isolation policy, whereby the children had no contact with the outside world, as that "reinforced the view that social work is inherently bad" [Winter, 1992: 21–25].

This "unchallenged dominant ideological framework" led a panicking public to accept the "common sense solutions" promoted in the press: only employ social workers with a "solid background rooted in experience"; overhaul the theoretically based training methods; and remove the legal immunity that had enabled social workers to promote their own agenda through government agencies [1992: 21–25].

Having drawn the standard contrast between the superiority of theory and analysis compared to public reliance on common sense based on experiential reality, Winter concluded by arguing that the social workers were really engaged in a "virtuous endeavor" because they had not been officially trained to uncover allegations of abuse; an allusion to the use of "disclosure therapy", a feminist method of helping children reveal abuse which was championed by *Social Work Today* [15.11.90 cited in Clapton, 1993: 18]. That endeavor was undermined by *The Daily Mail's* demand that the government should "sack the lot and start again" which initiated the moral panic, and the paper's ideology that the family was a safe haven for children within communities whose welfare and values were best served by the church [Winter, 1991: 25 and 27]. In other words, Winter used the structural politics popularized by the CCCS to contend that the motif of Christian Satan hunters referenced by Goode and Ben-Yehuda was used by Thatcherism to discredit progressive feminist social work which was uncovering the abuse that proved that the nuclear family was a dangerous place for children. In doing so, she revealed the progressive-feminist approach to child abuse. For if one reverses Winter's criticism of the press it becomes apparent that feminists believed: satanic abuse was real, it is perfectly acceptable to isolate children from the world to secure disclosures and display hostility to those professing innocence, and that there was nothing wrong with exploiting the power of public service to promote a political agenda. It is also apparent that they believed that social work is inherently good, and that one does not need any experience or evidence when armed with a theory that asserts children do not make false allegations.

SATANIC DAY CARE

Unlike Winter, de Young did not accept satanic abuse existed. Belief amounted to panic. The allegations which destroyed dozens of US DCCs between 1983 and 1986 [2004] were the result of the convergence and amplification of three master symbols reflecting the social strains of the 1980s that led to belief [2004: 11]. These symbols were:

- *The "vulnerable child"*: a secular symbol generated by feminist activism, which became a proxy for public fears about the "discomforting changes occurring in the family" and "in the traditional gender roles that sustain it", evidenced by working mothers' guilt at handing over their children to DCCs while going to work [2004: 11–12].
- *The "menacing devil"*: a sacred symbol in conservative Christian communities acting as a proxy for their fears about "America's immanent moral collapse", which would only be resolved by generating awareness of the source of all evil: Satanism. Promoted through their pro-child agenda targeting every threat to the family, from homosexuality and

pornography to divorce and dual income families, this symbol merged with the first symbol in the public imagination [2004: 13–14].
- *The "psychological trauma model"*: adopted by interest groups "organized around their own sense of injury and injustice", was linked to 'the vulnerable child' when feminists turned their attention to child abuse and became a public proxy for the pervasive anxiety that the future was "out of control" [2004: 15–16].

In other words, despite the obvious implications of Winter's account, de Young deflects attention away from the feminists role in the satanic panic by effectively claiming that the public turned the feminist's valid concerns about child abuse into a proxy for their own fears about social change because of the Christian moral enterprise during the 1980s.

SATANISM AND STRAIN BLAME

Despite that claim, de Young's account consists of a commentary on what clearly amounts to moral enterprise by numerous *urban* interest groups including highly educated academics, "clinicians", social workers, therapists, law enforcement officers, sexual abuse survivors, child advocates, and parents, as well as Christians [de Young, 2004: 43]. And there is a distinct lack of evidence for strain blame amongst the public. We are offered an opinion poll during the highly publicized McMartin DCC case [see Eberle and Eberle, 1993] which recorded near unanimity concerning the guilt of the accused, yet de Young never explained why the parents would need to create a "Believe the Children" movement if the public were already convinced [2004: 52–55; *Village Voice* 12.6.90]. As half of the DAs, judges, juries, and even parents involved in DCC cases dismissed the satanic allegations from the get-go [de Young, 2004: 41, 61, 65, 100, 115–165]; and other cases like the Children's Path preschool never made it to court [Meese, 1986: 713–71 4]; this panic was far from pervasive. Other polls conducted during the 1990s point to specific reasons for continuing belief including religious conviction and supermarket magazine readers [Cole, 2009: 436], so we need to consider the effect of the contemporary countervailing forces that de Young barely mentioned.

Apart from counter claims raised by defense committees [de Young, 2004: 37, 105–111], disputes appeared in communities like California's Kern county whenever the allegations emerged [Nathan and Snedeker, 1995; Humes, 1999], not least because the widely publicized searches for buried evidence failed to find any [Carlson and Larue, 1989]. Debbie Nathan, who had followed the allegations from the beginning also points out that the press had become skeptical, prosecutors began dropping the satanic angle, and even child protection personnel questioned the methods behind the allegations as early as 1985; long before most cases referenced by de Young went public [1991: 84]. While the Meese Commission recommended that the government establish a ritual abuse task force, due to feminist influence [1986: 612, 687–68 9], the allegations were dismissed by Attorney General Offices in Minnesota and California in 1985 and 1986 respectively [Humphrey, 1985; OAGSC, 1986]. This rapidly increasing scepticism may explain why popular critics of the "child abuse system" did not consider the satanic allegations important enough to feature in their condemnations [Pride, 1986; Gardner, 1991; Scott, 1994]. These problems in the thesis follow from de Young's assumption that social strain leads to panic rather than sends people reaching for a bottle, a copy of Nostradamus, or buying gold. Her evidence for strain consists of working mothers expressing guilt in a hearing and a couple of TV shows *after* the event [2004: 51 and 208]. As consequence *is not* cause, and parental guilt or panic could just as easily be explained by being told by an "expert" that their child could now be ruined for life, there is an obvious alternative, experiential, explanation for the parents' belief. Likewise, de Young's chronology of the social strain that led to public panic is all too convenient.

Although the public became obsessed with 'vulnerable children' during the 1980s, de Young does not consider how that followed from the child abuse crusades of the 1970s; and nothing else fits. There is an obvious difference between de Young's conception of the "menacing devil" and the Christian community's own belief in spiritual warfare that had also emerged in the previous decade [Bounds, 1972; Irvine, 1973; Penn-Lewis, 1973], and did so for religious reasons [Poloma, 1982; Hertenstein and Trott, 1993: 154–155]. Indeed, the satanic abuse allegations appears to have provided a boost for spiritual warfare if the reprinting, updating, and recycling of books on the subject are a guide [Watson, 1979; Cruz, 1985; Pratney, 1985; Lyons, 1988; Krupp, 1988; Ellis, 1989; Johnston, 1989; Larson, 1989; Pulling, 1989; Kjos, 1990; White, 1990; Subritzky, 1991; Boyd, 1991]. Some Christians continued to concentrate on other end time signs reflecting the increasing interest in the coming millennium [Hill, 1980 and 1982; Wimber, 1985; Larson, 1987]. More importantly, de Young never explained why Christians would fear rather than welcome the coming Rapture when God deals with the Devil and his heathen acolytes once and for all [Thessalonians 4: 17]; or why the secular public would suddenly believe in a devil as opposed to some 'perverts' in a satanic cult who apparently believed the devil did.

The major weakness when it comes to timing, however, concerns de Young's account of the role of Post Traumatic Stress Disorder (PTSD). Despite being included in the DSM in 1980, PTSD had nothing to do with the DCC allegations. The children were supposed to be suffering from Multi Personality Disassociation (MPD) caused by the repression of their traumatic satanic experience, whereas PTSD consists of the inability to stop the intrusive, conscious, thoughts generated by traumatic experiences. That was why the children needed "disclosure therapy" to "help" them "remember" their satanic abuse and prevent their multiple personalities appearing later in life [Gould, 1992]. That fatal *faux pas* demonstrates that de Young had not followed the allegations from the beginning and was continually turning consequences into causes. Most people would not have heard of MPD let alone PTSD until the early 1990s when "adult survivors" of alleged satanic abuse in their 1970s childhoods began to perform their split personalities on TV shows like *Sally* [12.2.91]. Previously unseen, they now appeared in great numbers to keep the claims alive as the DCC cases fell apart in appeal courts, Christians exposed bogus claims from within their own community [Passantino, Passantino, and Trott, 1989], insurance companies struck MPD off their list of funded medical conditions, and MPD therapists like Dr. Humenansky were sued by former patients for implanting false memories rather than recovering real ones [Wakefield and Underwager, 1994].

When the False Memory Society *immediately* appeared and offered an alternative explanation for the 'survivors' behavior on shows like *Sally*, too [7.12.92], it was at that point that satanic abuse proselytizers like Catherine Gould switched to PTSD rather than MPD despite the obvious conflict with their previous rationales. Their second attempt to keep the allegations alive as they came under increasing attack in the media [e.g. Rabinowitz, 1990], and in academia [e.g. Richardson, *et al.*, 1991] did not work either. They lost the public debate over repression, suggestibility, and recovered memories in "the memory wars" that followed [Loftus and Ketcham, 1994; Sinason, 1994; Ofshe and Watters, 1995; Campbell, 1998; Ceci and Bruck, 2000]; and they comforted themselves with the belief that that offered further evidence of society's denial of child abuse [Myer, 1994; Ryder, 1992; Sinason, 1994].

In any event, offering a structural reason why people may have believed or panicked about the allegations does not explain where the cases came from. Consequently, we need to look elsewhere for the source of the allegations, and we find it in de Young's [2004: 111] unjustified criticism that the academics who ultimately helped debunk the satanic myth [see Richardson, *et al*, 1991] were slow to react. That is unfair for three reasons. First, the debunkers efforts appeared at the same time that most of the publicity about satanic panic appeared [e.g. Manshel, 1990; Mayer, 1991], which reemphasizes the importance of the contemporary TV exposure. Even then, many 'true crime' authors ignored the DCC cases and continued to link satanic cults with serial killers [e.g. Mandelsberg, 1991]. Second, many of those debunking the claims, like Richardson, had been engaged in combating other elements of the wider 'satanic panic,' such as claims about suicide inducing rock music. Third, and most important, anyone in the 'wrong' department knowing what was going on before 1990 risked academic suicide if they questioned the received wisdom about children's trauma, based the model used by the feminist rape awareness movement the decade before [Davis, 2005], precisely because of the power exercised by believers in universities and government agencies referenced by de Young [2004: 40, 65, 69, 73]. That is why most of the early opposition to the psychobabble in progressive circles came from outside academia [Coleman, 1984] although some like Ofshe fought it in the courts having swapped sides [Ofshe and Watters, 1995].

The Unholy Alliance

The concepts of the vulnerable child, satanic cults, and trauma all played their part in public belief, but de Young's own account suggests that these were far less important than what linked them together in the beliefs and practice of the crusading interest groups and their allies in academia, medicine, and DA offices. Without exception they all believed in the pseudoscience that 'proved' the allegations: the false medical indicators of sexual penetration; the catch-all symptom checklists that turned children's everyday behavior and illnesses into signs of satanic abuse; and the iatrogenic "disclosure therapy" which generated rather than uncovered the allegations. As de Young discovered, convicting the innocent of non-existent crimes is precisely what happens when the accusers prefer theory to empiricism, rhetoric to scientific evidence, and reject healthy skepticism and critical thinking, otherwise known as common sense, in favor of the "evidence of intuition" on which the pseudoscience relied [2004: 39—45, 54–56]. That, of course, had far more to do with the non-scientific approach adopted by 'social scientists' than any structural strain [Gross and Levitt, 1998], which reflected the feminist critique of science during the previous decade [Fee, 1988; Tong, 1989]. Given that the academics and professionals involved were extremely successful in spreading their beliefs worldwide through their organizations, conferences, journals, seminars and workshops; that demonstrates that social science, professional qualifications, and progressive politics are no antidote to 'panic'; if by panic one means belief. As these groups also marginalized the religious proselytizers by securing ownership of the issue, evidenced by the switch from the "satanic" to the "ritual" abuse label, holding the Christian community and the public responsible for the 'panic' avoids apportioning blame where it really belongs [de Young, 2004: 44–52, 92–93; Chapter 7, this volume]. The Charismatic "satanic tale" would never have led to the DCC allegations and convictions without the academics, medics, and psychologists who promoted the pseudoscience and "evidence of intuition" in the courts [Ryder, 1992] already full of endemic errors in 'ordinary' cases of sexual abuse [Howitt, 1992]. In short, Young's strain blame had nothing to do with the 'panic' amongst the highly educated secularists promoting the cases in *urban* criminal justice systems.

Her arguments, as opposed to evidence, for public panic are also ironic, for de Young is oblivious to how they also rely on academic intuition and rhetoric. For example, her "master symbols" and explanation for public belief rely on ethereal concepts like *fin de siècle* and *Zeitgeist*. Her account of the court cases has people adopting the "Apollonian" and "Dionysian" approaches to the innate nature of children, whether they were aware of doing so or not. The explanation for the high incidence of satanic cases in the UK county of Lancashire amounts to the county being steeped in ancient lore about witches and ghosts [2004: 6, 77, 130, 177]! Once one removes these ethereal explanations the allegations can be seen for they were: the result of moral enterprise by progressive and feminist pediatricians, social workers, and academics peddling pseudoscience to promote their beliefs and their careers, while morally blackmailing the public to "believe the children" when they really meant "believe us" [de Young, 2004: 142–148; Bannister *et al*, 1990]!

One of the reasons it took so long to debunk the allegations is that having dumbed down due to the previous thirty years factional in-fighting between positivists and "interpretivists" [Abbott, 2001], social scientists who adopt a scientific approach to interpretations as well as material phenomena were greatly outnumbered by those preferring the "intuitive evidence" found in theories and models like moral panic. When the supposedly highly educated do that, blaming the public is more than questionable, especially when there is another obvious and less esoteric explanation for public belief. When local and regional newspapers, and national TV shows promote the claims being made by child protection "professionals", "experts", therapists, and DAs; suitably horrified looking reporters stand outside courthouses day after day reporting the prosecutions' claims but not those offered by the defense; juries convict on the basis of the 'medical evidence', everyone says exists; and the subsequent special reports, true crime books, and TV movies, which de Young admitted were vital, reinforce the claims made [2004: 81]; its no surprise the public might have believed. However, de Young never considered the fact that the public may have believed that "something must have happened" because "there is no smoke without fire" especially given the lack of awareness about false allegations at the time [Yant, 1991]. In short, de Young never demonstrated that belief in satanic abuse amount to the belief that the children had been *satanically* abused in the manner described. As some jurors voted to acquit despite all the "evidence" being thrown at them and, presumably, suffering from the same social strains as everyone else, she should have.

ATROCITY TALES AND STRAIN BLAME

The role ascribed to the master symbols highlights the paradigm's failure to ground the causes of panic in reality and cover the *social action* from which any symbol would emerge and gain significance. In this case, the symbols referenced by de Young would be meaningless without the increasing power of the child protection movement which promoted and then exploited public fears about threats to children through a series of exaggerated claims supported by suitable horror stories during the 1970s, both a cause and effect of the Mondale Act with its $80 million funding for child protection programmes and jobs for those making such claims. As a result, child protection became a growth industry and the public was sensitized to child abuse horror stories with the inference that there was a lot more to be uncovered [Best 1989; Johnson, 1989]. When children like Adam Walsh could disappear from under their parents' noses and 28 Atlanta children turned up dead in the early 1980s, real panics about pedophile clowns gripped six major cities [*Fate* 35.3. March, 1982: 53–55], estimates of 'stranger abductions' continued to grow, and Congress passed a Missing Children Act; it is easy to understand why the public might believe what they were told by protection personnel when the issue of satanic cults first appeared. Likewise, the common cause between university professors, psychologists, and crusading Charismatics was nothing new. It was evident in the anti-cult movement of the previous decade whose brainwashing conspiracy theories were boosted by the mass suicide at Jim Jones' People's Temple; although most religious abuse was found in charismatic churches [Bromley and Shupe, 1981; Bromley and Richardson, 1983; Lewis and Melton, 1994; Enroth, 1993].

That prehistory, the link with satanic abuse allegations [Kelly, 1988], an account of the influence of Alice Miller amongst feminists [1986], and similarity between adult survivors and the endless 'victims' paraded during the previous decade's crusade [Meese, 1986] would have been far more useful lines of inquiry. They would help explain how the master symbols built on the victimology of the 1970s became grounded in society, and encouraged the beliefs and actions of the social workers, mental health clinicians, and law enforcement officers who converted the "satanic tale" into legal allegations. Even good causes can have negative consequences if one does not stick to rational, evidential based scientific approaches. Likewise, we are nonplussed that anyone would try to account for the rise of satanic abuse allegations without covering the history and role of the overlapping conspiracy theories that encouraged satanic belief [Kahaner, 1988; Carlson and Larue, 1989; Steiger and Steiger, 1991; Colvin, 1992; Boyle, 1995]. The most important missing factor, however, concerns the nature of the medical and psychological "evidence" promoted by the protection movement and offered in court, which we cover below. While abuse awareness was to be welcomed, the medical and psychological 'evidence' offered in the growing number of child custody and care cases generated a large number of false allegations, but early critics who drew attention to these problems including psychiatrist Richard Gardner and the medics Lee Coleman and David Paul[4] were all but ignored in the subsequent ideological exploitation of child abuse [Coleman, 1984; 1985; Paul, 1977; 1986; Gardner, 1989; Wexler, 1990; Coleman and Clancy, 1999]. In short, the palpable problem with strain blame is that it does not *explain* so much as assert a link between social forces, a susceptibility to believe this or that, and subsequent social action, although every aspect can be accounted for. And where is de Young's account of the way the claims makers' rhetoric dispelled public incredulity, or how the claims makers exploited the court cases as evidence of their claims despite the obvious need to do so [Jenkins and Maier-Katkin, 1992]?

The same problem is apparent in Victor's assertion that strain blame accounts for those 'grass root' panics including Jamestown, NY on Friday the 13 May, 1988 following weeks of rumors and "talk up"[5] about a satanic cult [1993: 32–36]. Like de Young, Victor argued that the rumors acted as metaphors for the social, economic, and familial stresses faced by people in rural, small town areas without once demonstrating that those involved were adversely affected by those strains. Nor did he explain how those strains rather than their existing religious beliefs made them susceptible to believing Ken Wooden's seminal claims about satanic cults. That is why Bill Ellis' account of the satanic cult rumor which destroyed the Pennsylvania Panther Valley High School prom in May 1987 offers a better guide to how the religious satanic panic worked [Ellis, 1990].

TAMING STRAIN BLAME

For Ellis, the content of a belief was less important than the reason why people justified drawing the conclusions that they do from the facts as they understand them. He adopted that approach because folklore and social psychology had long since worked out that social group 'urban legends' and atrocity stories draw on the group's traditions and values, which are passed on from one member to another, validating their beliefs and commitment, reflecting their hopes and fears about the contemporary world [Hobbs, 1989; Beck, 1987; Ballard, 1984; Boyes, 1984; Toch, 1971]. Once one understands that, and how the "evidence" then selected reinforces the participants' belief system, it become apparent that rather than explain anything, the belief in concepts like master symbols and moral panic are the academic equivalent of social group myths. Panic explanations can not match the way folklorists like Ellis ground their accounts in social action.

The source of local 'social tension' in Panther valley was found in community members' religious conservatism and mythological world view which was offended by the satanic symbolism adopted by some teens as an expression of their rebellion against the dogma of the older generation, and that led to the ramifications of the "precipitating event", the unexplained suicide of a popular student. That incident explains why the high school jocks assaulted the Heavy Metal music loving students, which in turn provoked the rumors that "the cult" would exact revenge at the school's prom night. Although Ellis missed the possible role of the movie *Carrie* in what occurred, the preventative actions taken by parents, school authorities, local ministers and the police enhanced the belief that something was going to happen because the authorities wouldn't take precautions if there was no threat, would they? Nor should it come as any surprise that the sensitization to Satanism and metal music began five years before when a fatal child abuse case led the DA to establish a specially trained squad to avoid any repetition, and the trainer employed was none other than Ken Wooden [Ellis, 1990]. As the effect of social strains are not uniform, and susceptibility to a belief is related to people's interpretation of events based on their existing perspectives, generic explanations like strain blame are useless without the ethnographic back up deployed by scholars like Ellis. If one follows Ellis' example, one can easily account for the progressive social group moral enterprise, and the urban alliance that led to the DCC cases, without recourse to strain blame.

SECULAR SATANISM

As we saw in the previous chapter, the snuff movie legend demonstrates that the same atrocity tale can easily be adopted by different social groups and agencies whatever their religious or political outlook, and there is more than enough evidence to explain how and why feminists and progressives would have no problem "sharing" the "satanic tale" with Christians. They worked alongside each other in crusading social service departments [Raschke, 1990: 194–226]; they shared a faith in "intuitive" truths, although their precise objections to secular, male, science differed [see Sydie, 1987]; and they both embraced the growing emphasis on the therapeutic approach to social problems [Nolan, 1998]. The latter explains these allied groups' readiness to believe the satanic aspect of the allegations even though they were being induced in DCC children and adult survivors by the Children's Institute International, the International Society for the Study of Multi Personality Disorder (ISSMPD), and individual secular and Christian therapists [MacFarlaine, *et al*, 1986; Mulhern, 1991; Katchen and Sakheim, 1992; Wilkinson, 1991]. While commentators have underestimated the extent of Christian therapy and how it could act as another conduit [Hughes, 1981; Hancock and Mains, 1988]; there is no excuse for ignoring how secular feminist approaches also drew on intuitive approaches [Fee, 1988] to construct a problem that did not exist.

The most important reason for the crusading groups' willingness to believe was another manifestation of the mixture of theory, intuition, and rhetorical proof: the Child Abuse Accommodation Syndrome. This insisted that protection personnel had to believe every allegation and act as advocates for those making them in order to overcome society's continued denial that child abuse existed [Summit, 1983]. Armed with that conviction, the imperative to promote the allegations no matter how bizarre is easily explained as the key to the convergence in belief was the 'reality' of

MPD as much as Satanism. Although the psychiatrists and psychologists associated with the ISSMPD generated their patients' accounts of Satanism using the same methods as those uncovering "memories" of past-lives and UFO abductions, their medical credentials gave them far greater legitimacy. As their patients said they were satanically abused, they were, and protection personnel saw it as their responsibility to convince the skeptical public, and what better way to do that than 'prove it' in court.

In other words, the satanic panic is explained by the time old imperative to prove one's belief system and the subsequent social action directed towards that end rather than social strain in a decade *after* the rise of the belief in spiritual warfare and the concept of the vulnerable child, and *before* the widespread diagnosis of PTSD outside military circles. The convergence in the groups' beliefs and actions is better explained by the fact that these proselytizers all shared: a self—validating absolutist ethic, that they were compelled to promote in public; a fervently righteous advocacy, reflecting their convictions about an evil; self-righteousness, justifying their adoption of any means necessary and making them impervious to any criticism; and a belief that their self-selected mission was a moral and noble one, they were saving children from Satan. As these are the same ingredients Becker [1963] found behind the imperative to engage in moral enterprise, we have an explanation for the actions undertaken by the unholy alliance. The material, grounded, means of the convergence, involving each group's core beliefs is not difficult to find either: there was a massive pool of sexually abused people (feminist belief), who had repressed their experiences because it had terrified them (psychological belief), which, in this case, can be blamed on an evil cult (Christian belief). That explanation makes more sense than strain blame as it also applies to the rise and fall of the satanic abuse allegations in the UK, a world and a decade away from the proxies discerned by de Young in the US of the 1980s; and which involved Christian and secular proselytizers in equal numbers.

THE ROAD TO HELL

Initial media coverage of satanic abuse in the UK between 1988 and 1989 was steady but unsystematic, and somewhat unconvincing, consisting as it did of fantastic claims in supermarket magazines and the Sunday tabloid press emanated from Audrey Harper, who claimed that she had been forced to breed babies for satanic sacrifice [1990], and the Rev. Kevin Logan, whose previously hackneyed *Paganism and the Occult* [1988] revealed how opportune his switch to *Satanism and the Occult* was [1994]. Coverage of US cases had been almost nonexistent, and the UK public had no idea that the stream of sensationalism was related to a growing number of UK court cases because of the confidentiality clause covering children in care proceedings [e.g. *Chat* February, 1988: *The Independent* 17.10.88; *Sunday*

Sun, 19.3.89; *News of The World,* 14.5.89; *Friday Night Live,* Central TV, 19.5.87]. That explains why the panic paradigm can not offer any evidence that the UK public panicked about satanic abuse. On the other hand, Winter's claim that the public panicked about social workers, was backed by Kitzinger's [2004] focus group research, if you define fear of false allegations as panic. We don't; and the public had very good reasons to fear social workers.

One reason the satanic headlines had little effect was that the public were still preoccupied with the fate of the dozen missing children abducted over the previous decade because the police had yet to pin their demise on Cooke and his fellow gang of murderous hebephiles in the case of boys, and the truck driver Mr. Black who targeted girls [Oliver and Smith, 1993; Jenkins, 1992]. The publicity given to these missing children continued all the way up until 1992, when the trial of the first group took place, and 1994 when Black received 10 life sentences [*Daily Mirror* 23.10.92: 5; *The Guardian* 20.5.94: 1]. In between, horror-headlines like the "120 Hours of Evil" in which three other six and seven-year old children were snatched, raped, and found dead continued to reinforce fear about murderous pedophiles [*Today* 16.8.91: 1]. The constant horror-headlines about those missing children facilitated the growing power of the vocal child protection services as they dramatically switched from an emphasis on cruelty to sexual abuse with its demands that one "believe the children" and "take allegations seriously" that made it difficult for critics pointing out where that would led to get a hearing. As this switch has been covered in great detail by Phil Jenkins' excellent account [1992: 107–124], we concentrate on the back story and the features he missed that point to alternative interpretations of the very real panic about pedophiles.

While the protection services quickly adopted the feminist emphasis on incest, the missing children stories explains why the general public remained more worried about invisible threats including both stranger danger, and child pornography boosted by the *Cook Report's* fantastic claims about a massive child pornography industry based in Portsmouth despite being debunked by the local paper [*The News* 1.8.87: 1]. The protection services were not slow to exploit the widespread fear and tried to pull the public towards their perspective using moral blackmail. The public had to believe all allegations because their refusal to believe claims about cruelty to children and battered babies uncovered by caring professionals in the past had ensured that children had continued to suffer and ended up dead. As each new threat appeared, as the definition of incest continued to expand to include anyone who had contact with children from sports coaches to care workers, and the growing obsession with pedophile rings 'grooming' children for sexploitation, they were also added to the list of 'ignored' discoveries to maintain the momentum [Tate, 1990; 1991]. Despite the constant repetition of these claims on TV shows during the 1980s, reality was very different.

The public had always donated generously to child protection charities, tended to presume the guilt of anyone accused, and like the US public had readily accepted the legal reforms they were told were "needed" to secure convictions in otherwise disbelieving courts [Zgoba, 2004]. If anyone had "disbelieved" and not taken allegations seriously in the past it was the social workers in children's charities and social service departments. Their subscription to Freudian theory, familial ideology, and slum kid stereotypes had enabled Boy Scout leaders, reform school teachers, churchmen, incestuous dads, hebephiles, and pedophiles to indulge themselves with impunity for over a century. Rather than worry about sexual abuse, the social workers had been far too busy sending hundreds of thousands of children from poor families overseas into forms of indentured servitude and destroying their files to prevent any future attempt to contact their 'bad' families and relatives who smoke, drank, gambled, and did not go to church. They were still sending children abroad in the 1960s [Bean and Melville, 1990]. That is why you will not find sexual abuse covered in 1960s and 1970s social work texts on children [e.g. Clegg and Megson, 1968; Mays, 1972]. Feminist social workers were more preoccupied with blaming sexism in nursery school books and the concept of romantic love for women's emotional problems well into the 1980s that sex abuse [Berry, 1976; Dominelli and McLeod, 1989]. Likewise, the "experts" at Great Ormond Street Children's Hospital could be found promoting the virtue of family therapy for incest cases as late as 1983, having merely replaced the Freudian fantasy theory with one blaming inadequate mothers [Herman, 1981]. As a result, it is easy to understand why the public was more concerned with stranger danger than incest before the missing children decade, although they were also blamed for having done that too [Rush, 1980].

As Jenkins explained, all that changed with the CIBA foundation report in 1984; though he underestimated the imperative behind the switch to incest, which explains the social disaster that followed. The protection services were panicking having come under severe criticism for having repeatedly failed to protect several children battered to death despite all the warning signs highlighted by one Inquiry into their failures after another. While the switch to sexual abuse offered a means to absolution, the protection workers replicated their worst mistake, blind faith in theories; merely flipping from one set neo-Freudian theories about 'Lolitas' to a new equally erroneous set. One of the most important in this new bundle, enabling them to shift blame and ignore the cause of past mistakes, dismiss justified skepticism regarding their competence, and denounce the public's fear of stranger danger as a moral panic [Parton, 1985; 1991]. That is why the government was still trying to find a means to eliminate basic errors in 2002 [G2, 16.10.2002: 2–3]. Having ignored child sexual assault for decades, it is no surprise that once the protection services went looking they uncovered a phenomenal amount; and the horror-headlines that followed each new *un* covery, led the public to cocoon their own children and/or avoid others in case contact was misconstrued. The subsequent 'death of affection' was the least of the problems. As the child abuse industry expanded it also became politicized. It offered the radical feminists proof of the evils of patriarchy and male sexuality, the Christians a new explanation for sin, and lots of cash for therapists promising to save the victims from being ruined for life or worse, becoming abusers. The biggest winners however were pediatricians whose special 'expertise' in spotting sexual assault enhanced their lowly position in the medical hierarchy. In no time at all, the pedophile became the biggest folk devil in history, child abuse became synonymous with sex, and Britain really had an effective moral crusade on its hand generating real public panic [Bannister, *et.al*, 1990; Browne and Finklehor, 1986; Corwin, 1988; Finkelhor, 1985; Hughes and Blagg, 1989; MacFarlane, *et.al.*, 1986; Miller, 1986; Stanton Rodgers, *et al.*, 1986; *Feminist Review*, #28, Spring 1988; Norwich Consultants on Sexual Violence (NCSV), 1988; Katchen and Sakheim, 1992]. The combined result was an epidemic of false allegations and convictions running parallel with real ones, despite being exposed by the debacle known as Cleveland.

CLEVELAND

The Cleveland scandal involved the imposition of care orders on 121 children taken from 57 families during 1987 following a diagnosis of sexual assault by pediatrician Marietta Higgs and social worker Judith Richardson. Higgs had used the reflex anal dilation 'test' popularized by Hobbs and Wynne [1986], two feminist, WAVAW friendly, pediatricians from Leeds, which always produced a 'positive' result depending upon how it was conducted. That made it no more reliable than the signs of sex abuse promoted by Woodling and Kossoris [1981] and Cantwell [1983]. Despite being accepted in courts as evidence of assault because they had been promoted in medical journals none of these signs, from perihymenal erythema to 'scaring', had been scientifically verified and merely reflected the consensus amongst a small group of self appointed medical experts in the US. When they were finally subjected to controlled studies most turned out to be normal, common, anatomical variations in children's genitalia [McCann, *et al*, 1990a; 1990b]. What made their use in court even worse was that those promoting them like Dr. Astrid Heger were far more circumspect about the signs validity in the company of other medics [Coleman, 1989; Coleman and Clancy, 1989]. In some cases, like the four millimeter 'rule' whereby any larger hymeneal opening was deemed to be conclusive evidence of penetration [Cantwell, 1983], it was simply false. Others, like 'fissures' were commonly misdiagnosed, and even when present could be accredited to a dozen other causes [Paul, 1986]. As its name implied, the disclosure therapy used by the social workers to 'interview' the children presupposed that a sexual assault had occurred, and created a self-validating loop between the medical signs and the disclosure of abuse.

When the media supported the skeptical Stuart Bell MP and the female police surgeon, Dr. Raine Roberts, both of whom objected to the ideological origin of the allegations and the self-validating nature of the diagnosis, feminists denounced their preference for a scientific approach as a moral panic designed to negate the feminist medics and social workers expert status [Nava, 1988; NCSV, 1988]. That expertise amounted to the belief that Freud had uncovered widespread abuse but had switched to the oedipal theory after being criticized for doing so [Rush, 1980; MacLeod and Sagara, 1988]. That conviction ignored the facts. While patriarchal Vienna may have avoided facing up to incest, the problem with the cover up theory was that Freud did not so much uncover incest but had tried to convince his handful of patients that their problems were caused by sexual trauma in childhood, despite their lack of any memory of it, to prove his theory of repression [Webster, 1995]. Although the contemporary 'experts' were using disclosure therapy to do exactly the same thing, the difference was that they now had the bogus medical signs to confirm what ever they said. Despite that, feminists and progressives led by Beatrix Campbell rallied round the pediatricians and social workers, and used the panic paradigm to accuse the police, the press, and Bell of a sex abuse cover–up, proving their ideological belief that patriarchy was built on endemic incest [Campbell, 1989]. Contrary to Winter's account, the Cleveland media failed to derail that agenda [1992: 11–12]. The Inquiry which followed blamed everyone for a generic "break down in communication" in order to justify the government's existing plans to merge police and social services investigations into child abuse under a program entitled 'Working Together' [*Social Work Today* 13.9.90: 22–23]. By failing to outlaw the use of RAD, the other bogus medical signs, and disclosure therapy, the government made future intrusive interventions more rather than less likely. Although a *Memorandum of Good Practice* was supposed to reduce suggestive interviewing methods, it did not. Reluctant to impose a scientific standard on the medics, the government actually made the interview "crucial in constituting the nature of child abuse and the form that intervention should take". That ensured that there was nothing to stop anyone generating satanic or any other kind of allegation. Courts continued to accept the erroneous medicals, and simply took the interviewer's word that they had followed the guidelines [Clapton, 1993: 10]. As we discovered in over 200 cases involving over 1000 interviews, between 1990 and 2004, they rarely did.

Whether or not the Government made the decisions it did because admitting that the medics and interviewers were in error could led to hefty law suits by the falsely convicted, Winter's real complaint was that the government did not share her ideological conclusions about the extent and meaning of incest. That ensured the real "cover up" concerned the extent of the progressives' faith in pseudoscience and refusal to pay attention to the problems that had caused in the US [Gardner, 1989]. As the promotion and effects of bogus expertise has nothing to do with social strain and everything to do with the ideological construction of politically useful social problems, the ramifications of de Young's failure to address the progressives' belief in bogus abuse signs and disclosure therapy are obvious. On the other hand, the threat of false allegations had been planted in the minds of the British proletariat which now had a very good reason to rely on their common sense, and for being wary of social workers, experts, professionals, and sociologists.

BRITISH BRIMSTONE

As Campbell and the radical feminists were still preoccupied with trying to turn Cleveland into a cause célèbre, the satanic allegations were imported into the UK by US proselytizers flown in for a series of child protection conferences. The most important appears to have been the one held at Glasgow University in 1988. This featured both Kee McFarlane from the McMartin case and Lucy Berliner, the Seattle feminist who Roland Summit relied upon as a primary source for his Child Abuse Accommodation Syndrome. Like most controversial aspects of child abuse claims, including the bogus medical signs, this had emerged from the Los Angeles county Interagency Council on Child Abuse and Neglect, a very active group of moral entrepreneurs [Summit, 1983; MacFarlane and Waterman, 1986; Murry and Gough, 1991]. With the radical feminists otherwise engaged, Christian social workers and the Association of Christian Psychiatrists were quicker off the mark; and in no time the UK had generated most of the 80 satanic cases [Clapton, 1993: 41; La Fontaine, 1998; Pratt, 2005: 276]. Having had suspicions aroused, the Christians would call in the 'experts', the Reach Out Trust [*Sunday Telegraph*, 7.4.91:10], or Dianne Core who claimed to have uncovered the first satanic abuse case, although that amounted to slapping the label on some falsely accused priests [Core, 1991]. Like everyone else involved, this pair insisted that the public should "believe the children" and "take allegations seriously", although as Core revealed in an interview in *The New Federalist* they were not concerned with the patriarchy-incest theory.

The Christians' aim was to convince the public that spiritual warfare was real, and satanic abuse demonstrated the need to return to Christ before the immanent end time [*The New Federalist*, November 15, 1988: 4]. Core's reference to specific cases that were supposed to be confidential also suggests that the Christians, secularists, and the rapidly increasing army of experts were swapping details; and the most common means to do so was the Ritual Abuse Information Network (RAINS) organized by Jeff Hopkins at Keele University. Core's reference to poverty as a satanic recruiting tool alluded to the fact that many cases merely concerned dysfunctional families. As the incompetent parents would be incapable of organizing any-thing, that in turn proved that they were the minions of "high ranking civil servants, top industrialists, and prominent city figures" [Logan, 1994: 59]. Although that reflected the charismatic belief that anyone enjoying success but not conforming to their version of Christianity must have sold their soul to the devil; that approach also reinforced the feminist belief that "the establishment" was covering up patriarchal abuse. Despite being slower off the mark, Campbell and the radical feminists quickly caught up, making one of their cases, involving real intergeneration incest in a family from Nottingham, the seminal one by going public when the police refused to proceed with the satanic overlay. Two of the social workers, Dawson and Johnston, published articles in the social work and Left-wing press, Camp-bell fronted an exposé on the *Dispatches* TV show, and Valarie Sinason wrote a feature for *The Guardian* [*Community Care*, 30.03.89; *New States-man*, 5.10.1990; Channel 4: 3.10.1990; G2 3.11.90: 12–13]. The Marxist and radical feminists were more than happy to work with the Christian claims-makers, appearing together in the Evangelical Alliance video *Door-ways to Danger* and a series of conferences promoting satanic abuse symp-tom lists and disclosure therapy during 1989 and 1990. The 'Not One More Child' event held at Reading University during September 1990 was typical. It featured: Pamela Klein from the US, who went through a satanic abuse indicator list, Chicago 'cult cop' Jerry Simandl, who waved a satanic sacrifice body-bag around in the air, Maureen Davies, who "shared" her knowledge of UK cases, and Judith Dawson from Nottingham. The aim of these conferences was to sensitize attendees and ensure that they would call-in the organizer Norma Howes or another 'expert' when they found a case. That explains how issues like family disputes over a pregnancy scare quickly became satanic cases like $R^6 v M$ in which the accused parents committed suicide when their two *teenage* daughters denounced them after disclosure therapy. The fact that we cannot legally name that case, or other tragedies like the seized baby who having been adopted was not returned to the mother when the case collapsed three years later, demonstrates that the authorities were covering up the consequences of the false allegations rather than incest.

Secular social workers had no problems accepting the satanic angle which emerged in these cases for three reasons. The first was Finkelhor and Wil-liams *Nursery Crimes* [1988], which 'explained' the reality of US DCC cases in secular terms. They were the result of psychological disorders caused by the perpetrators' personal life stresses, neurological or psychological impairment which led to either: *pseudo-ritualistic abuse* which consisted of threats to use supernatural powers to secure the child's compliance; or *psycho-pathological ritualism* supposedly reflecting the perpetrator's inner conflict between their sexual desires and their religious beliefs [1988: 62–63]. Although the book really exposed how far theory and analysis can amount to self validating non-sense, given it was based on cases that were completely false, it enabled secular proselytizers to continue to "believe the children" no matter how bizarre the allegations became. The authors even claimed that the children had been deliberately drugged to make them sound implausible and encourage public skepticism! Likewise, these two 'experts' explained away the children's increasing distress the longer they were in discloser therapy by arguing that this reflected their repressed memory of sexual trauma coming back to consciousness [1988: 95, 116, 128]. This source's influence in UK cases is indicated by the constant appearance of features of the abuse that the authors drew their readers' attention too, especially games encouraging the children to undress [1988: 93–95]. As a result, it made no difference whether the satanic cases were initiated by Christian or feminist social workers; the believers believed [Boyd, 1991]. The second secular source was the video seminar *Ritual Child Abuse: A Professional Overview* featuring MPD expert Bennet Braun MD, Dr. Catherine Gould who penned a popular satanic symptom indicator list, and Roland Summit MD amongst others. Coming from UCLA, and being distributed by the prestigious Tavistock Clinic in London, the video promoted satanic abuse, castigated public disbelief, and emphasized the need for child protection personnel to vehemently support *any* disclosure. As UK protection personnel would also have been privy to the US literature like *Child Abuse and Neglect*, it's easy to see why secular social workers would believe in Satanic abuse [for example see Vol. 7, 1983]. The third source was RAINS formed in 1989, which acted as an unofficial clearinghouse of allegations having distributed Catherine Gould's satanic indicator list, and Ayrshire Lifeline which promoted Scottish cases. These organizations' members enable one to draw a link between Cleveland, Nottingham, and Orkney, demonstrating how our analysis of the failure of the Cleveland Inquiry was all too true.[7]

AFTER DARK

During 1990, coverage of satanic abuse allegations increased [Jenkins, 1992: 177–187] as any journalist seeking an expert to comment on sex abuse cases was now being told to look out for Satanism too [e.g. *The News,* Portsmouth, 5.2.90]. The key horror-headlines, however, appeared in September following the annual fundraising press conference held by the National Society for the Prevention of Cruelty to Children (NSPCC). The organization's status ensured that their claims to have uncovered half-a-dozen cases dominated the press and TV news; proving that you did not need parental guilt, a large Christian community, a widespread belief in the trauma model, or any social strain to explain why the public could and would have believed in satanic abuse. However, as the allegations fell apart in less than six months there was no time for panic.

The allegations collapsed during March 1991, for three reasons. A Rochdale judge castigated social workers for their naiveté by turning a child's account of TV shows and movies into satanic abuse allegations, after a working-class woman named Judy Parry used her common sense and encouraged the uneducated parents to fight back. That rare airing of issues in care proceedings led the Saturday night, three-hour round-table *After Dark* talk-show, popular with the opinion formers, to cover the subject. It then became the show to watch when news broke that the Royal Scottish Society for the Prevention of Cruelty to Children (RSSPCC), the Northern Constabulary (NC), and social workers from Orkney Islands Council (OIC) had carried on regardless and seized another nine children to save them from Satan. When Professor Mulhern and Dr. Bill Thompson systematically explained how MPD and disclosure therapy were iatrogenic, and neither Beatrix Campbell nor the feminist or Christian social work directors had an answer, the media set out to extricate itself from its uncritical coverage of the NSPCC's claims by pouring all over Orkney. This coverage bore no relationship to the standard horror-headlines. It was conducted by the UK's best journalists, such as Rosie Waterhouse and Barbara Jones, and they dug deep. The former, for example uncovered that Orkney was not the first Scottish case, but was modeled on one in Ayrshire, where the parents had been jailed [*Independent*, 14.4.1991]. No one had heard about it because of the confidentiality clauses 'protecting' children from publicity.[8]

Although this explains the dramatic switch in the focus of the press coverage of satanic abuse which the paradigm could not explain [Jenkins, 1992: 187]; rather than initiate a panic about social workers, what followed amounted to a battle between two belief systems. On one side, leading journalists like Alasdair Palmer criticized the fusion of religious metaphors and therapy, warned about the danger of false allegations, and that those falsely accused could find no relief within the current system. On the other, the professional press—*Social Work Today*, *Nursing Times*, *Community Care*, and *Young People Now*—dismissed the judge's criticisms about manufacturing evidence, which included turning an account of eating a can of tomato sauce-covered *Pasta Pets* into ritual sacrifice of animals, and fell back on the need to "believe the children" [Clapton, 1993: 18–20]. This ensured that the future of the allegations would now depend upon the outcome of the Orkney case, although the feminist-Christian alliance fell apart before then. The radicals in Nottingham attempted to have Andy Croall, the deputy director of social services dismissed for promoting the Christian rather than feminist perspective on *After Dark*.[9] Both sides were as bad as each other, and had been responsible for suicides by distressed teens they had been trying to convince had been satanically abused [*Mail on Sunday*, 17.11.91:5].

CHASING SATAN

The police, RSSPCC, and the OIC social workers convinced themselves that five families on the Island of South Ronaldsay in Orkney had held nocturnal meetings, dressed their children in Teenage Mutant Ninja Turtle costumes, and had made them dance in a ring around the local Church of Scotland to disco music by Kylie Minogue. After the Rev. Mackenzie had hooked the children into the middle using his Shepherd's Crook and performed "dirty stuff", the parents would then indulge themselves with each other's offspring. Highly organized, complete with arc lights, record decks, video cameras, and drugged orange juice; these "gatherings" allegedly followed the occult calendar. Rebuttals from other islanders that the local geography ensured that any gathering would have been seen and heard from miles around convinced the authorities that they must be Satanists too, or they would have reported what was happening.

Contrary to Winter's account, the case was sanctioned *and* funded by the government. The appeal court ruling against Sheriff Kelbie's decision to dismiss the care orders on the second group of children concerned a minor procedural error. The lack of any prosecutions is explained by the fact that it could easily be proven that the W children's allegations emerged from the same disclosure therapy criticized by the £6 million public Inquiry that followed. Despite that, the W children remained in care because their case, like the issues of Satanism and MPD, were deliberately excluded from the Inquiry's remit in order to maintain the fiction that the authorities' had no choice but to intervene despite what subsequently happened. The means by which the Inquiry was able to avoid addressing those issues despite being seminal was bizarre but effective. Unless you knew what was being referred to, hearing a lawyer ask a witness to "pick out Vol. 13 of the documentation files, thank you, please go to page 666, thank you, please look at paragraph 7, thank you, can you confirm whether or not you did that?" ensured that details like who trained Liz Mclean remained a mystery; although she went to Minneapolis which was a major site of MPD diagnosis at that time [Acocella, 1993; Orkney Inquiry witness, MacLean: 4.2.92].[10] Fortunately, as we know what to look for, we can use what emerged across the Inquiry to explain what occurred[11] and thereby demonstrate that the convergence of the themes of vulnerable children, Satanism and psychotherapy was a function of child protection "group think" rather than social strain.

THE W FAMILY

The case began in 1987 when the teenage children in the large W family, whose complaints had been ignored by the OIC for a decade, finally saw their father jailed for sex abuse, with the help of the local doctor. The RSSPCC, having embraced the belief in satanic abuse appeared offering to "assess' the half-dozen younger children in May 1988. They became annoyed when the mother refused to believe that her children would become abusers unless they received therapy, and the local children's panel sided with the mother. Panels consist of three people from a pool of community members who deal with family problems and delinquency, overseen by an independent Reporter. They try to find an equitable solution avoiding labeling the parties involved unless needs must, as in cases of sexual assault. Although the system is funded by local authorities, their Social Work Departments (SWDs) are supposed to accept the panel's decisions, although parents can appeal to the local sheriff's court.

Indignant that their 'expertise' did not lead to compliance, RSSPCC convinced the OIC SWD to execute a Place of Safety Order in June 1989 and ferried the younger Ws off to Scotland; but the Orkney panel promptly discharged the order, secured the children's return, and employed Scotland's leading child psychologist, Jack Boyle instead. He diagnosed "system abuse" and reminded everyone that they should follow the Cleveland guidelines. To avoid any hint of intergenerational abuse, the elder children left home, and the younger Ws spent 1990 being baptized, joining the Brownies and Boys' Brigade, and riding their ponies in gymkhanas; repairing the damage caused by their father [Lee: 5.9.91]. The possibility of a happy ending, however, did not last long. Following a supposedly unrelated dispute between the competent reporter and the incompetent SWD over the latter's inept running of the island's children's home [*Orcadian*, 4.5.89. and 11.5.89; 01.06.89.]; RSSPCC helped ensure that Katherine Kemp was suspended and replaced with their own nominee, Gordon Sloan, rather than the deputy reporter [Sloan: 20.1.92]. In no time at all, the SWD turned a sarcastic comment made by the eldest W girl that she had made "wild, passionate love" with the chronically ill Rev Mackenzie, hoping it would stop their persistent questioning, into another Place of Safety Order. The younger W children were then seized for a second time in November 1990 [Millar: 7.10.91]. Now in control, RSSPCC set about proving their satanic suspicions, in a manner not dissimilar to moral panic studies, as it relied more on beliefs than evidence.

DISCLOSURE THERAPY

The disclosure therapy began on 21 November, the same day that the Scottish Office warned Mrs. W not to talk to the press [SO Letter: JMD/00 22.1.10]. It consisted of repetitive questions about anything from what games the child played and with whom, through what they knew about sex, to listing people who had ever "hurt" them, in a probing, suggestive, and repetitive manner. Official sessions, when the police were present were proceeded by unofficial sessions when they were not. Unfortunately for the RSSPCC, the young Ws were neither willing nor suggestive subjects; they did not offer enough information to be reinterpreted and then convinced it meant something else. So, the social workers had to rely on other 'indicators' like turning the girls' agreement that they had played "horsey games" with Mrs. T (preparing for gymkhanas—eds.) into being sexually assaulted by the islanders who had helped the W's reintegration into the community after the first raid. The children's denial that anything untoward had happened and distrust of RSSPCC following their previous experience was seen as evidence that they were too traumatized to talk, and so the abuse must have been worse than normal. The lead interviewer, McLean became convinced that this had something to do with a secret "T club"; although the children had merely been referring to the Tea Club held for the elderly that preceded their Boys' Brigade and Brownies meetings in the church hall when they were asked about attending "gatherings" with adults [MacLean: 3.2.92]. McLean knew she was on the right track when she "analyzed" the cards and letters being sent to the children from Islanders worried about the isolation policy imposed upon the children. Maclean's conviction that "no one would send cards to abused children for innocent reasons" was confirmed by her ability to find sexual "trigger words" in the correspondence; though that amounted to turning innocent references to events like a rare snow fall on Orkney into sexual allusions like semen [MacLean: 3.2.92]!

Despite their efforts, the RSSPCC had only uncovered three dubious revelations by Christmas. The 10-year-old BW's agreement that an older brother *could* have "hurt" QW, his sister; the five-year-old SW's account of past bath times at home which they turned into sexual assaults "down there" by her mother; and QW's listing of her brothers by height order, which RSSPCC believed really meant their penis size! The method used to secure these "disclosures" was revealed by BW in an official session when he told the policewoman present that he had only agreed to that suggestion to secure a promised ride in a peddle car [Williamson: 19.2.92]. When the girls broke down, unable to cope with the persistent questions and constant demonstrations of how anatomically *in*correct dolls have sex "to help them remember" their abuse, RSSPCC concluded that the children had been pressured by the eldest boy, HW, into "group silence" even though the children had been isolated from each other [MacLean: 5–6.2.92].

MUTANT NINJA TURTLE ABUSE

When some of the Christmas cards and presents sent by Islanders to the children featured the popular Teenage Mutant Ninja Turtle cartoon characters, Maclean believed that she had uncovered the meaning of the T club and evidence of Satanism, because of the Charismatic Christian interpretation of what these and other "New Age" cartoon characters "really" meant [MacLean: 13.2.92; see Phillips, 1991]. Jeanette Chisholm was then hired to help "focus" the disclosures [Chisholm: 9.12.91]. This consisted of subjecting the worn-out MW to Lucy Berliner's "direct work", involving role playing abuse scenarios and telling MW that she had been raped [Chisholm: 9.12.91; Williamson: 19.2.1992]. MW was then "helped" to draw a huge panorama of the turtle circle abuse scenario to prove it [Williamson:

19.2.92]. Meanwhile the other children were subject to dozens of unre-corded sessions to "discuss the meaning of the mail" [MacLean: 10.2.92; 3.2.92], before they too were given "help" to copy the drawing, and to list their friends so that Mr. Lee, head of OIC SWD, could decide which fami-lies to target on 27 February [Trickett: 8.1.92]. In short, armed with both a prior belief and a self-validating form of analysis, RSSPCC created a case of satanic abuse out of everyday events.

PROFESSIONAL ABUSE

Convinced that their abuse theories were infallible, the social workers believed that Ms. W must have had "dubious motives" for refusing their help: non belief [Dreever: 16.9.91; 18.9.91]. That conviction was rein-forced by use of confirmatory bias, called "causes of concern" in child protection circles. The most absurd was convincing each other that there could be "no innocent reasons" for the Rev. Mackenzie's "influence over the W family, spiritual or otherwise", despite being the local vicar [Miller: 11.9.91; 12.9.91]! By failing to adopt a critical perspective, these professionals, experts, and social workers remained oblivious to how the turtle circle drawings followed from their suggestive methodology and self-referential interpretation of the children's accounts of their baptism. The children had stood around the font in a circle before being called "into the middle", before being treated to an open air party on their small holding complete with the disco music, dancing and as darkness fell, those arc lights.

The social workers lacked common sense. Millar was convinced it was all true because the themes detected by McLean in the mail promptly turned up in the children's next session [McLean: 10.10.92] and their urban igno-rance of farming communities led to more than one devious interpretation of "age inappropriate" activities for children mentioned in the mail [Millar: 8.10.91]. Their lack of critical faculties led them to believe that the draw-ings were "allegations", and allegations were "evidence" [Dreever: 16.9.91; 18.9.91]. They were also devoid of reason, explaining away the lack of medical evidence on the grounds that abuse (like exposure—eds.) does not always leave physical signs, even though they were supposed to be dealing with repeated multiple rapes! Proof of abuse was evident in the children's "inappropriate" sexual behavior, which included one girl readily open-ing her legs when asked to do so by the doctor during her medical exam [Williamson: 20.2.92]. Their understanding of theory was both superficial and inflated. Even the state's expert cited Gail Goodman as her source for the belief that children were unlikely to make false reports, in order to blame the W children for making the "allegations" [Trowell: 18.3.92]. Yet, the nearest Goodman ever came to saying that was suggesting that younger children's information is more likely to be true *if* what they said was completely free from suggestion, contamination, or any other influence [our emphasis—eds., cited in Spencer and Flinn, 1990: 241].

MPD

Although the Inquiry repeated Dr. Trowell's denunciation of the interview method as a "subjective interpretation of the children's answers to a high pressure questioning technique, in which the interviewers frequently supplied model responses", the children were *not* being interviewed [19.3.92]; and everyone involved in the investigation apart from the dumb cops knew that. As the euphemisms adopted by the social workers were dismissed as gibberish by the public and press alike, they missed the fact that Chisholm let slip that the children were being subjected to MPD therapy [9.12.91], a fact reinforced by the employment of MPD "expert" Dr. Stafford [MacLean: 17.2.92]. This became even more obvious in the social workers' rebuttals to the charges that they had made suggestions, contaminated accounts by telling one child what others had supposedly said, and had turned the children's answers to hypothetical questions like "how *could* you be taken into the middle" and "what *would* a bad man do to children", into "disclosures" of abuse. The social workers argued that they were merely "giving the children a focus" [Stevenson: 26.2.92], that they were "permission giving" questions, or "a peg" to help the child's "line of thought" [Chisholm: 12.12.91; 9.12.91]. The need for that was revealed in McLean's rationale for ignoring denials and the children's distress at not being believed. Ignoring denials did not "put pain into children", although it "sometimes touched that pain", because it was "painful" for children to disclose abuse, and the children's displays of anger, aggression, and crying were "expressions of that pain" [McLean: 9.12.91; 12.12.91]. The moment you substitute trauma, traumatic, or traumatized for pain in that exposition, it becomes apparent that the social workers believed that they were "helping" the children to overcome their "disassociation" which had led to repressing the trauma that they must have experienced during their turtle circle abuse [MacLean: 17.2.92; 17.2.92]. Confirmation that the RSSPCC saw the children's adverse reactions to disclosure therapy as abreacting their satanic rape trauma and that their repressed memories were coming back to consciousness can be found in Maclean's claims that the children's behavior was "the appropriate emotional response" and that their distress was "an expression of remembering" [MacLean: 17.2.92; 19.2.92]. If the parents, Islanders, and the press had realized what all this meant, and considered the psychological damage that implanting false memories could cause, the public reaction could have been far worse; which is why the government ensured that MPD, Satanism, and the W children were excluded from the Inquiry's remit. While those involved in the investigation *may* have been oblivious to the iatrogenic effects of this disclosure therapy, they were well aware that they were deliberately misleading the public by using the child protection argot, which had always confounded critics and frustrated the falsely accused alike because it did not reflect common usage. Like the references to MPD, the meaning of these expressions was found scattered across the Inquiry. For example, "giving children time on their own" was not leaving them alone, but team-interviewing a child who was on their own [Stevenson: 26.2.92]. For our purpose, the most important include: "awareness of abuse", which did not mean knowing sexual abuse occurs, but that it happens to most children [MacLean: 17.2.92]. "Supporting children", was "helping" them make an allegation [MacLean: 4.2.92]. A "settled child" was one who had agreed that they had been abused [MacLean: 10.2.92]; and "denial" was an expression of fear of the abuser [MacLean: 5.2.92].

These beliefs, common to child protection workers irrespective of their religious or political orientation, explains their gross overestimation of the "hidden extent of abuse" and the apparent paradox whereby no matter how readily the public accepted child protection truisms, social workers continued to insist that society was suffering from the accommodation syndrome. The public was deemed to be in denial because they did not accept that endemic abuse was proven by simple things like cuss words, a reflection of the profession's inclusive definition of abuse.

SATANIC ABUSE

Although the government would have preferred to avoid any references to satanic abuse emerging, they slipped out too, proving that the link between the search for Satan, the disclosure therapy, the validity of the "group think", and diabolical abuse was found in abreaction: the children acting out the abuse dissipating its emotional effects. For proof of abuse, you merely had to look at the children's reaction to questions about sex, which were not only seen as "inappropriate" for normal children but also "bizarre", proving that they "had knowledge but were unable to disclose" [Goodfellow: 5.12.91]. Those reactions alluded to the children throwing things around the room [MacLean: 14.2.92], attacking the interviewers, and saying things "out of context" [Stevenson: 27.2.92]. The primary offender was SB, from the second group of children, who had deliberately talked in opposites such as using "fat" for "thin", and kicked cuddly toys around the room while repeating cuss words because he quickly worked out that the social workers' horrified reaction disrupted their persistent questioning. He was not to know that by doing so, he would convince RSSPCC's satanic "expert" Sue Brown that they had all been abused [Brown: 6.1.92].

The cross—examination technique of RSSPCC's lawyer, Mr. Campbell QC, was also a good source for satanic references. When SB tried out his technique out on his foster parents he was being "blasphemous" [Mrs. B: 2.12.91] and "chanting" [Millar: 10.10.91]. The use of satanic abuse symptom lists emerged too; what else would a child's use of the word "wank" indicate [Greene: 13.1.92]? The same inference was applied to New Age "trigger words": rings, rainbows, and turtles [Chisholm: 9.12.91]. Like everyone else, Sue Brown was now using the term "ritual" rather than "satanic" [Brown: 7.1.92]. However, she not only constantly cited Finkelhor, Conte, Berliner, Summit, and Dr. Jonker's claims about satanic abuse, but she also revealed that the importance of trigger words had emerged in a government funded satanic survivors' conference organized by RSSPCC. Likewise, she defended disclosure therapy on the grounds that the fear engendered by "the conditioning techniques" used by Satanists made conventional interviewing techniques redundant [Brown: 7.1.92]. She then let slip that everyone believed that the local medic, Dr. Broadhurst was the real head of the cult and that he had manipulated the whole island to cover-up it's tracks [Brown: 8.1.92]. Brown also cited Berliner's speech at the Glasgow conference which included the claim that saving children from MPD would lead to the therapists being castigated by the public for daring to reveal the truth about satanic abuse, and insisted that was precisely what the Inquiry was doing [Brown: 7.1.92].

A forth source of evidence of Satanism came in answers covering the nature of the debriefing meeting held after the second raid. These revealed that the label "satanic" rather than "ritual" had been used throughout the meeting, that that those present had poured over the evidence of Satanism in the households including Metal music CDs [Millar: 15.10.91], novels with New Age themes [Millar: 15.10.91], and movies like *Friday the 13th* [Hersee: 6.12.91]. A fifth source was the foster parents who had been given the task of probing for satanic signs in the same way they had done so in the Nottingham case. As a result, the refusal to accept additive laden orange drinks became proof that the children had been given drugged orange juice [Hamilton: 13.12.91]. A description of a Quaker meeting became "sinister rituals in barns" [Foster Parent: 5.3.92]. The repetition of a father's advice to suck a cut finger because of the curative power of salvia became a disclosure that "her father drank blood" [Foster Parent: 5.3.92]. Innocent Orkney children's pastimes like the Viking Game reflecting the islanders' origins were deemed to have "three [sic] common components"—religion, violence, blood, and sex; and were therefore diabolical [Foster Parent: 12.12.91]. Children's fears that their pets might die while they were absent from home became proof of animal sacrifice [Foster Parent: 12.12.91].

BELIEVE THE CHILDREN

The OIC social workers' knowledge of Satanism and their level of competence turned out to be limited to reading the feminist articles in *New Statesman, Social Work Today,* and *Community Care* [Millar: 7.10.91; Dreever: 18.9.91]; but they were convinced of their expertise because they knew that if you did not "believe the children", the children would be "damaged". Chisholm summed up their approach by arguing that there were *no* false allegations of abuse because once you "worked with children" the allegations always turned out to be true! Likewise, allegations of abuse must be validated, and she could tell that the W children were abused because of their "inappropriate" behavior. That did not amount to a closed mind, because the only assumption that she ever made was the Ws had been abused [Chisholm: 11.12.91]! Their credentials for this advocacy was their ability to relate to abused children, evidenced by Dreever "breaking down" at the briefing meeting because she "empathized with the children's distress" [Dreever: 18.9.91]; and Ms. Finn "feeling the children's emotional pain", which "was shared by all those in the department" [Finn: 9.9.91].

FALSE CONVICTIONS

Over the course of the Inquiry it also became apparent that the protection personnel's confidence in what they were doing reflected how they had secured convictions for sexual abuse in the past.

The women police constables' (WPC) knowledge of child sexual assault was limited to one day courses run by Ouaine Bain, another bogus expert in the incestuous world of child protection personnel in Scotland [Bain and Sanders, 1991]. The police's role was merely to record what was needed for a prosecution: an allegation, where and when the event supposedly took place, and who was involved. They never recorded denials. They wrote their notes long after the sessions had taken place, which was why, when they were compared to the surviving audiotapes, they bore no relation to what had been said. When one was asked about the poor quality of her notes, she retorted that they had always sufficed in the past [McLaren: 25.2.92]. Another admitted that if she had missed anything important, she would have copied what WPC Hood said [Miller: 4.3.92]. WPC Williamson revealed that they had substituted their own words for the children's, and that she had seen a detective add something to one of the drawings [24.2.92]. The WPCs never considered the viability of the methodology employed. Williamson even argued that she had been convinced by her shock at the startling drawings, despite the fact that she had spent most of her time with the W children getting them to copy *her* versions of the turtle circle drawing until they could do so unaided [Williamson: 19–21.2.92].

Once again, the cross examination of other witnesses revealed even more. Although the officers' training was poor and none had read the Cleveland Report [Ross: 4.3.1992], they all knew that all disclosures should be believed [Mr. M: 27.11.91]. They accepted the veracity of the behavioral symptom checklists without question, and claimed that the drawings were spontaneous despite seeing them being constructed over several sessions [Gough: 19.11.91]. The Northern Constabulary refused to accept that the children had been prompted in any way [Mrs. H: 3.12.91]; and justified ignoring the children's denials because adult survivors had not disclosed abuse in their childhood [Heddle: 21.11.91].

THATCHERISM AND THE PANIC PARADIGM

As well as debunking Winter's radical feminist account, the Orkney Inquiry offers a perfect example of the dangers of prioritizing theory and professional 'expertise' over common sense grounded in empirical reality. Despite RSSPCC's religious convictions, they were able to justify everything they did by references to the theoretically backed "best practice" of the period found in the academic, feminist, and professional literature. No one cared that they ignored the children's legal rights, especially those concerning panel hearings [McLaren: 25.2.92]. Sloan still had not sent the second group of children or their parents the statutory legal notice concerning the grounds of referral for the raid by the time that the Inquiry met several months later! His defense, that he needed time to consider how to frame the grounds of referral, ensured that the raid on the second families was illegal which is one of the reasons that the Sheriff dismissed them, and sent the second group of children home [Sloan: 21.1.92]. The children were also let down by the court curators who are supposed to oversee the process, and guarantee that that the children's rights are not ignored [Peoples: 11.3.92]. While the second group of children lost six weeks of their lives, and discovered that Scottish child protection is anything but; the plight of the W children was far worse, as Sue Lowes letter to Dreever during January 1991 revealed. The constant pressure had made them too emotionally fragile to answer any questions about anything [MacTaggart: 16.1.92]; and yet, it was precisely at that point that the child Lowe identified as the most adversely affected, MW, was deliberately singled out and subjected to "direct work" to secure what RSSPCC wanted [MacLean: 5.2.92]. Despite everything that emerged in the Inquiry, the W children were kept in care; and when it was over subjected to an adoption proceeding to bury whatever they had to say about the origins of the allegations. Needless to say, when the second group of children were released they denounced their social workers as "kidnappers" and accused RSSPCC of lying about their experiences in care to the Inquiry [Mr. M: 27.11.91], the RSSPCC suddenly forgot that "children never lie about abuse", and the police insisted that they had merely done so to please their parents [Mrs. T: 4.12.91].

The only person involved who ever questioned what was happening was a working-class foster mother whose common sense, born of her experience of raising dozens of children, led her to believe that when children lock themselves in the bathroom to avoid disclosure therapy there had to be something wrong; and that when all the children denied that anything untoward had happened and wanted to go home, that suggested that whatever was wrong had not happened on Orkney. Her reward for revealing that when one child denied abuse had occurred the professionals responded by laughing and offering her a cup of additive full orange drink while they stuffed themselves with pizza, was to be struck off from her progressive council's foster parents list [FP: 17.12.91]! Far from opposing all this, the government had encouraged it. The Social Work Support Group (SWSG), part of the Home and Health Department supplied advice to the Secretary of State on social work policy, and guidance to local social work departments under Section 5(1) of the Children's Act 1968, usually in the form of circulars [Campbell: 9.3.92]. Despite its own guidelines including *Social Work Ethics in Child Abuse* [1986] and *Protecting Children and Effective Intervention* [1988] produced in the wake of Cleveland, the SWSG had given the OIC and RSSPCC the go-ahead, because they believed in satanic abuse too. It transpired that the SWSG and the Scottish Office (SO) had been involved ever since the Reporter and RSSPCC had argued over the W children back in 1989. They had briefed Cabinet Ministers about the November and February raids precisely because they believed that the investigation would lead to a major trial involving satanic abuse, evidenced by their own press releases [Campbell: 9.3.92]. As the RSSPCC was the major beneficiary of the SWSG power to grant funds under Section 10 (1) of the 1968 Act, the Government had also been funding RSSPCC and Scottish feminists' "work" with adult satanic abuse survivors [Campbell: 9.3.92].

Although the government attempted to absolve itself from culpability, the evidence was against it. The SO was supplied by Mr. Lee with constant updates after they had given the OIC the go ahead as an embarrassing memo revealed. The SO had lied to the Parents Action Group formed after the raids, claiming that they did not have the statutory powers to intervene when they did. The SO had also: agreed to both the suspension of the islands' reporter and replacing her with Sloan; told the OIC's press officer what to say; and provided the funds for the dawn raids, the isolation policy, and all those experts [Sinclair: 10.3.92; Lee: 29.8.91; Trickett: 8.1.92; Colwin: 10.3.92; Skinner: 10.3.92; Campbell: 9.3.92]. As overseeing interview methods was also part of the SWSG's remit, they had sanctioned the use of MPD therapy because they funded RSSPCC social workers' trips to the US to learn about MPD [Campbell: 9.3.92]. As their official policy included the videotaping the interviews, they had sanctioned the exceptions in this case and/or had sanctioned their destruction. Either way, that ensured claim to have been ignorant of RSSPCC's methods amounted to perjury [Sinclair: 10–11.3.92]. As they were also funding Scotland's adult survivor programs, they knew all about the relationship between MPD and satanic abuse claims [MacLean: 6.2.92; Skinner: 11.3.92]. As the authorities also blocked every legal move to have the younger W children released, and did nothing about the moves to have the youngest adopted [*Daily Express,* 22.11.92: 13]; the government was not covering up satanic abuse, but they had surely encouraged these false allegations. As every W child went home the moment they were old enough to leave care and the fundamentalist Christian families that they had been placed with, we can assume the only abuse they suffered after their father was jailed was perpetrated by the child 'protection' system.

WHO NEEDS SATAN?

Once again, the history behind the horror-headlines undermines the paradigm's accounts and explanations for panic; but this time it also offers even more. As the critical media accounts of events and the motivations behind them was accurate, far from generating moral panic, the press reported what had happened. If they deserve criticism it was their failure to demand that the Inquiry cover the W case, Satanism and MPD, or do so themselves. Otherwise, the claims that RSSPCC and the OIC SWD were out of control was accurate. They were generating false allegations of abuse for ideological purposes, and Winter's defense of disclosure therapy as a virtuous endeavor reveals what radical feminists were really doing. As a later report demonstrated that the media coverage was balanced [Skidmore, 1995], that demonstrates the purpose of the panic paradigm is a means to justify false ideologies and oppressive progressive practices.

Politically, the lesson to learn from Orkney is nothing new. When UK authorities make mistakes and ruin people's lives they waste millions covering it up rather than righting wrongs; ensuring that official histories are invariably false, and political responses not based on reality are a waste of time. The academic lesson to learn is not that different. Least anyone consider that our choice of Winter was an easy target, the publication of her dissertation demonstrates that it was representative and typical of what passed for moral panic in the UK. Nor was she alone. Kitzinger claimed that the media coverage masked the reality of abuse, undermining survivors' recovery in general and those abused on Orkney in particular [2004]. Soothill and Francis asserted that the collapse of the Orkney case was responsible for a decrease in the policing of incest cases [2002]. That recourse to moral blackmail, rather than admit that ideological based false allegations overload systems and undermine the scientific and common sense approaches which seek to distinguish between true and false victims in order to find a real solution to real problems, reinforces our claim that panic accounts are political. Those mainstream academics, like many feminists, still refuse to admit that they were forcing children to make false allegations when they failed to implant them, and that their belief in endemic incest rested on bogus medical evidence. As the ability of Christians, like the RSSPCC social workers to add Satanism to these myths was facilitated by secular child protection truisms and methods lauded as the feminist contribution to social work practice; the failure to point that out also undermines the interest group perspective's claims to political neutrality.

Although she dismissed satanic abuse as a fiction, de Young's use of strain blame made her account as bad as Winter's, if not worse. As well as criticizing debunkers for not doing so earlier, without explaining what she was doing at the time, her account amounts to an elongated excuse for this major blot on the history of feminism. Where was the revelation that feminists were using disclosure therapy to implant false memories of abuse in children by exploiting their position in protection services, or how they were using the power of the state to abuse children and send innocent people to jail for ideological purposes? The result of her thesis is the same as Winter's: whitewashing the downside of obsessive progressive causes. Despite effectively demonstrating that radical feminists and their academic allies were no less responsible for the DCC cases than Christians, some of whom at least admitted their mistakes [de Young, 2004: 193–198; 201]; de Young did not take the radical feminists involved to task for driving males out of the child care industry or the death of affection [2004: 209]. On the contrary, she shifted the blame onto Summit and the male psychologists by claiming that their seminars and workshops were bully pits forcing the 'skeptical' female protection workers to go chasing Satan, as if they were not willing participants. By also claiming that satanic abuse allegations involving women deflected attention away from the exclusive (sic) male crime of incest she appears oblivious to how she is repeating the ideology that led to the problem in the first place [de Young, 2004: 212–213].

While de Young was critical of the way the victimology of the 1980s encouraged those with victim status to believe that they had a "moral right to demand attention, compensation, justice and belief" [2004: 218–223] she failed to explore how the lack of logic, critical thinking, and empirical evidence exhibited was widely accepted and promoted by progressives who joined in the ideological assault on 'male' scientific standards by radical feminists with their preference for "intuition" [Tong, 1989]. To then suggest that the laws and measures that facilitated and followed the satanic panic were the work of a "control culture pumped up by moral panic" [2004: 215] also ignores how that part of the control culture was shaped by feminist ideology, evidenced by Janet Reno's lauded rise to power on the back of false convictions for satanic abuse in Florida which promptly led to the Waco debacle.

Consequently, the academic lesson to learn from Orkney is that there is no difference between the methods employed to construct satanic abuse and moral panic; and that the panic paradigm like the British establishment covers up its disasters rather than admits that it was wrong. What begins as a conviction based on faith in theory becomes in the hands of the professionals, 'experts', and sociologists a set of self-referential and self-validating rationales to bolster the original conviction. The panic paradigm enables people like Winter to promote their political perspective, playing fast and loose with the evidence, in an attempt to impose ideological closure on an issue. While she failed in her specific aim, 'proving' Orkney was a satanic case, she succeeded in demonstrate the *modus operandi* of so called progressive causes which steadfastly refuse to face up to their own failings. The panic paradigm does not like it, and becomes indignant when working-class women like Judy Parry, Mrs. W, the Orkney Reporter, and the foster mother invoke common sense to expose the oppressive results of theoretical fetishism and the way progressives also use state power when they are in control.

We prefer to lay the blame for the personal and social costs of Satanic abuse [de Young, 2004: 223–225], and Waco, where it belongs. Not on feminism or Charismatic Christianity, or even their metaphors *per se*, but on the politics and practice that follows from *any* uncritical conviction. Orkney demonstrates that when armed with uncritical theory, it does not matter whether or not the control culture reflects progressive power or 'reactionary' religious belief—there is trouble ahead. Goode and Ben-Yehuda have much to answer for too. Blaming rural Christians for DCCs followed on from refusing to face up to the obvious implications of the feminist anti-porn 'panic': blatant moral enterprise trying to force singular ideological beliefs on a pluralistic society. The UK experience, whereby the feminist academics and activists promoting "the truth" of satanic abuse were the same as those crusading against pin-up porn the decade before [see Itzin, 1992; 2000], may be an exception, but we doubt it. If the US boosters had dug deep enough they will find a connection between those promoting satanic abuse, myths and erroneous generalizations about pornography, bogus medical evidence in custody disputes, and all the rest. The reason for that is that they emerged out of the same belief systems and the imperative to impose it on others. To reinforce the point we need do no more than point out that that the moment the Orkney case fell apart, the radical feminists in the UK promptly generated a DCC case of their own.

HERE WE GO AGAIN

Cheered on by Campbell, using bogus medical evidence provided by Dr. Camille de san Lazero, who had been awarded an OBE for her 'services to children', and disclosure therapy yet again; this new feminist crusade wasted £millions. Refusing to accept that they had been wrong about Cleveland and Orkney, the feminists convinced Newcastle city council to adopt their perspective. Consequently, having panicked the parents and paid compensation for abuse that never happened; the authorities paid out again to have four "experts" including Johnson from Nottingham proclaim that the two acquitted care workers were really guilty, and had been handing the children over to others too, which was a complete fantasy. The authorities then had to pay out a third time when the maligned pair, Lillie and Reed, won the libel case in which san Lazero confessed that she had turned negative medical evidence into positives for ideological purposes[12] and the judge had to denounce disclosure therapy yet again [*Daily* Mail, 31.7.02: 16–17; Dyer, 2002].

When ideologues waste money that could be spent on child protection you have no need for Satan; but you have to ask what is going on when the panic paradigm denounces the Thatcher government as hiding satanic abuse when despite Orkney, its Department of Health wasted even more cash funding a RAINS 'study' of 'survivors' designed to prove that their satanic abuse was real [*New Christian Herald,* 5.10.96]. Crusading cops and social workers could also be found having a second go ten years later on Isle of Lewis in Scotland under Tony Blair's New Labour administration [*Sunday Herald,* 11.7.04: 1]. Having exposed the fact that the only difference between progressive moral entrepreneurs and any other is that they are deliberately trying to provoke 'moral panics', the next chapter will begin to answer those questions by demonstrating that covering up progressive oppression is not restricted to radical feminists. On the contrary, Orkney was merely a foretaste of the way that the paradigm was beginning to demonize the working-class for daring to prefer their common sense to experts, social workers, sociologists, and professionals whose convictions lack common sense.

Part III
The New Politics of Panic

Part I revealed that moral panic was a myth, a conceptual phenomenon with no grounding in reality. Having explained how that followed from the myth's foundations, Part II covered the how progressives had promoted the politics of panic as an integral part of their political agenda; demonizing their opponents and explaining away their failures. We discovered that there was little difference between the elite and the interest group perspectives. The former, be it Barker or Winter, offered an ideological account and explanation for events, misrepresenting the origins, nature, and effects of their subject matter. Although de Young detailed the activities of the interest group activity behind the horror-headlines, she also attempted to convince readers to accept a political perspective that was contrary to the evidence, invoking strain blame to deflect attention from the role of progressives in the satanic panic. In every case the label was being applied in a selective manner. Although it was used to stigmatize the beliefs, values, and truth claims made by moral entrepreneurs the authors did not approve of, especially when they appeared to have social influence amongst the public; when progressives engaged in moral enterprise using the same methods, everyone looked in the opposite direction or attempted to explain it away by blaming the public. When the media threw the spotlight on the progressives' activities that was denounced as moral panic, too. The authors' accounts reinforced the fact that the concept has no theoretical, methodological, or evidential integrity.

Part III explores why the panic paradigm uses a concept devoid of viability and explanatory value, by probing behind the issue of selectivity and considering the role of moral panic *in* progressive moral enterprise. Chapter 7 examines the bizarre case of the grass-root pedophile panic in Paulsgrove. Instead of denouncing the horror-headlines about a peaceful protest as a panic about phantom vigilantes, the paradigm swapped sides. It reinforced the media myth that the residents were violent vigilantes and asserted that they were panicking about a nonexistent threat because of the endemic abuse within their own families. As the omitted evidence, including video-tapes of the events, proves that the riots never happened, we have conclusive proof that our alternative accounts are not merely competing interpretations. In this case, the panic paradigm was projecting progressive fears and indignation onto phantom folk devils, as the paradigms and the progressive's past failings caught up with them.

The Conclusion explores the changing nature of progressive politics, which accounts for the theoretical and evidential problems we have uncovered in the myth of moral panic. It explains that the politics of panic is not restricted to selectivity but amounts to a form of fear inducing moral enterprise by the new postwar petit-bourgeoisie which has created an authoritarian control culture in order to impose its values on society: a mirror image of the seminal studies' folk devil: the old petit-bourgeoisie.

7 Streets of Fire

SCUM

On Friday, 4 August 2000, Britain woke to horror-headlines that had already gone global. "Scum with a deficit of intelligence" on a "sink estate".[1] Paulsgrove, whipped into frenzy by *The News of the World* (*NOW*), had formed a violent, vigilante lynch-mob and attacked the apartment of Victor Burnett, an alleged sex offender, before going on a rampage, fighting riot-police, and causing extensive property damage. Not content with that, the mob also spent the next week rioting, driving innocent people from their destroyed homes. All of which went to prove that the government was right to keep the sex offender registers closed to the British public because they clearly could not be trusted [Silverman and Wilson, 2002]. Despite the response to the horror-headlines being the nearest that a "precipitating event" has ever come to generating a moral panic as Cohen *defined* it; the panic paradigm sided with the politicians, and the socially accredited experts on the moral barricades, stereotyped the folk devils, and ignored the real amplification of deviancy that followed. As it did so *after* the subsequent court cases led to not guilty verdicts because the CCTV proved there was no riot, the paradigm was projecting its members' fears onto the folk devils and deliberately misleading readers.

This episode also belies the myth that the quality press steers clear of sensationalism [Goode and Ben-Yehuda, 2010: 94]. *The Guardian,* the UK's 'progressive' newspaper extended the myth to the whole city three years later to 'explain' why a gay math teacher preferred to fly to his death in the English Channel rather than rebut allegations that he had propositioned two boys:

> Portsmouth with its pent up sailors and poverty, and its tight grey streets encircled by sea and motorways, can be a slightly unforgiving place. And in recent times allegations of paedophilia have become a particular source of local outrage. Three years ago, anti-paedophile vigilantes mobilized on the Paulsgrove estate in the north of

the city, attacking innocent people on the flimsiest the evidence [*G2* 28.05.03: 2].

Every word was false. There was little poverty. The major naval base had long since become an upscale shopping mall. The city has some narrow streets like all British cities do, but plenty of wide ones too, as well as numerous peaceful public parks of more than one square mile, and seven miles of open beach front. It hosts the headquarters of IBM Europe, the Zurich Insurance tower, and a popular university with the best criminal justice department in the country. It has three marinas, a continental ferry port, numerous historic areas, buildings, and ships; and wonderful museums, including the one commemorating D Day opened by President Clinton. It is probably the cleanest big city in the UK too. *The Guardian*, like the panic paradigm, was pandering to its professional readership, absolving them from making the pedophile problem much bigger than it need have been; and that offers us the opportunity to consider the reality behind grass root 'panics', and the politics of panic hinted at in the previous two chapters.

ONE ROAD IN

According to Silverman and Wilson [2002], the riots were the inevitable result of the *NOW's* "common sense solution" to the "social strain" created by the government's attempt to reintegrate child-sex offenders into the community. Despite admitting that the program was underfunded, overloaded, paid little attention to reintegration, and that open registers had not led to that much 'vigilantism' in the US; the authors insisted that the non existent riots drove pedophiles underground, led to more assaults, prevented a public debate about reintegration, and masked the real problem besetting child protection: the sexualization of children in popular culture and internal familial assaults. By naming and shaming pedophiles, the *NOW* encouraged the factors that led to molestation, evidenced by the way the social construction of pedophilia (sic) and the labeling process had led to the massacre of a class of schoolchildren in Dunblane, Scotland because the perpetrator had been isolated by the local community. The vigilantes on the Paulsgrove estate, supposedly cut off from Portsmouth by motorways with only one road in to reinforce the image of a marginalized lumpenproletariat, believed that child abuse would disappear if they drove the pedophiles out. However, as their target was being monitored and had not been arrested since release, that lack of threat proved that the vigilantes were panicking about a nonexistent pedophile threat because of the *NOW*. Indeed, the rabble led by Katrina Kessell, who had failed to come to terms with her own childhood abuse, was not really worried about pedophiles at all. The real cause of the riot, exposed by the indigenous Labour MP, was the housing project's social problems, dysfunctional families, disaffected youth, and its long history of taking the law into its own hands. When those factors combined with the *NOW's* name and shame campaign, the hot weather, and the residents' intent to distract attention away from the ongoing abuse in their own families, the riots can be seen for what they were: acts of personal revenge masquerading as public concern, evidenced by the need to re-house four innocent families who had fled from the mob that was so moronic that when it tried to firebomb the critical MP's house, they destroyed the house next door instead [Silverman and Wilson, 2002: 33, 43–45, 59–61, 79, 126–129, 132–136].

As usual, when one examines the claims made by the paradigm, its account proves to be completely erroneous, beginning with that claim that there is only one road onto the estate. There are six: Leith Avenue, Portsview Avenue, Kelvin Grove, Washbrook Road, Ludlow Road, and Allaway Avenue.

WELCOME TO PAULSGROVE

Having spent the previous decade trying to stop the pedophile 'panic', start a public debate about the government's self-defeating approach to sex offender integration, and arrest the epidemic of false allegations encouraged by the child protection agencies, as others can attest [Sheldon and Howitt, 2007: 23]; we would have seen through Silverman and Wilson's apologia for professional malpractice even if we knew nothing about Paulsgrove; but we did. Despite failing to convince the Economic and Social Research Council that Paulsgrove was the perfect place to study the failure of public complaint procedures in the UK the decade before, our preliminary study for the grant proposal ensured that we knew all about residents' contempt for the authorities refusal to address working-class complaints and that history of taking the law into their own hands. Indeed, the latter ensured that the media reports made no sense at all, because if the residents *had* targeted Burnett the outside world would still be none the wiser.

The media reports' lack of veracity can be gauged by their failure to distinguish between two housing estates. The demonstrations included Wymering Garden City, the show piece of the governments 'homes fit for heroes' policy after the First World War. Paulsgrove was then built to accommodate those displaced by extensive Nazi bombing during the Second World War rather than former slum dwellers as Evans claimed [2003]. The response to the official neglect of the 1960s and 1970s on both estates was self—improvement during the 1980s and 1990s. As a result, the graffiti, decrepit cars, piles of trash, and other symbols of sink estates did not exist. The children's playgrounds only suffered natural wear and tear, the nets on community soccer field goal-posts lasted all season long; and although more than one Grannie grew her own, disruptive drug taking, like vandalism, was minimal. While some of the older houses in Wymering were past their best, Paulsgrove was not a sink estate, as you can see for yourself with the aid of *Google Maps* [Allaway Avenue, Paulsgrove, UK]

The reason for that was owner occupation had reached 55 percent as early as 1991, as it had on most housing projects [Jones, 2011: 206]. Thanks to extensive self-employment, unemployment was only 5.9 percent during the 1990s [Williams, 2004]. Paulsgrove people were proud of their estate, and rightly so. Allaway Avenue, scene of the first demonstration, could win the Britain in Bloom competition if former housing projects were allowed to enter. All this made Paulsgrove an extremely unlikely venue for a riot, and certainly not by a lumpenproletariat that did not live there. The residents' history of do-it-yourself justice was based on the concept of the "fair fight" and support for the underdog, as more than one bully or deadbeat dad had discovered to their cost. Consequently, the assertion that the residents' had targeted innocents made even less sense than blaming the *NOW* for riots that never were.

RANDOM THREATS

The creation of the Paulsgrove myth began four weeks before, with the horror-headlines covering the abduction of eight-year-old Sarah Payne some 20 miles along the coast from Portsmouth in the neighboring county of West Sussex. Although missing invariably means murder, *every* paper and TV news report devoted an increasing amount of space to the parents' hapless hope that Sarah would be found alive [*The Sun*, 04.07.00; *The Sunday Times*, 09.07.00], premised on the remote possibility that she was being sexploited by a pedophile ring [*Sunday Times*, 09.07.00: 7]! As the search across the beautiful South Downs that stretch from Portsmouth to Brighton dominated the news for the next two weeks, the inevitable contrast between the formerly happy home and stranger danger emerged, illustrated by *The Sun's* 'Our Sarah Is Out There—And Alive' feature, including "poignant pictures of missing Sarah" playing "in the safety of her garden at a family christening party" [06.07.00: 9]. Academics and child protection "experts" who claim that the media emphasis on stranger danger masks the reality of the greater threat to children from within the family are clearly incapable of understanding why abduction-murder stories capture more attention and have greater salience for the majority. As most parents do *not* maltreat or molest their children, strangers *do* represent a greater threat than the family to most children. As most parents also see their primary duty as protecting their children, the statistical chances of abduction are far less meaningful to them than the fact that their children can be snatched like Sarah was, within a hundred yards of her grandmother's house. The fear invoked by these random threats reflects that fact that one slip can lead to a lifetime's regret. Likewise, while the "deathly silence" that immediately descended upon playgrounds nationwide that summer [*The Sun*, 02.08.00: 3] looks like closing the barn door after the horse had bolted, it offers an insight into the parental perspective and helps explain why the pedophile panic of the previous decade, promoted and exploited by progressive professionals for ideological purposes, had had such a deleterious effect on UK children and was about to backfire. The even tighter control that parents exercised over their children after Sarah's abduction was explained by a Paulsgrove father:

> We were trying to encourage my daughter to try and spread her wings a little bit and go outside, out into the Close and it just totally stopped ... We've got a nice big garden, so we've always, up until then, we've always said, you know, the kids are fine in the garden, but then [E] was saying, "I want to ride my bike outside", "I want to go outside", but it just threw doubt into it. I was constantly looking at people and I was thinking, 'I don't know you. Who are you? What are you doing in our Close?' [Respondent 51].

Once Sarah's body was discovered on 18 July, the media coverage not only doubled when the pathologist confirmed that death had occurred within hours [*Daily Mail*, 19.07.00: 2], public angst turned to the anger reflected in *The Sun's* headline "Nail the Bastard" [18.07.00:1]. Having been drawn into the Payne's heartache for over two weeks, thoughts of revenge amongst the public were common, but the claim that the NOW turned that anger into vigilantism is simply not true.

NAMING AND SHAMING

Although the NOW will forever be associated with the phone bugging scandal which led to its demise in 2011, its response to Sarah's abduction was primarily political. The day before the discovery of the body, it launched the *For Sarah* campaign [17.07.00: 1]. Feature articles and a dedicated *For Sarah* website urged the public to lobby their MPs for a UK version of Megan's Law, giving the public access to the sex offender registers in order to engage in self-protection. The government said no, insisting that opening the registers would lead to vigilantism although the US experience suggested otherwise [Thompson and Greek, 2010]. Consequently, the following Sunday, the NOW also launched a name and shame campaign to force the government's hand. The six page spread, including a list of fifty people convicted of child sex offences, their mug-shots, their last known whereabouts, and a short description of their offense, ended with the threat to publish another fifty every week until the government changed its mind. The justification offered was that with "110,000 child sex offenders in Britain, one for every square mile", Sarah's death proved that "the police monitoring of these perverts is not enough" [*NOW*, 24.7.00: 1]. Given that the chief suspect, who proved to be the killer *was* a registered sex offender that claim was not misplaced, although the campaign was symbolic as it would take forty years to cover everyone already registered. The *NOW* also advised people in a prominent sidebar not to engage in do-it-yourself justice but contact the authorities if any problem arose. Despite the rest of the news media uniting in condemnation of the *For Sarah* campaign, and doing so all week long, the fact that an independent Mori poll found 88 percent in support of open registers should prove once and that media horror-headlines are no guide to public opinion [*NOW*, 23.07.00: 6]. If anyone was panicking, it was those opposed to a UK Megan's Law.

GET THE VIGILANTES

Given the extent and ferocity of the media criticism of the *For Sarah* campaign, Silverman and Wilson's claim that "no alternative analysis" appeared in press exposes the formulaic nature of that claim in the panic paradigm. On the contrary, apart from *The Sun* the rest of the news media insisted vigilante violence was inevitable [Williams, 2004: 224–235]; and their opposition increased after the name and shame feature. The public appears to have dismissed the evidence on offer, and probably did so because of the on-going 'vigilante debate' ignored by paradigmatic accounts.

During the previous two decades, the public had become increasing annoyed that have-a-go-heroes were being punished more harshly than the criminals that they tried to stop. The key issue concerned the amount of 'reasonable force' that one was entitled to use when confronted by violent criminals. As we saw in Chapter 3 the police had considered indicting a mugging victim because he was a martial artist, whose hands and feet were considered offensive weapons! While he escaped prosecution, Russell Burrows was found guilty of injuring an escaping burglar he had wrestled to the ground as he had no need to "assault" the criminal to protect himself, even though a police officer doing the same thing would have been applauded for capturing the crook [*Daily Mail* 15.09.94: 23]. The debate reemerged in 1992 when the Director of Public Prosecutions, Barbara Mills, agreed that the law should be changed, but was deposed before she could act [*Sunday Telegraph* 21.06.92: 14; *Daily Telegraph*, 29.10.92: 3]. The following year, when Duncan Bond and Mark Chapman were sentenced to five years jail-time for assaulting a local teen behind a spate of motorcycle thefts, the Bishop of Norwich and cabinet minister John McGregor joined in the widespread condemnation given that criminals who *killed* have-a-go-heroes got far less [*Sunday Telegraph,* 13.06.93: 3; *The Telegraph*, 15.06.93: 4; *The Daily Mail*, 18.06.93: 29]! When John Taylor was beaten to death by half-a-dozen drunken youths trying to destroy his garden fence in Alverstoke "for a laugh", the youth who landed the fatal blow only got two-and-a half years jail-time; and he was not the only thug turned killer [*Daily Mail*, 12.12.92: 12–13]. As a result, *The Sun* was not alone in its belief that the criminal justice system was betraying the public [30.05.94: 1].[2] After dozens of other cases, the issue finally came to a head in 1999 when a farmer, Tony Martin, was found guilty of manslaughter after fatally wounding a fleeing burglar. Although he did not need to shoot, the public understood why he did; over a dozen frustrating unsolved thefts from his decaying farm in recent years. As a result of the public outcry, the New Labour government promised to redraw the guidelines on reasonable force. As they had yet to keep that promise before the *NOW* launched its name and shame campaign, that helped ensure that the claims made about the threat of vigilantism did not have the impact its proselytizers hoped that it would, not least because they could offer no evidence that mobs had maimed and killed innocent people in the past having mistaken them for sex offenders [*The Guardian*, 24.07.00: 3].

The source of the mob rule myth was the National Association for the Care and Resettlement of Offenders (NACRO), which asserted that:

> Past experience shows that when paedophiles are publicly identified some of them go to ground, fearing vigilante attacks. They move elsewhere and change their names, making it difficult or impossible for the police to track them. This may in fact increase the risk to children [*The Independent*, 23.07.00: 1].

The same claim was repeated *ad nausiam* in a local media blitz by NACRO's policy director, Paul Cavadino, and on TV by talking heads like Val Howarth from the abuse hot-line, Childline; although no one offered any substantiation for the "40 cases" the Association of Chief Officers of Probation was supposed to have on file [*The Sentinel*, Stoke, 23.07.00: 2; *The Guardian*, 24.07.00: 1; *The Daily Record*, 03.08.00: 28; *The Guardian*, 24.07.00: 3].

The public was not convinced. They suspected those "cases" referred to a series of angry protests that followed the two child serial killers, Oliver and Cooke, responsible for many of missing children over a decade before, as they went from town to town on their release in 1997 and 1998 looking for somewhere to stay. Having served short time for manslaughter because of evidential technicalities and having refused to reveal the whereabouts of other suspected victims to avoid further prosecution, no one wanted them in their town [*The Sun* 06.10.99: 17]. The rowdy protests had finally turned into a violent confrontation with the police outside a Bristol PD after Cooke's whereabouts had been exposed by the local *Evening Post* [23.04.98: 10–11; 24.04.98: 1]. As this pair of serial child killers were obviously atypical, having literally got away with murder, and had fled back to prison rather than go underground, they did not prove the generalized threat of vigilantism. Faced with the unpleasant but understandable reaction to the release of a gang of child sex killers, the Government opened a special unit to house them

[*The Guardian*, 20.7.99: 6]. When the probation service finally turned their "cases" over to Duncan Campbell, it transpired that these had nothing to do with vigilantism either. The list did not include the worst case of anti-pedophile violence on record; the fatal shooting of William Malcolm two years before, because the case was ambiguous. Malcolm had a prior conviction but may have been innocent of the allegation that led to his death at the hands of the thuggish friends of his 'victim'. The Partington family who had fled their home in July 1997 and the James Cameron case in Kilmarnock also highlighted the threat posed by false allegations [*G2* 11.8.98: 2–3]. Another half-a-dozen incidents turned out to be 'nonce bashing' following incendiary 'outings' in the local press. Campbell joined in that hypocrisy by forgetting to remind his readers that the violent protests involving the Cooke, Oliver and another member of the gang, Lennie Smith, had also been provoked by horror-headlines concerning police opposition to their release because they obviously posed a real risk to the public, or how the reaction had encouraged the government to explore 'preventative detention' at the end of killers' sentences [*The Sun*, 18.6.99: 12–13; *The Guardian*, 16.2.99: 9]. As the "ugly mobs" that often appeared outside courts when child killers were indicted [*Daily Mail* 23.2.93: 1] were not included in the list, we can discount them too. In short, as public protest, 'nonce bashing' and revenge attacks do not amount to vigilantism, the alleged threat relied on two dubious examples of "lynch mobs". *The Guardian*'s "Tabloid Sets Vigilante Terror on Innocent Man" which dominated the media before Paulsgrove turned out to be no more than persistent taunting by local delinquents, and the innocent bore no resemblance at all to his alleged name and shamed doppelganger. While that was no comfort to the target because of his fears of worst-case scenario, it is impossible to determine whether it was the *NOW* or the anti-vigilante press that had encouraged the incident. What is not in doubt is that this case concerned harassment not vigilantism [*The Daily Mail* 24.07.00: 8; Williams, 2004: 231–245]. The second, the alleged "attack" on the pediatrician because of her name-plate, promoted *after* Paulsgrove by *The Guardian* [30.09.00: 1], was completely false as a local folklore buff explained:

> the story was almost immediately exaggerated in the telling. The underlying confusion about the words was true, but there was no mob. The doctor woke up one morning and found the word "paedo" on her walk and front steps, and decided to leave for a while. I think that falls somewhat short of being "forced" to "flee" by a "mob". No flaming torches, no bricks through windows, not even a group of people. It could have been the work of one person [alt.folklore.urban[3] 07.07.01; see Williams, 2004].

In short, as the public could distinguish between vigilante lynch mobs, public protests against freeing unrepentant child serial killers, violence following a false allegation, 'nonce bashing', and false reports about name and shame vigilantism; the only people panicking were the authorities, the children's charities, and the professional classes. Whether or not the professional classes' disproportionate response reflected fears that their exploitation of the pedophile over the previous decade for political purposes had now backfired, it definitely masked the fact that the monitoring system, with rare exceptions like Cleveland PD, was a sham. That is why, when the residents of Paulsgrove attempted to expose that fact, they were denounced as violent vigilantes by superimposing accounts of the anti-Cooke protest in Bristol two years before onto a peaceful protest [*Bristol Evening Post* 24.04.98: 1; Williams, 2004]! The professional classes had to create a vigilante threat to maintain their position on closed registers to hide their own failures.

THE BIGGER THE LIE

The national papers' uniform response to the Paulsgrove protest, like the Clacton reaction, can be accredited to the stringers from the local paper, *The News*. Its horror-headline "Streets of Fire: Naming of Paedophile Leads to City Riot" set the tone for the rest of the coverage [04.08.00: 1]. Generic plurals and the other rhetorical devices endemic to panic press were evident in a report that prefixed the supposed target with the qualification "alleged" [*The News*, 04.08.00: 1]! Although the demonstrators had *not* attacked Burnett's apartment and only one car was destroyed, *The News* claimed that *homes* had been bombarded with bricks and *cars* had been torched by the violent mob [*The News*, 04.08.00: 2]. The authenticating details including "children as young as six, their faces contorted with fury, began hurling stones at the Ford Fiesta", never happened. They were copied almost verbatim from the report of the anti-Cooke protest [*The News*, 04.08.00:2; Bristol *Evening Post*, 24.04.98: 1].

Over the next two days, *The News* and the national media, now encamped on the former housing project, churned out a 100 articles a day, an average of six per paper. The result was a media amplification spiral in which *The Independent's* "battle scene" motif was the most distorted [06.08.00: 21]. Provincial newspapers all ran the story too, either emphasizing the "ex" offender motif like Newcastle's *Evening Chronicle* [04.08.00: 2]; or implying potential innocence like *Leicester Mercury's* "Mob Attacks Home of Suspected Sex Offender" [04.08.00: 9]. What made this coverage even more ridiculous than usual was that the press reinforced its previous warnings by making Paulsgrove the exemplar of lynch mob violence elsewhere, even though no other lynch mobs appeared [e.g. *Evening News*, Edinburgh, 04.08.00: 6].

CLACTON II

The Paulsgrove press followed the Clacton reaction step by step, as we have shown in more detail elsewhere [Williams, 2004]. With one solitary exception, the press agreed that the riot in Paulsgrove was a warning come true, and that the name and shame campaign had led to lynch mobs. The effect was so powerful that it convinced many people that they *saw* a week of rioting on their TV screens!

Exaggeration and Distortion

The predominant image was of vigilantes rampaging through the streets, hell bent on destruction:

> A furious mob went on the rampage last night outside the home of a paedophile 'named and shamed' by the News of the World. Rioters hurled stones and bottles at Victor Burnett's home before attacking cars parked outside [*Daily Mail*, 04.08.00: 7].

The melodramatic rhetoric, complete with over reporting and rumors presented as facts, created the impression that a housing project was being besieged by a mob in the same way that Clacton was supposed to have been overrun by mods and rockers [Cohen, 2003: 20]. As Cohen predicted, the local paper, *The News,* added caveats because readers would be aware of the truth. The most prominent was that "a vocal but peaceful demonstration" had "turned into a riot", although that was also false [*The News*, 04.08.00: 2]. The most important was Hampshire County Police spokesman, Bob Golding's hint at a police press conference that the demonstration had little to do with the *NOW*:

> What has happened tonight is utterly outrageous and disgraceful. *If* it happened as a result a result of naming and shaming in the *News of the World*, it is a clear indication of the destructive effects of the paper's actions [Our emphasis—eds. *The Daily Mail*, 04.08.00: 7].

Unaware that the CCTV camera covering events would prove otherwise, these caveats were ignored by the national press in favor of Deputy Chief Constable, Ian Redhead's assertion that:

> The majority of people on the streets of Paulsgrove were not concerned parents. They were using the debate over sex offenders as an excuse to carry out disorder and violence [*Independent*, 05.08.00: 3].

Prediction

Paulsgrove was prediction personified, proof that naming and shaming *had* led to vigilantism. All three pre-Paulsgrove media themes—vigilantes, innocents attacked, and molesters going underground—used by critics like Malcolm Savidge MP to demand that the *NOW* suspend its campaign "before someone gets killed" [*Aberdeen Evening Express*, 02.08.00: 8] were immediately applied to Paulsgrove. *The Guardian,* for example, insisted that Burnett had disappeared despite printing an interview with him [05.08.00: 1; 13.08.00: 14]. *The News* had even published a front page story 'Paedophile Vigilantes Target Man' [03.08.00: 1] four hours *before* the demonstration started! As the reports of the subsequent demonstrations served as follow-up stories, it is not surprising that the only other example of "vigilantism", the non attack on the Newport pediatrician, became associated in the public imagination with Paulsgrove. By deliberately *not* reporting several other peaceful demonstrations like one held in Yate, Bristol and constantly referring to Paulsgrove as the most violent manifestation of vigilante violence [e.g. *The Guardian*, 05.08.00: 1], the end result was a folk memory of a summer full of lynch mobs, evidenced by Lawler's later account [2002: 103]. When the residents responded to the initial misrepresentation with more demonstrations, these were reported in the same way as the first:

> Last night predictions that the baying crowd would continue to threaten suspected paedophiles in the area proved correct. A mob of up to 300 men, women and children hurled missiles at the home of another man 300 yards away from Thursday night's violence [*The Independent*, 05.08.00: 3].

Once it became apparent that Burnett *was* still active, the press desperately scrabbled around for evidence to substantiate their claims, typified by *The Daily Mail's* "Innocent Families Flee Mob: Pedophile Vigilantes Defy Police Pleas to Halt the Attacks":

> Galvanized by the 'naming and shaming' of a local sex offender by the *News of the World*, crowds of up to 300 have rampaged through the streets of a council estate burning cars and smashing up the homes of suspected child abusers. The protesters, gathering for a sixth night of violence last night, claim to have evidence of at least 20 paedophiles living on the Paulsgrove estate in Portsmouth and say they will be targeted until they leave [10.08.00: 6–7].

Images and Symbolization

Although *no one* was attacked, the orientation and symbolization deployed in the press ensured that readers believed that they had been. The "sharpening up process", complete with its "emotionally toned symbols", quickly generated the image of a "social disaster", as in "we don't want another Paulsgrove" [Williams, 2004: 30]. That image was reinforced by accrediting every minor incident and crime amongst all 30,000 residents, solely to the mob. This was achieved by using the shotgun approach, identified

by Knopf, whereby every act becomes an incident, every incident a disturbance, and every disturbance a riot, evidence by the claims made by *The
Guardian* [24.07.00: 3; Knopf, 1970: 20 cited in Cohen, 2003: 20].

Deviance Amplification

In this case, the paradigm ignored the way that the media *had* for once
increased the deviancy in three ways. First, the protest continued into the
following week for four reasons. The protesters were annoyed that: the
media did not explain the real reason for the demonstration; the local council instead of addressing their complaint declared that it would sack any
employee and evict any tenant found to have been present; and that the
police had literally occupied the estate instead of admit that they had failed
to monitor Burnett [Williams, 2004; Williams and Thompson, 2004a and
2004b]. Second, by linking every adverse event to the protest to 'prove'
that the vigilantes were "out of control", the horror-headlines increased the
deviancy by offering cover to anyone intent on criminal activity knowing
that the protesters would be blamed, as often happens [Cloward and Ohlin,
1961]. Although there were not that many criminal acts during this period,
the dramatic firebomb incident ensured people believed there were. It had
nothing to do with the protesters, who believed that the local MP was
"a complete wanker" for thinking that they considered him that important [R80]. Third, the most significant falsehood, the myth of four families
fleeing their homes, was disproven by its very source: *The News'* feature
"Innocent Families Being Forced Out" [09.08.00: 5; 11.08.00: 1].

As the one "innocent" cited claimed to have found three of their windows
broken when they returned from work on 10 August, they could not have
been "forced out" by the protest [Police Statement I90, 24.10.00: 1]. The
demonstrations not only took place in the evening, they had been suspended
the day before [*The News*, 11.08.00: 4–5]. The most likely explanation is
that these "innocents" were exploiting the image of the protesters stoning
houses to secure an otherwise difficult council house transfer. Whether or
not they were targeted by others for some other reason, as the firebombed
house had been, the fact remains that no one has ever uncovered a single
example of anyone, be they sex offender or innocent, being attacked by any
of the protesters. Although the commercial exploitation was limited to the
media coverage and the sale of syndicated reports and photographs, the
ideological exploitation of the incident was huge.

Orientation and Sensitization

As the real origin of the protest was only mentioned in one article [*The
Daily Express,* 12.08.00: 10–11], and a TV documentary which was pulled
by Channel 4 at the last minute for reasons that have never been explained,
Paulsgrove was subjected to ideological closure. The public was led to believe

that Paulsgrove was in the hands of a lynch mob. They were sensitized to the new image of the folk devil, complete with its spurious attributions and specific auxiliary status. This did not replace the emotive symbolic label of vigilante but added to it; putting a name to it to "structure the situation", in the same way that "mods and rockers" became the face of vandalism.

The vigilantes were "the chavs" from sink estates even though Paulsgrove wasn't one. Believed to originate from the Romany word for child, chav had become an acronym for several imaginative slurs including "council house and violent". It is a hate term, but like the US equivalent of "white trash" it is deemed perfectly acceptable by the politically correct despite being as vicious as the 'n word' when used to disparage blacks [Jones, 2011]. The reason for that is exemplified by David Aaronovitch's "Why I am so scared of Paulsgrove Woman", which also explained the new politics of moral panic and why the paradigm switched sides [2000]. Aaronovitch was no ordinary commentator. He was one of the leading figures steering the National Union of Students away from militancy and towards the politics of political correctness during the 1970s, which shaped the perspective of the professional Left in the 1980s, and went mainstream under Tony Blair's New Labour Governments after 1997. Aaronovitch began by admitting that he was disappointed that:

> when working-class women and their children take to Portsmouth's streets, it isn't in support of the NHS,[4] or to demand better nurseries, but out of a desire to hang, burn or castrate some of their neighbours [Aaronovitch, 2000].

His rationale for that myth regarding violent intent was the Left-wing folklore about fascism we covered in Chapter 3:

> This depressing failure of the proletariat to perform their historical task is slightly reminiscent of those days in 1968, when dockers and meat-porters marched—not for socialism or against the Vietnam war—but in support of Enoch Powell [Aaronovitch, 2000].

That self-referential justification, ignoring the duplicity of the professional generated pedophile panic we covered in the last chapter, was reinforced by his dismissive caricature of the protesters:

> mums (no dads), faces studded, shoulders tattooed, too-small pink singlets worn over shell-suit bottoms, pallid faces under peroxide hair telling tales of a diet of hamburgers, cigarettes and pesticides [Aaronovitch, 2000].

Having promoted the stereotype belied by the demographics of the protest, Aaronovitch then revealed the source of the fear and loathing that the working-classes now invoked amongst progressives. By admitting that "Paulsgrove Woman are an alien race to me", Aaronovitch drew attention to the fact that progressives had long since abandoned political agitation amongst the working-class in favor the new petit-bourgeois social movements, and justified doing so on the grounds that the chavs had no views on serious subjects, lacked ambition and aspiration, and exhibited an arrogant immaturity, woeful irresponsible, and a lack of respect for law. What made that echo of the spurious attributes listed in *Folk Devils* ironic was that many of the Paulsgrove protesters had been mods in their youth. It got worse. As Jones explained in his study of the perspectives adopted by the UK's political classes, when the sections of the working-class impoverished by Thatcherism objected to being abandoned in favor of the positive discrimination for petit-bourgeois members of ethnic minorities irrespective of need, the Left denounced that as racial bigotry. They then employed that as an excuse for leaving the unemployed and underemployed to their fate, as well as blaming them for their enforced dependency on welfare. For example, determined to end subsidized housing projects, Thatcherism sold off the public housing stock, ensuring that what was left, the most run down, had to be used to house the most in need and the most hopeless. Hence the rise of 'sink estates' with their demoralizing social deprivation and generation of exasperation that others were being compensated for the problems of the past when many of those gaining the benefit had not even been born [Jones, 2011].

As the Left's response had made all sink estate protest guilty by association with the activities of small neo-fascist groups who tried to exploit the progressives political neglect, it was no surprise when Paulsgrove exposed the progressives' parallel fear of "the mob" Aaronovitch played the racist card. Determined to stigmatize the carnivalesque atmosphere on the demonstrations seen on TV which belied the mob image found in the press, Aaronovitch claimed that it reminded him of "the smiling faces you see in lynching photographs from the Old South . . . especially when there's very little interest in guaranteeing that the next victim is actually guilty" [2000]. That perfect illustration of Jones' revelations about the closet class hatred amongst the professional Left as it becomes more and more divorced from the working-class, also explains why Aaronovitch's "excuse" for the supposed ignorance of the mob was also wide of the mark:

> a significant number of the women are single mothers, some of whom have been mistreated or abandoned by men. They're used to feeling like the bottom of the social heap. Yet here are blokes living among them whom even they can despise, and on behalf of the one thing that does belong to them: their children. A telling comment from one interview was that drug-dealing had now become part of the scenery in Paulsgrove, but that paedophilia never would be; they may have failed in every other way to protect their families, but not in this [Aaronovitch, 2000].

That claim belied by the demographics we uncovered [Williams, 2004], was a function of the deliberate use of Katrina Kessel by the press to promote the chav stereotype, although like Blake in Cohen's study, Kessel was in a minority of one in the local action group, Residents Against Pedophiles (RAP). As a result, the most profound thing that Aaronovitch wrote was his admission that the Left was using the same language to dismiss the protesters as every other commentator on TV and in the press [2000].

Causation

With everyone agreed that the riots had been caused by chavs who read the *NOW* and whose prejudices had been unleashed by the name and shame campaign despite Bob Golding's big "if", we need say no more here than that was very convenient. Before the death of Sarah Payne, media coverage of integration program problems revolved around two issues: housing officials complaining that every other agency was in favor of placing released offenders on sink estates; and the hypocritical claim that peaceful protests against that policy was nimbyism [*The Guardian*, 13.10.99: 8–9]. Now that it needed to prove the *For Sarah* campaign would lead to vigilantism, the press conveniently forgot what it had said before.

THE PUBLIC REACTION

Although it is rare for the paradigm to offer any evidence for public panic, the hate mail sent to the Paulsgrove protesters, which arrived in its hundreds, provided plenty of evidence that sections of the public accepted the stereotype of the chavs that appeared in the press. It also came complete with the *same* derogatory comments and phrases seen in the 30 pieces of Handsworth hate mail complete with vigilante style threats! The authors clearly believed that Paulsgrove was full of ignorant, uneducated, single-mothers living off welfare. Several suggested naming and shaming the demonstrators so that everyone would know who to avoid and prevent their "own children playing with such offspring and becoming contaminated". As several also referred to "breeding monsters" and insisted that the mothers should "have their tubes tied", these authors prove that these phrases had nothing to do with race, but are common *sexist* insults directed at working-class women in the news [Williams, 2004]. On the other hand, the protesters also received hundreds of support letters from people who had ignored the misleading media barrage and realized that this was a protest against the authorities, although a lot appeared to believe that the protest reflected their own pet hates. The author who believed it was targeting gay child molesters was typical of this sub group. As a result, we concluded that major news stories mobilize cranks with a surfeit of postage stamps on both sides of the political and educational divide; and that if hate mail reflects an authoritarian personality, chav hating progressives have one too. The same can be said of the posts on internet-based newsgroups, which also ignored the issue of open registers in their determination to condemn, which they did in an even more derogatory fashion, evidenced by those found on *free.uk.talk. portsmouth.*[5] They were obsessed with benefit scrounging:

> 24.08.00 The very parents who complain and go to the streets probably beat their kids at night or just leave them to roam the streets. What a load of *scum* they are—reactionary, ill informed, vulgar and DHSS *scroungers*. They have done the best thing to tell the public that Paulsgrove is the pits and full of hatred.

The following example from *uk.local.hampshire*[6] was representative of the themes and insults contained in the hate mail too:

> 10.08.00 About 250 people . . . are they representative of the presumably large number of people on that estate, or are they basically intimidating other people who disagree with them? Shouldn't the Police be taking action to stop them rather than timid requests to call it a day? Do people really want that *sub-section of society* calling the shots, I mean really? And is anyone prepared to nip it in the bud?
>   No-one seems like they dare do it, for fear of being called a "paedo-sympathiser". It's total madness R I agree, and at the end of the day it's just a mob of *thick-as-shit* typical Paulsgrove *scum* looking for an excuse to burn cars and brick windows with impunity. Did anyone see the interview on the BBC breakfast programme this morning with *that ape* from Paulsgrove [Lee someone or other] in the baseball cap and women's earrings, backed by a few other members of his lynch mob? Now THAT was one *thick twat* even by Paulsgrove standards☺. Fucking hypocritical *white-trash bastards*, pretending that "normal" people on Paulsgrove are the "salt of the earth", what crap, I mean don't get me wrong there are some decent types there but these few are outnumbered by the vast majority of *scummy single-parents* who got *up the spout at 12 years* old, and are *propagating the latest generation of baseball-cap wearing numbshulls (sic) who'll be busting into your cars in a few years time to nick your stereo, alcoholic, sky TV-watching chain smokers who haven't worked in decades, knob heads* like that bloke on the TV this morning who start pub brawls for fun, and other assorted morons whose so-called "SOCIAL" problems [ie they're *fucking lazy and mentally ill*] keep a whole army of social-workers, probation officers, and "counsellors" in jobs.
>   If I had the choice of having a former paedophile or one of those Cro Magnon (sic) *pillocks* living next door to me, I know who I'd choose [Emphasis in original—eds.].

As well as reinforcing our criticism of the self-serving nature of the paradigm's "analysis" of common pejorative terminology; this example illustrates how prejudice once formed, ignores countervailing evidence to the contrary. Despite the ideological closure in the mainstream media, live talk shows offered one of the few opportunities to raise the real cause of the protest, although the protesters quickly learnt that doing so was the quickest way to be charged with riot. The police monitored every word as DW and we discovered when they interrupted our interview about his contribution to the popular *Kilroy* show and arrested him. He had to be ring leader because he was articulate, and exposed the real problem behind the protest. The most revealing feature of the hate mail was the number who repeated the criticisms in the elite press concerning the children's clothing, placard slogans, appropriate bedtime, and the hypocrisy of parents putting their children at risk by taking them to violent riots. These complaints demonstrated that the supposedly educated classes are only too willing to suspend their criticism of mainstream media when it confirms their own prejudice. The references to sexualizing children, an allusion to light clothing on a hot evening, amount to blaming the victim. While some placards looked hate filled they had been deliberately sought out by the media to reinforce the theme of hate-filled people. Sending children to bed before dark during a humid summer is somewhat authoritarian, and no one complains when the Left take children on demonstrations because, of course, that is an indication of peaceful intent [Williams, 2004].

RIOT BY RHETORIC

As Jock Young defended the panic paradigm's reliance on conjecture when covering the social control culture on the grounds that their motives were usually secret [1971: 1–4]; we decided to test that excuse by setting out to secure copies of both the police statements and the CCTV footage so that we could compare them. While UK freedom of information laws do not extend to that material, we correctly believed it would not prove difficult for the ethnographically orientated. The police statements, written *a month* after the event, were constructed to conform to the requirements of Section 1.1 of the Public Order Act, 1986:

> Where 12 or more persons who are present together use or threaten unlawful violence for a common purpose and the conduct of them [taken together] is such as would *cause a person of reasonable firmness present at the scene to fear for his personal safety, each of the persons using unlawful violence for the common purpose is guilty* of riot' [Our emphasis—eds. HMSO, 1986].

This intent to create a rhetorical riot was immediately apparent in Police Constable D's account[7] of the scene outside Burnett's apartment when he

arrived *before* the demonstration had begun. He claimed that he was confronted by a group of "clearly excited women holding placards" who were
"too agitated" to discuss the "concerns" that he tried to raise with them
"to calm them down" [PC D: 13.09.00: 3]. Unfortunately for Operation
Sackville,[8] he was promptly contradicted by Inspector T:

> There was some shouting and *chanting but the mood of the demonstra-
> tors was not aggressive* [Our emphasis—eds. Inspector T, 22.09.00: 1].

Both versions, and Inspector T's contradictory claim that the protesters
attempted "to goad" the police into "a debate", were belied by the CCTV.
The tape revealed that there were only half-a-dozen women with a single
placard between them at this point, and that they were talking to the single
police officer present while waiting for the rest of the demonstrators to
arrive [PC D: 13.09.00: 2]. Likewise, at the very point that Inspector T
claimed to have withdrawn his officers because the demonstrators' refused
to disperse [22.09.00: 2], and PC D attempted to "firm up" that account
with his claim that he "feared for" the safety of his probationary officer in
the face of a riotous mob [13.09.00: 3], the CCTV revealed that the demonstration had not even started! The protesters had only just arrived, and
were unfurling their banner. When PC D claimed that as he "returned to
my post at the rear of the property" he was told by acting sergeant BR that
"we're losing control of this", and so he "realized that what was occurring
was a riot", which he defined as a "dangerous frenzy with people looking
for violence" [3.09.00: 4–5]; he was contradicted by both Inspector T's
timeline and the CCTV's clock [Inspector T: 22.09.00: 4]. Similar problems emerged within and between every officer's account concerning *every*
aspect of the protest. The same applied to the statements taken from hand
picked elderly residents who would not have fulfilled the legal requirement
of "reasonable firmness" even if they had been able to see events from their
windows, which many could not [Williams, 2004].

THE LONG SLOW FUSE

The 3 August demonstration was not only peaceful; it had little to do with
the *NOW* and was directed at the authorities rather than Burnett. The criminal damage that occurred was the equivalent of the "fringe delinquency"
that the paradigm had always dismissed in the past. It was committed, as
the local councilor and magistrate Mr. Horne immediately confirmed, by
"the usual yobbos" who took advantage of the demonstration as such elements often do [Rosenbaum and Sederberg, 1976]. The police, the media,
Silverman and Wilson all knew that, and so did the *British Journal of
Criminology,* which declined to publish a more detailed account of what
follows, although *The Police Journal* did [Williams and Thompson, 2004a

and 2004b]. The protest's 18-month etiology is best told by delineating the different groups that appeared on Allaway Avenue. The first group, were the *complainants*,[9] included Mrs. W, referenced uncritically but erroneously in the Hampshire Constabulary official report as an organizer [Case Summary, Operation Sackville, 2000: 1–3]. The W family had complained that Burnett had approached their son to go to his apartment, a year before the protest. When they tried to follow-up that complaint by calling the local PD, their failure to remember the officer's number ensured that they drew a blank [R98]. Feeling embarrassed that the lack of action may indicate that they had overreacted, the Ws kept their experience to their close friends. Others insist that this was not the only complaint, and point to Burnett's disappearance for a week while his front door was replaced by a fire resistant one as proof that they collected a petition presented to the local council [R71].

Silverman and Wilson dismissed both claims as false, and insist that Burnett was no threat, in the face of the police acknowledging the W's claims. The confusion surrounding the second complaint may reflect the fact that the local monitoring system did not act on referrals from the public, let alone complaints to councilors; but there is no doubt that Burnett was a threat. He had fled Weymouth four years before, having been exposed for doing the same thing [*Sunday Mirror,* 25.8.96]. Be that as it may, the complainants were annoyed that Burnett had not been subject to a Sex Offender Order under the Crime and Disorder Act 1998 following the W's complaint. They feared that while the residents had been informally monitoring known ex-offenders for years, the authorities' failure to act might indicate that other offenders were being secreted into the estates' shrinking public housing stock without their knowledge [R80].

The second group, the *hospitables*, consisted of the older residents who had been befriended by the seemingly "very helpful" Mr. Burnett. Now, having read their *NOW,* they realized that his cover story about being denied access to his children by his ex-wife had been a ruse. Far from expressing irrational fears about a harmless 'ex' offender as Silverman and Wilson would have you believe, this group were annoyed at Burnett for taking advantage of their typical Paulsgrove trust [R62], *and* at themselves for having dismissed the complainants' suspicions in the past. It was this group that alerted others who did not read the *NOW,* quietly advised Burnett to leave the estate, and compiled the list of teens seen in his company in order to alert their parents. Meanwhile, the complainants having had their suspicions confirmed, turned to the internet where they discovered that Burnett had been a member of Britain's "biggest known paedophile ring" [*Daily Mail,* 3.2.89: 5]. On release he had settled in Weymouth, but fled having foolishly boasted to a *Sunday Mirror* reporter that he could "have any child he wanted within minutes of meeting them" and that "there is nothing, nothing at all, that parents can do to thwart a determined child molester" [25.8.96]. It was that article, outlining the same *Modus Operandi* that he had used in Paulsgrove rather than the *NOW* that led to the decision to demonstrate.

Far from being angry, the initial reaction had been one of shock, which then turned to angst at the sight of the forty distressed families adversely affected by Burnett. Hiding the real reaction behind the lie that that the protesters were covering up their own internal familial abuse as Silverman and Wilson did should be a sociological scandal. Although prevalence levels would ensure that some protesters families would have experienced an internal assault in the past, Paulsgrove was a clear case of stranger danger. The first two groups' response was speculation about the authorities continuing refusal to act against a very active Burnett, evidenced by all the texts he had continued to send to the teens. Given the history of do-it-yourself justice on the estate, the fact that the hospitables had warned Burnett to leave and the complainants decided to hold a peaceful demonstration on the following Thursday, when he brazenly returned, demonstrates that the protesters were exercising extreme restraint.

In any event, the protest was directed at the local authorities because they had failed to follow the government's *Potentially Dangerous Offenders Protocol,* activated in October 1998, supposed to guide the actions of local Multi Agency Public Protection Panels, (MAPPPs). Originally conceived to encourage and allow the UK's county based PDs to respond to specific crime patterns in their area and rearrange their budgets according, they became Multi Agency Public Protection Arrangements (MAPPAs) under s5–7 of the Crime and Disorder Act 1998, and s67–69 of the Criminal Justice and Court Services Act 2000 amounted to the formalization of police and probation services use of the sex offender registers created in 1997. The inability of most PDs to reallocate sufficient funds in their already tight budgets ensured that monitoring was far from comprehensive. This was not the PDs fault. The government had spent considerable sums on sex offender programs in prisons which hastened release, but far too little on reintegration. Most people did not know that MAPPAs existed and were oblivious to the poor state of monitoring in the UK [Nash and Williams, 2008 and 2010]; but that did not apply to the more informed from Wymering and Paulsgrove.

Given the W family's complaint, and the indisputable evidence that he was still active, the police could and should have made Burnett subject to a Sex Offender Order to make him desist. Their failure to do so and the excuse they offered illustrate the consequences of underfunded MAPPAs, and the lack of forethought regarding reintegration that we had highlighted as far back as 1991 on BBC's *Week In: Week Out* following a public protest in Wales. The attempt by Hampshire PD to excuse their failure by arguing that even the best protocol "can never guarantee that potentially [sic] dangerous offenders do not slip through the net" is moot given what happened in Weymouth, the Ws complaint, and the extensive evidence of activity that emerged once he had been "outed" [Hampshire MAPPA 3rd Edition,

2002: 2]. What made this failure worse was that Burnett's history, his *MO*, and recent activities replicated the example of the hypothetical Mr. 'X' in the Home Office guidelines for imposing an order to the letter. The residents feared that the failure of Hampshire MAPPA to issue more than a dozen orders since its inception meant that the authorities were engaged in less official monitoring than their own unofficial efforts over the previous decade. The fact that Hampshire MAPPA still did not consider public complaint a good enough reason to impose a sex offender order two years later demonstrates both the failings of the monitoring system and the need for open registers [3rd Edition 2002: 7 and Appendix 1]. Yet, when it came to apportioning blame, the residents did not blame the police, but the authorities as a whole:

Interviewer: Who were you blaming for that?
R87: The council; you know, everyone. The police, you know, everyone let you down. It's not just one department, it's the government as a whole . . . It's down to the probation service, the police, the lot, yeah?

FEAR AND FRINGE VIOLENCE

The third and largest group involved in the demonstration consisted of friends of the other two groups, those drawn in by the rapidly spreading news, and even passers-by on the night. They were there not because of the name and shame campaign, or the past complaints, but their fear of the pedophile generated by child protection experts, the *Cook Report* and *Dispatches* TV shows, and the previous decade's nonstop horror-headlines about missing murdered children. These were "the fearful" whose susceptibility had been reawakened by the Sarah Payne coverage. These married or divorced mothers had subsequently suffered their own and working neighbors' children under their feet or cooped-up in the back yard all day long for the previous three weeks. Consequently, once the demonstration "was on", the release of that pressure ensured that all the issues involved became encapsulated in the single catch-all demand that the authorities prioritize the rights of the children over those of a single, active, sex offender that they had failed to monitor. That pressure also explains why, having been denied their usual freedoms to visit friends, use the play parks, or roam Portsdown Hill, you could not have kept the children away from the protest if you had tried.

The forth group in attendance that night, hiding amongst the couple of hundred onlookers, were those *"usual yobbos"*. As the subsequent trials demonstrated that these half-dozen miscreants were not connected to the protest, no one has any excuse for maintaining the myth that they were; except one. Unlike the mods, the muggers, and the skinheads that the paradigm had paraded as symbolic rebels in the past, this group turned out to be just that. When we finally got the chance to explore their motives we were rightly made to feel foolish. It transpired that the yobbos had trashed his apartment to ensure that Burnett could not use it again. The first car set on fire was a diversionary tactic to get at the Lada which they erroneous believed to be Burnett's sister's car [Witness Statement 5, CE: 04.08.00: 1–3]. The brick through the Housing Office window was payback for not removing Burnett. The stone thrown at the constable was nothing to do with them, as the trials proved [TUY].[10] Here for the first time in the history of the paradigm were some yobbos actually engaging in "resistance", consciously, instrumentally, and deliberately, and the paradigm missed it! That failure not only followed from the paradigm's political bias, recourse to strain blame, and promoting the chav stereotype, but its refusal to explain popular protest as one must, by differentiating between the groups involved, and reconstructing the interaction between them [Wright, 1978: 92]. What makes that failure worse in this case is that the paradigm like every other academic deliberately ignored the evidence that emerged in the trials [Silke, 2001; Evans, 2003].

RIOT! WHAT RIOT?

The timeline revealed in the courts, with the aid of the CCTV that overlooked Allaway Avenue proved that the protest never turned violent. Burnett's windows were smashed at 6:30 pm, and the apartment trashed while he was being escorted to Cosham PD, an hour *before* the demonstrators had even gathered on the park opposite the Allaway Avenue shopping plaza at 7:30 pm [Statement PC D: 13.09.00: 1–2]. The 100 or so female protesters with their children then took half an hour to take up their position, some 20 to 30 yards from the entrance to Burnett's apartment block at 8:00 pm. Another 200 or more onlookers and the women's husbands decided to observe from the sidewalk. The demonstration grew over the next hour as still others, like one married woman who had gone to the shopping plaza with her husband and had asked what was going on, joined in too [R81]. The diversionary tactic, the fired car in Bourne Road, behind the Allaway Avenue shopping plaza occurred shortly after 8:00 pm, out of sight of the demonstration. When the smoke generated by extinguishing the fire began to drift over the plaza roofs, the demonstrators can be seen on the CCTV marshalling the children away. Despite their intent, it took another hour before the yobbos set about destroying the Lada. Once it was set alight, the CCTV confirms that the organizers decided to "call it a day" and began to disperse because they did not want to be associated what had happened [R 62 and 87]. The brick thrown at PC BR occurred at 9:10 pm, and amounted to an act of bravado by an impressionable youth who having seen his heroes flip the Lada decided he would prove himself too. The final incident followed shortly afterwards when one of the yobbos threw a brick through the plate glass window of the council housing office on the shopping plaza.

The CCTV confirmed that the criminal damage had nothing to do with the peaceful protest, which had dispersed long before the riot police, who had been ever present, were finally deployed at 11 pm in order to protect the integrity of the crime scenes from later onlookers. Otherwise, there was no rampaging through the streets, no one besieging homes, no one firebombing anything; no one, apart from a impressionable youth, attacking anyone, no one fighting with the police, and no orgy of destruction. As you can see from the CCTV extract [Figure 7.1], those flipping the Lada while the police looked on were not part of the demonstration, and yet the myth of riot became more preposterous with each telling. Academics, like the news media, vied with each other to produce the most dramatic account, with the prize going to Hughes and Edwards [2002: 2] who added more imagery details for effect:

> over 100 people *carrying the picture* of an *alleged sex offender*, as it appeared in the News of the World, *besieged and ransacked his home, fire-bombed his sister's car* and then *assaulted the police who were protecting the suspect* [Our emphasis—eds.].

There was no picture of Burnett, no besieging the apartment, no fire-bombing of the car, or mass assault on the officers at the scene; and Burnett was ensconced in the Cosham PD a mile away. While they no doubt had their own reasons for doing so, Hughes and Edwards were burying the real issue: the failure of the public protection panels to protect the public. Likewise, in the same way that the CCTV exposed the myth of the riot on the first night, the police videos covering the subsequent protests prove that these authors' claim that "five nights of rioting" followed was equally false. On the contrary, the videos prove that what followed amounted to the revival of the ancient British proletarian tradition of rough music.

ROUGH MUSIC

The week of rough music replicates the second phase of Cohen's model with its amplification of deviancy and show of force by the police, although other features like moral enterprise were not necessary as the alleged problem was already illegal and widely condemned.

The decision to continue the protest was taken by the complainants and hospitables the next morning when they woke to discover that they that were being denounced as vigilantes, the yobbos' handiwork was being written up as a riot, and that the TV were talking to the fearful.

Figure 7.1 The Lada incident.

Top Left: The demonstrators can be seen spreading out across the road, with the bulk on the south side of Allaway Avenue (left), opposite Wastwater House, Burnett's apartment block. A car unable to convince the demonstrators to let it through is turning around. The majority of onlookers are out of sight of the CCTV in the foreground left and right. You can see one youth smashing a window of the Lada. **Top Right:** As the disappointed driver completes the U turn, you can see two other youths approach the Lada. **Middle Left:** Two more youths approach the Lada. **Middle Right:** The youths can be seen kneeling down to tip the Lada. **Bottom Left:** Two youths flip the Lada. **Bottom Right:** The Lada is now on its side. The demonstrators remaining on the north side of the Avenue can be seen breaking ranks to the other side of the roadway. Inspector T and PC BR can be seen in the foreground watching these events.

Note: the distances between these three groups of participants are much greater than they appear because of the camera angle, but can be gauged by the relative size of the figures.

So they selected spokespersons, had a quiet word with attention seekers, elected to emphasize children's rights to gain more sympathy, worked out how to stop the yobbos, and formed Residents Against Pedophiles [R87, R64]. Their first decision as an organized group was to continue the demonstrations until the authorities and the news media address the threat that Burnett had posed and explain why the previous complaints had been ignored. Their second decision was to find out how many other unknown offenders were on the housing estate. The rough music in Paulsgrove between the 4 and 9 August took the same form. Residents having assembled on the park would parade off at 7 pm. They took a circular route to include all the addresses of the offenders in Paulsgrove and Wymering that they had uncovered during the day. As they did so, they would wave their placards and odd banner in the air, and would begin to chant as they neared the targeted property. When they got to the address, they would stop, form ranks, and continue to chant *at the house* of the sex offender to make their protest, before moving on to the next address until they arrived back at the park to disperse.

Without realizing what they were doing, the residents were replicating the tradition of organizing a noisy parade to the homes of anti-social people warning them of what could happen if they did not desist, mend their ways, or clear off. Compared to the past, when participants would blow horns and bang on pots and pans if they didn't have drums, and hang or burnt effigies of the trouble makers outside the residence, the Paulsgrove protesters restricted themselves to inflammatory placards and chanting. Although the placards attracted adverse comment in the press, they were meant to be intimidating, but were *not* a call to action. The demand "pedophiles out" reflected the annoyance they were not being housed in middle-class areas. Others saying more were an encouragement to leave of their volition, and the widespread but not unanimous belief that child killers did not deserve to live. Until the 1860s and in some places like Portsmouth up until the 1890s, authorities turned a blind eye precisely because this form of protest dissipated community anger, encouraged public order, and prevented further wrongdoing [Thompson, 1993]. Rough music was the antidote to vigilantism; but the pedophiles had to go.

As both academic and non academic accounts insist that the following week was full of riots, it is possible, for once, to assert that the horror-headlines like "Rioters Clash with Police: Vigilante Britain" had a uniform effect [*The Daily Mirror* 09.08.00: 17]. Indeed, the effect was so powerful that two very short scuffles of the kind that often occurs on otherwise peaceful demonstrations became a mass folk memory of *seeing* rioters clashing with riot police on TV screens. As we have explained in detail elsewhere; both incidents involved mothers trying to rescue young teens dawdling behind the parade being seized by snatch squads. The protesters claim that the police were "out of order" for "picking on the kids", not least because the initial pushing and shoving led to the immediate deployment of batons and mace. The women intervened knowing, as occurred in one case, that if any male protester attempted to do so, that they would be "kicked to fuck". The police countered those claims with their own: teens, lagging behind the protest, had been throwing stones at the targeted houses [R68, 71; Williams, 2004; Williams and Thompson, 2004a and 2004b].

Whatever the truth, it is indisputable that progressives would have immediately denounced what happened as heavy handed policing as they had during the miners strike of 1984. Even Britain's police apologist, Peter Waddington, admitted that incidents like this are common during the policing of demonstrations by women [1992]. Yet no one in the panic paradigm took account of that, or has ever mentioned how the estate was effectively occupied by the police, or addressed the incidents of police goading and provocation seen on the demonstrations. We were subject of intimidation when we videoed police behavior on the unreported protest march to the PD. Otherwise, as every action undertaken by the protesters conformed to those delineated by E.P. Thompson as the "ritualised expressions of hostility", we have no need to justify the label 'rough music' [Thompson, 1993: 469]. As the protest also stopped the moment the council agreed to talk, the real purpose is not in doubt either. While the police videos reveal that the house calls were very noisy, they did not involve any physical altercations at all. For example, the one produced at Ms. Kessell's court hearing shows that the sex offender standing ignored and unmolested outside his house only yards from the 250-plus crowd chanting at a property in Braintree Road. Indeed, these videos explain why so few indictments followed the rough music, and that the only people convicted of any crime, apart from the one stone thrown youth, had pleaded guilty to those catch all charges like "obstruction" that Cohen scathingly denounced when they were used against the mods at Brighton. The reason for that plea was that they did not want to risk being labeled a rioter, because pleading not guilty meant you were in for a show trial.

THE LIST

During the period when they were unable to find any innocents being attacked, the media became obsessed with "the list" of targets RAP supposedly drew up in order to find "an innocent" on it. This nonsense has also featured in paradigmatic accounts even though the legend of "the list" played the same symbolic role that paying fines by bank check did in *Folk Devils*. Silverman and Wilson inferred that the failure to produce the list for media inspection proved the protesters were targeting innocents. That typical example of non evidence was surpassed by Evans, who despite speculating that the list probably did not exist, made other ironic inferences as a result:

> Paulsgrove residents [sic] made much of a 'list' of suspected paedophiles that had been drawn up and was used as the basis for their actions.

However, there was no consensus between them as to the sources for this list. Neither has it ever been clear that such a list had a real existence; according to one account there is no firm evidence that anyone other than the protesters 'saw' it [Evans, 2003: 165].

Evans then used this nonexistence to proved that there was a subconscious link between "the vigilante state of mind" and the "mind of the state" reflecting "the strain" caused by the governments "ambiguous" approach to sex offenders [Evans, 2003: 163–165]. As the protesters believed that the authorities were duplicitous, the policy was underfunded rather than ambiguous, and Evans' source was Silverman and Wilson who relied on media disinformation despite being told by residents what had really happened; the only "strain" evident here is the academic peer review process that passes this nonsense as fit to print. Whenever we raised the issue, the respondents became agitated because "we never had a bloody list" [R80]; and the reason for that was the three sources they used to find targeted houses. The major source was research at the local library and on the internet, but others could be suddenly added to that 'list' when the police "gave the game away" by either standing guard outside other properties or referring to others on their unsecured police radio communications. In other words, there was no permanent list. It not only changed daily as a result of RAP's research, but could also change in an instant before and during the protest. Moreover, as RAP was determined to *avoid* targeting innocents because of their awareness of the extent of false allegations, that often meant holding back an address until after further research. Apart from the properties inadvertently revealed by the police, which confirmed the estate *was* being used to house released offenders, RAP were determined that no house would be subjected to "a rude cacophony of controlled hostility" [Thompson, 1993: 467] unless there was conclusive proof that it was occupied by a convicted offender [Williams and Thompson, 2004a and 2004b].

RESIDENTS AGAINST PEDOPHILES

As well as concentrating on the personal history of Ms Kessell, rather than the fourth generation home owning residents like Sharon Mills, to promote the stereotype of a sink estate full of chavs; the press ignored the male spokespersons. The press and the panic paradigm imposed a blackout on RAP's other activities as they would undermine the mob myth. RAP held a candlelight vigil; collected a petition in support of open registers; held sidewalk sales and a pantomime to raise funds; engaged in extensive research on the Web; held educational classes about the law and sex offender policies; and swapped experiences with other people organizing peaceful protests that were not reported in the press. The most important omission was the fact that despite all the horror-headlines, RAP was included in the city's deputation to the prime minister, and that it was their Letter of Protest concerning the widespread failure to issue Sex Offender Orders, the lack of funding for monitoring, and the need for MAPPAs to include a member of the public that led to a change in the law when the show trials collapsed.

VIGILANTES OR VIGILANCE

The lack of any evidence for riot ensured that Operation Sackville proved a complete failure. After dozens of charges were dropped; and pleas whittled the 37 charged with minor offenses to "the ringleaders", a synonym for pleading not guilty, the four show trials at the local crown court took place a year later. However, the "ringleaders" were also found not guilty because the judge decided that the court would watch the CCTV tape rather than the police's heavily edited version of it. Needless to say, the mainstream media failed to cover the collapsing cases in any detail, or review the meaning of the verdicts, leaving it to Portsmouth's *The News* to try and explain it all away:

> Prosecutors and police officers were today picking up the pieces after the £2m Paulsgrove riots investigation resulted in just one jury conviction . . . [because] . . . the evidence was not strong enough . . . but with so few court successes the public is left asking whether it has got its money's worth [24.10.01: 7].

The answer, of course, was "no" because wasting £2 million on trying to demonize peaceful proletarian protest rather than spending it on monitoring and reintegrating sex offenders into the community would never be worth it. Despite armed police, 92 witness statements claiming that they had seen a riot, a crime-mapping expert, a face-mapping expert, edited CCTV tapes, and pointless forensic evidence; all four juries used their common sense and believed what they saw on the CCTV rather than what the media had said the year before. A desperate attempt to save the day by subjecting *us* to a Third Party Disclosure Order in the vain hope that our research notes would reveal evidence of a conspiracy to riot did not work either. The prosecutor, who believed in the rule of law, accepted our legal arguments why he should leave our offices empty handed, and when the police seized our research papers several months later they still found nothing, because like the CCTV, our notes proved the opposite. Once the show trials were out of the way, and Roy Whiting was tried, convicted, and imprisoned for the murder of Sarah Payne in December, 2001, the new Home Secretary, David Blunkett met the Payne Family in a blaze of publicity and announced that a lay individual would be appointed on every MAPPA [*The Express*, 18.12.01]. Although this was widely seen as a concession to the *For Sarah* campaign, as the *NOW* campaign had not included that demand, the government's decision, like the sudden increase in the use of Sex Offender Orders across the country, can be accredited to RAP and the Paulsgrove protest.

NAMING AND SHAMING

Yet again, the social reality behind horror-headlines had little in common with the paradigm's account, which paid no attention to the causes of precipitating events; and thanks to the CCTV and the police videos there can be no equivocation as to why, and what that means. One only has to compare the myth of Paulsgrove to other accounts of violence during other political protests to see how progressive ideology determines their approach. When real riots broke out in Oldham, Burnley, and Bradford during the summer of 2001, and the local Pakistani and Bangladeshi youth put over 200 police officers in hospital as well as caused extensive property damage, the academic Left had its explanation ready. As the police had failed to protect the Asians from racists, the teens' violence was "reactive", the only choice left for the violated and victimized community [Poynting and Mason, 2007: 74]. As that justification could just as equally be applied to Paulsgrove where the fringe delinquency and two short altercations do not compare to the riots in northern English towns, we are clearly dealing with double standards when it comes to the politics of community protest. The same applies to academic criticism of media coverage. When the press focused on the *deliberate* violence perpetrated by minority on the otherwise peaceful anti-capitalist demonstrations across Europe during the decade after Paulsgrove, progressives denounced the selectivity in the media and leapt to the demonstrators' defense [Donson, *et al*, 2004; Rosie and Gorringe, 2009].

It would appear that while anti-capitalist and politically correct protest is acceptable, woe betide the proletariat if they dare think and act for themselves, especially when they are exposing the failings of the progressive petit-professional classes. As we saw in the previous chapter, while the rise in child protection was to be welcomed, the battle for ownership to exploit it for ideological ends was not. The hundreds of false allegations that followed—Cleveland, satanic abuse, Newcastle, and care homes—had wasted £millions, leaving MAPPAs in counties like Sussex and Hampshire unable to monitor an increasing number of released offenders to make way for the "innocents" being sent to jail by progressives. Far from Paulsgrove inhibiting the desperate need for a public debate about the reintegration and monitoring of ex-offenders, the panic paradigm ensured that was the case by promoting rather than challenging the myth of Paulsgrove. Having raised the need for that debate over and over again in mainstream media since 1991, pointing out that the ideological exploitation of pedophilia was generating false convictions, was leading to an increase in attacks, and would have dire consequences one day we take no pleasure in being right. Those dire consequences, however, were *not* the nonexistent riots by phantom vigilantes who have been blamed for two deaths [McAlinden, 2010: 384]. They were the consequences of the lack of funding for monitoring and integration because the system was overloaded with the falsely convicted. That enabled hebephiles like Burnett to generate widespread distress and pedophiles like Whiting to murder another working-class child. The paradigm helped create that social disaster by constantly denouncing disquiet about progressive promotion and exploitation of false allegations as moral panic, failed to explain the fear of random threats, and dismissed popular fears of pedophiles as a conspiracy theory about upper-class perverts [Jenkins, 1992; 2009: 57–58]. Now that the subsequent experiment in open registers demonstrates that the fear of vigilantism was always exaggerated, and never justified excluding the public from 'public protection panels', Paulsgrove was clearly a disproportionate professional panic rather than a grass root one [Kemshall and Wood, 2010].

What makes this case the worst example of moral panic malfeasance in our files, despite the social disaster of satanic abuse, was the means chosen to cover up progressive culpability this time around. In order to do so, the paradigm flip-flopped, lied about every indicator of panic while masking its own, and encouraged its audience to project their fears onto the folk devil and cheer for the riot police when they took the stage in the morality play unfolding on the Paulsgrove estate. The level of hypocrisy involved reached unprecedented heights. Having spent two decades ignoring how progressive theory and practice was sending hundreds of innocents to jail, they now claimed to be concerned about "innocents", and generated some more fake victims to do so. As a result the working-class residents had to rely on their common sense to work out that "something did not add up" when Burnett was not subject to a Sex Offender Order. Having never had the 'privilege' of taking a class in moral panic they were oblivious to the paradigm's role, but they soon worked out that the professional classes were more interested in promoting, maintaining, and furthering their own interests than the reality of child abuse. The hospitables were also incensed at Aaronovitch's racist card having gone out of their way to help an Asian family move in, on the estate the year before.

Rather than being condemned, the Paulsgrove protesters should be lauded for exposing the incompetence of the authorities, the *lack* of monitoring, and the progressives' determination to deny the public a say in its own protection. We are grateful to them for enabling us to debunk the myth of spontaneous grass root panic and the tenuous nature of strain blame. The week of peaceful protest only became a grass root panic because the paradigm was willing to lie about the history and nature of the protest. The paradigm was more than willing to rely on horror-headlines to do so, its claim about ideological closure was formulaic, it picked the wrong paper when it apportioned blame for provoking the 'riot', and ignored the ambiguous effects. Despite the media crusade against open registers, the public continued to support the concept despite the "summer of rioting". The contents of hate mail revealed that the headlines confirmed the authors existing beliefs and offered new rationales for them. If hate mail reflects an authoritarian personality, progressives would win the prize. Paulsgrove also put the final nail in the paradigm's supposed political neutrality.

The political lesson to learn from Paulsgrove *is* disheartening, but a very different one from that promoted by the paradigm. The protesters made mistakes, as they admitted they had, and constantly argued with one another over the right course of action, what the negative reaction meant, and what to do next because of their lack of experience. Kessell was not alone in her belief that David Ike may be on to something. As we have noted elsewhere the protesters were desperate to learn about the government's sex offender policies that had been overshadowed by the torrent of moral enterprise emanating from the TV over the previous decade [Williams and Thompson, 2004a and 2004b]. Avoiding the temptation to go native was extremely frustrating, it led to many awkward moments and difficult decisions, but it ensured that we saw the most intriguing aspect of the whole affair. With no one to guide them, and the world against them, the protesters reinvented rough music, and the rising generation learnt that no matter what the media said, direct action can get results even at risk of jail. It was as if we were watching some form of embryonic class consciousness emerging, before it dissipated.

Having exposed how the paradigm's theoretical, methodological, and evidential integrity had now reached rock bottom, we now turn our attention to why the paradigm swapped sides, demonized this isolated proletarian protest, and covered up professional culpability.

Conclusion
Carry on Panicking

BEHIND THE HORROR HEADLINES

The more we explored the worlds behind the horror-headlines and compared what we found to the paradigm's accounts we discovered that it made no difference when the descriptive gave way to generic panics. No one appeared to be panicking apart from the author. Claims to the contrary amounted to insisting that horror-headlines, be they generated or exploited by various interests, and the odd poll result meant much more than they did. Proof of panic, those "more sociological explanations", consisted of misrepresenting the social actor's motives, promoting a mass of assumptions, and omitting countervailing evidence.

The mods and rockers proved that the media did not have the effects ascribed to it and Paulsgrove confirmed that effects are invariably ambiguous. Orkney revealed that the media sometimes gets it right. Video nasties and Paulsgrove reinforced the lesson from Clacton, that stigma is in the eye of the beholder and need not adversely affect the folk devil at all; the videos were back on the shelves in no time and the 'vigilantes' helped change the law. The exception, pedophilia, followed from the nature of the sexual preference and fear of worst-case scenarios. Otherwise, common values were as difficult to find as a link between social strain, the deviants, and their condemnation. The nearest we got was zero tolerance of violence; but exceptions were evident too. There was more mutual dependence between the horror-headlines and the authors than between the deviants and their accusers. The moral entrepreneurs were trying to change society's values rather than restore them. The progressive attack on the chavs demonstrated that social group values, or rather what they said they were, can readily change too. Give or take the "reporting effects" that produce poll results, the general public tended to be spectators unless they were victims of circumstance. Orkney, a microcosm of contemporary western societies, confirmed that. Despite the allegations, the children's hearings, the activities of the Parents Action Group and councillor Cyril Annal, the Inquiry, and the polarization between the authorities and the accused; most islanders went about their daily business and considered the claims and counter claims as they would any other: in terms of their existing beliefs and/or who their friends were. The folk devils reacted to their demonization in different ways. While the Paulsgrove protesters and the 'Satanists' joked about it, the Orkney island social work department fulfilled their ascribed role to the letter. Timely intervention of a dose of common sense and a demand for evidence went a long way to undermining the satanic abuse and pin-up porn crusades. Paulsgrove confirmed the importance of visibility *and* invisibility. The media and the authorities manufactured visible vigilantes because their examples of nonce bashing had failed to curtail the demand for open registers. Invisibility explained public fear of random threats. Once Burnett's outing in the *NOW* explained what his recent behavior really meant, the protesters were determined to make the threat, the lack of monitoring, visible. The video nasties and pin-up porn crusades confirmed that moral enterprise claims-making is designed to justify coercive reform. From what we saw, while the religious were aware that changing the law need not reinforce their values, progressives hoped that it would. Appeals to the public could be a genuine attempt to gain wider support, or a tactic to imply that there was a public demand. Satanic abuse and Paulsgrove suggested that social and interest groups pursue their own agenda irrespective of what the public wanted. From mods and rockers to Paulsgrove, the police did what police do, and from the Lima disaster analogy to the rhetorical riot, the paradigm consistently got it wrong.

In every case, the panic paradigm failed to cover let alone explained what "was really happening". On the contrary, like the CCCS, it deliberately omitted the evidence that would. Once we reinserted that evidence, the events conformed to the US model of the social construction of social problems. The moral entrepreneurs adopted coercive reform because they knew that they could not and would not convince the majority of the public to agree with them. The 'public panic' amounted to slapping the label on the media coverage, the activities of the moral entrepreneurs, and their perceived effects. Indeed, the nearest we got to 'panic' was the expositions offered by the CCCS, Winter, and Barker. Far from panicking, the grass root Paulsgrove residents were engaged in what progressives used to call political protest. Otherwise, progressive or religious, voluntary activist or paid employee, state agency or NGO, competent or incompetent, it made no difference; the moral entrepreneurs were determined to impose their perspective and values on society by constructing social problems and securing government backing; though that is where the difference ended. We never saw the activists in Valour, CARE, or CSAs with whom we interacted on a regular basis engage in anything other than a rational, if determined manner. Like most of the maligned we met, they were always offering to discuss things over cups of tea. The same could not be said for progressives involved in the anti-porn and satanic abuse crusades. Indeed, these members of social groups which claimed that they had no power in society while demonstrating that they had far too much, constantly displayed their indignation and worse in front of us, time and time again. Otherwise, the horror-headlines were not generating 'panic' so much as supersizing the entrepreneurs' claims.

As we suspected, hanging out with PACS and Mary Whitehouse, NCROPA and the Soho Society, the residents on Orkney and the Paulsgrove vigilantes, while interviewing and observing many others, taught us more about moral panic than academia did. It quickly became obvious that moral panic claims-making was a form of moral enterprise. The panic accounts we covered were divorced from reality because they rewrote rather than described or explained what was "really happing" to promote a political message, although that message began to change over time. The first three case studies turned the religious moral entrepreneurs into sociological folk devils. They were seen and denounced as an irrational threat to the 'rational' values of panic proselytizers, and those experts, professionals, social workers, and sociologists who, apparently, knew better than the public because of its subscription to common sense. The entrepreneurs and the public were assumed to have 'panicked' because unlike progresses they really did not have any values. Every one on the moral barricades was a reactionary; and the public was stupid. Winter, de Young, and Silverman and Wilson were not that different; the public was now reactionary as well as stupid. These erroneous accounts were no mistake, they were deliberate. One only had to look at Paulsgrove to see that something "did not add up". Having spent thirty years dismissing fear of crime and the public zero tolerance of violence as moral panic, when some real teen rebels finally turned up, the paradigm turned their political vandalism on one housing estate into a national threat posed by irrational lynch mobs full of chavs. This concluding chapter considers why they did that, and the purpose behind the moral panic myth.

A PROBLEM WITH POLITICS

As the road from Clacton to Paulsgrove was full of moral entrepreneurs from both sides of the political divide rather than a panicking public, we need to consider why the panic paradigm spent four decades claiming otherwise, despite a complete lack of evidence. It is not for want of warning. A growing number of critics raised the same questions about the label's indiscriminate use, the failure to differentiate between 'panics' about deviancy and crime, the way proselytizers ignored moral entrepreneurs' perspectives in favor of their own interpretation of it, and its political selectivity. When generic panics appeared more complaints emerged. These included the failure to differentiate between, let alone integrate the role of 'the public', social group moral enterprise, or economic and political interest groups in any systematic way; the distinct lack of any commonality, phenomenological or analytically, between the events and reactions covered by the paradigm; and the growing reliance on disproportionality, despite its ontological and methodological limitations, to justify the label. An increasing number began to ask where was the evidence that the general public had *ever* succumbed to moral panic because of horror-headlines [Sumner, 1981: 282–283; Watney, 1987: 41; McRobbie and Thornton, 1991: 560, 565–570; Tester, 1994: 85; Hunt, 1997: 645; Jenkins, 1992: 8–9; Cornwell and Linders, 2002: 314; Waiton, 2008: 104, and 112–131; Garland, 2008: 10–11, 15, 20–24; Rosie and Gorringe, 2009].

One reason the warnings were ignored relates to the nature of socio-logical criticism. As it frequently amounts to one theoretical perspective claiming that another is in error, it can be ignored for that reason; so what if Burgett noticed the paradigms "political stance towards the object of analysis" was related to structuralism? [2008: 76] The most important reason, however, was that the critics had failed to grasp that the paradigm's academic failings followed from its politics, and selectivity was merely a symptom. That is why we concentrated on the evidence offered and omitted in the case studies, and demonstrated that far from being a metaphor, 'panic' was a means to delegitimize alternative truth claims, beliefs, ideologies, and policies as innately flawed. Doing that encouraged readers to rely on the authors' account of what "really happened" so that they would then accept the political explanation offered for the 'panic'. Peel the sticker off all the US accounts of moral enterprise and put them aside, and you are left with a pile of political propaganda. We knew that demonstrating that the authors' version was not "really happening" at all would not change their minds, but it would undermine their claims that what had happened was moral panic. Indeed, in Cohen's case, having shown how the national moral entrepreneurs, the public, and parliamentarians not only failed to play their ascribed role but did the complete opposite, we proved that 'moral panic' did not exist! The fact that the other studies we debunked have all been lauded in progressive circles despite failing to justify what amounts to a meaningless label reveals that selectivity is not the issue. As the authors and their audience were either unaware or did not care that the concept *and* the evidence offered by Cohen were theoretical and rhetorical constructions, the use of the label and belief in its viability demonstrates that it is a political perspective, *per se*. Barker and Winter even used it to justify political comment diametrically opposed to their own 'evidence': Thatcherism was permissive rather than censorious; and while the media accounts of Orkney helped explain the lack of prosecutions, that was because the coverage was correct. Like everyone else, their analysis and claims-making owed more to their ideological and political fears than 'reality'. That is why we have to cross swords with Goode and Ben-Yehuda.

REVISIONISM

Goode and Ben-Yehuda's post Reno makeover is a seminal case study in how not to address criticism. Rather than admit that Cohen's concept was a theoretical construct based on rhetorical evidence, they avoided the issues of validity and explanatory value in favor of a new summary of events that extended the myth, rewriting the motives behind Cohen's PhD repeated parrot fashion by de Young, and adding more myths for effect. The most fraudulent was turning the Prime Minister, Macmillan's famous phrase "most of our people have never had it so good" reflecting the fact that the working classes living standards had increased into a common complaint that the youths' "never had it so good" to bolster Cohen's claim's about the teens materialism [2009: 25]. Despite what is recorded in *Hansard*, they covered up the fraud in *Folk Devils* by perpetuating the myth that:

> the *dominant mood* among politicians and legislators toward youth crime in the period following the initial incident *was angry, self-righteous, vindictive, condemnatory, and punitive"* . . . Politicians and legislators joined the bandwagon against offending youth, making proclamations, statements to the press, and speeches that expressed *a vindictive self-righteous punitive stance towards youth crime* [Our emphasis–eds; Goode and Ben-Yehuda, 2009:26; 32–33].

Needless to say, having rewritten history, the boosters' international text book on moral panic was never going to review Cohen's lack of evidence for the "cognitive processes" that supposedly justified the concept and the label [2009: 21–31]. As it is futile trying to define something that does not exist, it is not surprising that their attempt to save the label led to further problems. Rather than deal with the politics of panic, they avoided it by concentrating on selectivity. Despite finally admitting that progressives engaged in moral enterprise, they argued that moral panic amounted to something more, even though without those "cognitive processes" the "anxiety" offered to indicate a generic panic was in progress remains anxiety, no matter how "intense" the "concern". That is why their examples of generic panics were inscrutable; vague or self-defeating. Likewise, rather than clarify how Cohen's consensual model could have ever withstood the ramifications of Moralgate and the rise of National Valour, they invented sectional panics and pretended pluralism was something new. While that 'solution' enabled them to hive off the embarrassing feminist pornography 'panic', it did not resolve the fundamental problem: no one has ever justified the label or its use. Having ducked all the evidential problems we identified as well by declaring that their new 'elements' could be quantified; they made no attempt to do so when they engaged in academic imperialism, turning everything from slave revolts to religious pogroms into moral panic [2009: 3–5; 169–196]. No wonder the free-for-all that followed multiplied the criticism: the result was nothing to boast about.

Attempts to conform to either the descriptive and generic guidelines were rare and formulaic [Paterson and Stark, 2001; Rothe and Muzzatti, 2004]. Others did not conform to any criteria at all [Moorhouse, 1991; Wright,

2000; Van Den Hoonaard, 2001; Clegg and Flint, 2006; Humphrey, 2007; Smith, 2010]. The label was slapped on any issue with negative connotations that attracted media and academic interest; a primary culprit being falling educational standards [Aitkin, 2001a; Hawdon, 2001; Valentine and Holloway, 2001; Yates *et al*, 2001; Lawler, 2002; Miller and Leger, 2003; Smith, 2003; Stanton, 2005; Barron and Lacombe, 2005; Clegg and Flint, 2006; Neuilly and Zgoba, 2006; Fahmy and Johnson, 2007; Smith, 2007; Aguirre and Lio, 2008; Cole, 2009; Smith, 2010]. It was applied to examples of moral enterprise, crime waves, and understandable reactions to real threats, without enlightening readers why the alternative explanation did not suffice [Saux 2007; Zatz, 1987; Doezema, 1999; Soothhill and Francis, 2002; Chapkis, 2003; St. Cyr, 2003; Welch *et al*, 2004; Liew and Fu, 2006; Wilson *et al*, 2006; Armstrong, 2007; Durington, 2007; Robinson, 2008; Weidner, 2009]. The vast majority, however, continued to stick the label 'moral panic' on 'Right-wing' and/or religious claims-making during culture wars, political debates, and censorship crusades whether those "must have" features or that extraordinary level of "anxiety" was present or not [Murray with McClure, 1995; Boddy, 1996; Lawson and Comber, 2000; Erjavec, 2003; Zgoba, 2004; Grillo, 2005; Macek, 2006; Anderson, 2007; Saux, 2007; Toor, 2007; Burgett, 2008; Cassell and Cramer, 2008; Davies, 2008; Fejes, 2008; Ferguson, 2008; Timmerman and Schreuder, 2008; Poynting and Mason, 2010]. The fact that generic panic made matters worse is clearly indicated by the increasing number of case studies in which the evidence offered undermined the application of the label and/or contradicts others' accounts of the same 'panic' [Rogers and Coafee, 2005; Miller, 2006; Humprey, 2007; Lattas, 2007; Robinson, 2008; Luzia, 2008]. Similar tendencies and problems can be found in the growing number of historical studies rebranding the popular politics of the past 'moral panic', and the same applies to law [McGarry, 2000; Williams, 2001; Rapp, 2002; King, 2003; Lombardo, 2004; Marx, *et al*, 2007; De Vananzi, 2008; Lemmings and Walker 2009; Patry, 2009].

Although the concept had become extremely popular, it was invariably being used as a means to promote a political perspective. From Ungar [1990] to Altheide [2006], the paradigm reversed the standard academic process. With rare exceptions, like those formulaic panics, no one was using their case study to *test* the viability of the concept or its constituent parts as other academics, like historians, used to do when we were undergraduates. Case studies did not even consider the difference between the latent and overt functions of the social actions that they described, let alone displayed any awareness of the label's conceptual problems. The only systematic attempt to review the concept's viability not only restricted itself to the label's application, it was undermined by its own methodology [Critcher, 2003]. Rather than compare the claims made and evidence offered in published studies to the criteria used to assess them—Cohen's description (renamed the processional model) and the definition features in generic panics (the attributional model)—Critcher used his own assessment of events and his own definition of the two models to draw his conclusions. The problems that accrued can be seen in the general rationales offered for dismissing the fearful reaction to AIDS in the UK as moral panic.

As the extent of the threat posed to the heterosexual majority *was* minimal, despite the predictions about impending pandemics, Critcher's declaration that AIDS claims-making was not disproportionate is questionable. If we applied another contention, rapid institutionalization of problems negates panic, across the paradigm all those panics about crime and drugs which are already institutionalized would disappear [2003: 36–40]. Critcher's specific rationale for dismissing the AIDS panic was undermined by his selective account, and the now constant problem of demarcating where moral enterprise ended and generic panic began. If sections of the public did not overreact to the medical projections about impending pandemics as Critcher claimed, he can not explain where the demands for compulsory testing and quarantining of those found positive came from. His subsequent assertion that no panic followed because no one exploited those two demands is contradicted by the fact that moral entrepreneurs *within* the gay community promptly did just that. Scare mongers pointed to both those demands to assert that the community was under a panic attack from the New Moral Right; and they did so to 'panic' gays into abandoning their hedonistic lifestyle and return to the good old days of the Marxist, Gay Liberation Front and its political agenda. As they did so by using the same techniques in the gay press that the paradigm condemned when used by mainstream media, it offered a perfect example of progressive moral enterprise [Annetts and Thompson, 1992].

Despite having over twenty five years to deal with the problems being raised again and again after 1989, the paradigm's responses have generated even more, and did so for the same reason for 'the poverty of sociological theory' in general [Mouzelis, 1993]: its politics gets in the way. Further evidence of that can be seen in the lack of criticism emanating from inside the paradigm and the way it ignored its outside critics until it came under political attack from the UK press.

PANIC IN THE PARADIGM

When students schooled in the panic paradigm became journalists during the 1980s and Barker popularized the label, the concept quickly appeared in the liberal leaning *Guardian, New Statesman, New Society*, and the *Independent*. As the UK press had always presented diverse perspectives despite the paradigm's claims, 'panic' soon turned up in the conservative *Telegraph, Times,* and *Sunday Times* as well, although critical comment was not far behind. The most common complaint concerned the paradigm's tendency to minimize real problems:

Moral panic is one of those deflating phrases used by sociologists and other alleged impartial students of human behavior to condescend to excitements amongst the general populace . . . The Doctoral message is calming: do not worry, we have been here before, your concerns are an ersatz compound manufactured by the media, a few odd bishops, strident voices from the left and the right, moralists and nostalgists of all kinds [*Independent On Sunday* 21.9.93 cited in Hunt, 1997: 641].

Others were even more discerning, drawing attention to the fact that whatever you called them; moral panics and moral crusades really amounted to an attack on the working-classes by their betters rather than reflect any common popular sentiment:

The anti smoking movement . . . is only the latest in a long line of coercive crusades and moral panic, by means of which the upper and middle class elites seek to impose their lifestyles and preferences upon the working classes [*Sunday Times*, 18.10.92. cited in Hunt, 1997: 641].

Instead of seeing this coverage as a wake-up-call, Cohen denounced it as a Thatcherite plot to discredit the Left [2002: xxxii], and a battle of blame broke out within the paradigm.

One side, made up of newcomers, attempted to absolve Cohen and the concept from culpability by pointing to the "much more partisan definition" offered by the CCCS [Hunt, 1997: 632 and 635]. Garland insisted against all evidence that the concept was "rigorously defined" and "empirically grounded", and blamed Cultural Studies for the "lack of care and precision"; the same approach adopted by the US boosters [2009: 9 and 20]. Innes, not wishing to cause offense, offered a generic excuse for university professors' inability to distinguish between a definition and a description, although it was just as embarrassing:

Concepts such as moral panic, that enter the standard lexicon of the discipline, do so through a process in which they are configured in a particular fashion. They come to assume a standardized and accepted interpretation, wherein many of the original complexities, complications, and equivocations detailed by the author are stripped away [Innes, 2005: 107].

The Marxists were was not going to accept that, play the patsy, or abandon their politics, and fought back in dogmatic fashion. Kenneth Thompson not only defended the elite perspective, he insisted that it was the only viable one. Although the rise in pluralism had led to increasing social group value conflict, those involved were still "alarmed by the apparent fragmentation or breakdown of the social order" which threatened their interests. Their campaigns' success remained dependent on the press and politicians for success. Despite proving Innes correct by invoking Wallis' original, jettisoned, analysis of Valour's motives and the simplistic version of status discontent to do so, Thompson then dismissed the interest group perspective as a "mid-range theory" which only dealt with the immediate causes. The problem with "the Americans" was that they did not understand that cultural conflict at the superstructural level followed changes in the economic base, evidenced by the fact that interest group panics had emerged during a period of capitalist restructuring. In any event, unless a panic had the support of the elite and promoted social control it was doomed to failure [Thompson, 1998: 11, 18–19, 140].

The problems with that rebuttal are obvious. It confused the timing of the US boosters' claims about interest group panics with the appearance of social and interest group moral enterprise which went back centuries, presumably because Thompson ignored Weber's warning that conflict does not always take a pure class form. The reference to the 'breakdown motivation' merely exposed the Left's refusal to explore the purpose behind most moral enterprise: to secure legislation to further the entrepreneurs' interests whatever the consequences for 'society'. His criticism of "the Americans" contained a core contradiction. If superstructural responses followed developments in the economic base, the social group value conflict Thompson referenced would reflect *previous changes*, and the effects of the contemporaneous restructuring would appear later, as we saw it did in the previous chapter when the progressives attacked the main losers, the chav underclass, that they denied existed when Charles Murray said otherwise in 1989. Thompson's rationales draw attention to a generic problem in sociology. When a mismatch between social reality and its theoretical accounts become too obvious to ignore, sociologists have a habit of insisting that the world has suddenly changed. Their explanations for change, masking problems in the original theory, are then presented as an "advance" in theory, and history and reality becomes the chronology of those explanations. As we have demonstrated elsewhere, the panic paradigm is not alone in this. It purveys sociology. Tony Walter's misleading explanation for changes in the British way of death revolved around the contemporary social factors he observed when he finally noticed that a change had occurred, rather than the factors that had led to the change decades before [Thompson, 2000]. In this case, whatever their disagreements, the 'debate' between the US boosters and Thompson reinforced the myth that value pluralism only emerged in the UK and the US from the mid 1980s, a misnomer reinforced by their class orientated analysis, which had written previous social and interest group conflict out of the script, and ignored how subscription to values need not take an overt political form. Progressives had never liked the concept of pluralism because they associated it to the consensus school in US political science during the cold war, which celebrated a limited definition of 'pluralism' as an antidote to the ideological conflict perspective promoted by progressives in the past and contemporaneously by the New

Left. To admit that Moralgate exposed the effects of secular humanism would undermine more than Cohen's consensual model.

The only real advance as opposed to makeovers and mistakes, criticism and erroneous explanations for "sudden change", was Critcher's attempt to explain when and why horror-headlines did and did not lead to panic [2006]; although he avoided addressing the specific criticism that had encouraged him to do so [Williams, 1999]. Despite becoming convinced that moral panic should be subsumed under the concept of moral regulation, another Marxist model covering the relationship among ideology, state legitimacy, and what the author believes the masses think [Critcher, 2009; Hier, 2002: 325–329]; Critcher finally addressed this long-standing weakness. The success or failure of horror-headlines depended upon five [sic] factors. These were the crucial construction of folk devils by the media, and the reaction amongst the public, 'pressure groups', politicians, and the police. Successful panics required a unanimous media, claims-makers accredited with expert status to make the claims convincing, an alliance between at least two of the four social and interest groups, the support of the elite, and an attainable remedy perceived to be effective. Divisions amongst the elite and/or the media, the existence of counterclaims-makers, high-status folk devils, and a lack of public support guaranteed failure [2006: 2–11]. Although his schema did not resolve the label's lack of veracity, it finally offered the paradigm a means to establish uniformity by setting a research agenda, as well as offering a means to assess the label's application; but as it was ignored by those who found the label convenient, that ensured there was no debate over its drastic ramifications, including eliminating 'classic' panics like video nasties, and turning strain blame into a prerequisite rather than explanation.

THE STATE OF THE PARADIGM

The failure of the paradigm to take advantage of Critcher's framework meant that the major effect of the critical media coverage was to force the paradigm's politics out into the open. In contradistinction to the US boosters' attempts to play down the politics of panic, others became quite candid about its purpose. McRobbie and Thornton celebrated the way it had "challenged the moral guardians" [1991: 560 and 572]; Garland extolled its virtue as a "critical tool with which to discredit overzealous law enforcement and moral conservatism" [2008: 19]; and Jenkins admitted that progressives in the US were unlikely to label their causes panic [2009: 36]. The most important admission, however, was Young's which confirmed the open secret that the paradigm reflected the revolutionary spirit of 1968, and that the original purpose was to prove that capitalism created the contradictions that Merton accredited with causing crime [1938, cited in Young, 2009: 11]. When Cohen finally responded with what amounted to a 'state of the paradigm address', he also demonstrated that he could not be absolved from the paradigm's politics or the "lack of care and precision" that followed.

Cohen's review of the "seven familiar clusters of moral panic" amounted to a series of political dictates. For example, when covering panics about working-class youth, Cohen compared those that followed the death of James Bulger and the black youth Stephen Lawrence at the hands of a gang of London racists. He dismissed the latter on the grounds that no one 'panics' about black victims or could turn the police into folk-devils [2002: xxii]. That was debatable. Incidents like the beating of Rodney King quickly become as symbolic for progressive moral enterprise as Waco was for Second Amendment advocates. Veno also had no problem helping outlaw bikers in Australia turn the tables on the police as well as the horror-headlines and politicians after they had been targeted [2007]. Cohen's comments covering child abuse panics were just as doctrinaire and even more dubious. Despite now being ambivalent about Cleveland on the grounds that there was "no consensus about the whole episode", he insisted that satanic abuse was "one of the purest cases of moral panic". This was, apparently, proven by being "superimposed on the real phenomenon of child sexual abuse", although no one had justified "superimposition" as an indicator before, there was no evidence of public panic in the UK, and Cohen appears to have relied on de Young. Cohen then insisted that the epidemic of historic abuse allegations concerning care homes was an exercise in denial rather than panic, though that reflected *his* contemporary preoccupation with societal denial and was contrary to all the evidence [2002: xvi; Cohen, 2001].

As we explained in Chapter 3, the care home scandals appearing up to 25 years after the alleged events followed from the stupidity of putting the hard-core hooligan in the new therapeutically oriented care homes during the 1960s. The method used to contain the inevitable contagion of violence as the depraved preyed on the deprived, 'pin-down', was initially lauded as a progressive response because of its therapeutic elements, but it became "abusive" during 1989 when it offered the 'evidence' for claims about sex-exploitation that were otherwise difficult to substantiate. Although there is no doubt that some staff took advantage of the teens sexually, the credibility of other claims can be gauged by the way that they were shaped by the contemporary preoccupation with finding pedophile rings making snuff movies that had crossed over from WAVAW's anti-pornography crusade. Although that feature faded when the police went trawling through every care home on the orders of Virginia Bottomley [*Independent*, 4.6.91: 2], their suggestive methods led to far more dubious allegations than real ones. Once the Waterhouse Inquiry into one home had "validated" the allegations by failing to consider their self validating nature exposed by a Home Office Select Committee during 2002, the UK was treated to another progressive mass miscarriage of justice. Dozens of innocent care home workers were jailed along with the guilty before it became apparent that they were the victims of compensation fuelled false allegations by the former hard-core delinquents, long since turned hard-core if incompetent criminals, who now had an 'abuse excuse' for their drug addiction too [Webster, 1998; 2005]. In contrast, although Cohen's observation that child abduction-murder 'panics' were never contested had merit; it certainly was not proven as he claimed that it was by "the *primitives* whose *atavistic forces* were whipped up by the *News of the World*" in Paulsgrove for the reasons we saw in the previous chapter [our emphasis—eds. Cohen, 2002: xvi].

Having reinforced our contention that 'panics' are a function of the authors' preoccupations, politics, and antipathy towards those supposedly panicking rather than the evidence; Cohen turned his attention to resolving the admitted "lack of compatibility" between the seven clusters of panic. After confirming that the concept *was* innately political, recounting how *Folk Devils* had "fused" labeling theory, cultural politics and "critical sociology" [2002: xxii], Cohen endorsed Goode and Ben-Yehuda's new generic panic as the means to establish uniformity. He then undermined their claims about political neutrality, their critique of the elite perspective, and the viability of "sectional panics" by simultaneously endorsing Ken Thompson's rebuttal: moral panic required the support of "the majority of the elite and influential groups, especially the mass media" [2002: xxii–xvii]. If that was not enough to bamboozle readers his unilateral declaration that criminal acts should now be considered "harms" rather than an assault on consensual values, and his dismissal of disproportionality as an indicator of panic, should have [2002: xxiii–xxvii]. As well as embarrassing his US boosters, those two changes undermined several of the panics Cohen had just sanctioned in his review.

Cohen's justification for his conflicting endorsements was a perfect example of those "theoretical advances" necessitated by "sudden change". Without explaining how it retained the label's meaning, Cohen claimed that the new definition was needed because the "traditionally disinterested" like "the helping professions" and the new "multicultural and identity groups" had *suddenly* begun to engage in moral enterprise; a claim belied by the simple historical fact that they all owed their existence to value conflict moral enterprise [Platt, 1977; Banks, 1981; Bouchier, 1983; Adam, 1987; Roberts and Klibanoff, 2007]. Furthermore, as we shall see below, the "sudden change" Cohen alluded to concerned the adoption of critical theory to justify these groups' moral superiority, rather than the groups' appearance and motives. Cohen's second justification, that *recent* public skepticism towards the authorities and the police meant that the effects of media coverage and the cognitive process behind panic could no longer be taken for granted, was also moot. Moralgate, his surveys, and the Parliamentary response in Chapter 2, and the police corruption scandals and the juries' decisions in Chapter 3 meant that they never could.

Cohen concluded with three contentious claims about the political problems besetting the paradigm. First, he asserted that he had never meant to imply that panics were irrational but were merely misplaced fears "slanted in a particular ideological direction" despite his analogies with mass delusion and hysteria. Second, he chided those sneering at the small mindedness, Puritanism, and the intolerance of reactionaries, as if his comments about Whitehouse, Earl Longford, and Blake in *Folk Devils* never did. Third, he then blamed these consistent features in the paradigm on the use of concept [sic] in the UK press; and had the temerity to do so despite admitting that the paradigm's tendency to criticize conservative ideologies and to dismiss popular anxieties as irrational was so ingrained that it could not be reversed [2002: xxxii–xxxiii]! The potential debacle these dictates should have caused was avoided by the predictable paradigmatic practice of ignoring revisions.

HAPPY ANNIVERSARY

No one appears to have paid much attention to the ramifications of the articles published in the *British Journal of Criminology* on the 35th anniversary of *Folk Devils*. Ben-Yehuda, as expected, claimed that moral enterprise and sectional panics were "theoretical innovations" needed to cover the rise of pluralism, without justifying his time scale [2009]. Jenkins "reminded" everyone that the concept had always referred to the novelty, the sudden explosive growth, and the menace the folk devils posed to "vulnerable groups and individuals" as well as values; effectively dismissing Cohen's emphasis on 'the reaction', those "cognitive processes", and his claim that the violence suffered by the elderly on the beaches was irrelevant [2009]. While rewriting history was now so common these contributions hardly mattered, the simultaneous appeal by Young to "get back to basics" should have. Young's new revelation about the concept's hidden history undermined its viability completely [2009]. It now transpired that it not only relied on Erikson's habit of rearranging the evidence to facilitate the unproven link between the boundary crises, the deviants, and the restoration of values; but that the source of those all important "cognitive processes" was Ranulf's *Moral indignation and middle class psychology*. The obvious problem with that, of course, is that Ranulf not only *dismissed* the psychology of petit-bourgeois projection of economic fears as pure guesswork; he had questioned the power of stigma in contemporary societies, pointed out that capitalism had long since abandoned the values that the panic paradigm later relied upon, and traced the role of "moral indignation" in politics back to its origins: the fear of God's collective judgment on the community [1964]! In short, the concept of moral panic relied on a gross misreading of a source that would support our critique.

The paradigm was sinking, but the passengers were careless that every attempt by the Captain and crew of this academic Titanic to plug the breach had only succeeded in punching more holes in the hull. The failure to address the problems identified in the press above the waterline and the academic critics below it reminded us of the response adopted by the motley crew in charge of satanic abuse. Instead of steering clear by offering proof that the phenomenon existed, or abandoning ship when the truth poured in over their cargo of pseudoscience, the band played on to the tune of new labels, definitions, and dimensions in the hope that no one would notice [see Sakheim and Devine, 1992]. Having failed to deal with the politics behind the lack of theoretical, methodological, and evidential bulkheads, any attempt to chart a new course by redefining "the substantive scope and conceptual parameters of moral panic studies", was a waste of time; especially when the relief crew readily blamed the "lack of focus" that led to the collision on the "the popular use of the moral panic concept amongst journalists and politicians" rather than the ideologues manning the bridge [Hier, 2011: 2]. Jumping ship, and rowing a 'provision-less-lifeboat' towards a desert island shrouded in the fog of "social fear" will not help; it merely delays the inevitable. In order to understand why the paradigm's guardians responded in this fashion, we need to explore their politics of panic in more detail; and we can find numerous clues in the three rival theories that subsequently emerged after the panic in the paradigm.

RISKY FEARS

One of those "fall of the Berlin Wall" theories, projecting academic fears about the "end of ideology" onto a general public that was never beholden to them, risk theory claimed that everyone was panicking now because of the never-ending series of disasters and problems, from bio-hazards to global warming, caused by "late-modern" technology.[1] Panic allegedly followed the incapacity of the traditional problem solver, government, to control the potential outcome of new technologies. That was asking too much because by its very nature new technology was impossible to pretest and avoid the unintended consequences discovered after the fact. While some like Garland [2008] and Heir [2002 and 2003] believed that a merger between both types of panic was possible, Ungar insisted otherwise [2001]; and his rationales draws attention to the problematic nature of turning politics into panic.

Ungar made much of the paradigm's inability to cope with the "open, variable, and problematic" claims-making process covering real risks by the "informed public" in interest groups and social movements, without calling it progressive moral enterprise; and he pointed to its failure to cover all the 'panics' found on talk radio and the internet, otherwise known as the political Right [Ungar, 2001: 271–280]. But he promptly replicated every other problem we have found within the paradigm. The most important was the typical failure to differentiate between the varied causes and consequences of public concern about risks that create the social fears that we expect will be the next home for the moral panic label. The type of 'panic' that follows horror-headlines that the world's major manufacturer of breast implants has been using industrial rather than medical grade silicone [*Associated Press*, Paris 26.1.12], that neighborhood nuclear plants are melting down, or that the UK government is engaging in countryside genocide to eliminated Bovine Spongiform Encephalopathy or Aphtae epizooticae, is as different as their causes. The only common factor in Ungar's account appears to be the *lack* of any evidence that the public reaction amounts to a "loss of faith in science" leading to risk panic [2001: 286–287]. *Panicking* about potentially poisonous plastic breasts, *fear* of being eradiated, and *over caution* about eating beef that hasn't been fed dead sheep are very different phenomenon. Whereas the first two generate real panic, worrying about BSE and hoof and mouth disease is enhanced by the claims and counter claims about sources, estimates, and government agency incompetence. When the public do not know what to believe, worry is an inevitable result [*G2* 28.2.01: 8; *The Guardian*, 25.9.01: 11]. The same may explain why more people are wary about GM foods' potential consequences [*The Guardian*, 19.5.99: 11; *Independent, Business Review*, 21.4.99: 3]. The key question to ask in these cases is why rational fears about the link between agribusiness and food risk are deemed panic [*The Guardian*, 27.10.00: 1]?

That question becomes more pertinent when one considers the way that progressives have 'ignored' the panic over human generated CO2 global warming. Although this followed the successful moral enterprise of the IPCC, progressives become very indignant and worse if anyone dare suggest that they are spreading panic. All of a sudden, public anxiety and social fear are lauded as enlightening and welcomed even though the history of the climate crusade fulfils the requirements of generic panic to the letter, including turning Lord Moncton into an international folk devil. The crusade came complete with atrocity tales about drowning polar bears, and disproportionate claims about 'extreme' weather patterns, "the worse since "records began", a mere century ago! Those involved attempted to enforce ideological closure with the constant refrains that 'the debate was over" and that "all scientists agree" over the causes, although they were clearly false. It was not only belied by Professors Tim Ball (US), Nir Sahviv (Israel), Ian Clarke (Canada), and Phillip Stott (UK), all leading authorities in their specialisms; but Richard Lindzen, Paul Reiter and John Christy who were cited by the IPCC also disassociated themselves from 'the consensus', denounced it as a political conclusion, and pointed out that many of those being touted as "leading scientists" were activists or reviewers.

Ignoring all that, Demeritt's confession that he provided politicians with the data that they wanted in return for future funding [2001], the fact that Al Gore's popularization relied on a deliberate dubious base year, and the obvious problems with relying on worst case computer models, clearly amounts to more than political selectivity. As we are 13,000 years into this warming cycle, extreme weather is explained by the interaction between solar flares and wind, ice core research suggests CO2 increase may follow from rather than 'cause' warming, and no one factors in the issue of 'peak oil,' there is still a lot to discuss. The same applies to the solutions, including whether 'cap and trade' and curbing soccer mum's SUVs would be efficacious than protecting freshwater supplies and planting a lot more trees. Those observations draw attention to how the absence of human generated climate change 'panic' from Ungar's thesis enabled him to ignore how risk panics can depend as much on moral enterprise and the politics of fear as they do on technology, not to mention popular ignorance about science [Huber, 1993]. On the other hand, Ungar can be absolved from a charge of political selectivity because he adopted a very pessimistic approach to the politics of protesting risk because of his belief in "the end of ideology". Risk panics, apparently, do no one any good:

Rainbow coalitions of victims, oppositional scientists, sympathetic journalists, labor unions and other organizations often create moral outrage by prying open hidden institutional behaviors and violations [despite being] normal, inevitable, and predictable features of institutions . . . the exposure and accumulation of oversights, ineptitudes, and violations tends to engender a marauding sense of disbelief and anger. But this is generally different to moral panic . . . Rather than serving as a force of social control or cohesion, risk society accidents tend to create 'corrosive communities' as the different actors try to deny their culpability and pass the hot potato. In this foraging process, public trust is the ultimate victim [Ungar, 2001: 283].

We do not agree for two reasons. First, as panic induced social cohesion was a theoretical assertion, and declining public trust reflects growing awareness that the corporate and political classes are in cahoots, Ungar can not justify the panic label. Second, even if a risk panic did not provide the resolution for the indignation/outrage allegedly found in moral panic, because culpability becomes embroiled in the vagaries of the legal-political system for years; that does not entitle Ungar to dismiss public protest as irrational because *he* believes that risk is inevitable and considers attempts to apportion blame a pathetic trawl for scapegoats [2001: 282–284]. On the contrary, the growing awareness that needless risk has increased since corporate capitalism secured deregulation in the 1980s not only questions the viability of dismissing political responses as 'panic', but points to the purpose behind panic politics. As permanent groups like Greenpeace and citizens who mobilize, like the families of those lost aboard the Derbyshire supertanker, have constantly demonstrated that many risks *were* avoidable and could *easily be eliminated*,[2] Ungar's diagnosis and prognosis is false. We could just as easily argue that fears about Frankenstein food feeding anti-corporatism on both sides of the political divide, evidenced by the simultaneous coverage on Alex Jones' populist *Infowars.com* and the libertarian-progressive *The Young Turks* on current TV, points to alternative political conclusions: the problem exposed and posed by risky fears is the failure of all those aware of the links between 'risk', corporate greed, lobbyists, and the political classes to put aside their other differences and find the common cause needed to reduce risk. Ungar's thesis can not be saved by his versions of complicity—the desperate demand that new drugs are released before the side-effects are known, or disproportionality— Greenpeace overestimated the amount of pollution sinking the Brent Spar oil platform in the North Sea would cause. On the contrary, the alleged duplicity in the demand to release HIV antiretroviral drugs is insignificant compared to Big Pharma paying psychiatrists to push psychotropic drugs on the population through the medicalization of everyday problems. Likewise, rather than proving panic, the Brent Spar incident points to something else entirely. The subsequent boycott of Shell gas stations, the firebombing of the company's installations in Germany and the high profile invasion of the platform clearly amount to politics rather than 'panic', When the law and order lobby picked on the mods and rockers, the religious moral entrepreneurs on Video Nasties, WAVAW on sexstores, Campbell on Cleveland, and Greenpeace literally jumped aboard the platform; it mattered not whether an academic considered these responses irrational or disproportionate. Every one of these moral entrepreneurs was adopting a political response, exploiting the 'threat' to promote their value-laden agenda.

Ungar's panic analysis is no different from the paradigm's. He was promoting his political perspective, when others are readily available; and the selectivity displayed concerned the evidence that might point the reader towards those alternatives. It displayed the same lack of academic integrity by failing to differentiate between causes and effects, and between ad hoc pressure groups, moral enterprise, and social movements before throwing labels around [Eder, 1985]. There is however, more to the paradigm's approach than that, and we gain another set of insights by reviewing what fear theory has to say.

FEAR THEORY

The politics behind the US variant is revealed by its subtitle: "why Americans are afraid of the wrong things". According to Glassner [1999] they do so because the media generates a culture of fear to deflect public attention away from 'real issues', although *he* never has a problem working out what they are. LA freeway shooting stories? Taking the heat off transport policies he does not like. The same can not be said of Furedi's UK version.

Rather than blame the media, the end of ideology, or technological risk for the increase in fear in contemporary societies, Furedi concentrated on the role of social relationships in shaping peoples' perceptions of reality which spread fear, and shed a lot of light on the politics behind the panic paradigm as he did so [1997]. Furedi argued that the Thatcher's economic and social policies led to a rise in anomie between 1979 and 1997. By undermining working-class communities and the institutions of civil society, the UK's social orientated outlook collapsed and led to widespread cynicism towards the authorities, fear of other people, and that increased sensitivity to risk. These fears were enhanced rather than resolved by Tony Blair's New Labour governments after 1997 because the professional Left had abandoned the politics of class struggle in favor of the politics of political correct victimology with its emphasis on the "virtues of caring and suffering". Despite the rhetoric of empowerment, the therapeutic solutions promoted by New Labour generated a widespread sense of vulnerability reinforcing people's social isolation [Furedi, 1997: 40–42, 62–67]. The counseling culture that emerged was a new form of social control, encouraging people to adjust to circumstances rather than attempt to change them by exaggerating threats, treating theoretical possibilities as definites, and relying on ideological metaphors rather than quantifiable evidence. By also emphasizing real "harms" from the past, like discrimination against blacks and women, to secure the moral high ground this progressive perspective encouraged people to adopt the position of victims as a means to gain recognition. By turning any perceived slight, misunderstanding, or disagreement into a politically incorrect crime on the basis of the 'victim's' overblown subjectivity, victim based social groups increased division in society and undermined a collective response to new problems [1997: 19–40; 79–83]. The increase in sensitivity to risk followed the progressive panics from child abuse to violence in popular culture based on radical feminist ideology and myths; and the progressives' failure to denounce risk panics like skin cancer and toxic shock as gross exaggerations. This recourse to the politics of fear by progressives encouraged and facilitated a convergence in the social control policies on both sides of the political divide, which had Kafkaesque consequences. For example, parents could no longer take snapshots of their toddlers in the nude without being accused of, and prosecuted for, child pornography [1997: 21–25, 33–41, 53, 74–77, 83–87].

Although we could criticize Furedi for adopting a one-size-fits-all approach to fear, he not only tried to ground his claims about social fears in social action, he recognized that the panic paradigm had played an important part in this process:

> Those involved in the child protection industry interpret the targeting of Cleveland social workers by sections of the media as an exemplar of the classical moral panic, but it never occurs to the authors that the invention of an epidemic of child abuse in Cleveland, by doctors and social workers, was in scale a far more significant event. It helped unleash widespread anxieties and fears which affected millions of people. It seems that many social scientists and social workers distance themselves from the concerns of wronged parents in Cleveland and other places. They feel aloof from the effects that accusations of child abuse and satanic abuse panics have had on the life of parents and are

extraordinary indifferent to their plight . . . The view that moral panics are targeted against caring professionals and not against wronged parents is systematically pursued in a collection of essays, *Scare in the Community, Britain in Moral Panic* [Furedi, 1997: 46–47].

Whether or not Cleveland was *the* source of the "culture of fear" in the UK, it *was* indicative of the progressives' promotion of the politics of fear which they simultaneously denounced when used by others, and that raises a far more damning set of criticisms. As *Scare in the Community* was edited by Geoffrey Pearson, another revolutionary from the class of 1968 [1983], and the special issue of *Feminist Review* [1988] demonstrated that Campbell and the radicals were alone in defending Cleveland, the progressives were not merely being selective. They were either woefully ignorant of the issues involved, demonstrating how their politics amounts to a preference and that their 'analysis' is completely useless; or they were in favor of implanting false memories of abuse in children and manufacturing the medical evidence to 'prove' them, and their 'analysis' was very useful when it came to masking manufacturing crimes to promote the progressive agenda. Both options raise questions about the nature of progressives' supposed concern for innocents, be they sexually assaulted children or those who *were* harassed during the NOW name and shame campaign. While conservatives have always been castigated by the paradigm for exploiting crime victims for political purposes, at least their victims were real [Elias, 1993]. In order to uncover why progressives adopted these methods to strengthen the agencies of social control that they inhabited, we can consider the clues offered by another form of panic analysis.

RIGHT ANSWER: WRONG REASONS

Like Furedi, Waiton [2008] rejected the supercilious sociology of risk in favor of another socio-political explanation that simultaneously undermined Garland's lauded *Culture of Control* which laid the blame for the rise of "penal-welfare state" on the political-Right although New Labour had created six times as many new criminal offenses as Thatcher [2002]. Waiton's disagreement with Furedi concerned the role of progressive panics. Rather than promoting *moral* panic, the expression of a collective response to a transgression of social and moral norms, Waiton argued that progressives had promoted *amoral* panics reflecting the decline in collective values [2008: 10–11, 82, 89, 131, 137].

According to Waiton, when progressives lost their faith in alternatives to capitalism and active moral subjects because of the "end of ideology", they abandoned the attempt to transform society in favor of regulating, controlling, and monitoring individual behavior. Social and welfare problems became regulatory rather than class issues [2008: 131–135]. As the

Conservative party abandoned their appeals to traditional morality at the same time, the public became confused. No longer able to tell right and wrong, the public lost faith in the political system and panicked, making them susceptible to the therapeutic solutions offered by the regulatory state. That response was understandable. Society had become more asocial precisely because the progressives' therapeutic approach encouraged the introspection that inhibited collective social action, which generated the feeling of impotence that produced the fear of and overreaction to anti-social behavior that progressives then exploited to their advantage [Waiton, 2008: xiii–xvii, 140–145, 155–160]. When Thatcherism fanned the flames of the fear of crime, undermined organized labor, and blamed social problems on the underclass that it had created, its emphasis on crime victims' rights and 'the politics of vulnerability' opened the door for the Labour party [2008: 45–49; 52–59, 79]. Having lost three elections, Labour had reinvented itself under Tony Blair as New Labour. Having abandoned its commitment to socialism in favor of political correctness, and adopted Left Realism's re-conceptualization of crime as "harm", it become the party of law and order by turning the politics of crime into the politics of safety, and exploited the public's zero tolerance for violence and amoral panics like child abuse, while promising to protect the public from anti-social behavior. As a result, it won the election in 1997 [Waiton 2008: 9, 50, 63–66, 133–136]. Once in power, the effect of New Labour's policies was the opposite of its public rationales.

Hailed as the antidote to working-class political disengagement as well as crime, the Crime and Disorder Act 1998 created the foundations of the regulatory state especially on "sink estates", evidenced by Waiton's case study into a Scottish housing project curfew. The curfew was sold to the public through horror-headlines about "streets of fear" exaggerating the vandalism and underage drinking, and promised to save the community from the unsupervised teens, and the teens from their own risky behavior. Lauded by the Left as the means to rebuild communities devastated by Thatcher's economic policies, it really amount to social control [Waiton, 2008: 3, 13, 32]. Despite picking up dozens of youths ignoring their civil liberties in the process, the police only uncovered three cases of poor parental supervision, but increased the level of fear as they did so; and rather than empowering the residents, the policy promoted passive reliance on the authorities [2008: 28–35, 38–41]. That outcome, reflecting the change in public housing policy from an issue of provision to regulating the behavior of those who had one, was replicated by the surveillance measures inserted into other social policies. As a result, the populace became convinced that they were incapable of dealing with problems because of the stress, trauma, and psychological damage involved; which is why they embraced the regulatory state [Waiton, 2008: 76, 91–92, 101, 113, 135, and 152].

Although that account of progressive oppression, described by *The Observer* as a moral crusade [5.9.99: 1], undermined Garland's selective claims-making, it had its own limitations. Waiton, like Furedi was proffering "sudden change" and was suffering from a panic paradigm hangover too. Convergence was apparent long before the "end of ideology" sent a confused public running for cover under the umbrella of safety when a shower of anti-social teens appeared; and although a definitive account would require a book of its own, we can draw attention to six factors that could and should have been considered before Waiton and Ferudi offered their chronologies.

THERAPEUTIC POLITICS

Social work-therapeutic doublespeak emerged in public long before New Labour. During the early 1980s petit-professionals began to "share" their dogmatic "feelings" about "inappropriate" behavior whether you wished to hear them or not, the youth who could afford to do so expressed their "care" about third world politics and other issues by attending all-day rock concerts rather than mobilize politically, and everyone let you know when "abuse" of one kind of another had caused them "offence". While child abuse awareness played its role in spreading this self validating language, it can be traced back to the 'politics of self' promoted by the therapy movement hailed by feminists as the antidote to oppressive male psychiatry and the solution to the 'feminine mystique' in the early 1970s. Neither Waiton nor Furedi considered how easy it was to sell Tony Blair's subsequent appeals to "caring and sharing" after the Conservative government's 'Back to Basics' campaign blew up in their faces, as libertarians warned that it would [*The Times*, 11.11.93: 16]. Launched in 1993, after 'Black Wednesday' when the stock market collapsed, it was overtly deflective; stressing, for example, the amorality of single mothers while ignoring that exhibited by banksters. When it fell apart amid horror-headlines about Thatcherite MPs' hypocritical personal habits *and* the financial gains cabinet members accrued from denationalizing state assets, Blair could not lose.

Although the failure of Back to Basics would have been a good enough reason to abandon moralizing, the Conservative party had little choice. The Christian community it was aimed at had already switched sides as we saw in Chapter 4. Oblivious to the history of religious-progressive alliances, Waiton and Furedi also missed the links between the rise of communitarianism in the Christian community and Tony Blair's version of the Third Way, though it was evident in Gidden's justification for turning the Labour party from a vehicle for socialism into a nebulous social democratic party [1989]. That is why, under New Labour, the progressive version of "diversity' suddenly included "faith groups"! Blaming the decline of the UK's communal outlook on Thatcherism was also less than half the story. It had long since been undermined by the welfare state which provided the services previously offered by the Co-operative societies with their medical services, friendly societies (insurance), and building societies (savings and loans) which had created the socially orientated outlook the two authors alluded because of their participatory nature [Pollard, Liddle, Thompson, 1994]. The steady demise of this 'self help' socialism' ensured that there was nothing left to fall back on when Thatcher destroyed the militant unions, which inadvertently increased the power and influence of white-collar unions while doing so. Full of politically correct academics, social workers, and local government employees, these bastions of the new petit-bourgeois petit-professionals employed by the state helped facilitate what Waiton and Furedi describe as New Labour's switch from class to therapeutic politics; which is where their analysis falls apart.

Therapeutic politics is class politics: the politics of the progressive petit-professionals from the new petit-bourgeoisie. As we saw in Chapter 5, the professional feminists were counting on the votes of these white-collar unions to turn Liberty, the UK's ACLU, into an organ of progressive censorship back in 1990. That attempt reflected the fifth factor: the reason why critical criminologists who previously dismissed concerns about rising crime as moral panic suddenly embraced Left Realism. As Jock Young revealed to Sarah Benton, it was not because they had been mugged by reality, but had adopted feminist victimology [*New Statesman* 21.11.86: 12–14]. Another "advance in theory", this one now defined crime as "male", and Young provided the proof that the world had suddenly changed by claiming that the 'macho culture' behind the contemporary crime wave had been encouraged by Thatcherism [*The Independent*, 10.10.92: 5]; enabling the paradigm to ignore the obvious ramifications of Left Realism for the seminal studies. Consequently, while 'amoral panics' and New Labour's crusade against anti-social behavior help explain why it won the election in 1997 by "connecting directly with the insecurities of working families", and the crusade against anti-social teens were an important step on the road to the therapeutic state [2008: 74, 99, 119–121, 127–129], we need to look elsewhere for the source of the progressives' switch to the politics of victimology, and the paradigm's switch to political correctness. Fortunately, our accidental ethnography offers an insight, the sixth factor.

WHO'S OPPRESSING WHOM?

The progressive progeny of the new petit-bourgeoisie attending UK colleges during the 1970s and 1980s were theoretical revolutionaries. Raised on Frankfurt School structuralism, they believed that being critical amounted to rejecting "mainstream values", deemed Right-wing by concepts like moral panic, rather than developing and exercising their own critical faculties. Having foolishly believed that the revolution was just around the corner until Thatcher proved it wasn't, they took their

264 The Myth of Moral Panics

indignation out on fellow students. As they could not convince, they began to impose their politically correct policies on Student Unions,[3] and anyone taking their studies seriously was regard as a greater threat than conservatives because they could see through the justifications being offered, and what the Leninist approach being adopted would lead to. Serious students would discover that the real history of popular protest behind the ideological accounts was a never ending series of 'sell-outs' by 'revolutionaries', those adopting objective criteria for assessing social problems would see that the campaigns against discrimination were being exploited by those with least experience of it, and anyone wary of authoritarianism need look no further that WAVAW supporters' sexual politics. In short, it was obvious that the 'revolutionaries' were not interested in securing equal opportunity *for all,* but in power for themselves. The Cultural Revolution in both its theoretical form, 'critical theory', and its Maoist manifestation complete with its inane sloganeering had come to the UK.

As the late 1970s turned into the 1980s, these cultural revolutionaries took their PC political perspective with them when they secured employment in the local government bureaucracies and to NGOs, which dramatically expanded during the Thatcher years while working-class unemployment soared. Although radical Left councils were their preferred choice, conservative led councils also depended upon this college cohort to staff their social service and educational bureaucracies as well. That ensured local government became a major site of social control convergence long before New Labour, not least because between 1989 and 1995 Thatcher's policy of expanding surveillance was overseen by Virginia Bottomley: a former social scientist, social worker, Child Poverty Action Group researcher, and Chairwoman of the Inner London Juvenile Court. This conduit offers a real word alternative to Waiton's more esoteric explanation about a confused public desperately subscribing to the therapeutic paradigm because it could no longer tell what was right from wrong because the political classes had abandoned philosophies that they never believed in [2008: 151, 140]. Likewise, the casualties of Thatcherism adopted the therapeutic perspective before New Labour because any demand for redress already depended upon it. What the victims of de-industrialization, rationalization, asset-stripping and out-sourcing did not understand was that official victim status and subsequent benefits only apply when it furthered the progressive's discriminating agenda. Hence the Paulsgrove protesters' stunned surprise when they were denounced as vigilantes despite setting out to defend their children from a sex offender. Their reaction also explains the real reason for working-class disengagement from politics. The hard data clearly demonstrates that it *followed* rather than proceeded New Labor's policies [UK Elections, 2012]. The claim to the contrary refers to their lack of enthusiasm for PC politics and their refusal to mobilize around that agenda in the previous decade.

INCORRECT POLITICS

Solutions to social problems do not always work out the way that their promoters hope. They frequently generate other problems because much depends upon the original typification and the method chosen to deal with the original claims. The way PC politics was applied in the UK was a questionable as the progressives' 'Powell panic' in 1968. There was a problem, but pretending that it was bigger than it was would have an adverse corollary in the real world; and so it proved. PC politics did nothing to arrest the increasing power of the elite and crony capitalists. On the contrary, New Labour made as many deals with banksters and corporate titans like Murdock as Thatcher had. Its policy of 'inclusion' went no further than the 'oppressed minorities' amongst the new petit-bourgeoisie who could take advantage of it, particularly in the public sector where it conferred immediate benefits [Jones, 2011: 162, 171, 256]. Meanwhile, working-class women, ethnic minorities, and gays were forced like the rest of the proletariat to take minimum wage jobs, rely on welfare, and/or get into debt traps to secure the needless academic degrees required for marginally better paying jobs and by taking out a mortgage in order to have somewhere to live [Jones, 2008: 117, 139–144, 176]. The plight of Bangladeshi community in depressed areas was typical. Like the white working-class they were forced to depend on the state whether they had jobs or not, while the rich got richer no matter what their race, gender, or sexual orientation, because company profits had never been higher [Jones, 2008: 156, 163]. Militants, whistleblowers, and anyone else trying to keep the old working-class causes alive for the benefit of all found themselves on employment blacklists organized by the Consultant Association amply aided by the New Labour's police forces.

New Labour's meritocracy was no better than the old. Teens from the richest fifth were seven times more likely to make it to university than those from the poorest 40 percent, even though the percentage going to university increased from around 15 to 50 percent over New Labour's life-time [Jones 2008: 159, 180]. If that was not bad enough, PC politics proved to be as pernicious as the problems it allegedly addressed. As jobs disappeared, unionism declined, families fell apart, and the demoralized took to drugs, illegal and prescribed; those 'revolutionaries' readily began to blame the chavs for their predicament, tarring them with the PC crime of racism to symbolize their unworthiness, even though that characterization was false [Jones, 2008: 152, 186–188]. The majority of poor residing on sink estates had jobs; they were simply badly paid. As UK Asians and blacks were just as concerned about immigration, knowing that it was exploited to maintain a low wage economy, its use as a proxy for racism was nonsense. The majority of UK working-class are far from racist, which is why 50 percent of black British males, and 33 percent of black British females have white partners, as do 20 percent of those from India and Africa. It was the progressives' emphasis on race rather than class, ignoring the fact that most of the minorities' contemporary problems were shared by their white working-class neighbors, that explains why the proletariat began to disengage [Jones, 2008: 166, 203, 222–238, 240–246, 253]. There was nothing in PC politics for them, and they were fed up with being made guilty by association with the residual of racist thugs now using militant Islam as their latest excuse.

As Aaronovitch revealed, the demonization of the chavs was an expression of progressive indignation that the working-classes treated them and their agenda with contempt; and did so for good reasons. Experiences like Paulsgrove taught them that progressive sloganeering from "workers control" to "inclusion" reflected their route to power rather than their aims. Like the 'care and concern' in social work doublespeak, it was phony; a means to impose the values of the new petit-bourgeoisie on society rather than promoting a truly diverse one in which *everyone's* life-style preference would be accommodated having had the *equal opportunity* to secure it.

DÉJÀ VU

Many of the tendencies accredited to the political-Right by the panic paradigm, like the promotion and exploitation of the fear of crime, have their origins in the nineteenth century feminist-progressive-religious alliance [Ghatak, 2007]. As we saw in Chapter 2, the justification offered was that the masses needed more direction because urbanization had produced anomie. When that merged with the progressive fear that the masses were fascistic too after the Second World War, it not only led to moral crusades against horror comics, or railing against the baneful influence of TV on Teddy boys; progressives could convince themselves that the masses were so irrational that they had to be controlled. Despite attempts to hide this, it was apparent in the CCCS's condemnation of the working classes, before Cohen could no longer contain himself and let everyone know that he believed the masses were atavistic primitives. What, of course, progressives had really meant all along was that the working-classes were alienated from *their* concept of a perfect society, which was true. Like today's chavs, the nineteenth-century masses and the organized working-classes in between preferred the idea of an equitable society to a regulated one. The progressive-feminist-religious alliance had other ideas, and welcomed the new 'science' of sociology to provide them with the evidence to justify their agenda [Greek, 1992; Boyer, 1992]. During the 1930s, sociology exams included questions regarding the benefits of Mussolini's regime and 'social-hygiene' policies, the progressive code word for eugenics which they tried to sell to the respectable working-class [Thompson, 1983]. Although this tendency was masked by the New Left hiatus and the rewriting of history we covered in Chapter 4, when the new petit-bourgeoisie appeared in large enough numbers and took over the ever expanding 'social services' in local government, progressives set about fulfilling Comte's vision for sociology.

Despite their pretentions, the Marxists were no different as all those references for the need to heed the experts, professionals, sociologists, and social workers in the panic paradigm's seminal studies demonstrate. Although they would have preferred some form of socialism as opposed to Comte's Kings and Capital when it came to politics and the source of material wealth, Marxists have subsequently proven that they were all too willing to assume their Comte given role of telling everyone else what to do in order to live harmoniously with 'the system', whatever form it takes. As long as they believed that the proletariat was their route to power, they produced a wealth of theories and self-serving histories about them, but once the workers failed to deliver, the Marxists cynically switched to the new social movements that emerged from the new postwar petit-bourgeoisie. The growth of white-collar state employment, including publicly funded Non Governmental (sic) Organizations ensured that the politics of identity—based around the Marxist interpretation of the demands of women, ethnic minorities, and gays—would provide a new route to power, and one in keeping with their bourgeois values. The switch was not that difficult. The academic Left, drawn from the UK's middle classes had always preferred the easier task of training those future experts, professionals, sociologists, and social workers attending college to agitation amongst the working-classes, including proletarian women and ethnic minorities. By emphasizing the harms caused by racism, sexism, and homophobia they had found a new vision, a justification for their social control policies, and an easier argument. Anyone who disagreed, no matter what the reason, could be dismissed as the embodiment of evil, an oppressor, a victimizer: a racist, sexist, homophobe. No debate. The extent of the switch can be illustrated by Rose's search on the *MLA International Bibliography* data base of academic publications which revealed 13,820 results for "women", 4,539 for "gender", 1,862 for "race", 710 for "postcolonial", and a mere 136 for the "working class" between 1991 and 2000 [cited Jones, 2011: 255]. Left-realism also provided the means to turn those interests into Governance. It did so by merging law and order and radical feminist victimology to create 'the politics of safety', and they way they did it was stunning. The CCCS had no qualms at all about turning the thuggish teen folk heroes of the paradigm's past into the reactionary working-class 'Essex man' who voted Conservative, while Jock Young turned their children into Thatcherite thugs to justify New Labour's social control policies [Waiton, 2008: 85–88, 121–123]. In reality, the rise of 'yobbo culture' had far more to do with the three decades of progressive failure to heed Ms Bacon's warning to distinguish between the depraved and the deprived and offering the depraved 'abuse excuses' while the paradigm dismissed fears about the inevitable consequences as moral panic. The fact that they could switch so easily and exploit the social-disaster that their policies had created shows how opportunistic these Marxists were.

No longer needing to accommodate the organized working-class who had lost the battle of living standards with Thatcherism, progressives simply picked up where they had left off because of the Second World War. New Labour was the modern equivalent of the feminist-progressive-religious alliance; only this time, being in Government, they could now extend Thatcher's social service surveillance and control with little hindrance. Like the nineteenth-century variant, the contemporary alliance's agenda emerged from its power bases in universities, local government social work, philanthropic organizations, and even judicial institutions [Ghatak, 2007]. Whereas the latter had been the means to introduce the original 'therapeutic' solution to delinquency a hundred years before, it now imposed a therapeutic perspective on the rest of the population.

THE NEW AUTHORITARIANS

Our brief account of the antecedents behind the tendencies observed by Furedi and Waiton does not begin to cover the complexity of its progress and set backs, its ambiguities and incongruities, and the convergence of latent effects with overt intent; although for every caveat, we could add another link, like Thatcher's Home Office funding for progressive victimology studies. The main purpose was to draw attention to the fact that ideology did not end with the fall of the Berlin Wall, its façade did. Puritanical progressivism could always be found on the aging British road to socialism, and only became more obvious when the panic paradigm joined the new petit-bourgeoisie on the politically correct super highway being subsidized by Thatcherism, where the toll booths handed out free passes to drivers in the 'victims only' lane, and a PC road test for everyone else. By the time insightful commentators like Catherine Bennett noticed that progressives creating a generation at "the mercy of dogma, unfounded scares, and anyone with a vested interest in ignorance" [cited in Calcutt, 1997: 163], it was too late, it had already happened. Everyone was rushing towards the bridge to nowhere.

As we discovered, and covered in the Preface, anyone warning that the recourse to the politics of fear and victimology to build US-style voting blocks around 'the oppressed' would ensure that the next Labour government would be far worse than the mythical 'strong state' was demonized [Annetts and Thompson, 1992]. While we spent the next decade devoted to clearing up one progressive miscarriage of justice after another, and helped build United Against Injustice[4] in a desperate attempt to stop even more, we sometimes joked about a SWAT team smashing down the door, and whether they would use crack, chemicals, or child pornography as the excuse. Once in power, New Labour confirmed our suspicions. The infamous ASBOs (Anti-Social Behavior Orders) were the least of their assault on civil liberties, but were typical of the methods. Breaking one could lead to jail time for an offence that otherwise would not, with no right of defense. New criminals included prostitutes carrying condoms, charity soup workers feeding homeless people in city centers, non aggressive beggars, kleptomaniacs, those exhibiting their tattoos, and anyone playing soccer in the street. No debate or new law needed [NAPO, 2005]. While we are ambivalent about Waiton's complaint that bad behavior in schools and the annoying habits of typical teens were relabeled anti-social tendencies because, for some, that was the right label, we were not surprised that independent working-class protest was labeled pathological vigilantism because there was more to it than that [Waiton, 2008: 87, 99, 121–123, 146–147].

Turning the working class into chavs, and the chavs into "the unwashed mob" of yesteryear, exposed both the fears and the authoritarianism found in those progressive experts, professionals, social workers, and sociologists. As Waiton also pointed out, Paulsgrove was not the only "false alarm" in New Labour's proletarian panic, spread with the aid of the deal struck with Murdock to manage the news [*The Guardian*, 24.5.04: 8]. When the prophesized rise in Islamophobia and racist attacks failed to materialize after the 7/7 London bombings in 2005 and hate crimes actually fell, the police simply turned any allegation, irrespective of the evidence, into a hate crime, making reality under New Labour what progressive claims-makers insisted it was [Waiton, 2008: 137–138, 149]. That proof positive that the features the paradigm ascribed to Right-wing moral panic were anything but; and also applied to themselves can also be seen in the US.

RUNNING DOWN THE DREAM

While racism, sexism, and homophobia were extensive in the 1950s, the progressives contemporary approach today is as questionable as lauding and rewarding Rosa Parks for staying put when the accolade belonged to the teen rebel Claudette Colvin who received a beating from the cops before being abandoned by the NAACP because she was too working-class, independent, and sexual active [Hoose, 2011]. While 'respectability' may have been a useful tactic at the time, not admitting the truth since is counterproductive.[5] If one was to believe progressive claim-making, repeated night after night by their TV boosters, who match the politics of fear found on *Fox News*, scare for scare [Avlon, 2010], nothing has changed. It enables them to explain away the continuing difficulties faced by the black community, despite the gains made by its middle-class. However, as the same problems and their symptoms, from high school drop out rates to child-poverty traps, purvey northern, white, rural communities, there is obviously something wrong with their analysis and explanation. Friendly critics have been pointing out the contradictions in progressive philosophy and the self defeating nature of policies based on it for 20 years [Franca *et al*, 2000; D'Souza, 1992]. Yet whenever contradictions appear, like Asians being excluded from Californian universities because the success undermined the quotas designed to make admissions match the state's demographics, academics like Glassner continue to insist that 'inclusion' policies are justified by past exclusion, with no regard for the real consequences [1999: 13]. In this case, the 'beneficiaries," who had known nothing but positive discrimination, were often left unprepared and unable to cope because of other PC failures lower down the educational system; and, as Golden [2006] pointed out, that had done nothing to address the real inequities perpetuated by the Ivy League system. Although combating discrimination is laudable, maintaining methods that do not work is not; and dismissing any and all attempts to consider what's gone wrong as racism merely demonstrates that progressives do not want to face the answer, which is not difficult to find.

According to Wagner, the puritanical streak in the progressivism of yesteryear returned when the student rebels of the 1960s became the teachers, social workers and other petit-professionals of the 1970s; and their PC policies facilitated the policing of personal behavior from college campuses to corporations in the 1980s. Although these revolutionaries denounced the political-Right's familial ideology because it stood in the way of their agenda on abortion and gay rights, they also prioritized personal politics rather than economics having adopted the radical feminist's definitions of male sin [1997: 104, 112–116, 135–139]. The switch from class to PC politics was symbolized by the content of *Mother Jones* magazine which despite being named after a radical labor organizer was also more concerned with the consumption of fatty foods, cigarettes, and other personal "failings' [Wagner, 1997: 145–146]. Indeed, although the attack on the tobacco industry was supposed to be a stalking horse strategy leading to the regulation of corporate malpractice, the consumer quickly became the main target; and we all know what happened because of that [Wagner, 1997: 146–150]. Likewise, Wagner argued that that the dual panics from cyberspace to satanic abuse promoted by progressives and conservatives explained the "totally administered society" that the former blamed on the latter [Wagner, 1997: 151–173]. Jenkins [2006: 108–152, 203, 80–81] more extensive review of the politics of the period designed to explain the origin and nature of contemporary social fears, may have placed more emphasize on the way that the progressive crusades had played into the hands of the political-Right, but he also drew attention to the fact that while race was still a factor, the Left had ignored many others that were equally important, and were drawing the wrong inferences as a result. We could not agree more. When we attempted to explore the "selective issues" that Jenkins alluded to, which led working-class Catholics to vote Republican, by looking at the last white bastion in the Bronx, Throgs Neck, we found the nature of the racism so offensive we could not put up with it, even for the benefit of social science; on the other hand, when we followed the survival strategies of black dope dealing recidivists we discovered that they were not impressed with progressive perspective either; and once we began to hang out with rednecks in upstate New York, the situation became even more complicated.

It did not take us long to discover that when race is divorced from class it guarantees little progress in other areas, even when issues like death row demographics are clearly a question of race. By ignoring the common problems within the criminal *in*justice system that enabled race to effect the outcome, like the lack of any imperative to conduct a full investigation before imposing multiple indictments, progressives inhibit the broad based campaigns needed for reform. Concentrating on incidents like the beating of Rodney King by the Blue Klux Klan while ignoring the far more drastic ramifications of Ruby Ridge and Waco for everyone's constitutional protections because the victims had the wrong politics and religion, had enabled successive administrations to rip up the Bill of Rights, and did nothing to address the economic issues that account for continuing ethnic conflict. Denouncing those who point to these problems as conspiracy theorists only added to the confusion that is contemporary US politics. By 'ignoring' Waco because of *their* apocalyptic paranoid style, progressives alienated large sections of the working class in rural areas where the welfare and criminal process systems are operated like fiefdoms by the elite of both parties to control 'the rednecks'. The cost of that control annoys the working-class who call themselves the middle-class, even though it supplies many of their jobs; and as they do not want to pay for this *white* welfare, they vote GOP for those 'lower tax' policies that tend to benefit 'the one percent', although they spend all day complaining about 'big government' subsidies for business. This should come as no surprise, given the history of the redneck. While blaming the chavs for their fate in the UK is a recent development, blaming the redneck for their plight is nothing new. Originally denounced as the evil "lubbers" by the fearful colonial rulers, they evolved into the "crackers" of the mixed race anarchistic frontier communities which angered the indigenous population, before being forced to work for the local middle-classes by the first regulators who sold the blacks back into slavery. Having then been re-stigmatized as "white trash" by no less than Harriet Beecher Stowe in *Dred* [1856]; they finally became the infamous 'redneck' in upstate New York thanks to the eugenic orientated sociology of Doug Dale [Wray, 2006]. They only escaped being subjected to progressive social-hygiene policies *en masse* because the holocaust gave eugenics a bad name, although 60,000 redneck and hillbilly women were still subjected to enforced sterilization because of their supposed feeble mindedness [Black, 2003; *The Guardian*, 4.5.02: 21]. While it is easy to dismiss them as Obama did by throwing them in with the religious petit-bourgeoisie who held Tea party rallies when he made his infamous quip about clinging to their churches and guns in times of crisis; life is not that simple. The rednecks have not forgotten that the Democrats had no qualms about burning the Branch Davidians at the stake, and so were galvanized by Ron Paul because of his social libertarianism, even though his free market fundamentalism was not in their immediate interest. What made that even more bizarre was that the rednecks could have readily supplied the constituency the Democrats were looking for when it came to issues like universal health care and infrastructural investment if it were not for their simplistic approach to gun control. None of this makes any sense, unless one abandons the simplistic dichotomies and stereotypes employed by progressives, and looks at the experiential sources of political positions; but that is unlikely to happen anytime soon.

One of the reasons is that the popularity of moral panic stateside has paralleled the contradictions in PC policies, not least because it enables progressives to reach for the panic stickers the moment their coercive reforms go belly up. When the Trafficking Victims Protection Act 2000, failed to uncover the hundreds of traffickers and thousands of deceived victims its backers claimed that it would because of the disproportionate claims based on the ideological definition of 'exploitation', Wilson *et al* [2006] could not cope with reality. They explained that away as a function of the cops' preoccupation with their [sic] stereotype of national organized crime networks, which ensured they could not spot the trafficked victims in their locales. Back in 1910, when the brothels were full of exploited immigrants, first wave feminists had blamed the cops' failure to find the blue-eyed, blond haired Aryans from the heart lands seduced in their thousands in ice cream parlors on local graft [Bell, 1910]. Having observed the contemporary results of the raids on San Francisco's massage parlors, Leigh offered an alternative explanation. It transpired that the foreign female sex workers involved did not fit the feminist stereotype. They had knowingly made deals with facilitators in exchange for transportation to the US which, of course, meant that they were not entitled to the support services the Act provided for trafficked victims, despite being forced to be material witnesses. Consequently, Leigh [2005] argued that it was time to consider that the source of and solution to sexploitation was found in their women's working conditions. However, as decriminalization of prostitution and enforcement of labor codes was the last thing feminists would want, as that would undermine the symbolic role of the sex industry in their sexual politics, Wilson et al [2006] blamed the cops. Instead of admitting that the alliance with the Moral Right which secured the law had backfired, Chapkis [2003] had already claimed that the 'persecution' of the foreign sex workers was the really a moral panic about sexuality and immigration control. That not only undermined Wilson's claim the public had supported the bill; it enabled professional feminists and the Coalition Against Trafficking Women to avoid facing the fact that *they* had effectively reinforced the distinction between good 'victims' who gained a road to citizenship and 'bad girls' who have chosen their fate. If the progressives promoting the Act really believed that the outcome would be any different as Leidholt [cited in Chapkis, 2003: 927] claims that they did, that demonstrates the extent of the gap between progressive theory and reality, their refusal to learn from history [Thompson, 1994a], and the fact that de Young is not the only one using generic panics to explain away progressive disasters.

Twenty years on, when desperate hope and a handful of change is all the poor working-classes have left when a progressive president bailouts banksters rather than saves Main Street, makes it easier to declare martial law, and tries to take down dissenting voices on the internet while corporations like Monsanto continue to grab control of everything from seed generation to human genes [Resnik, 2004; Laughlin, 2008; Koepsell, 2009]; it's not surprising that the paradigm is proving even more popular. It has become the progressive's answer to what they see as the political-Right's recourse to conspiracy theory. As an increasing number of populists like Alex Jones identify the "the new world order" with the cabal of banksters, corporate fat cats, and the political class*es* rather than some shadowy secret society like the Illuminati, progressive critics like Chip Bertlet have become increasing fearful that an increasing number on the political-Left are also tempted to consider that the seminal division in society is between that cabal and the masses [Fenster, 2008: 44]. Like David Aaronovitch's [2010] conspiracy theory about US conspiracy theories, Bertlet reaches for the crisis-fascist card rather than consider that the disaffected have noticed that PC politics has left banksters free to rake in the profits from outsourcing, war profiteering, speculating on substitutes for stocks and hedging futures markets, while forcing a low wage economy on everyone else washed down with a dose of HFCS or aspartame. That problem is not restricted to a few 'sacrifice zones' [Hedges and Sacco, 2012].

As long as progressive typification is determined by ideology rather than reality the contradictions will continue to grow, and recourse to moral panic will not solve the problem that resides in the progressives' tendency to assess evidence on its perceived ramifications for their existing agenda rather than anything their opponents are doing. University of Texas at Austin's Mark Regnerus was immediately accused of academic fraud simply because his study into the effects of homosexual parentage did not produce the results some members of the gay community would have liked. Rather than check his methodology and data, and consider what the results might mean, they wanted him fired immediately. Yet, despite the unimpeachable evidence concerning all those medical false positives in the child abuse crusades we covered in Chapter 6, no one called for those proselytizers to be reigned in. On the contrary, progressives ignored the evidence by attacking the messengers who were denounced as child abuse "deniers" who were putting victims at risk of disbelief. Unfortunately, that response is all too typical. SUNY have sacked the untenured because they don't agree with Al Gore about the causes of global warming, fail to subscribe to progressive victimology, or object to the medicalization of students on campus. John Jay, of all places, steers clear of anyone who has been accused of these and other PC crimes. Progressive professors are more than happy that they do so because they do not believe in real diversity as that would require them to justify their truth-claims, tolerate activities like prostitution, smoking, and gun ownership which they would prefer to eliminate, and face the fact that Pally's [2011] study of liberal Charasmatics confirmed that they know far less about social reality than Glenn Beck! Progressives can not justify their strategies either. While living in the Catskills, literally surrounded by *mixed race* couples on minimum wage subsidized by food stamps, HUD, and HEAP, who could not afford a gun and did not go to church unlike the progressive elite; we were frequently asked by rednecks why they were blamed for the sins of someone else's forefathers and did not have a college fund when they were just as disadvantaged, though they did not use that word. So, we told them in language that they would understand that by doing so, the progressive middle classes could pretend that it was "all your fault" while they grab some rather large crumbs from the crony capitalists' table in return for inventing a much better form of social control. We did not bother to mention moral panic.

THE MYTH OF MORAL PANIC

The moral panic paradigm is and always was a political perspective. It reflected and promoted the social values and interests of the secularized, educated, progressive wing of the postwar petit-bourgeoisie. As it shared the aims of the new secular social movements emerging from that class, it set itself the task of identifying the barriers to their success to win them over to overthrowing capitalism rather than remain single issue crusades. The paradigm denounced the old petit-bourgeoisie as the cultural enemy, the font of the prejudice that stood in the way of the new movements' aspirations. Despite the lack of evidence, the moral entrepreneurs were not only deemed to be capitalism's source of support in major crises, but the cause of every progressive set back too. When it became apparent that the working-class was not going to deliver, and the paradigm needed to switch, Cohen called in "the Americans". In return for an academic Marshall plan to deal with the ravages after Reno, they could inherit the empire. When the Marxist elite objected that he had no right to give away their share, Cohen offered a compromise to keep the peace; the press had been bad enough, but it would not be long before someone else noticed what was going on.

Instead of being sociological, the paradigm used sociology to legitimize its politics. Cohen turned his PhD on vandalism into a thesis on the oppression of rebellious youth, the victims of a prejudicial society, whose social disasters could only be solved by sociologists, experts, professionals, and social workers who were taking on the reactionaries who confused the working-class [Cohen, 1973]. Ten years on, the CCCS abandoned all the metaphors; this was, after all, *the* crisis. Moral panic was propping up capitalism, and the reactionaries in the petit-bourgeoisie were really neo-fascists. However, although the middle-class students and feminists, and the 'revolutionary' muggers had exposed Capital's cultural and economic contradictions, the working class blew it because they were racist. What is worse is that they refused to do as they were told by all those sociologists, experts, professionals, and social workers because of their subscription to common sense [Hall *et* al, 1984]. The contradictions within the paradigm could and should have been laid bare by Barkers video panic. Although he claimed that Thatcherism was bamboozling everyone with familial ideology [Barker, 1984b] and had blocked the progressives' agenda for women and gays, he had just exposed where that simplistic reasoning had led to in the 1950s, when the Communist Party's crusade to ban them had undermined the horror commix subversive approach to myopic perspectives [Barker, 1984a]. Having popularized the politics of panic, Barker deflected attention away from the rise of the progressive-feminist-"faith group" alliance that was moving towards the therapeutic state. By the time that Winter appeared [1992], the petit-professionals were now exercising considerable power in the state bureaucracies, turning the students' cultural revolution into the social control policies that would be adopted and extended by New Labour. Winter's exasperation may have reflected her frustration but it also offered evidence for the widespread acceptance in academia that the working-class was now the main enemy. The progressives were not manu-facturing false allegations of abuse to 'prove' that patriarchy was built on endemic abuse; the working-class was incestuous as well as racist.

Strain blame and panic also enabled de Young to draw attention away from progressives' willingness to jail innocents to promote their thera-peutic philosophy in the US, and more: the radical feminist's adventurism into satanic abuse had proven even more embarrassing than porn. Having almost given the game away twice, the public had to be blamed for satanic abuse. Consequently, it was their adherence to familial ideology that had induced the guilt that made them susceptible to the claims of the religious Right and led them to "superimpose" the 'satanic tale' on the extensive child abuse exposed by the caring and concerned feminist movement. Yes, feminist social workers had been involved, but Summit had made them do it. He had bullied them. No need to mention that 'his' accommodation syn-drome theory was really Lucy Berliner's, Kee McFarlane had invented and promoted disclosure therapy to implant false memories in children, femi-nist pediatricians were peddling unscientific proof of blunt force trauma, and feminist psychiatrists and psychologists were turning every day chil-dren's troubles into signs of molestation in the same way that Dr. Kellogg had turned them into signs of 'self abuse' a century before [2004]. Goode and Ben-Yehuda, who had enough problems explaining away the feminist anti-porn panics, ducked this one completely. By blaming the 'satanic tale' on the Christians, and ignoring the DCC cases, they wrote a decade of torturing children in disclosure therapy by progressives out of history.

When the progressives' response to Thatcherism backfired in Paulsgrove, Wilson and Silverman simply lied about a nonexistent vigilante mob of chavs to cover up the fact that the sociologists, social workers, experts, and professionals the panic paradigm had lauded for 30 years were creating social disasters. No matter if they had to turn the paradigm's model inside out to do so. Blaming the chavs drew attention away from the fact that PC politics and victimology had given capitalism free reign to finish off the now leaderless working-class. As the chavs were racist, incestuous, atavistic, primitives, they only had themselves to blame. It had nothing to do with the progressives' exploitation of child abuse generating mass miscarriages of justice to overload the system, leaving nothing left for monitoring offenders facilitating the abduction, rape, and murder of another working-class child, Sarah Payne. Progressives could wipe the blood off their hands on a grass root panic.

ACADEMIC STRAIN

This academic class warfare targeting those wary of the progressives' cultural revolution was promoted by the same means that Cohen denounced when used by the media: exaggerating and distorting events, constructing false causations, sensitizing readers to the author's orientation, promoting false images, demonizing alternative belief systems and criticism, creating folk devils, and dramatizing and amplifying their evils; and as we just did, to make the point, making no distinction between overt and latent intent and effects. Though, in this case, the effect can not be denied. The progressive petit-professional classes responded to the alleged threats identified by the panic paradigm and the progressive agenda offered by critical theory by experimenting with new forms of social control on college campuses, perfecting them in local government social work departments, and extending them under New Labour which then gave the former class of 1968 government grants to justify the very problem the paradigm claimed that it had exposed: the extension of social control through the politics of fear.

In contradistinction to the claim that value pluralism did not exist in the 1960s, the panic paradigm is proof that it did. It was a product and manifestation of the value conflict *within* the new post war petit-bourgeoisie between the religious and secular factions. The only reason it looked different was that Cohen and company claimed that the religious were the old petit-bourgeoisie. In reality, Cohen began his PhD at the same time that the Charismatic revival took off, and the NFOL mobilized the socially conservative amongst the new petit-bourgeoisie a mere two years before *Folk Devils* appeared, as the battle began in earnest. The fact that Cohen misread Ranulf, the CCCS ignored Wallis, and Barker was woefully ignorant of the politics within the Christian community and so focused on Valour makes no difference. Neither does the fact that panic paradigm's problems with progressive moral enterprise reflected the tensions that inevitably arose when the religious and secular factions effectively aligned to promote the therapeutic politics of the new petit-bourgeoisie. The radical feminists obsession with pornography and convictions about satanic abuse may have proved embarrassing; but as CARE's communitarianism moved from the religious fringe to the political center under New Labour, it is far more significant that Valour's Marxist critics, having abandoned the working-class, proved they were "petit-bourgeois deviationists" too and set about the atavistic primitives who lacked ambition and aspiration, had no views on serious subjects, and revelled in their arrogant immaturity, while the corporate Kings did their own thing.

Like many others, we once foolishly believed that the authoritarian night-mares presented in *Animal Farm, 1984, Brave New World,* and *Fahrenheit 451* would emerge from the political-Right, because the Left claimed to have learnt the lessons of the corrupt communist regimes. A dose of college divested us of that because those nightmares never alluded to naked force alone, but the self interested who dreamed of power, Big Brother surveillance, soma, and eliminating dissent by destroying its source, free inquiry, symbolized by book burning. While some of the author's own politics made us wince, they all held a candle for free thought, the source of real diversity. When we looked at the paradigm's truth claims about the source and nature of coercive reform and ideological closure in contemporary society, we discovered the same problem that we had encountered in college; as Reich had warned, one found as many authoritarians on the Left as the right. The myth of moral panic has been misleading its readers about the nature and purpose of moral enterprise on all sides of the political divide for four decades, especially its own. The end result is that the fat cats on corporate welfare have been laughing all the way to their next bail out, while the rest of us now live in the brave new world of 'inclusive' social control because of all those sociologists, experts, professionals, and social workers. That's why we prefer common sense based on the experiential truths that we were offered by the panic paradigm's folk-devils when it was dispensed over a cup of tea and cookies.

Notes

NOTES TO THE PREFACE

1. When we use the word 'progressive' in this volume it reflects US usage, covering a range of perspectives from social democrat to Marxist. The terms professional Left and professional feminist refers to politicians, academics, and those employed in any other organization including local government where they can combine their employment and politics.
2. When we use the term in this volume, we are alluding to any act by any social or interest group that promotes its values by engaging in political activity designed to secure/exploit government support for their preferred social policy agenda.

NOTES TO THE INTRODUCTION

1. http://www.onpedia.com/encyclopedia/moral-panic, retrieved 01/01/2009.
2. See http://everything2.com/title/The+war+on+Iraq+as+a+moral+panic, retrieved 23/05/2013.
2. As children have no "use" we would prefer not to use the term "abuse," but given its popular usage we have retained it for this volume.
3. Jenkins' *Intimate Enemies* is also a perfect example of the limitations of the "interest group perspective." Despite his exemplary account of the moral enterprise involved behind the headlines, unless one 'was there' you cannot appreciate or understand the influence of Ray Wyre of the Gracewell Centre. He dominated popular TV shows from the late 1980s, spreading myths about pedophilia, pornography, and sex crime; and then between 1989–94, did so as part of a 'double act' with Mike Hames of the Obscene Publication Squad. They were also major players in the feminist crusade against pin-up porn we cover in Chapter 5, and the satanic panic we cover in Chapter 6, although because of space we have had to cut their particular contributions from the script.
4. The failure of this limited understanding of history became apparent to us when we lived in the Catskills but never met a redneck who watched *Fox News,* listened to 'Right-wing radio,' or went to church. We also gained the impression that if progressives had spent the same amount of time mobilizing the rural poor as Acorn did municipal minorities, they might had the constituency who would vote for universal health care, infrastructural investment, and regulating banksters. Ironically, church attendance amongst the progressive elite was as extensive as the local GOP.

NOTES TO CHAPTER 1

1. This refers to The Beatles being awarded Member of the British Empire status in 1965 by the Queen following the recommendation of the Labour Party, then in power.

NOTES TO CHAPTER 2

1. Hansard House of Commons debates can be retrieved from http://hansard. millbanksystems.com/commons/1964/
2. MAR1 source URL—http://www.britishpathe.com/results.php?search= mods+and+rockers
3. Hansard HOC debates can be found at http://hansard.millbanksystems.com/ commons/1964/. Hereafter, all HOC references can be found at this URL.
4. MAR2 source URL—http://www.youtube.com/watch?v=EFWnaAQjbK4
5. Property owners exploiting the housing shortage.
6. The philosophy behind the Clean Up TV campaign.
7. This major omission becomes central in Goode and Ben-Yehuda's rewrite of Cohen's account, without any explanation [2010: 29].
8. Acquisitiveness was a euphemism for Covetousness'—a sin denounced in the 10th Commandment.
9. Canon Collins was a radical cleric. He not only led the Campaign for Nuclear Disarmament which organized the Ban the Bomb marches, but also favored civil disobedience as a tactic. The reference in the debate alludes to the public disorder that occurred on the 1963 march.
10. A Christian argument long before John Gagnon turned it into a sociological one.
11. Rag weeks consisted of numerous events designed to raise funds for charities but often became an excuse for binge drinking and destruction.
12. It had suggested raising the age of criminal responsibility to 12 years, and recommend further attention to be paid to 13-21 year olds; hence the proposed Royal Commission.
13. The voting age; then at 21.
14. One Plus One URL—www.oneplusone.org.uk/ICOR/StatisticsDetails. php?Ref=41, retrieved 13/04/09.

NOTES TO CHAPTER 3

1. That expression alludes to the way public political 'debate' tended to amount to people listening to politicians on TV rather than the centuries old habit of mass meetings in public, effectively denying the public any voice.
2. While employed as an attorney's clerk researching Chapter 5, we jumped at the chance to work on a fraud case in front of the equally infamous Judge Argyle. We were not disappointed. The trial was delayed while Argyle threatened a Rastafarian in the preceding case with a longer sentence unless he removed his tam; and at the end of the prosecution phase of our trial, he threatened our client with the maximum penalty if he dared waste the court's time with his "useless defense"! We turned the tables, and our client avoided jail.
3. A non-existent confession.
4. This followed and attempt by the police to arrest a man for "parking a Mercedes, while black" in south London, who turned out to be a Nigerian diplomat [see Moore, 1975: 66].

5. Lobster was a magazine, and it's now a web site—www.lobster-magazine.co.uk.

NOTES TO CHAPTER 4

1. The 1960s sociological argot for petit-bourgeoisie [see Tracey and Morrison 1976: 278].
2. Abortion, obscene publications, moral education in schools, Sunday trading, tax breaks for family, embryo experimentation, and surrogacy.
3. The European equivalent of a voodoo doll.
4. Though their motives were similar we wish to reiterate that none of the moral entrepreneurs we met, including Mary Whitehouse, revealed any hint of Mather's authoritarianism let alone his megalomania.

NOTES TO CHAPTER 5

1. The sources used in this chapter are based on the contents of the files collectively known as 1/27 in Portsmouth City Council's records office (PCC). This included the correspondence between the Planning Committee and council officers, and between the planning committee and the Department of Environment (DOE), both indicated by the material's official file codes; and in this case a letter from the City's MPs. The protest letters and petitions were also found under this file number. As were the relevant Committee's minutes. We acknowledge the access granted by Portsmouth City Council to research and cite this material, which first appeared in Thompson [1987] in return for a ten-year moratorium.
2. For Hansard HOC debate please refer to URL - http://hansard.millbanksystems.com/commons/1981/nov/25/, retrieved 16th April 2013.
3. We apologize for the lack of page numbers in some newspaper references. They were not *de rigueur* at the time, and the cuttings file we utilized during this period did not record the page number.
4. See http://hansard.millbanksystems.com/commons/1981/mar/23/, retrieved 16th April 2013.
5. See http://hansard.millbanksystems.com/commons/1979/jan/26/, retrieved 16th April 2013.
6. See http://hansard.millbanksystems.com/commons/1982/jul/, retrieved 16th April 2013.
7. At the time, the popular term for a politically correct person was "right-on".
8. At the time a 15 certificate meant those under that age could watch the movie as long as they were accompanied by an adult.
9. See http://hansard.millbanksystems.com/commons/1986/apr/25/act-to-apply-to-television-and-sound, retrieved 16th April 2013.
10. From 1990, we were constantly contacted by attorneys whose clients were being accused of selling snuff movies; although, following our reports detailing the origin of the movies and the alleged 'victims' next one, the charges were always dropped. We did, however, have to appear as a witness in the case of *"Minnie's 3rd Love, or: Nightmare on Polk Street"*, a cartoon strip written and drawn by Phoebe Gloeckner, published in the 1994 feminist collection *Twisted Sisters*. The not guilty verdict led to an assurance by HM Customs to review its practices.

NOTES TO CHAPTER 6

1. Sheriffs are judges in Scotland.
2. As most of the media material cited is from British, we have used the day-month-year rather than the US system; and once again apologize when we have relied on cuttings services which did not record the page number.
3. We have retained the popular use of "abuse" despite our philosophical, political, and linguistic objections to its deliberate nebulous nature.
4. We were fortunate enough to have worked with Dr. Paul on two cases before his untimely death.
5. We explain this feature with appropriate examples below.
6. In the UK the prefix *R* in legal cases stands for Regina (indicating the queen) and represents the state or crown.
7. We acknowledge the extensive investigative work by Derek Prigent.
8. Our analysis of the remaining interview notes helped reopen this case. As some of the children were much older and contested McLean's interpretation of the interviews too, the parents successfully appealed against their conviction.
9. Although we believed that they were all knaves or fools, our hang up about honesty compelled us to offer evidence on behalf of Croall, whose contribution to the TV show was being misrepresented by his detractors; and so helped him escape false allegations.
10. Hereafter, testimony is indicated by the name of the witnesses and the date of their evidence. Although we could usually cite several, to save space we only refer to the major witness.
11. We became involved when the Parents Action Group asked for our help. We were then engaged by their lawyers. However, having got our hands on the only copies of the copious case files that had officially been 'lost', correctly transcribed the remaining audio tapes of the disclosures, and spent 6 months reconstructing what had happened, we were excluded from giving oral evidence because we could prove what had really happened and why. We were then subject to a gagging order.
12. That was nothing new either. We added that claim to our critic of the interview methods adopted in the Bishop Auckland satanic case several years earlier; but the authorities dropped the whole case rather than put that to the test, enabling her to continue her 'services to ideology'.

NOTES TO CHAPTER 7

1. This has a similar connotation to "ghetto," when used in the US to describe a housing project.
2. One of the authors twice faced prosecution. The first followed his defense of a senior citizen being threatened by three thugs, because he had used a weapon (a piece of wood), although one of the thugs was armed with an axe! The second followed catching two teens attempting to invade the home of his neighbor. The charge: kidnapping. The charges were not pursued because of infringements of statutory duties by the police. Yet, academics ignore this problem when accounting for the Bystander effect.
3. Alt.folklore.urban was an old usenet discussion group, which unfortunately no longer exists.
4. National Health Service, the state of which is the Left's major barometer of the balance of forces in UK politics—eds.
5. free.uk.talk.portsmouth is a local newsgroup which is still active. Unfortunately, this newsgroup thread is no longer available [see Williams, 2004: 355].

6. uk.local.hampshire was a local newsgroup which, unfortunately, is no longer available [see Williams, 2004: 355-356].

7. As most police officers were acting under orders, we do not blame them. On the contrary, we believe that their decisions on the first night were an exemplary example of public order policing, and it's a pity that example was lost in what followed.

8. The official name given to the investigation reflecting the attempt to construct a rhetorical riot.

9. These labels are ours reflecting the groups' core attributes.

10. We maintain complete confidentially in this case.

NOTES TO THE CONCLUSION

1. Like most theories of this ilk, it is simplistic and is defied by its chronology. The 'Right-wing' version, based on Francis Fukuyama's 1989 essay The End of History, suggested that liberal democracy was the 'highest' form of evolution in governance. That was an easy claim to make once the major alternative, state communism fell apart. Its obvious weakness was that it relied on an evolutionary model of thought and development. The Left-wing version which followed and has numerous sources, argued that whereas people and governments were once inspired by ideologies, they are now both guided and governed by fear. Its obvious weakness is that it relies on a dichotomous model belied by the rebirth of libertarianism, the dramatic growth in fundamentalist environmentalism, and numerous other ideologies. It also takes government 'fear' at face values, and refuses to consider it as a deliberate tactic. Like this volume's subject matter, these developments owe far more to interpretation than social reality.

2. This concerned the loss of the super tanker Derbyshire in the fall of 1980, during a typhoon off Japan, and the loss of the 42 crew members. The relatives had to engage and endure a two decade-long campaign before the manufacturers and the UK government would admit that there was a design fault which also explained the sinking of dozens of other tankers. Thanks to the unheralded efforts of the Derbyshire Family Association, the Oceaneering Technology Company which located the wreck and the underwater forensic team from the Oceanographic Institute of Massachusetts, the ship was finally located and real cause uncovered. On 8 November 2000 the crew was exonerated of all blame, and the design of bulk carriers improved from then on.

3. British student unions were a world away from the Greek Societies found on US campuses. They were autonomous; had their own buildings, bars, and concert halls. They funded the students' sports and social clubs; and represented student interests both locally and nationally. They also offered a training ground for future politicians.

4. Much more than the equivalent of the US Innocence Project, it consists of numerous groups dedicated to opposing false allegations and convictions.

5. This is not to dismiss Parks' real contribution to the civil rights movement covered in Danielle L. McGuire's At the Dark End of the Street; but the failure to accredit Colvin is indicative of the way the black teens' vital contribution in securing civil rights, bailing out the revered 'leaders' time and time again, left future generations of black high-school students with no political role models of their own.

References

Aaronovitch, D. (2000). Why I am so scared of Paulsgrove woman. *Independent*, retrieved 11 August 2011, from http://www.independent.co.uk/opinion/commentators/why-i-am-so-scared-of-paulsgrove-woman-697018.html.

Aaronovitch, D. (2010). *Voodoo history: the role of conspiracy theory in shaping modern history*. New York: Riverhead Books.

Abbott, A. (2001). *Chaos of disciplines*. Chicago: The University of Chicago Press.

Abbott, K. (2007). *Sin in the second city: madams, ministers, playboys and the battle for America's soul*. New York: Random House.

Abercrombie, N. and Turner, S. T. (1978). The dominant ideology thesis. *British Journal of Sociology*, 29(2). pp. 149–170.

Acocella, J. (1993). *Creating hysteria: women and multiple personality disorder*. New Jersey: Jossey-Bass.

Adam, B.D. (1987). *The rise of a gay and lesbian movement*. Boston: Twayne Publishers.

Adorno, T.W., Frenkel-Brunswik, E., Levinson, D.J., Nevitt Sanford, R. (1950). *The authoritarian personality*. New York: Harper.

Aguirre, A. and Lio, S. (2008). Spaces of mobilization: the Asian-American-Pacific islander struggle for social justice. *Social Justice*, 35(2). pp. 1–17.

Aitken, S.C. (2001a) Schoolyard shootings: racism, sexism, and moral panics over teen violence. *Antipode*, 33(4). pp. 593–600.

Aitken, S.C. (2001b). *Geographies of young people: the morally contested spaces of identity*. London: Routledge.

Akdeniz, Y. (1997). Governance of pornography and child pornography on the global internet: a multi-layered approach. In L. Edwards, and C. Waelde, (Eds.). *Law and the internet: regulating cyberspace* (pp. 223–241). Portland, OR: Hart Publishing.

Ali, T. (1972). *The coming British revolution*. London: Jonathon Cape.

Altheide, D.L. (2006). Terrorism and the politics of fear. *Cultural Studies: Critical Methodologies*, 6(4). pp. 415–439.

Ammerman, N.T. (1987). *Bible believers*. New Brunswick: Rutgers University Press.

Anderson, D. (Ed.). (1992). *The loss of virtue: moral confusion and social disorder in Britain and American*. London: The Social Affairs Unit.

Annetts, J. (1998). *Queer motivations: gays, aids, and social movement theory*. Unpublished PhD Thesis, University of Reading, UK.

Annetts, J. and Thompson, B. (1992). Dangerous activism. In K. Plummer (Ed.). *Modern homosexualities: fragments of lesbian and gay experience* (pp. 237–246). London: Routledge.

Armstrong, E.G. (2007). Moral panic over meth. *Contemporary Justice Review* 10(4), pp. 427–442.

Assiter, A. and Carol, A. (Eds.). (1993). *Bad girls and dirty pictures: the challenge to reclaim feminism*. London: Pluto Press.

Ault, J. (1987). Family and fundamentalism: the Shawmut Valley Baptist church. In J. Obelkevich, L. Roper, and R. Samuel (Eds.), *Disciplines of faith: Studies in religion, politics, and patriarchy.* London: Routledge and Kegan Paul.

Avlon, J. (2010). *Wingnuts: how the lunatic fringe is hijacking America.* New York: Beast Books.

Bain, O. and Sanders, M. (1990). *Out in the open: a guide for young people who have been sexually abused.* London: Virago.

Ballard, L.M. (1984). Tales of trouble. In P. Smith (Ed.), *Perspectives on contemporary legends.* Sheffield: Sheffield University Printing Unit.

Banks, O. (1981). *Faces of feminism.* Oxford, UK: Blackwell Publishers.

Banner, S. (2002). *The death penalty: an American history.* Cambridge, MA: Harvard University Press.

Bannister, A., Barrett, K. and Shearer, E. (Eds.). (1990). *NSPCC, listening to children: the professional response to hearing the abused child.* Harlow: Longman.

Barker, M. (1984a). *A haunt of fears: the strange history of the British horror comics campaign.* London: Pluto Press Ltd.

Barker, M. (Ed.). (1984b). *Video nasties: freedom and censorship in the media.* London: Pluto Press Ltd.

Barlow, G. and Hill, A. (1985). *Video violence and children* London: Hodder and Stoughton.

Barron, C. and Lacombe, D. (2005). Moral panic and the nasty girl. *CRSA/RCSA, 42*(1). pp. 52–69.

Barry, K. (1979). *Female sexual slavery.* New York: New York University Press.

Bean, P. and Melville, J. (1990). *Lost children of the empire.* London: Unwin Hyman Limited.

Bebbington, D. (1995). The decline and resurgence of Evangelical social concern 1918–1980. In J. Wolffe (Ed.), *Evangelical faith and public zeal* (pp. 175–197). London: SPCK.

Beck, E. (1987). Occupational identity and legend decline: the meat that never spoils. In P. Smith (Ed.), *Perspectives on contemporary legends.* Sheffield: Sheffield University Printing Unit.

Becker, H. (1963). *Outsiders: studies in the sociology of deviance.* New York: Free Press.

Beecher Stowe, H. (1856). *Dred: a tale of the great dismal swamp.* Boston: Phillips, Sampson and Company.

Bell, E.A. (1910). *Fighting the traffic in young girls, or war on the white slave trade.* Chicago: G.S. Ball.

Bell, S. (1988). *When Salem came to the boro: the true story of the Cleveland child abuse crisis.* London: Pan.

Ben-Yehuda, N. (2009). Moral panics: 36 years on. *British Journal of Criminology, 49*(1). pp. 1–3.

Benson, R. and Saguy, A. C. (2005). Constructing social problems in an age of globalization: a French-American comparison. *American Sociological Review, 70.* pp. 233–259.

Ben-Yehuda, N. (1984). The sociology of moral panics: towards a new synthesis. *Sociological Quarterly, 27*(4). pp. 495–513.

Bercovitch, S. (1980). *The American jeremiad.* Madison: University of Wisconsin Press.

Berry, J. (1976). *Social work with children.* London: Routledge & Kegan Paul.

Best, J. (1989). Dark figures and child victims: statistical claims about missing children. In J. Best (Ed.). *Images of issues* (pp. 21–37). New York: Aldine De Gruyter.

Best, J. (1999). *Random violence: how we talk about new crimes and new victims.* Berkeley: The University of California Press.

Best, J. (2001). *Damned lies and statistics: untangling numbers from media, politicians, and activists.* Berkeley: University of California Press.

Best, J. (Ed.). (1989). *Images of issues: typifying contemporary social problems.* Hawthorne: Aldine de Gruyter.

Bewes, W. A. (1923). *A manual of vigilance law* (4th ed.). London: National Vigilance Association.

Bewes, W. A. and Thompson, G. (1923). *A manual of vigilance law.* National Vigilance Association and the International Bureau for the Suppression of Traffic in Women and Children. London: Skinner & Co.

Black, G. (1994). *Hollywood censored: morality codes, Catholics, and the movies.* Cambridge: Cambridge University Press.

Blythe, R. (1963). *The age of illusion: England in the twenties and thirties 1919–1940.* Harmondsworth, UK: Penguin.

Boddy, W. (1996). Approaching "the untouchables": social science and moral panics in early sixties television. *Cinema Journal,* 35(4). pp. 70–87.

Boero, N. (2007). All the news that's fat to print: the American "obesity epidemic" and the media. *Qualitative Sociology,* 30. pp. 41–60.

Bottomley, K. and Coleman, C. (1984). Law and order: crime problem, moral panic, or penal crisis? In P. Norton (Ed.). *Law And Order And British Politics* (pp. 38–59). Aldershot, UK: Gower Publishing Co. Ltd.

Bouchier, D. (1983). *The feminist challenge: the movement for women's liberation in Britain and the United States.* London: Macmillan Press.

Bounds, E. M. (1972). *Satan: his personality, power, and overthrow.* Grand Rapids: The Baker Book House Company.

Boyd, A. (1991). *Blasphemous rumors: is satanic ritual abuse fact or fantasy? An investigation.* London: Fount.

Boyer, P. (1968). *Purity in print: book censorship in America.* New York: Charles Scribner's Sons.

Boyer, P. (1992). *Urban masses and moral order in America, 1820–1920.* Cambridge, MA: Harvard University Press.

Boyer, P. and Nissenbaum, S. (1974). *Salem possessed: the social origins of witchcraft.* Cambridge, MA: Harvard University Press.

Boyes, G. (1984). Belief and disbelief: an examination of reactions to the presentation of rumour legends. In P. Smith (Ed.). *Perspectives on contemporary legends.* Sheffield: Sheffield University Printing Unit.

Boyle, J. J. (1995). *Killer cults: shocking true stories of the most dangerous cults in history.* New York: SMP.

Brierley, P. (Ed.). (1989). *UK Christian handbook.* Bromley, Kent, UK: Marc Europe.

Bristow, E. J. (1977). *Vice and vigilance: purity movements in Britain since 1700.* London: Gill and MacMillan Rowan and Littlefield.

Bristow, E. J. (1982). *Prostitution and prejudice: the Jewish fight against white slavery 1870–1939.* Oxford, UK: Clarendon Press.

Britain First. (1976). #40. August–September.

Bromley, D. G. and Richardson, J. T. (1983). The brainwashing/deprogramming controversy: sociological, psychological, legal, and historical perspectives. *Studies in Religion and Society, Vol. 5.* New York: The Edwood Mellen Press.

Bromley, D. G. and Shupe, A. D. (1981). *Strange gods: the great American cult scare.* Boston: Beacon Press.

Brown, B. (1984). Exactly what we wanted. In M. Barker (Ed.). *The video nasties: freedom and censorship in the media* (pp. 68–79). London. Pluto Press.

Brown, K. D. (1995). Nonconformist evangelicals and national politics in the late nineteenth century. In J. Wolffe (Ed.). *Evangelical faith and public zeal* (pp.138–154). London: SPCK.

Brown, L. B. (1987). *The psychology of religious belief.* London: Academic Press.

Browne A. and Finkelhor D. (1986). Impact of child sexual abuse. *Psychological Bulletin, 99.* pp. 66–77.

Bruce, S. (1988). *The rise and fall of the new Christian Right.* Oxford: Clarendon Press.

Bunyan, T. (1977). *The history and practice of the political police in Britain.* London: Quartet Books.

Burgett, B. (2008). Sex, panic, nation. *American Literary History,* 21(1). pp. 67–86.

Burnham, J. C. (1993). *Bad habits: drinking, smoking, taking drugs, gambling, sexual misadventure, and swearing in American history.* New York: New York University Press.

Burstyn, V. (Ed.). (1985). *Women against censorship.* Vancouver: Douglas and McIntyre.

Bushaway, B. (1982). *By rite: custom, ceremony, and community in England, 1700–1880.* London: Junction Books.

Calcutt, A. (1997). *Arrested development: pop culture and the erosion of adulthood.* London: Cassell.

Calder, M. (Ed.). (2004) *Child sexual abuse and the internet: tackling the new frontier.* Lyme Regis, UK: Russell House Publishing Ltd.

Campbell, B. (1989). *Unofficial secrets: child sexual abuse: the Cleveland case.* London: Virago Press.

Campbell, B. and Jones, J. (1999). *Stolen voices: an exposure of the campaign to discredit children's testimony.* London: The Women's Press.

Campbell, H. (2004). *Anne Bradsheet and her time.* New York: Globusz.

Campbell, T. W. (1998). *Smoke and mirrors: the devastating effect of forced sexual abuse claims.* New York: Insight Books.

Cantwell, H. B. (1983). Vaginal inspection as it relates to child sexual abuse in girls under the age of thirteen. *Child Abuse and Neglect,* 7(2). pp. 171–176.

CAPC. (1989). *Campaign against pornography and censorship policy statement.* London: CAPC.

Carlson S. and Larue G. (1989). *Satanism in America.* El Cerrito: Gaia Press.

Carol, A. (1994). *Nudes, prudes, and attitudes: pornography and censorship.* Cheltenham, UK: New Clarion Press.

Cassell, J. and Cramer, M. (2008). High tech or high risk: moral panics about girls on-line. In T. McPherson (Ed.), *Digital youth: innovation and the unexpected* (pp. 53–76) Cambridge, MA: MIT Press.

Caulfield, M. (1975). *Mary Whitehouse.* London: Mowbrays.

Ceci, S. J. and Bruck, M. (Ed.). (2000). *Jeopardy in the courtroom: a scientific analysis of children's testimony.* Washington, DC: The American Psychological Association.

Chalmers, D. M. (1976). *Hooded America: the history of the ku klux klan.* New York: New Viewpoints, Franklin Watts.

Chambliss, W. J. and Mankoff, M. (Eds.). (1973) *Whose law? What order?* New York: John Wiley.

Chapkis, W. (2003). Trafficking, migration, and the law: protecting innocents, punishing immigrants. *Gender and Society,* 17(6). pp. 923–937.

Chaplin, J. (Ed.). (1992). *Politics and parties: when Christians disagree.* Leicester: Intervarsity Press.

Chen, C. M. (1996). *The sex side of life: Mary Ware Dennett's pioneering battle for Birth control and sex education.* New York: The New Press.

Chibnall, S. (1977). *Law and order news: An analysis of crime reporting in the British press.* London: Tavistock Publications Limited.

Clapton, G. (1993). *The Satanic abuse controversy: social workers and the social work press.* London: University of North London Press.

Clarke, J. (1996). The Skinheads and the magical recovery of community. In S. Hall and T. Jefferson (Eds.), *Resistance through rituals: youth subcultures in post-war Britain* (pp. 99–102). London: Routledge.

Clegg, A. and Megson, B. (1968). *Children in distress*. Middlesex: Penguin Books.

Clegg, S. and Flint, A. (2006). More heat than light: plagiarism in it's appearing. *The British Journal of Sociology of Education*, 27(3). pp. 373–387.

Cloward, R. and Ohlin, L. (1961). *Delinquency and opportunity: a theory of delinquent gangs*. London: Routledge and Kegan Paul.

Cocca, C. E. (2002). From "welfare queen" to "exploited teen": welfare dependency statutory rape, and moral panic. *National Women's Studies Association Journal*, 14(2). pp. 57–79.

Cohen, S. (1966). Mods, Rockers and the rest: community reactions to juvenile delinquency. Lecture presented to the Howard League, 6th December. *Howard Journal of Penology and Crime Prevention*, Vol. XII. No. 2.

Cohen, S. (1969). *Hooligans, vandals and the community: a study of societal reaction to juvenile delinquency*. Unpublished PhD Thesis, University of London, UK.

Cohen, S. (Ed.). (1971). *Images of deviance*. London: Penguin Books.

Cohen, S. (1972). Vandalism: its politics and nature. In J.B. Mays (Ed.), *Juvenile delinquency, the family and the social group* (pp. 307–317). London: Longman.

Cohen, S. (1973) *Folk devils and moral panics: the creation of the mods and rockers*. St. Albans, UK: Paladin.

Cohen, S. (1985). *Visions of social control: crime, punishment and classification*. Cambridge, UK: Polity Press.

Cohen, S. (2001). *States of denial: knowing about atrocities and suffering*. Cambridge, UK: Polity Press.

Cohen, S. (2003). *Folk devils and moral panics: the creation of the mods and rockers* (3rd ed.). Oxford: Blackwell Publishers.

Cohen, S. and Young, J. (Eds.). (1973). *The manufacture of news: social problems, deviance and the mass media*. London: Constable and Co.

Cole, S. A. (2009). Cultural consequences of miscarriages of justice. *Behavioral Sciences and the Law*, 27. pp. 431–449.

Coleman, L. (1984). *Reign of error: psychiatry, authority and the law*. Boston: Beacon Press.

Coleman, L. (1985). False allegations of child abuse: have the experts been caught with their pants down? *Forum: Journal of the Californian Attorneys For Criminal Justice-Los Angeles*, Jan–Feb 1985. pp. 12–21.

Coleman, L. (1989). Medical examinations for sexual abuse: have we been misled. *Issues in Child Abuse Accusations*, 1(3). pp. 1–9.

Coleman, L. and Clancy, P. (1999). *Has a child been molested? The disturbing facts about current methods of child abuse investigations*. Walnut Creek, CA: Berkeley Creek Productions.

Colvin, R. (1992). *Evil Harvest: A true story of cult murder in the American heartland*. New York: Bantam Books.

Cone, J. H. (1969). *Black theology and black power*. New York: Seabury Press.

Cone, J. H. (1989). *Black theology and black liberation*. New York: Orbis Books.

Corby B., Doig, A. and Roberts V. (2001). *Public inquiries into residential abuse of children*. London: Jessica Kingsley Publishers.

Corcoran, C. (1989). *Pornography: the new terrorism*. Dublin: Attic Press.

Core, D. (1991). *Chasing Satan*. London: Gunter Books.

Cornwell, B and Linders, A. (2002). The myth of moral panic an alternative account of LSD Prohibition. *Deviant Behavior: An Interdisciplinary Journal* 23, pp. 307–330.

Corwin D.L. (1988). Early diagnosis of child sexual abuse: diminishing the lasting effects. In G.A. Wyatt and G.J. Powell (Eds.), *Lasting effects of child sexual abuse* (pp. 251–269) Newbury Park: Sage.

Cox, B. (1975). *Civil liberties in Britain*. Harmondsworth: Penguin.

Cox, B., Shirley, J. and Short, M. (1977). *The fall of Scotland Yard*. Harmondsworth, UK: Penguin.

Crain, R. L., Katz, E. and Rosenthal, D. B. (1969). *The politics of community conflict: the fluoridation decision*. Indianapolis: Bobbis-Merrill Co. Inc.

Crichlow, F. (2010). *Standing tall against racism, an interview by Hassan Mahamdallie*, retrieved 22 May 2013 from http://www.socialistreview.org.uk/article.php?articlenumber=11443.

Critcher, C. (2000). *Government, media and moral crisis: paedophilia in the British press in the summer of 2000*. Paper presented at the conference on 'Communication In Crisis: The Media, Conflict And Society', Naples University.

Critcher, C. (2003). *Moral panics and the media*. Buckingham, UK: Open University Press.

Critcher, C. (Ed.). (2006). *Moral panics and the media: critical readings*. Buckingham, UK: Open University Press.

Critcher, C. (2009) Widening the focus: moral panics as moral regulation. *British Journal of Criminology*, 49(1). pp. 17–34.

Critchlow, D. T. (2005). *Phyllis Schlafly and grassroots conservatism: A woman's crusade*. Princeton: Princeton University Press.

Cruz, N. (1985). *Satan on the loose*. Bristol, UK: Don Summers.

David, M. (1986). Moral and marital: The family in the right. In R. Levitas (Ed.). *The ideology of the new right*. Cambridge, UK: Polity Press.

Davies, C. (2008). Proliferating panic: regulating representations of sex and gender during the culture wars. *Cultural Studies Review*, 14(2). pp. 83–102.

Davis, J. E. (2005). *Accounts of innocence: sexual abuse, trauma, and the self*. Chicago: Chicago University Press.

De Grazia, E. and Newman, R. K. (1982). *Banned films: movies, censors and the first amendment*. New York: Bowker.

D'Sousa, D. (1992). *Illiberal education: the politics of race and sex on campus*. New York: Vintage Books.

De Vananzi, A. (2008). Social representations and labeling of non-compliant youths: the case of Victorian and Edwardian hooligans. *Deviant Behavior*, 29. pp. 193–224.

de Young, M. (2004). *The day care ritual abuse moral panic*. Jefferson, NC: McFarland.

Demeritt, D. (2001) The construction of global warming and the politics of science. *Annals of the Association of American Geographers*, 91(2). pp. 307–337.

Dillon, P. (2003). *Gin: the much lamented death of Madam Geneva*. Boston: Justin, Charles & Co.

Dixon, D. (1991). *From prohibition to regulation: bookmaking, anti-gambling and the law*. Oxford: Clarendon Press.

Doezema, J. (1999). Loose women or lost women? The reemergence of the myth of white slavery in contemporary discourses of trafficking women. *Gender Issues*, 18(1). pp. 23–50.

Doherty, T. P. (2002). *Teenagers and teenpics: the juvenilization of American cinema in the 1950s*. Boston: Unwin Hyman.

Dominelli, L. and McLeod, E. (1989). *Feminist social work*. Basingstoke, UK: Macmillan.

Donson, F., Chesters, G., Welsh, I. and Tickle, A. (2004). Rebels with a cause, folk devils without a panic: press jingoism, policing tactics and anti-capitalist protest in London and Prague. *Internet Journal of Criminology*. Retrieved 22 October 2012 from http://www.internetjournalofcriminology.com/Donson%20et%20al%20-%20Folkdevils.pdf

Dreher, N. H. (1997). The virtuous and the verminous: turn of the century moral panics in London's public parks. *Albion*, 29(2). pp. 246–267.

Dunning, E., Murphy, P. and Williams, J. (1988). *The roots of football hooliganism*. London: Routledge and Kegan Paul.

Durham, M. (1991). *Sex and politics: the family and morality in the Thatcher years*. Basingstoke, UK: Macmillan.

Durington, M. (2007). The ethnographic semiotics of a suburban moral panic. *Critical Arts,* 27(2). pp. 261–275.

D'Souza, D. (1992). *Illiberal education: The politics of race and sex on campus*. New York: Vintage Books.

Dyer, C. (2000). Gynaecologist struck off the medical register. *British Medical Journal,* 321:258.1.

Eberle, P. and Eberle, S. (1993). *The abuse of innocence: the McMartin preschool trial*. Buffalo, New York: Prometheus Press.

Eden, M. (1993). Domestic Politics. In M. Eden (Ed.), *Britain on the brink: major trends in society today* (pp. 41–54). Nottingham: Crossway Books.

Eder, K. (1985). The 'new social movements': moral crusades, political pressure groups, or social movements? *Social Research,* 52(4). pp. 869–890.

Elias, R. (1993). *Victims still: the political manipulation of crime victims*. London: Sage.

Ellis, B. (1990). The devil worshippers at the prom: rumor panic as therapeutic magic. *Western Folklore,* 49(1). pp. 27–49.

Ellis, R. (1989). *The occult and young people*. Eastbourne, UK: Kingsway Publications.

Engels, F. (1969). *The condition of the working class in England*. London: Panther.

England, E. (1982). *The spirit of renewal: an open window on the charismatic movement*. Eastbourne, UK: Kingsway Publications.

Enroth, R. M. (1993). *Churches that abuse*. Grand Rapids, MI: Zondervan.

Erikson. K. T. (1966). *Wayward puritans: a study in the society of deviance*. New York: John Wiley & Sons.

Erjavec, K. (2003). Media construction of identity through moral panics: discourses of immigration in Slovenia. *Journal of Ethnic and Migration Studies,* 29(1). pp. 83–101.

Evans, J. (2003). Vigilance and vigilantes: thinking psychoanalytically about anti-paedophile action. *Theoretical Criminology,* 7(2). pp. 163–189.

Evers, E. (1982). *The Catskills: from wilderness to Woodstock*. Woodstock, NY: The Overlook Press.

Everywoman. (1988). *Pornography and sexual violence: evidence of the links*. London: Everywoman.

Fahmy, S. and Johnson, T. J. (2007). Mediating the anthrax attacks: media accuracy and agenda setting during a time of moral panic. *Atlantic Journal of Communication,* 15(1). pp. 19–40.

Family Base (1987). *The family charter*. Cambridge. UK: Jubilee Centre.

Fanon, F. (1963). *The wretched of the earth*. New York: Grove Press.

Fanon, F. (2008). *Black skin, white masks*. New York: Grove Press.

Fee, E. (1988). Critiques of modern science: the relationship of feminism to other radical epistemologies. In R. Bleir, *Feminist approaches to science* (pp. 42–56). New York: Pergamon Press.

Fekete, J. (1995). *Moral panic: biopolitics rising*. Montreal: Robert Davies.

Feminist Review Collective. (1988). *Family secrets: child sexual abuse,* Special Issue, No. 28, Spring.

Fenster, M. (2008). *Conspiracy theories: secrecy and power in American culture*. Minneapolis: University of Minnesota Press.

Ferguson, C. J. (2008). The school shooting/violent video game link: causal relationship or moral panic? *Journal of Investigative Psychology and Offender Profiling,* 5(1–2). pp. 25–37.

Ferrell, J. and Hamm, M. S. (Eds.). (1998). *Ethnography at the edge: crime deviance and field research*. Boston: Northeastern University Press.

Finkelhor D. (1985). The traumatic impact of child sexual abuse: a conceptualization. *American Journal of Orthopsychiatry,* 55(4). pp. 530–541.

Finkelhor, D. and Williams, L. M. (1988). *Nursery crimes: sexual abuse in day care.* Newbury Park, CA: Sage.

Fishman M. (1978). Crime waves as ideology. *Social Problems,* 25(5). pp. 531–542.

Fishman, M. (1989). *Where do crime waves come from?* Paper presented to the 41st annual Meeting of the American Society of Criminology, Reno, November 1989.

Forster, R. (1986). *Ten new churches.* Bungay, UK: The Charcer Press.

Foster, J. (1974). *Class struggle and the industrial revolution: early industrial capitalism in three English towns.* London: Weidenfeld and Nicolson.

Frith, S. (1978). *Sociology of rock.* London: Constable and Co.

Frith, S. (1983). *Sound effects: youth, leisure and the politics of rock 'n' roll.* London: Constable and Co.

Fryer, P. (1988). *Staying power: the history of black people in Britain.* London: Pluto Press.

Fulce, J. (1990). *Seduction of the innocent revisited: comic books exposed.* Lafayette, LA: Huntington House Publishers.

Furedi. F. (1997). *Culture of fear: risktaking and the morality of low expectation.* London: Cassell.

Gallagher, N. (1981). *The porno plague.* Minneapolis: Bethany House Publishers.

Gardner, D. E. (1969). *A warning to the nation.* London: Marshall, Morgan and Scott.

Gardner, D. E. (1983). *The trumpet sounds for Britain: Vols. 1 & 2.* Altringham: Christian Foundation Publications.

Gardner, R. A. (1989). Differentiating between bona fide and fabricated sex abuse allegations in children. *Journal of the American Academy of Matrimonial Lawyers,* 5. pp. 1–12.

Gardner, R. A. (1991). *Sex abuse hysteria: Salem witch trials revisited.* Cresskill, NJ: Creative Therapeutics.

Garland, D. (2002). *The culture of control: crime and social order in contemporary society.* Chicago: University of Chicago Press.

Garland, D. (2008). On the concept of moral panic. *Crime, Media, Culture,* 4(1). pp. 9–30.

Gelsthorpe, L. (2005). Folk devils and moral panics: a feminist perspective. *Crime, Media, Culture,* 1(1). pp. 112–116.

Gerassi, J. (1966). *The boys of Boise: furor, vice and folly in an American city.* New York: Collier Books.

Ghatak, S. (2007). *Anti-vice mobilizations and the development of criminological knowledge in progressive era America.* Paper presented at the American Sociological Association New York. August 11–14, 2007.

Gibbs, E. (Ed.). (1984). *Ten growing churches.* Bromley: UKSTL Books.

Gibson, P. (1989). Gay and lesbian youth suicide. In M.R. Feinleib (Ed.), *Report of the secretary's task force on youth suicide.* United States Government Printing Office.

Giddens, A. (1989). *The third way: the renewal of social democracy.* Cambridge, UK: Polity.

Gilbert, J. (1986). *A cycle of outrage: America's reaction to the juvenile delinquent in the 1950s.* Oxford, UK: Oxford University Press.

Gilbert, R.A. (1993). *Casting the first stone: the hypocrisy of religious fundamentalism and its threat to society.* Shaftsbury, UK: Element.

Gillies, V. (2006). *Marginalised mothers: exploring working class experiences of parenting.* Abingdon, UK: Routledge.

Gist, R. and Lubin, B. (Ed.). (1989). *The psychosocial aspects of disasters.* New York: John Wiley and Sons.

Glassner, B. (1999). *The culture of fear: why Americans are afraid of the wrong things*. New York: Basic Books.

Gloss, M. (1990). The Halifax slasher and other 'urban maniac' tales. In G. Bennett and P. Smith. *Perspectives on contemporary legend V*. Sheffield, UK: Sheffield Academic Press Ltd.

Goddard, S. (Ed.). (1986). *See it god's way: the best of buzz magazine*. Reading, UK: Word Publishing (UK) Ltd. Cox and Wyman Ltd.

Goffman, E. (1990). *Stigma: notes on the management of a spoiled identity*. London: Penguin Books.

Golden, D. (2006). *The price of admission: How America's ruling elite buys its way into elite colleges—and who gets left outside the gates*. New York: Crown Publishing Group.

Goode, E. and Ben-Yehuda, N. (1994). *Moral panics: the social construction of deviance*. Cambridge, MA: Blackwell.

Goode, E. and Ben-Yehuda, N. (2010). *Moral panics: the social construction of deviance* (2nd ed.). Cambridge, MA: Blackwell.

Gould, C. (1992). Diagnosis and treatment of ritually abused children. In D.K. Sakheim and S.E. Devine (Eds.). *Out of darkness: exploring satanism and ritual abuse* (pp. 207–248) New York: Lexington Books.

Greek, C. (1992). *The religious roots of American sociology*. New York: Garland Publishing Inc.

Greek, C. and Thompson, B. (1992). Anti-pornography campaigns: saving the family in America and England. *International Journal of Politics and Culture and Society*, 5(4). pp. 597–612.

Greene, H. Sir (1969). *The third floor front: a view of broadcasting in the sixties*. London: Bodley Head.

Griffiths, B. (1982). *Morality and the marketplace: Christian alternatives to capitalism and socialism*. London: Hodder and Stoughton.

Griffiths, M. (Ed.). (1985). *Ten sending churches*. Bromley: UKL STL Books.

Grillo, R. (2005). 'Saltdean can't cope': protests against asylum seekers in an English seaside suburb. *Ethnic and Racial Studies*, 28(2). pp. 235–260.

Gross, P.R. and Levitt, N. (1998). *Higher superstition: the academic left and its quarrels with science*. Baltimore: Johns Hopkins University Press.

Grubin, D. and Prentky, R. A. (1993). Sexual psychopathic laws. *Criminal Behaviour and Mental Health*, 3. pp. 381–392.

Gusfield, J. R. (1963). *Symbolic crusades: status politics and the American temperance movement*. Urbana, IL: University of Illinois Press.

Guth, J. L. (1983). The politics of the Christian right. In A. J. Cigler and B. A. Loomis (Eds.), *Interest group politics* (pp. 60–83). Washington, DC: CQ Press.

Hacker, A. (1973). Getting used to mugging. In W. J. Chambliss and M. Mankoff (Eds.), *Whose law? What order?* (pp. 215–224). New York: John Wiley.

Hall, D. D. (Ed.). (1999). *Witch hunting in 17th century New England: a documentary history, 1638–1693*. Boston: North Eastern University Press.

Hall, S., Critcher, C., Jefferson, T., Clarke, J. and Roberts, B. (1984). *Policing the crisis*. London: Macmillan.

Hall, S., and Jefferson, T. (Ed.). (1996). *Resistance through rituals: youth subcultures in post-war Britain*. London: Routledge.

Hampshire MAPPA (2002). *Potentially dangerous offenders protocol* (3rd ed.). Hampshire and Isle of Wight Constabulary.

Hancock, M. and Mains, K. B. (1988). *Child sexual abuse: a hope for healing*. Crowborough, UK: Highland Books.

Harper, A. (1990). *Dance with the devil*. Eastbourne, UK: Kingsway Publications.

Harris, T. (Ed.). (1995). *Popular culture in England c. 1500–1850*. Basingstoke, UK: Macmillan.

Hawdon, J. E. (2001). The role of presidential rhetoric in the creation of moral panic, Regan, Bush, and the war on drugs. *Deviant Behaviour: An Interdisciplinary Journal*, 22(5). pp. 419–445.

Hedges, C. and Sacco, J. (2012). *Days of destruction, days of revolt*. New York: Nation Books.

Henslin. J. (1977). *Deviant lifestyles*. New Brunswich, NJ: Transaction Books.

Herdt, G. (Ed.). (2009). *Moral panics, sex panics: fear and the fight over sexual rights*. New York: New York University Press.

Herman, J. W. with Hirschman, L. (1981). *Father-daughter incest*. Cambridge, MA: Harvard University Press.

Hertenstein, M. and Trott, J. (1993). *Selling satan: the evangelical media and the Mike Warnke scandal*. Chicago: Cornerstone.

Hicks, R. D. (1991). *In pursuit of satan: the police and the occult*. Buffalo, New York: Prometheus Books.

Hier, S. P. (2002). Conceptualizing moral panic through a moral economy of harm. *Critical Sociology*, 28(3). pp. 311–334.

Hier, S. P. (2003). Risk and panic in late modernity: implications of the converging sights of social anxiety. *The British Journal of Sociology*, 54(1). pp. 3–20.

Hill, C. (1980). *Towards the dawn*. London: Collins, Fount Paperbacks.

Hill, C. (1982). *The day comes*. London: Collins, Fount Paperbacks.

Hillsborough. (2011). Hillsborough: prosecutions likely over the 'biggest cover-up in history', *The Telegraph*, retrieved 19 April 2013 from http://www.telegraph.co.uk/sport/football/teams/liverpool/9539424/Hillsborough-prosecutions-likely-over-the-biggest-cover-up-in-history.html.

Himmelstein, J. L. (1983a). The new right. In R.C. Liebman and R. Wuthnow (Eds.), *The new Christian right* (pp. 15–30). New York: Aldine de Gruyter.

Himmelstein, J. L. (1983b). *The strange career of marihuana: politics and ideology of drug control in America*. Westport, CT: Greenwood Press.

Hobbs S. (1989). Enough to constitute a legend. In Burnett G. and P. Smith (Eds.), *The questing beast: perspectives on contemporary legends IV* (pp. 55–75). Sheffield, UK: Sheffield Academic Press.

Hobbs, C. J. and Wynne, J. M. (1986). Buggery in childhood: a common syndrome of child abuse. *Lancet*, 2(2). pp. 792–796.

Hobsbawm, E. and Rude, G. (1973). *Captain swing*. Harmondsworth, UK: Penguin University Books.

Hobsbawm, E. J. (1963). *Primitive rebels: studies in archaic forms of social movement in the 19th and 20th centuries*. Manchester, UK: Manchester University Press.

Holstein, J. and Miller, G. (1993). *Reconsidering social construction*. Hawthorne, NY: Aldine de Gruyter.

Home Office (2002). *Protecting children from potentially dangerous people: an inter agency inspection on children's safeguards*. London: Her Majesty's Stationary Office.

House of Commons (1983, 8ᵗʰ November). *Video nasties: a background to the video recordings bill 1983–84*. Background Paper, #130. House of Commons Library Research Division.

Hoose, P. (2011). *Claudette Colvin: twice toward justice*. New York: Square Fish Books.

Hosken, A. (2007). *Nothing like a dame: the scandals of Shirley Porter*. London: Granta.

Houghton, W. E. (1957). *The Victorian frame of mind: 1830–1870*. New Haven: Yale University Press.

Howard, P. (1963). *Britain and the beast*. London: Heinemann.

Howard, R. (1997). *Charasmania: when Christian fundamentalism goes wrong*. London: Mowbray.

Howitt, D. (1992). *Child abuse errors: when good intentions go wrong.* New Brunswick: Rutgers University Press.

Huber, P. W. (Ed.). (1993). *Galileo's revenge: junk science in the courtroom.* New York: Basic Books.

Hughes, G. and Edwards, A. (Eds.) (2002). *Crime control and community: the new politics of public safety.* New York: Willan Publishing.

Hughes J. and Blagg H. (1989). *NSPCC, child sex abuse: listening, hearing and validating the experiences of children.* Harlow UK: Longman.

Hughes, S. (Ed.). (1981). *The Christian Counselors Journal*, 3(2).

Humes, E. (1999). *Mean justice; a true account of a town's terror, a prosecutors ower, and a betrayal of innocence.* New York: Pocket Star Books.

Humphrey, H. H. (1985). *Report on Scott County investigation.* St. Paul, Minnesota: Minnesota Attorney General's Office.

Humphrey, M. (2007). Culturalising the abject: Islam, law, and moral panic in the west. *The Australian Journal of Social Issues*, 42(1). pp. 9–25.

Humphries, S. (1981). *Hooligans or rebels? An oral history of working class childhood and youth 1889–1993.* Oxford, UK: Blackwell.

Hunt, A. (1997). Moral panic and moral language in the media. *British Journal of Sociology*, 48(4). pp. 629–648.

Inglis, B. (1972). *Poverty and the industrial revolution.* London: Panther.

Innes, M. (2005). A short history of the idea of moral panic. *Crime, Media and Culture*, 1(1). pp. 106–111.

Irvine, D. (1973). *From witchcraft to Christ.* Cambridge, UK: Concordia Publishing.

Itzin, C. (Ed.). (1992). *Pornography: women, violence, and civil liberties.* Oxford, UK: Oxford University Press.

Itzin, C. (Ed.). (2000). *Home truths about child sexual abuse: influencing policy and practice. A reader.* London: Routledge.

Jaeger, M. (1956). *Before Victoria: changing standards and behavior 1787–1837.* London: Chatto and Windus.

James T. and Goudie C. (1986). *Local authority licensing of sex shops & sex cinemas.* Chichester, UK: Wiley.

Jeffrey, S. (1985). *The spinster and her enemies: feminism and sexuality 1880–1930.* London: Pandora.

Jeffreys, S. (ed.) (1987). *The sexuality debates.* New York: Routledge & Kegan Paul.

Jeffreys, S. (1993). *Anticlimax: a feminist perspective on the sexual revolution.* London: The Women's Press.

Jenkins, P. (1992). *Intimate enemies: moral panics in contemporary Great Britain* Hawthorne, NY: Aldine de Gruyter.

Jenkins, P. (2009). Failure to launch: why do some social issues fail to detonate moral panics? *British Journal of Criminology*, 49(1). pp. 35–47.

Jenkins, P. and Maier-Katkin, D. (1992). Satanism: myth and reality in a contemporary moral panic. *Crime, Law, and Social Change*, 17(1). pp. 53–75.

Johnson J.M. (1989). Horror stories and the construction of child abuse. In J. Best (Ed.), *Images of issues* (pp. 5–19). New York, Aldine De Gruyter.

Johnston, J. (1989). *The edge of evil: the rise of Satanism in North America.* Dallas: Word Publishing.

Johnston, O. R. (1976). *Christianity in a collapsing culture.* Exeter, UK: The Paternoster Press.

Johnston, O. R. (1979). *Who needs the family? A survey and Christian assessment.* Sevenoaks, UK: Ecclesia Books, Hodder and Stoughton.

Johnston, O. R. (1990). *Caring and campaigning: making a Christian difference.* London: Marshall Pickering.

Jones, O. (2011). *CHAVS: the demonization of the working class*. London: Verso Books.

Kahaner, L. (1988). *Cults that kill: probing the underworld of a cult crime*. New York: Warner Books.

Katchen, M. H. and Sakheim, D. K. (1992). Satanic beliefs and practices. In D. K. Sakheim, and S. E. Devine (Eds.), *Out of darkness: exploring Satanism and ritual abuse*. New York: Lexington Books.

Kavanagh, D. (1987). *Thatcherism and British politics: the end of consensus*. Oxford, UK: Oxford University Press.

Kelly, S. J. (1988). Ritual abuse of children dynamics and impact. *Cultic Study Journal*, 5(2). pp. 228–236.

Kemshall, H. and Wood, J. (2010). *Child sex offender review (CSOR) public disclosure pilots: a process evaluation (2nd Edition)*. Research Report 32. London: Home Office.

Keyes, R. (2006). *The quote verifier: who said what, where and when*. New York: St. Martin's Press.

King, A. (1993). Mystery and imagination: the case of pornography effects studies. In A. Assiter and A. Carol (Eds.), *Bad girls and dirty pictures: the challenge to reclaim feminism* (pp. 57–87). London: Pluto Press.

King, P. (2003). Moral panics and violent street crime 1750–2000: a comparative perspective. In B. S. Godfrey, C. Emsley, and G. Dunstall (Eds.), *Comparative histories of crime*. Oxford, UK: Oxford University Press.

Kitzinger, J. (2004). *Framing abuse: media influence and public understanding of sexual violence against children*. London: Pluto Press.

Kjos, B. (1990). *Your child & the new age: how parents can help their children recognize and resist new age deceptions*. Wheaton, IL: Victor Books.

Klocke, B. V. and Muschert, G. W. (2010). A hybrid model of moral panics: synthesizing the theory and practice of moral panic research. *Sociology Compass*, 4(5). pp. 295–309.

Knight, D. (1982). *Beyond the pale: the Christian political fringe*. Leigh, UK: CARAF Publications Limited.

Koepsell, D. (2009). *Who owns you: the corporate gold-rush to patent your genes*. Chichester, UK: Wiley-Blackwell.

Kostogriz, A. (2006). *On strangers, 'moral panics' and neo liberalization of teacher education*. Paper presented at the Annual Conference the Australian Association for research in education. Adelaide, Australia, November 27–30th.

Krinsky, C. (Ed.). (2008). *Moral panics over contemporary children and youth*. Burlington, VT: Ashgate.

Krupp N. (1988). *The church triumphant*. Shippensburg, PA: Destiny Image Publishers.

Lacey, D. (2010). *Derby day is the best time to fall out with your*, retrieved on 29 October 2010 from http://www.guardian.co.uk/football/blog/2010/oct/29/premier-league-derbies.

La Fontaine, J. (1998). *Speak of the devil: tales of satanic abuse in contemporary England*. Cambridge, UK: Cambridge University Press.

Lanning K. V. (1990). *Multi-dimensional child sex rings*. Unpublished Paper.

Lansbury, C. (1985). *The old brown dog: women, workers, and vivisection in Edwardian England*. Madison: The University of Wisconsin Press.

Larkin, R. W. (2007). *Comprehending columbine*. Philadelphia: Temple University Press.

Larson, R. (1987). *Larson's book of rock*. Wheaton, IL: Tyndale House Publishers.

Larson, R. (1989). *Satanism: the seduction of American youth*. Nashville, TN: Thomas Nelson Publishers.

Lattas, J. (2007). Cruising: moral panic and the Cronulla riot. *The Australian Journal of Anthropology*, 18(3). pp. 320–335.

Laughlin, R. B. (2008). *The crime of reason: and the closing of the scientific mind.* New York: Basic Books.

Lawhead, S. (1989). *Rock on trial.* Leicester, UK: Intervarsity Press.

Lawler, T. (2002). Mobs and monsters: independent man meets Paulsgrove woman. *Feminist Theory,* 3(1). pp. 103–113.

Lawson, T. and Comber, C. (2000). Censorship, the internet and schools: a new moral panic? *The Curriculum Journal,* 11(2). pp. 273–285.

Lemert, E. (1964). Social structure, social control and deviation. In M.B. Clinard (Ed.), *Anomie and deviant behavior* (pp.57–97). New York: Free Press.

Lemmings, D. and Walker, C. (2009). *Moral panics, the media and the law in early modern England.* New York: Palgrove/McMillan.

Leveritt, M. (2002). *The devil's knot: the true story of the West Memphis three.* New York: Atria Books.

Lewis, R. (1984). *Enoch Powell: principle in politics.* London: Cassell.

Lewis, J. R. and Melton, J. G. (1994). *Sex, slander, and salvation: investigating the family/children of God.* Stanford, Cal.: Center For Academic Publication.

Levitas, R. (1986). *The ideology of the new right.* Cambridge, UK: Polity Press.

LGYM (1985). *Are Holocausts made of leather belts?* London: Lesbian and Gay Youth Movement.

Liebman, R. C. (1983). Mobilising the moral majority. In R. C. Liebman and R. Wuthnow (Eds.), *The new Christian right* (pp. 50–73). New York: Aldine de Gruyter.

Liew, K. K. and Fu, K. (2006). Conjuring the tropical spectres: heavy metal, cultural politics in Singapore and Malaysia. *Inter-Asia Cultural Studies,* 7(1). pp. 99–112.

Lingua, F., Brenkma, J. Llyod, E. and Albert, D. (Eds.). (2000). *The Sokal hoax; the sham that shook the academy.* Lincoln: University of Nebraska Press.

Link, W. A. (1992). *The paradox of southern progressivism, 1880–1930.* Chapel Hill, NC: University of North Carolina Press.

Livesey, R. (1986). *Understanding the new age: preparations for antichrist's 1-world government.* Tiptree, UK: The New Wine Press.

Loftus, E. and Ketcham, K. (1994). *The myth of repressed memories: false memories and allegations of sexual abuse.* New York: St. Martin's Griffin.

Logan, K. (1990). *Paganism and the occult.* Eastbourne, UK: Kingsway.

Logan, K. (1994). *Satanism and the occult: todays dark revolution.* Eastbourne, UK: Kingsway.

Lombardo, R.M. (2004). The black hand: a study in moral panic. *Global Crime,* 6(3–4). pp. 267–284.

Lowery, S. and DeFleur, M. L. (1983). *Milestones in mass communications research.* White Plains, NY: Longman Inc.

Lummis, T. (1994). *The labour aristocracy, 1851–1914.* Aldershot, UK: Scolar Press.

Luzia, K. (2008). Daycare as battleground: using moral panic to locate the front lines. *Australian Geographer,* 39(3). pp. 315–326.

Lyons, A. (1988). *Satan wants you: The cult of devil worship in America.* New York: Mysterious Press.

MacArther, Jr., J. F. (1992). *Charismatic chaos.* Grand Rapids, MI: Zondervan Publishing House.

MacCleod, M. and Sagara, E. (1988). Challenging the orthodoxy: towards and feminist theory and practice. *Feminist Review,* 28. pp. 16–55.

Macek, S. (2006). *Urban nightmares: the media, the right, and the moral panic over the city.* Minneapolis: University of Minnesota Press.

MacFarlane, K. and Waterman, J. (Ed.). (1986). *Sexual abuse of young children.* London: Cassell.

MacKay, C. (1989). *Extraordinary popular delusions and the madness of crowds.* New York: Barnes and Noble Books.

Manchester, C. (1986). *Sex shops and the law*. Bungay, UK: Richard Clay.

Mandelsberg, R. S. (Ed.). (1991). *Cult killers: their secret rituals always ended in death*. New York: Pinnacle.

Manshel, L. (1990). *Nap time: the true story of sexual abuse at a suburban daycare center*. New York: Zebra Books.

Marone, J. A. (2003). *Hellfire nation: the politics of sin in American history*. New Haven: Yale University Press.

Marsden, G. M. (1980). *Fundamentalism and American culture: the shaping of the twentieth-century evangelism, 1970–1925*. Oxford, UK: Oxford University Press.

Marshall, P. (1984). *Thine is the kingdom: a biblical perspective on the nature of government and politics today*. Basingstoke, UK: Marshall, Morgan and Scott.

Martin, D. and Fine, G. A. (1991). Satanic cults, satanic play: is "dungeons and dragons" a breeding ground for the devil? In J. Richardson, J. Best and D. Bromley (Eds.), *The Satanism scare* (pp. 107–144). New York: Aldine de Gruyter.

Marx, K. and Engels, F. (1975). *Articles on Britain*. Moscow: Progress Publishers.

Marx, P. A., Alcabes, P. G. and Matsumura, J. (2007). Unfaithful wives and dissolute labourers: moral panic and the mobilization of women into the Japanese workforce 1931–45. *Gender & History*, 19(1). pp. 78–100.

Masters, P. and Whitcomb, J. C. (Ed.). (1988). *The charismatic phenomenon*. London: The Wakeman Trust.

Mayer, J. (Ed.). (1994). *The backlash; child protection under fire*. Thousand Oaks, CA: Sage.

Mayer, R. S. (1991). *Satan's children: shocking true accounts of satanism, abuse, and multiple personality*. New York: Avon Books.

Mays, J. B. (1972). *Juvenile delinquency, the family, and the social group*. London: Longman.

McAlinden, A. (2010). Punitive policies on sexual offending: from public shaming to public protection. In M. Nash and A. Williams (Eds.), *Handbook of public protection* (pp. 380–398). New York: Willan Publishing.

McCann, J., Wells, R., Simon, M., and Voris, J. (1990a). Comparison of genital examination techniques in prepubertal girls. *Pediatrics*, 85(2). pp. 182–187.

McCann, J., Wells, R., Simon, M., and Voris, J. (1990b). Genital findings in prepubital girls selected for nonabuse: a descriptive study. *Pediatrics*, 86(3). pp. 428–439.

McCarthy, J.D. and Zald, M.N. (1977). Resource mobilization and social movements: a partial theory. *American Journal of Sociology*, 82(6). pp. 1212–1241.

McCarthy, M.A. and Moodie, R.A. (1981). Parliament and pornography: the 1978 child protection act. *Parliamentary Affairs*, XXXIV(1). pp. 47–61.

McGarry, M. (2000). Spectral sexualities: nineteenth-century spiritualism, moral panic, and the making of US obscenity law. *Journal of Women's History*, 12(2). pp. 8–29.

McGuffin, J. (1974). *The guineapigs*. Harmondsworth: Penguin.

McGuire, D. L. (2011*). At the dark end of the street: black women, rape, and resistance—a new history of the civil rights movement from Rosa Parks to the rise of black power*. New York: Vintage.

McRobbie, A. and Thornton, S. (1995). Rethinking "moral panic" for multi-mediated social worlds. *British Journal of Sociology*, 46(4). pp. 559–574.

McWilliams, P. (1993). *Ain't nobody's business if I do: the absurdity of consensual crimes in a free society*. Los Angeles: Prelude Press.

Meese, E. (1986). *Attorney General's commission on pornography*. Washington DC: US Department of Justice.

Miller, A. (1986). *Thou shalt be aware: society's betrayal of the child*. New York: Meridian.

Miller, A. (Ed.). (1987). *For your own good: the roots of violence in child-rearing*. London: Virago.

Miller, G. and Holstein, J. (1993). *Constructionist controversies: issues in social problem theory*. Hawthorne, New York: Aldine de Gruyter.

Miller, P. (1982). *Into the arena: why Christians should be politically involved*. Eastbourne, UK: Kingsway Publications.

Miller, T. (2006). A risk society of moral panic: the US and the 21st century. *Cultural Politics*, 2(3). pp. 299–318.

Miller, T. (2008). Panic between the lips: attention deficit hyperactivity disorder and ritalin. In C. Krinsky (Ed.), *Moral panics over contemporary children and youth* (pp. 143–165). Burlington, VT: Ashgate.

Miller, T. and Ledger, M. C. (2003). A very childish moral panic: ritalin. *The Journal of Medical Humanities*, 24(1/2). pp. 9–33.

Miller, T. G. (1975). *On dealing with student unrest*. Unpublished internal document. Committee of Directors of Polytechnics, Portsmouth Polytechnic.

Miroff, B. (2009). *The liberal's moment; the McGovern insurgency and the identity crisis of the democratic party*. Lawrence: University of Kansas.

Mitchell, S. (2004). Douglas-home, the Conservative party and the threat of rebellious youth: 1963–64. University of Sussex Journal of Contemporary History, retrieved on 1 August 2004 from http://www.ac.uk/Units/HUMCENTER/usjch/smitchell4.html.

Moorcock, S. (1990). Lesbian chainsaw massacre. *The Pink Paper* #116, 1.4.1990. pg. 8.

Moore, R. (1975). *Racism and black resistance in Britain*. London: Pluto Press.

Moorhouse, H. F. (1991). Football hooligans: old bottle, new whines? *Sociological Review*, 39(3). pp. 498–502.

Morin, E. (1971). *Rumour in orleans: Jews accused of white slaving, a modern myth examined*. London: Anthony Blond.

Morone, J. A. (2003). *Hellfire nation: The politics of sin in American history*. New Haven: Yale University Press.

Morrison, D. E. and Tracey, M. (1978). American theory and British practice: the case of Mrs. Mary Whitehouse and the National Viewers and Listeners Association. In R. Dhaven and C. Davies (Eds.), *Censorship and obscenity*. London: Martin Robertson.

Morrison, D. E. and Tracey, M. (1980). Beyond ecstasy: sex and moral protest. In W. H. G. Armytage, R. Chester, and J. Peel (Eds.), *Changing patterns of sexual behaviour* (pp. 1–12). London: Academic Press.

Mort, F. (1987). *Dangerous sexualities: medico-moral politics in England since 1830*. London: RKP.

Mouzelis, N. (1993). The poverty of sociological theory. *Sociology*, 27(4). pp. 675–695.

Mulhern, S. (1991). Satanism and psychotherapy: a rumour in search of an inquisition. In J. Richardson, J. Best and D. Bromley (Eds.), *The Satanism scare* (pp. 145–172). New York: Aldine de Gruyter.

Murji, K. (1998). *Policing drugs*. Aldershot, UK: Ashgate.

Murray, K. and Gough, D.A. (1991). *Intervening in child sexual abuse*. Edinburgh, UK: The Scottish Academic Press.

Murray T. with McClure, M. (1995). *Moral panic: exposing the religious right's agenda on sexuality*. London: Cassell.

Myers, J.E.B. (1994). *The backlash: child protection under fire*. Thousand Oaks, CA: Sage.

Musgrove, F. (1974). *Ecstasy & holiness: counter culture and the open society*. London: Methuen and Co.

Nash, M. and Williams, A. (Eds.). (2010). *Handbook of public protection.* Cullompton: Willan Publishing.

Nathan, D. (1991). Satanism and child molestation: constructing the ritual abuse scare. In J. Richardson, J. Best, and D. Bromley (Eds.), *The Satanism scare* (pp. 75–94). New York: Aldine de Gruyter.

Nathan, D. and Snedeker, M. (1995). *Satan's silence.* New York: Basic Books.

National Campaign for the Repeal of the Obscene Publications Act (1985). *Obscene publications (protection of children etc.) amendment bill. a critique.*

National Deviancy Conference (1980). *Permissiveness and control: The fate of sixties legislation.* Basingstoke, UK: Macmillan.

Nava, M. (1988). Cleveland and the press: outrage and anxiety in the reporting of child sexual abuse. *Feminist Review, 28.* pp. 103–121.

NCSV (1988). Norwich consultants on sexual violence: claiming our status as experts—community organising. *Feminist Review, 28.* pp. 144–149.

Neuilly, M.A. and Zgoba, K. (2006). Assessing the possibility of a pedophilia panic and contagion effect between France and the United States. *Victims and Offenders, 1.* pp. 225–254.

Newburn, T. (1992). *Permission and regulation: laws and morals in post-war Britain.* London: Routledge.

NFOL (1981). *The proliferation of sex stores.* London: Nationwide Festival of Light.

Nolan, J. L. (1998). *The therapeutic state: justifying government at century's end.* New York: New York University Press.

OAGSC (1986). *Report on Kern County child abuse investigation.* California: Office of the Attorney General.

Obama, B. (2004). *Dreams from my father: a story of race and inheritance.* New York: Crown Publishers.

Ofshe, R. and Watters, E. (1995). *Making monsters: false memories, psychotherapy, and sexual hysteria.* London: Andre Deutsch.

Oliver, T. and Smith, R. (1993). *Lambs to the slaughter: a web of evil to rival the moors murders.* London: Warner Books.

Pally, M. (2011). *The new evangelicals: expanding the vision of the common good.* Grand Rapids, MI: W.B. Eerdmans Publishing.

Parker, R. (1997). Healing ministries and their potential for harm. In L. Osborn and A. Walker (Eds.), *Harmful religion: an exploration of religious abuse* (pp. 65–81). London: SPCK.

Parsons, S. (2000). *Ungodly fear: fundamentalist christianity and the abuse of power.* Oxford, UK: Lion.

Parton, N. (1985). *The politics of child abuse.* Basingstoke, UK: Macmillan.

Passantino G., Passantino B. and Trott, J. (1989). Satan's sideshow. *Cornerstone,* December 1989. pp. 26–28.

Paterson, B. and Stark, C. (2001). Social policy and mental illness in England in the 1990's: violence, moral panic, and critical discourse. *Journal of Psychiatric and Mental Health Nursing, 8*(3). pp. 257–267.

Parton, N. (1991). *Governing the family: child care, child protection and the state.* Basingstoke, UK: Macmillan.

Patry, W. (2009). *Moral panics and the copyright wars.* New York: Oxford University Press.

Paul, D. M. (1977). The medical examination in sexual offences against children. *Medicine, Science and the Law, 17*(4). pp. 251–258.

Paul, D.M. (1986). What really did happen to Baby Jane? The medical aspects of the investigation of alleged sexual abuse of children *Medicine, Science and the Law, 26*(2). pp. 85–102.

Payne, R. (2008). Virtual panic: children online and the transmissions of harm. In C. Krinsky (Ed.). *Moral panics over contemporary children and youth* (pp. 31–45). Burlington, VT: Ashgate.

Pearce, F. (1976). *Crimes of the powerful: marxism, crime, and deviance.* London: Pluto Press.

Pearl, C. (1955). *The girl with the swansdown seat.* London: Robin Clark.

Pearson, G. (1983). *Hooligan: a history of respectable fears.* Basingstoke, UK: Macmillan.

Pearson, R. (1972). *Worm in the bud: the world of Victorian sexuality.* Harmondsworth, UK: Penguin.

Pendergrast, M. (1995). *Victims of memory: incest accusations and shattered lives.* Hinesburg, VT: Upper Access, Inc.

Pengally, J. and Waredale, D. (1992). *Something out of nothing: the myth of 'satanic ritual abuse' and the truth about paganism and witchcraft. A handbook for childcare and other professionals.* London: The Pagan Federation.

Penn-Lewis J. (1973). *War on the saints.* Erith, UK: Diasozo Trust.

Peretti, F. (1990). *This present darkness.* Eastbourne, UK: Monarch Publications.

Perry, M (Ed.). (1987). *Deliverance: psychic disturbances and occult involvement.* London: SPUK.

Petrow, S. (1994). *Policing morals: the metropolitan police and the home office 1870–1914.* Oxford, UK: Clarendon Press.

Phillips, D. (1973). The press and pop festivals: stereotypes of youthful leisure. In S. Cohen and J. Young (Eds.), *The manufacturer of news: deviance, societal problems, and the mass media* (pp. 323–333). London: Constable.

Phillips, P. (1986). *Turmoil in the toy box.* Erith, UK: Diasozo Trust.

Phillips, P. (1991). *Saturday morning mind control.* Nashville, TN: Oliver-Nelson.

Phillips, P. and Robie, J. H. (1987). *Halloween & Satanism.* Lancaster: Starburst Publishers.

Pijpers, R. (2006). Help! The poles are coming: narrating a contemporary moral panic. *Geografiska Annaler,* 88(B). pp. 91–103.

PIMCO. (1987). *It's your business: a history of the Portsea Island mutual co-operative society limited.* Portsmouth, UK: PIMCO.

Platt, A. M. (1977). *The child savers: the invention of delinquency* (2nd ed.). Chicago: University of Chicago Press.

Plotnikoff, J. and Woolfson, R. (2000). *Where are they now? An evaluation of sex offender registration in England and Wales.* London: Home Office.

Plummer, K. (Ed.) (1992). *Modern homosexualities: fragments of lesbian and gay experience.* London: Routledge.

Pollard, S., Liddle, T. and Thompson, B. (1994). *Towards and more co-operative society: ideas on the future of the British Labour movement and independent healthcare.* London: IHA.

Poloma, M. (1982). *The charismatic movement: is there a new pentecost?* Boston: Twayne Publishers.

Porter, D. (1986). *Children at risk.* Eastbourne, UK: Kingsway Publications.

Porter, D. (1989). *Children at play.* Eastbourne, UK: Kingsway Publications.

Poynting, S. and Mason, V. (2007). The resistible rise of Islamophobia: anti-Muslim racism in the UK and Australia before 11 September 2001. *Journal of Sociology* [Australia], 43(1). pp. 61–86.

Pratney, W. (1985). *Devil take the youngest.* Shreveport, LA: Huntington House.

Pratt, J. (2005). Child sexual abuse: purity and danger in an age of anxiety. *Crime, Law and Social Change,* 43. pp. 263–287.

Pride, M. (1986). *The child abuse industry: outrageous facts about child abuse and everyday rebellions against a system that threatens every North American family.* Westchester, IL: Crossway Books.

Prothero, I. (1979). *Artisans and politics in early nineteenth century London, John Gast and his times.* London: Methuen and Co. Ltd.

Prothero, I. (1997). *Radical artisans in England and France 1830–1870.* Cambridge, UK: Cambridge University Press.

Pulling, P. (1989). *The devil's web: who is stalking your children for Satan?* Shreveport, LA: Huntington House.

Rabinowitz, D. (1990). From the mouths of babes to a jail cell. *Harper's Magazine,* May, 1990. pp. 52–63.

Randall, I. M. (1995). The social gospel: a case study. In J. Wolffe (Ed.), *Evangelical Faith and Public Zeal* (pp. 155–174). London: SPCK.

Ranulf, S. (1964). *Moral indignation and middle class psychology* New York: Schocken Books.

Rapp, D. (2002). Sex in the cinema: war moral panic, and the British film industry 1906–1918. *Albion: A Quarterly Journal Concerned with British Studies,* 34(3). pp. 422–451.

Raschke, C.A. (1990). *Painted black: from drug killings to heavy metal–the alarming true story of how satanism is terrorizing our communities.* San Francisco: Harper and Row.

Reich, W. (1975). *The mass psychology of fascism.* Harmondsworth, UK: Pelican Books.

Reiner, R. (1985). *The politics of the police.* Oxford: Oxford University Press.

Resnik, D. B. (2004). *Owning the genome: a moral analysis of DNA patenting.* Albany: State University of New York Press.

Rhodes, D. and McNeill, S. (Ed.). (1985). *Women against violence against women.* London: Onlywomen Press.

Richardson, J. T., Best, J. and Bromley, D. G. (Eds.). (1991). *The satanism scare.* New York: Aldine De Gruyter.

Ritchie, J. (1991). *The secret world of cults: inside the sects that take over lives.* London: Angus and Robertson.

Roberts, D. (1994). *The Toronto blessing.* Eastbourne, UK: Kingsway.

Roberts, G. and Klibanoff, H. (2007). *The race beat: the press, the civil rights struggle and the awakening of a nation.* New York: Vintage Books.

Roberts, M. (2003). *Related to bigotry: the repression of swingers in early 21stC Britain.* Unpublished paper, London: Feverparties.com.

Roberts, N. (1986). *The front line; women in the sex industry speak.* London: Grafton Books.

Robinson, K.H. (2008). In the name of childhood innocence: a discursive exploration of the moral panic associated with childhood and sexuality. *Cultural Studies Review,* 14(2). pp. 113–129.

Rock, P. and Cohen, S. (1970). The Teddy boy. In V. Bogdanor and R. Skidelsky (Eds.), *The age of affluence 1951–1964* (pp. 288–320). London: Macmillan.

Rodgers, B. (1990). Pornography: the debate goes on. *Everywoman,* #Dec 1990-Jan 1991.

Rogers, P. and Coafee, J. (2005). Moral panics in urban resistance: policy, tactics, and youth in public space. *City,* 9(3). pp. 321–340.

Rose, L. (1986). *The massacre of innocence: infanticide in Britain, 1800–1939.* London: Routledge and Kegan Paul.

Rose, L. (1991). *The erosion of childhood: child oppression in Britain 1860–1918.* London: Rutledge.

Rosenbaum, J. and Sederberg, P. (Eds.). (1976). *Vigilante politics.* Philadelphia: University of Pennsylvania Press.

Rosie, M. and Gorringe, H. (2009). The anarchists world cup: respectable protest and media panics. *Social Movement Studies,* 8(1). pp. 35–53.

Ross, A. (1989). *No respect: intellectuals and popular culture.* New York: Routledge.

Rothe, D. and Muzzatti, S.L. (2004). Enemies everywhere: terrorism, moral panic, and US civil society. *Critical Criminology,* 12(3). pp. 327–350.

Royal, E. (1981). *Chartism.* Harlow, UK: Longman.

Rubington, E. and Weinberg, M. S. (1989). *The study of social problems: six perspectives.* Oxford, UK: Oxford University Press.

Rudé, G. (1981). *The crowd in history: a study of popular disturbances in France and England 1730–1848*. London: John Wiley and Sons Ltd.

Rush, F. (1980). *The best kept secret: sexual abuse of children*. Blue Ridge Summit, PA: TAB Book.

Ryder, D. (1992). *Breaking the circle of satanic abuse: recognizing and recovering from hidden trauma*. Minneapolis: CompCare Publishers.

SAFF (1991). *The Satanic ritual abuse myth*. Leeds, UK: Sorcerer's Apprentice Legal Fighting Fund.

Sakheim, D. K. and Devine, S. E. (1992). *Out of darkness: exploring satanism and ritual abuse*. New York: Lexington Books.

Samara, T. R. (2008). Marginalized youth and urban revitalization: a moral panic over street children in Cape Town. In C. Krinsky (Ed.), *Moral panics over contemporary children and youth* (pp. 187–202). Burlington, VT: Ashgate.

Saux, M. S. (2007). Immigration and terrorism: a constructed connection. The Spanish case. *European Journal on Criminal Policy and Research*, 13(1/2). pp. 57–72.

Scala, M. (2000). *Diary of a teddy boy: a memoir of the long sixties*. London: Headline Books.

Schaeffer F. A. and Koop, C. E. (1982). *Whatever happened to the human race?* London: Marshall, Morgan and Scott.

Schissel, B. (1997). *Blaming children: youth crime, moral panics, and the politics of hate*. Halifax, Nova Scotia: Fernwood Publishing.

Schissel, B. (2008). Justice undone: public panic and the condemnation of children and youth. In C. Krinsky (Ed.), *Moral panics over contemporary children and youth* (pp. 15–29). Burlington, VT: Ashgate.

Scott, B. (1994). *Out of control: whose watching our child protection agencies*. Lafayette, LA: Huntingdon House Publishers.

Sheldon, K. and Howitt, D. (2007). *Sex offenders and the internet*. Chichester, UK: John Wiley and Son.

Shiman, L.L. (1988). *Crusade against drink in Victorian England*. Basingstoke, UK: Macmillan Press.

Short, C. (1991). *Dear Clare . . . this is what women feel about Page 3*. London: Hutchinson Radius.

Shupe, A. D. and Bromley, D. G. (1983). Apostates and atrocity stories: some parameters in the dynamics of deprogramming. In B. Wilson (Ed.), *The social impact of new religious movement* (pp. 179–215). New York: The Rose of Sharon Press.

Silke, A. (2001). Dealing with vigilantism: issues and lessons for the police. *The Police Journal*, 74. pp. 120–133.

Silverman, J. and Wilson, D. (2002). *Innocence betrayed: paedophilia, the media and society*. Cambridge, UK: Polity Press.

Silvermoon (1992). *Silvermoon: the wicked*, 2(2).

Sinason, V. (Ed.). (1994). *Treating survivors of satanic abuse*. London: Routledge.

Sinclair, A. (1965). *Prohibition: the era of excess*. London: Four Square.

Sivanandan, A. (1982). *A different hunger: writings on black resistance*. London: Pluto Press.

Sked, A. (1987). *Britain's decline*. Oxford: Blackwell.

Skidmore, P. (1995). Just another moral panic? Media reporting of child sexual abuse. *Sociology Review*, April, 1995. pp. 19–23.

Sloman, L. (1979). *Reefer madness: a history of marijuana*. St. Martin's Griffin.

Sloman, L. (1983). *Reefer madness: a history of marijuana*. New York: St Martin's Griffin.

Smail, T., Walker, A. and Wright, N. (Eds.) (1995). *Charismatic renewal: the search for a theology*. London: SPCK.

Smith, E. (2003). Failing boys and moral panics: perspectives on the underachievement debate. *The British Journal of Educational Studies*, 51(3). pp. 282–295.

Smith, E. (2010). Underachievement, failing youth, and moral panics. *Evaluation and Research in Education,* 23(1). pp. 37–49.

Smith, J. (2007). 'Ye've got to 'ave balls to play this game, sir!' boys, peers, and fears: the negative influence of school-based 'cultural accomplices' in constructing hegemonic masculinities. *Gender and Education,* 19(2). pp. 179–198.

Snedeker M. (1988). The rise and fall of the devil in Kern County, California. *Californian Prisoner,* 4 and 5.

Solomos, J. (1987). *From equal opportunity to anti-racism: racial inequality and the limits of reform.* Policy Paper in Ethnic Relations No. 17. John Birkbeck Public Policy Centre, Department of Politics and Sociology Birkbeck College, University of London.

Soothill, K. and Francis, B. (2002). Moral panics and the aftermath: a study of incest. *Journal of Social Welfare and Family Law,* 24(1). pp. 1–17.

Spector, M. and Kitsuse, J. (2001). *Constructing social problems.* New Brunswick: Transaction Publishing.

Spencer, J.R. and Flinn, R.H. (Eds.). (1990). *The evidence of children: the law and psychology.* London: Blackstone.

Springhill, J. (1998). *Youth, popular culture and moral panics: penny gaffs to gangsta rap 1830–1996.* New York: St. Martins Press.

Springhill, J. (2008). The monsters next door: what made them do it? Moral panics over the causes of high school multiple shootings. In C. Krinsky (Ed.), *Moral panics over contemporary children and youth* (pp. 47–68). Farnham, UK: Ashgate.

St. Cyr, J. L. (2003). The folk devil reacts: gangs and moral panic. *Criminal Justice Review,* 28(1). pp. 26–46.

Stanton, B. (2005). School drug education in new south wales: moral panic and the individualization of youth drug use. *Social Alternatives,* 24(4). pp. 50–54.

Stanton Rogers, W., Hevey, D. and Ash, E. (1989). *Child abuse and neglect: facing the challenge.* London: Oxford University Press.

Starker, S. (1991). *Evil influences: crusades against the mass media.* New Brunswick: Transaction.

Steiger, B. and Steiger, S.H. (1991). *Demon deaths: shocking true crimes of devil worship.* New York: Berkley Books.

Stott, J. (1984). *Issues facing Christians today; a major appraisal of contemporary social and moral questions.* Basingstoke, UK: Marshalls Paperbacks.

Subritzky, B. (1991). *How to cast out demons and break curses.* Auckland, New Zealand: Dove Ministries Limited.

Summit, R. (1983). The child sexual abuse accommodation syndrome. *Child Abuse and Neglect,* 7. pp. 177–193.

Sumner, C. (1981). Race, crime, and hegemony: a review essay. *Contemporary Crisis,* 5(3). pp. 277–291.

Sutherland, E. H. (1950). The diffusion of sexual psychopathic laws. *The American Journal of Sociology,* 56(2). pp. 142–148.

Sutherland, J. (1982). *Offensive literature: decensorship in Britain, 1960–1982:* London: Junction Books.

SWP. (1976). *Mugging: the facts.* Socialist Worker Pocket Pamphlet #4. London: Socialist Worker Party.

Sydie, R. A. (1987). *Natural women: cultured men: a feminist perspective on sociological theory.* Milton Keynes, UK: Open University Press.

Tam, C. R. (1992). *'Junk science' in action: critical notes on the Environmental Protection Agency.* London: Freedom Organization for the Right to Enjoy.

Tate, C. (1999). *Cigarette wars: the triumph of the little white slaver.* New York: Oxford University Press.

Tate T. (1990). *Child pornography: an investigation.* London: Methuen.

Tate, T. (1991). *Children for the devil: ritual abuse and satanic crime.* London: Methewn.

Taylor, I. R. (1971). Soccer consciousness and soccer hooliganism. In S. Cohen (Ed.). *Images of deviance* (pp. 134–164). Harmondsworth, UK: Pelican Books.

Taylor, L. (1984). *In the underworld.* Oxford, UK: Blackwell.

Tester, K. (1994). *Media, culture and morality.* Routledge: London.

Thompson, B. (1983). *The women's Co-operative Guild: a study of branch activity in Portsmouth and Colchester.* MA Oral History Project. University of Essex, Essex.

Thompson, B. (1987). *PornWars—Moral enterprise, sexuality & social policy: the Local Government (Miscellaneous Provisions) Act 1982.* Unpublished PhD Thesis, University of Essex.

Thompson, B. (1989). *PornWars: moral panics, pornography and social policy.* Paper presented at the American Society of Criminology annual meeting, Reno.

Thompson, B. (1990). *Puff and nonsense: parents against tobacco & the political exploitation of children.* FORREST Conference, London.

Thompson, B. (1991a). *Snuff, sex and Satan: the social construction of satanic ritual sex abuse.* Paper presented at 8th International Conference on Contemporary Legend. Sheffield University.

Thompson, B. (1991b). Written submission–The Clyde Inquiry into Orkney Islands child protection service procedures.

Thompson, B. (1992). Britain's moral minority. In B. Wilson (Ed.), *Religion: contemporary issues, the All Souls seminars in the sociology of religion* (pp. 64–91). London: Bellow.

Thompson, B. (1994a). *Softcore: moral crusades against pornography in Britain and America.* London: Cassell.

Thompson, B. (1994b). *Sadomasochism: painful perversion or pleasurable play?* London: Cassell.

Thompson, B. (1997). Charismatic politics: the social and political impact of renewal. In S. Hunt (Ed.), *Charismatic christianity: sociological perspectives* (pp. 160–183). Basingstoke, UK: Macmillan Press Ltd.

Thompson, B. (2000). *There was a baby lying dead in a window: a critique of death in the media.* Paper presented at 5th International Conference on Death, Dying, and Disposal. Goldsmith College, London.

Thompson, B. and Annetts, J. (1990). *Soft-core: a content analysis of legally available pornography in Great Britain 1968–90 and the implications of aggression research.* Reading University Monograph, Reading, UK.

Thompson, B. and Annetts, J. (1992). *Guilt by association: questions of homosexuality.* Paper presented to the Lesbian and Gay Studies Conference, Institute of Romance Studies, London.

Thompson, B. and Greek, C. (2010). Sex offender notification, policy imperatives, effects and consequences in the USA. In M. Nash and A. Williams (Eds.), *Handbook of public protection* (pp. 295–315). Cullompton: Willan Publishing.

Thompson, B. and Williams, A. (2003). Virtual offenders: the other side of internet allegations. In M. C. Calder (Ed.), *Child sexual abuse and the internet: tackling the new frontier* (pp. 113–132). Lyme Regis, UK: Russell House Publishing.

Thompson, E. P. (1972). *The making of the English working class.* Harmondsworth, UK: Penguin Books.

Thompson, E. P. (1975). *Whigs and hunters: the origin of the black act.* London: Pantheon Books.

Thompson, E.P. (1993). *Customs in common: studies in traditional popular culture.* New York: The New Press.

Thompson, G. (1923). *A manual of vigilance law.* London: National Vigilance Association.

Thompson, K. (1998). *Moral panics.* London: Routledge.

Thompson, K. (1992). *Emile Durkheim*. Chichester, UK: Ellis Horwood. Ltd.

Tierny, K. J. (1989). *The social and community context of disaster*. In R. Gist and B. Lubin (Eds.), *The psychosocial aspects of disaster* (pp. 11–39). New York: John Wiley.

Timmerman, G. and Schreuder, P. (2008). Pedagogical professionalism and gender in daycare. *Gender and Education*, 21(1). pp. 1–14.

Toch, H. (1971). *The social psychology of social movements*. London: Methuen and Co.

Tomkinson, M. (1982). *The pornbrokers*. London: Virgin.

Tong, R. (1989). *Feminist thought: a comprehensive introduction*. London: Unwin Hyman.

Tonry, M. (2004). *Thinking about crime: sense and sensibility in American penal culture*. New York: Oxford University Press.

Toor, S. (2007). Moral regulation in a post-colonial nation-state: gender and the politics of Islamization in Pakistan. *Interventions*, 9(2). pp. 255–275.

Tracey, M. and Morrison, D. (1979). *Whitehouse*. Basingstoke, UK: Papermac/ Macmillan.

Troyer, R. J. and Markle, G. E. (1984). Coffee drinking: an emerging social problem? *Social Problems*, 31(4). pp. 403–416.

Trudgill. E. (1976). *Madonnas and magdalenes: the origins and development of Victorian sexual attitudes*. New York: Holmes and Meier.

Ungar, S. (1990). Moral panics, the military-industrial complex, and the arms race. *Sociological Quarterly*, 31(2). pp. 165–185.

Ungar, S. (2001). Moral panic verses risk society: the implications of the changing sites of social anxiety. *British Journal of Sociology*, 52(2). pp. 271–291.

Ungar, S. (2008). Don't know much about history: a critical examination of moral panics over student ignorance. In C. Krinsky (Ed.), *Moral panics over contemporary children and youth* (pp. 167–180). Burlington, VT: Ashgate.

VACSG (1990). *Violence against children study group: taking child abuse seriously*. London: Unwin Hyman.

Valentine, G. and Holloway, S. (2001). On-line dangers? Geographies of parents' fears for children's safety in cyberspace. *Professional Geographer*, 53(1). pp. 71–83.

Van Den Hoonaard, W. C. (2000). Is research-ethics review a moral panic? *CRSA/ RCSA*, 38(1). pp. 19–36.

Vance, C. (1984). *Pleasure and danger: exploring female sexuality*. London: Pandora Press.

Veno, A. and Van Den Eynde, J. (2007). Moral panic neutralization project: a media-based intervention. *The Journal of Community and Applied Social Psychology*, 17(6). pp. 490–506.

Victor, J. S. (1993). *Satanic panic: the creation of a contemporary legend*. Chicago: Open Court.

Waddington, P. (1986). Mugging as a moral panic: a question of proportion. *The British Journal of Sociology*, XXXVII(2). pp. 245–259.

Waddington, P. (1993). Dying in the ditch: the use of police powers in public order. *The International Journal of the Sociology of Law*, 21. pp. 335–353.

Wagner, D. (1997). *The new temperance: the American obsession with sin and vice*. Boulder: Westview Press.

Waites, B., Bennett, T. and Martin, G. (Eds.). (1981). *Popular culture: past and present*. London: Croom Helm.

Waiton, S. (2008). *The politics of anti social behaviour: amoral panics*. New York: Routledge.

Wakefield, H. and Underwager, R. (1994). *Return of the furies: an investigation into recovered memory therapy*. Chicago: Open Court.

Walker, A. (Ed.). (1988). *Restoring the kingdom: the radical Christianity of the house church movement*. London: Hodder and Stoughton.

Wallis, R. (1972). Dilemma of a moral crusade. *New Society,* July 13th 1972. pp. 69–72.

Wallis, R. (1976). Moral indignation and the media: an analysis of the NVALA. *Sociology* 10(2), pp. 271–295.

Wallis, R. and Bland, R. (1978). Who rallied to the call? *New Humanist: Journal of the Rationalist Press Association,* Autumn, 1978. pp. 55–57.

Wallis, R. and Bland, R. (1979). Purity in danger: a survey of participants in a moral-crusade rally. *The British Journal of Sociology,* XXX(2). pp. 188–205.

Walsh, F. (1996). *Sin and censorship: the Catholic church and the motion picture industry*. New Haven: Yale University Press.

Washington, P. (1989). *Fraud: literary theory and the end of English*. London: Fontana.

Watney, S. (1989). *Policing desire: pornography, AIDS and the media* (2nd ed.) Minneapolis: University of Minnesota Press.

Watson, D. (1979). *How to win the war*. Wheaton, IL: Harold Shaw Publishers.

Watson, D. (1989). *Hidden warfare: conquering in the spiritual conflict*. Eastbourne, UK: Kingsway Publications.

Weber, M. (1982). Science as a vocation. In H. H. Gerth and C. Wright Mills. *From Max Weber* (pp.129–156). London: Routledge and Kegan Paul.

Webster, R. (1995). *Why Freud was wrong: sin, science and psychoanalysis*. New York: Basic Books.

Webster, R. (1998). *The great children's home panic*. Oxford, UK: Orwell Press.

Webster, R. (2005). *The secrets of Bryn Estyn: the making of a modern witch hunt*. Oxford, UK: Orwell Press.

Weeks, J. (1981). *Sex, politics & society: The regulation of sexuality since 1800*. London: Longman.

Weeks, J. (1985). *Sexuality and its discontents: meanings, myth, and modern sexuality*. London: Routledge and Kegan Paul.

Weidner, R (2009). Methamphetamine in three small midwestern cities: evidence of a moral panic. *The Journal of Psychoactive Drugs,* 41(3). pp. 227–239.

Welch, M. (2000). *Flag burning: moral panic and the criminalization of protest*. Hawthorne, New York: Aldyne de Gruyter.

Welch, M., Price, E. and Yankey, N. (2004). Youth violence and race in the media: the emergence of 'wilding' as an invention of the press. *Race, Gender, and Class,* 11(2). pp. 36–48.

Welsh, M. (2003). Detained: immigration laws and expanding INS jail complex. *Political Science Quarterly,* 118(3). pp. 520–521.

Wertenbaker, T. J. (1947). *The puritan oligarchy: the foundation of American civilization*. New York: Grosset and Dunlap.

Wexler, R. (1990). *Wounded innocence: the real victims in the war against child abuse*. Buffalo, New York: Prometheus Press.

White, T. (1990). *The believers guide to spiritual warfare*. Eastbourne, UK: Kingsway Publications.

Whitehouse, M. (1971). *Who does she think she is?* London: New English Library.

Whitehouse, M. (1977). *Whatever happened to sex?* Hove, UK: Wayland.

Whitehouse, M. (1982). *A most dangerous woman*. Tring, UK: Lion Publishing.

Whitehouse. M. (1985). *Mightier than the sword*. Eastbourne, UK: Kingsway Publications.

Whitehouse, M. (1993). *Quite contrary* London: Pan Books.

Widgery, D. (1976). *The Left in Britain: 1956–68*. Harmondsworth, UK: Penguin.

Wilkins L.T. (1964). *Social deviance: social policy, action, and research*. London: Tavistock.

Wilkinson, H. (Ed.). (1991). *The Christian Counselor* 1(2).

Williams, A. (2004). *"There ain't no peds in Paulsgrove": social control, vigilantes, and the misapplication of moral panic theory*. Unpublished PhD Thesis, University of Reading, Reading, UK.

Williams, A. and Thompson, B. (2004a). Vigilance or vigilantes: the Paulsgrove riots and policing paedophiles in the community. Part I: the long slow fuse. *The Police Journal,* 77(2). pp. 99–119.

Williams, A. and Thompson, B. (2004b). Vigilance or vigilantes: the Paulsgrove riots and policing paedophiles in the community. Part II: the lessons of Paulsgrove. *The Police Journal,* 77(3). pp. 199–205.

Williams, B. (1979). *Report on the committee on obscenity and film censorship.* London: Her Majesty's Stationary Office.

Williams, J. A. (2001). Ecstasies of the young: sexuality, the youth movement, and moral panic in Germany on the eve of the first world war. *Central European History,* 34(2). pp. 163–189.

Williams, N. (1991). *False images: telling the truth about pornography.* Eastbourne, UK: Kingsway Publications.

Willis, P. (1982). The motor-bike and motor-bike culture. In B. Waits, T. Bennett and G. Martin (Eds.), *Popular culture: past and present* (pp. 284–293). London: Open University Press, Croon Helm Ltd.

Wilson, D. G., Walsh, W. F. and Kleuber, S. (2006). Trafficking in human beings: training and services among US law enforcement agencies. *Police Practice and Research,* 7(2). pp. 149–160.

Wilson, E. (1983). The context between pleasure and danger: the Barnard conference on sexuality. *Feminist Review,* 13. pp. 35–41.

Wilson-Thomas, C. and Williams, N. (1996). *Laid bare: a path through the pornography maze.* London: Hodder and Stoughton.

Wimber, J. (1985). *Power evangelism: signs and wonders today.* London: Hodder and Stoughton.

Winter, K. (1992). *The day they took away our children: ritualistic abuse, social work, and the press.* Social Work Monographs, #113. Norwich, UK: University of East Anglia.

Wood, M. and Hughes, M. (1984). The moral basis of moral reform: status discontent vs. culture and socialization as explanations of anti-pornography social movement adherence. *American Sociological Review,* 49. pp. 86–99.

Woodiwiss, M. (1988). *Crime, crusades and corruption: prohibitions in the United States 1900–1987.* London: Pinter Publishers.

Woodling, B. A. and Kossoris, P. D. (1981). Sexual misuse: rape, molestation and incest. *Pediatric Clinics of North America,* 28(2). pp. 481–499.

Wray, M. (2006). *Not quite white: white trash and the boundaries of whiteness.* Durham: Duke University Press.

Wright, N. (1986). *The radical kingdom: restoration in theory and practice.* Eastbourne, UK: Kingsway.

Wright, R. (2000). 'I'd sell you suicide': pop music and moral panic in the age Marilyn Manson. *Popular Music,* 1(3). pp. 365–385.

Wright, S. (1978). *Crowds and riots: a study in social organization.* London: Sage.

Yablonski L. (1962). *The violent gang.* New York Macmillan & Co.

Yant, M. (1991). *Presumed guilty: when innocent people are wrongly convicted.* Amherst, NY: Prometheus Books.

Yates, R., Powell, C. and Beirne, P. (2001). Horse maiming in the English countryside: moral panic: human deviance, and the social construction of victimhood. *Society and Animals,* 9(1). pp. 163–175.

Young, J. (1971). The role of the police as amplifiers of deviancy, negotiations of reality and the translators of fantasy: some consequences of our present system of drug control as seen in Notting Hill. In S. Cohen (Ed.), *Images of deviance* (pp. 27–61). Harmondsworth, UK: Pelican, Penguin Books.

Young, J. (2009). Moral Panic: its origins in resistance, ressentiment, and the translation of fantasy into reality. *British Journal of Criminology,* 49(1). pp. 4–16.

Zajdow, G. (2008). Moral panic: the old and the new. *Deviant Behavior,* 29(7). pp. 640–664.

Zatz, M. S. (1987). Chicano youth gangs and crime; the creation of a moral panic. *Contemporary Crises,* 11. pp. 129–158.

Zgoba, K. M. (2004). Spin doctors and moral crusaders: the moral panic behind child safety legislation. *Criminal Justice Studies,* 17(4). pp. 385–404.

Zurcher, L. and Kirkpatrick, R. (1976). *Citizens for decency.* London: University Texas Press.

NEWS PAPERS/PERIODICALS & OTHER PRIMARY SOURCES

Care News (1987 and 1988)

CACP: Campaign Against Pornography & Censorship flyer 1989

Case Summary, Operation Sackville, 2000

Clarion (Soho Society)

Cornish Community Standards Association Newsletter

Child Abuse and Neglect

Daily Express

Daily Mail

Daily Mirror

Daily Telegraph

Evening News (London)

Evening Standard (London)

Family Magazine (1985)

HMSO: Public Order Act, 1986

LGYM: Lesbian and Gay Youth Movement flyer, 1985

Local Government Chronicle

London Standard

Newham Recorder, London

New Lambethian

News of the World

Orkney Inquiry

PCC: Portsmouth City Council Archives

Portsmouth Association for Community Standards Newsletter

Potentially Dangerous Offenders Protocol

Private Eye

Screen International

The Christian Democrat (1991 and 1995)

The Guardian

The Journal, Portsmouth

The Listener

The News (Portsmouth)

The Sun

The Times

The Sunday Times

The Viewer and *Listener*

WIRES: Women's Information Referral and Enquiry Service newsletter

Index

Lightning Source UK Ltd.
Milton Keynes UK
UKHW020632140619
344410UK00009B/128/P